KW-553-972

SOUTH ASIA ON A SHORT FUSE

SOUTH ASIA ON A SHORT FUSE

Nuclear Politics and the Future of Global Disarmament

Praful Bidwai and Achin Vanaik

Praful Bidwai
Achin Vanaik

OXFORD
UNIVERSITY PRESS

OXFORD
UNIVERSITY PRESS

YMCA Library Building, Jai Singh Road, New Delhi 110001

Oxford University Press is a department of the University of Oxford. It furthers the University's objective of excellence in research, scholarship, and education by publishing worldwide in

Oxford New York

Athens Auckland Bangkok Bogota Buenos Aires Calcutta
Cape Town Chennai Dar es Salaam Delhi Florence Hong Kong Istanbul
Karachi Kuala Lumpur Madrid Melbourne Mexico City Mumbai
Nairobi Paris Sao Paolo Singapore Taipei Tokyo Toronto Warsaw

with associated companies in Berlin Ibadan

Oxford is a registered trade mark of Oxford University Press
in the UK and in certain other countries

Published in India
By Oxford University Press, New Delhi

© Oxford University Press 1999

For sale only in South Asia, including India, Pakistan, Sri Lanka,
Bhutan, Nepal, Bangladesh and Myanmar

The moral rights of the author have been asserted
Database right Oxford University Press (maker)
First published 1999

All rights reserved. No part of this publication may be reproduced, stored in a retrieval system, or transmitted, in any form or by any means, without the prior permission in writing of Oxford University Press, or as expressly permitted by law, or under terms agreed with the appropriate reprographics rights organization. Enquiries concerning reproduction outside the scope of the above should be sent to the Rights Department, Oxford University Press, at the address above

You must not circulate this book in any other binding or cover and you must impose this same condition on any acquirer

ISBN 0 19 565178 2

Typeset in Bembo with Officina display
by Eleven Arts, Keshava Puram, Delhi 110035
Printed in India at Pauls Press, New Delhi 110020
Published by Manzar Khan, Oxford University Press
YMCA Library Building, Jai Singh Road, New Delhi 110 001

Beg my boy's pardon!
Apologize on your knees
Those who made the atomic bomb!

(Extracted from the poem, 'I wanted to Live,' by the mother of Fumiki Nagoya, who died in Hiroshima at the age of seven.)

This book is dedicated to the memory of the victims of Hiroshima and Nagasaki, and to the struggle for the abolition of nuclear weapons worldwide.

Preface

The South Asian Tinderbox

Kargil as the Short Fuse

When we settled on the title for this book's South Asian edition, the border conflict had not yet broken out at Kargil on the Kashmir border. The two month-long confrontation, India's biggest military mobilization since 1971, was a touch-and-go affair. It showed just how grimly appropriate is the term 'Short Fuse'. Kargil was the first military conflict in nearly 30 years between the two recently nuclearized rivals, and *the only large-scale conventional engagement ever between any two nuclear states.* (The Ussuri River conflict between China and the USSR never involved air strikes nor had the same escalation potential.) Kargil took a toll of nearly 1300 lives (according to the Indian government) and over 1750 (according to Pakistan). And yet, there is a potential for more Kargils. Pakistan Prime Minister Nawaz Sharif makes no bones about this.

Kargil confirms some of our worst fears and gives rise to new ones. Nuclearization has not only failed to instill greater confidence or maturity in either India and Pakistan or in their mutual relations. It has actually reinforced mutual distrust, fear, suspicion and paranoia. Conflicts like Kargil, however limited, are militarily and politically destructive because they undermine the potential for improvement in regional security. Worse, they make a nuclear confrontation considerably likelier.

Indian and Pakistani high officials exchanged nuclear threats, whether directly or indirectly, no fewer than 13 times in just five weeks during the Kargil crisis. These varied from warnings that they won't hesitate to use 'any weapon', to threatening devastation in answer to the adversary's nuclear 'threat'.

It would be the height of irresponsibility to play down the significance of such threat-mongering. Cold War adversaries confronted one another in various forms. They escalated military preparations and fought countless proxy battles and full-scale wars through surrogates. But it is hard to think of an instance after the Cuban Missile crisis of 1962 where the US and the USSR exchanged serious threats of nuclear devastation so casually and cavalierly. It would be even harder to think of Washington and Moscow so easily resorting to purely military means without first exploring diplomatic possibilities.

However, what about the much touted Prime Ministerial Summit between A.B.Vajpayee and Nawaz Sharif on February 20–21, 1999 which culminated in the launch of the first-ever direct bus service between Delhi and Lahore and in the Lahore Declaration that was to inaugurate a new era of *qualitative* improvement in mutual relations? While all efforts at dialogue and reducing tensions between the two neighbours must be welcomed, India, having initiated a nuclear arms race in the region, had a vested interest in making some gesture of moderation and 'responsibility'. It is noteworthy that this Summit did not emerge from a purely unilateral or even bilateral initiative. US mediation was crucial to it with deputy secretary of state Strobe Talbott visiting New Delhi and Islamabad beforehand.

However, the bomb lobbies of both countries went hyperbolical about what Lahore had accomplished. Given the nuclearization of the region, such lobbies felt compelled to claim all kinds of security-enhancing properties for deterrence, making the Summit an example of its supposed virtues. Hawks on both sides claimed that with nuclearization, conventional wars would be averted. Rarely could so many 'nuclear experts' have suffered so swift, embarrassing and comprehensive a comeuppance and exposure of the falsity and naivety of their arguments.

As for the Lahore Declaration, it contained not one serious measure or even promise of nuclear restraint. Indeed, the agreement reached at the poorly prepared Summit, on extremely limited confidence-building (or rather, transparency) measures like informing each other beforehand of ballistic missile tests, effectively legitimized the very process of both countries' further nuclearization! On future bomb tests, the left hand took what was presumably given with the right—e.g. the moratorium on further nuclear tests in both the countries would continue unless the 'national interest' dictated otherwise!

The Kargil crisis, then, was not the total and blatant violation or negation of the 'Lahore process' that it was made out to be. India and Pakistan's verbal nuclear war-mongering and one-upmanship during the conflict, and their failure afterwards to undertake any serious soul-searching, are hard to explain solely by reference to the nature of their regimes, the revanchism and bitterness of their hawks, or even the severe crisis of legitimacy facing their rulers. It is crucial to understand that their search for nuclear weapons (more emphatically, India's) was not driven primarily by considerations of security and real, felt, dangers and how best to meet them.

That is why it has been so easy for New Delhi and Islamabad to practise a *confused and deeply contradictory nuclear policy*. On the one hand, they claim they need nuclear weapons for their security; and on the other, they sever and disconnect nuclear weapons from security to the point of jeopardizing it by brandishing nuclear threats against each other. Had their search for nuclear weapons been organically linked to security, rather than to false notions of prestige and status, they would not have behaved in such a grossly irresponsible manner.

This is obviously not the place for a lengthy discussion of the genesis of the Kargil crisis, Pakistan's wrongful violation of the Line of Control status quo, or the larger Kashmir conflict.[1] But the Kargil confrontation is best understood through three factors or phenomena. First, it derives from long-term India–Pakistan hostility and what either or both regard as 'unresolved' issues, including Kashmir, and attempts to force a resolution of disputes. Thus, sections in India's and Pakistan's armed forces and secret services, backed by political leaders, have always wanted to 'get even' with one another through covert operations, and low-cost, low-intensity warfare to alter the status quo.

Pakistan's army leaders clearly saw the Kargil LoC as an Indian Achilles' Heel, where infiltrating a few hundred troops/guerrillas could destabilize the situation. They were emboldened by New Delhi's failure to anticipate this or heed intelligence warnings. Even if this misadventure had succeeded, it would not have given Islamabad significant strategic advantage. The fact it was launched, at considerable political–diplomatic cost to Pakistan, speaks of the strength of the bitterness among Islamabad's hawks.

Secondly, although its planning may have preceded the Lahore meeting, the Kargil operation must also be seen as an attempt to undermine whatever positive momentum and spirit of conciliation the Summit generated. There has been strong resentment against conciliation within the Pakistan military establishment and the political–religious right. True, the Summit, coming barely nine months after the crossing of the nuclear threshold, was largely symbolic in importance. But then, so was the absence of Pakistan's defence chiefs at Vajpayee's arrival in Lahore.

The resentment towards Lahore was stronger in Pakistan, where those who bore it saw in the Lahore Declaration Islamabad's retreat from an aggressive Kashmir agenda or agreement to put that issue temporarily on the backburner. To these hardliners, crossing the LoC around Kargil, and masking it as a *mujahideen* or 'freedom-fighter'-led 'spontaneous' act (inconceivable without Pakistani army support at that altitude), must have seemed a worthwhile low-cost strategy. If it failed, the (military) costs would not be high. If it succeeded, Pakistan would have in effect not only altered the LoC alignment, but also internationally highlighted the Kashmir issue as never before. Even Sharif was probably tempted to try this out.

However, the third, and extraordinarily important, factor was related to South Asia's nuclearization. This seems to have created a false sense of complacency in India coupled with greater willingness in Pakistan to embark on a military misadventure. As we argue below in Chapters 4, 5, 8 and 9 and in Box 2, many political and military leaders and strategic 'experts' in the two countries permit themselves the dangerous self-delusion of invulnerability on account of their Bombs. Their sordidly boastful claims of superior military-nuclear prowess are part of a mindset which drives the temptation to raise the conventional danger threshold, to see how far you can irritate and harass the adversary at the sub-war level. You believe the opponent will only make a nuclear threat *in extremis*, once many levels of tolerance have been crossed. And then too, there is the 'realistic' hope that external intervention would defuse the threat. Ergo, brinkmanship is in order. Besides, you have your own deterrent to rely upon.

As is usual with most such military 'plans', this game-theory scenario failed to account for one vital factor—*politics* and the role of the international community. The world was horrified at Kargil's potential for something far more destructive than limited conventional warfare. The Big Powers got active. A three-way 'mediation' or 'dialogue-facilitation' process began at the initiative of the US, which favoured India's stand on the LoC, and led to Pakistan's isolation, and finally to the 4 July Clinton–Nawaz Sharif meeting in Washington, resulting in a phased pullout of Pakistan-backed forces.

Both India and Pakistan ended up paying heavily for Kargil. Pakistan was politically weakened, winning little support from its old friend China, leave alone the US. Internally, Kargil dealt another blow to democratization, further weakened the crisis-ridden economy, and aggravated the regime's legitimacy crisis. The explosion of religious bigotry and Islamic fanaticism on Kashmir was a severe setback to Pakistan's healthy development.

India lost hundreds of men—410 according to the government. (This is almost certainly a gross underestimate. The number of wounded was said to be 594, when an injured-death ratio of 4 or 5 to one is the accepted Indian norm. The casualties were probably much higher.) The economic cost for India was over Rs. 10,000 crores ($ 2.5 billion) in direct expenses—just to recover its own territory in 'peacetime'. The economic toll will mount as the Kargil LoC becomes a super-Siachen to be patrolled round the year. (Siachen glacier is the highest point of military confrontation anywhere in the world. Since 1984, India and Pakistan have lost over 10,000 lives patrolling it, at the expense of $ 10 million a day.) Even more onerous have been the social costs: outbreak of jingoism and religious chauvinism, celebration of militarism, male-supremacism, growth of intolerance, media manipulation and censorship, and suppression of debate and dissent.

The specifically *nuclear lessons* of Kargil are also clear. The conflict dramatically highlighted South Asia as *the* most likely place in the world where a nuclear exchange can take place. This judgement is not the concoction of motivated propagandists, but obvious common sense. It is when war-time or near war-time conditions prevail, that a nuclear outbreak becomes most likely—whether because brinkmanship is practised, hostile emotions and suspicions get out of hand, or the dynamic of military escalation careens out of control.

Kargil revealed the horrific absurdity of relying on nuclear deterrence. The most faithful Indian adherents of this doctrine repeatedly declared during the conflict that Pakistan is a 'rogue state', its leaders are 'irrational' and irresponsible and could not be trusted *not* to use nuclear weapons, for which India, therefore, had to be 'prepared'. Again, many of them declared that the US would somehow ensure that Pakistan would not use its nuclear weapons. What then became of the assured efficacy that these same people attributed to the workings of *mutual* India–Pakistan deterrence?

One of the more dangerous outcomes of the whole Kargil crisis was the fillip it gave to the practice of 'demonizing the Other' and therefore to religious fundamentalist forces in both countries, which are the ones most willing to sustain this process. Such behaviour only 'essentializes' mutual hostility (e.g. rooting it in the fundamentally 'incompatible' nature of Islam and Hinduism) leading to the false conclusion that the sources of conflict are permanent and inescapable, and therefore lie beyond the issue of Kashmir which is at least in principle resolvable. This is a recipe for political disaster. On the nuclear front, such demonization just feeds on itself, reinforcing the tendency in each country to prepare for or even pre-empt the worst that is expected from the other side, namely the use of nuclear weapons.

Disturbing as the possibility was of a nuclear exchange (whether triggered by design, miscalculation or accident) during the Kargil crisis, it can only be magnified once India and Pakistan openly deploy nuclear weapons.

The nuclear warning from Kargil is clear. India and Pakistan must move firmly towards denuclearization, beginning with an immediate freeze on nuclear and missile development and fissile material production—no further weaponization, no induction and no deployment. Both countries must accede to the CTBT, and be pressed to carry out actual dismantling of their nuclear-fission assemblies. Nuclear and military tensions between them must be systematically reduced. This is unlikely to happen through bilateral talks alone, which themselves, like Lahore, would be a response partially to external pressure.

There is indeed a strong case for some external encouragement, if not intervention, to defuse India–Pakistan nuclear rivalry, especially across the LoC where they confront each other menacingly. It would be morally or politically hard to oppose external, multilateral, intervention to separate Indian and Pakistan forces physically should they move towards nuclear engagement. One positive, if unintended, 'gain' from Kargil is that it has focussed world attention on the volatility of the India–Pakistan strategic situation and the critical importance of Kashmir. Of course, in order to be fair, equitable, effective and sustainable, such intervention must be multilateral, non-manipulative and strictly neutral.

India and Pakistan have to accept a bitter lesson. India crossed the nuclear threshold largely out of its grandiose ambition to influence world affairs. Pakistan wanted to match India's status. It was also not immune to exaggerated ideas about enhancing its world stature when it decided to go nuclear. Both countries now have to pay a price: to have the world influence *their* affairs. Kargil underscores this even as it darkens the nuclear shadow over the one-fourth of humanity that lives in South Asia.

However, a good deal of the impetus towards denuclearization must come from within. Kargil highlighted the vacuity of the dogmatic assumption that nuclear weaponization would prevent a nuclear exchange between India and Pakistan. Large numbers among the Indian and Pakistani public became distinctly uneasy about the existence of nuclear weapons in the armouries of the two bellicose rivals which could so easily move into intense hostility. Many who had welcomed the tests of May 1998 too were affected by such unease. But this *unease* is yet to be translated into *active opposition* to nuclear weapons and a practical demand for their non-manufacture, non-deployment and rapid dismantling.

Indeed, at least in India, media-cultivated jingoism and false euphoria over 'victory' in Kargil threatens to submerge these stirrings of uneasiness. In Pakistan too, the bomb lobby will try to provide false assurances that nuclear weapons remain necessary for the country's security. The translation of this unease into a powerful sentiment and force of public opposition to nuclearism is a moral and political imperative. We hope this book can contribute to that worthy goal.

Praful Bidwai, Achin Vanaik
New Delhi, 26 July 1999.

Note

1 We contributed numerous articles on the Lahore summit and the Kargil crisis to the press, which were critical of both governments' handling of the issue, warned against escalation, and took a strong stand against jingoism and chauvinism. Most of them can be accessed through the website of 'South Asians Against Nuclear Weapons' [www.mnet.fr\aiindex\NoNukes.html]. Here is a non-exhaustive list:

Praful Bidwai, 'From Pokharan to Kargil: the Nuclear Danger is No Fantasy', *The Times of India,* New Delhi, 2 June 1999; 'India–Pakistan Hold Reins to World's Nuclear Future', *The Daily Star,* Dhaka, 1 January 1999; 'Bus Diplomacy', *Mid-Day,* Mumbai, 17 February 1999; 'Pakistani–India Ties: Talking Peace but Far from Detente', *Dawn,* Karachi, 25 February 1999; 'Indo–Pak Conciliation: The Nuclear Shadow Must Go', *The Times of India,* New Delhi, 20 March 1999: 'Voices for Peace', *Frontline,* Chennai, 26 March 1999; 'Can there Ever be Peace between India and Pakistan?', *The Sunday Times of India,* New Delhi, 2 June 1999; 'Sack George', *Mid-Day,* Mumbai 6 June 1999; 'Information War', *Mid-Day,* Mumbai, 16 June; 'Playing with Fire in Kargil', *Frontline,* Chennai, 18 June 1999; 'Kosovo, Kargil, Kashmir: towards South Asia's Denuclearisation', *The Times of India,* New Delhi, 19 June 1999; 'Border Situation Becomes more Dangerous', *Inter Press Service,* 30 June 1999; 'And now, Information Warfare', *Frontline,* Chennai, 2 July 1999; 'Between Two Stools: BJP's Flawed Kargil Strategy', *The Kashmir Times,* Jammu, 4 July 1999; 'No Place for Triumphalism: don't Demonize Pakistan', *The Kashmir Times,* Jammu, 12 July 1999; 'Voice of Reason', *Mid-Day,* Mumbai, 14 July 1999; 'The Charade over Kargil: no 'Secret Deal', Mr Vajpayee?', *The Kashmir Times,* Jammu, 19 July 1999; 'The Mind War', *Mid-Day,* Mumbai 21 July 1999; 'Kargil Raised Risk of Nuclear Confrontation', *Inter Press Service,* 27 July 1999; 'Misplaced Triumphalism', *Frontline,* Chennai, 30 July 1999; 'A Kargil Post-Mortem: Now Comes the Hefty Bill', *The Kashmir Times,* Jammu, 26 July 1999; 'What a Waste!', *Mid-Day,* Mumbai, 28 July 1999.

Achin Vanaik, 'The Politics of Symbolism', *The Hindu,* New Delhi, 18 March 1999; 'Mediation is the Message', *The Telegraph,* Calcutta, 26 July 1999; 'No Paradigm Shift', *The Hindu,* New Delhi, 23 July 1999.

For a longer discussion of the Kashmir issue, see Achin Vanaik, *India in a Changing World,* Orient Longman, Delhi, 1994, chapter 5; and Praful Bidwai, 'Face to face with Janus?: Kashmir's Challenge to Nationalism', *Frontline,* Chennai, 3 December 1993; 'Narasimha Rao's Kashmir Gambit: A Recipe for Trouble', *Frontline,* Chennai, 1 December 1995; 'New Opening in J&K: The Art. 370 plus Solution', *Newstime,* Hyderabad, 7 October 1996.

Acknowledgements

We would first and foremost like to thank Phyllis Bennis, of the Institute for Policy Studies and Interlink Publishers, who persuaded us, indeed insisted, that we should write this book now and that we should—and could—meet her extraordinarily demanding deadlines. This is our book but it has emerged from her pushing, cajoling, and encouragement and hence owes a singular debt to her. However, she should not be held responsible for any deficiencies for which we alone must plead guilty.

We would also like to thank a number of other people, adult and junior, who have in one way or the other helped and inspired us. Special thanks are due to Zia Mian, Pervez Hoodbhoy, and A.H. Nayyar of Pakistan, all of them scientific experts and courageous anti-nuclear activists both in their home country and internationally. We owe much to our discussions with them. Their practical solidarity in the common cause of regional and global nuclear disarmament has always been a source of strength to us, as has been the work and passionate concern of yet another scientist–peace activist, M.V. Ramana. Our gratitude also to Kanti Bajpai for his unstinting support and helpful suggestions.

Those familiar with the path-breaking critiques of political realism by Justin Rosenberg and Fred Halliday, both of the London School of Economics, (International Relations Department), will recognize the measure of our indebtedness to them. Fred Halliday, a former colleague at the Transnational Institute of Amsterdam, of which we are both Fellows, has been a stimulating source of ideas. We cannot fail to mention other TNI colleagues, in particular Fiona Dove, its present director and labour movement fighter against apartheid.

Thanks are also due to the following. To Olle Nordberg of the Dag Hammarskjold Foundation, Uppsala, who has been a great source of encouragement and who earlier published our joint little book, *Testing Times: The Global Stake in a Nuclear Test Ban* (1996); to Neloufer de Mel, of the University of Colombo, who made several valuable comments on the manuscript; to Ritu Menon of the remarkable publishing venture, Kali for Women, on whose authority of judgement in publishing matters we have relied heavily; and to Krishna Raj, who edits that unique Mumbai-based journal, *Economic and Political Weekly*, where we have had an occasional column, 'Nuclear Notebook', for over 15 years, and who never tires of encouraging worthy causes.

We are deeply indebted to Akila Seshasayee for the design of this edition, and to Rafeeq and Bina Sarkar Ellias and Mangesh Rane, all of the splendidly produced *Gallerie* magazine from Mumbai, for the design of the cover.

Our friends in MIND (Movement in India for Nuclear Disarmament), of which we are proud activists, deserve a special mention, as do numerous others such as Admiral L. Ramdas, Amartya Sen and author Arundhati Roy, who showed the courage of their convictions by swimming against the tide when it mattered the most.

Pamela Philipose has given us moral and practical support without which we could not so effectively have concentrated on the task at hand. Our thanks to Shri Ram Gupta for invaluable secretarial help; to Anish Vanaik, whose computer expertise made him our regular troubleshooter/problem-solver in this regard; and finally to Samar Vanaik, who carried out innumerable errands for us despite occasional murmurs (good-humoured we hope) about the use of child labour.

Contents

Abbreviations

ABM	anti-ballistic missile (treaty)
ACBA	Arms Control and Disarmament Agency (of the US)
AEC	Atomic Energy Commission
AERB	Atomic Energy Regulatory Board (of India)
AEW	Airborne early warning
ANC	African National Congress (of South Africa)
ASCI	Accelerated Strategic Computing Initiative (of the US)
ASEAN	Association of South East Asian Nations
ASP	Airborne surveillance platform
ATV	Advanced Technology Vessel (code-name for India's nuclear submarine project)
BBC	British Broadcasting Corporation
BJP	Bharatiya Janata Party
BMD	ballistic missile defence
CANDU	Canadian Deuterium (-moderated and cooled) Natural Uranium (reactor)
CBM	confidence building measure
CD	Conference on Disarmament (of the UN in Geneva)
CIRUS	Canada–India Research Reactor, United States (India reactor, commissioned 1960; source of plutonium for the 1974 test)
CND	Campaign for Nuclear Disarmament (Britain)
CNN	Cable News Network
CPI	Communist Party of India
CPM	Communist Party of India (Marxist)
CTBT	Comprehensive Test Ban Treaty
CTBTO	Comprehensive Test Ban Treaty Organization (at Vienna)

DAE	Department of Atomic Energy
DARHT	Dual Axis Radiographic Hydrodynamic Test Facility (of the US)
DIA	Defence Intelligence Agency (of the US)
DRDO	Defence Research and Development Organization (India)
EC	European Community
EEC	European Economic Community
FMCT	Fissile Materials Cut-off Treaty
G–21	Group of 21 (non-aligned states in the CD)
GATT	General Agreement on Tariffs and Trade
GDP	Gross Domestic Product
HNE	hydro-nuclear experiment
IAEA	International Atomic Energy Agency
IAF	Indian Air Force
ICBM	Inter-continental ballistic missile
ICF	Inertial confinement fusion
IMF	International Monetary Fund
IMS	International monitoring system (under the CTBT)
INF	Intermediate Nuclear Forces (Treaty)
INSSAP	International Network of Engineers and Scientists Against Proliferation
IPKF	Indian Peace-Keeping Force (in Sri Lanka)
KANUPP	Karachi Nuclear Power Plant (Pakistan)
LCA	Light Combat Aircraft (Indian Project)
LCNP	Lawyers Committee on Nuclear Policy
MAD	mutual assured destruction
MARG	Market Analysis and Research Group (India)
MBT	main battle tank
MIA	Multilateral Investment Agency
MIRV	Multiple independently-targetable re-entry vehicle
MNWC	Model Nuclear Weapons Convention
MPLA	Portuguese acronym for Popular Movement for the Liberation of Angola
MTCR	Missile Technology Central Regime
MW	megawatt
NAFTA	North American Free Trade Agreement
NAM	Non-Aligned Movement

NATO	North Atlantic Treaty Organization
NGO	non-governmental organization
NIF	National Ignition Facility (US)
NMD	national missile defence
NNWSs	non-nuclear weapons states
NPT	Nuclear Non-Proliferation Treaty (1970)
NPR	Nuclear Posture Review (of the US)
NRDC	Natural Resources Defense Council (US NGO)
NWC	Nuclear Weapons (abolition) Convention
NWFZ	nuclear weapons free zone
NWS	nuclear weapons state (often used here interchangeably with the P–5)
OECD	Organization for Economic Cooperation and Development
OSI	on-site inspection
P-5	the five 'recognized' NWSs (US, Russia, UK, France, China)
PCI	Italian acronym for Communist Party of Italy
PML	Pakistan Muslim League
PMO	Prime Minister's Office (India)
PNE	peaceful nuclear explosion
PPP	Pakistan People's Party
PTBT	Partial Test Ban Treaty (1963)
RSS	Rashtriya Swayamsevak Sangh (National Volunteer Corps)
SAC	Strategic Air Command (US)
SALT–1/2	Strategic Arms Limitation Treaty (between the US and the USSR)
SBSS & MP	Science-based Stockpile Stewardship & Management Programme
SCE	sub-critical experiment
SDI	Strategic Defence Initiative (US)
SIOP	Single Integrated Operational plan (US)
SIPRI	Single Integrated Operational Plan (US)
SPD	German acronym for Social Democratic Party
SSMP	Stockpile Stewardship and Management Programme
SSOD–IV	Special Session on Disarmament–IV (held by the UN General Assembly, 1988)
START–I/II/III	Strategic Arms Reduction Treaty–I/II/III
SWPS	Strategic War Planning System

THAAD	Theatre High Altitude Area Defence (US)
TMD	Theatre Missile Defence
TNC	transnational corporation
VHP	Vishwa Hindu Parishad (World Hindu Council)
VVER–1000	Name of a Russian pressurized water nuclear reactor of 1000 megawatts capacity
WB	World Bank
WMD	weapons of mass destruction
WMDFZ	weapons of mass-destruction-free zone

CHAPTER ONE

The Top Story of the Century

The nuclear bombing of Hiroshima and Nagasaki remains the top news story of the twentieth century. That is the conclusion of a survey of opinion of top US journalists and scholars, conducted by 'Newseum', an archive on news gathering, and released in February 1999.

Hiroshima and Nagasaki was unquestionably the first choice, well ahead of Astronaut Neil Armstrong's walk on the moon, Japan's bombing of Pearl Harbour, and President Kennedy's assassination. It scored several ranks higher than Watergate, the invention of penicillin, the invention of the microchip-based personal computer, and above the extension of franchise to women, and the desegregation of schools along racial lines in the US.[1]

Hiroshima and Nagasaki might well be the topmost news stories of the century in many other countries as well.

Nuclearism: Sanctification or Popularization?

The shattering impress on the public mind of those climactic moments of twentieth century history came from the revelation of the two inextricable dimensions of nuclear weapons, the first relating to its incredible power and the second to the unconscionable destruction and unimaginable suffering that they embody and symbolize. Nuclear weapons evoke awe and revulsion, wonder and horror. They have continued to do so ever since.

The most ardent advocates of nuclear weapons have constantly sought to invest these weapons with a virtually religious authority and importance, and to give them an accepted and respectable place in the mass popular culture of our times. What better way is there to legitimize their existence than to do one or both of these things! If nuclear weapons can come to acquire the same 'profound value' as the sacred symbols that supposedly condense the meaning and purpose of a religion, and if the discourse surrounding them can seem as arcane and complex as the higher reaches of religious philosophizing can be for the ordinary believer or the uninitiated, then we have surely succeeded in making the politics and ideology of the possession of nuclear weapons virtually incontestable. After all, to sacralize something is precisely to remove it from the domain of normal contestation except for the 'qualified' few!

The other approach also seeks to make the presence of nuclear weapons and the discourse that justifies it incontestable, but it does so not by seeking to place it on a pedestal to be revered from afar or below. Rather, it so immerses it in the web of everyday life and values of a mass society that their presence is 'normalized' and considered unexceptional and unobjectionable. These two approaches, the religious and the cultural–popular, may appear to work at cross-purposes, but they do not. Indeed, the greatest success is achieved when the two can be fused; when the religious–sacred is both revered and seen as an unproblematic and normal part of everyday life.

The great dilemma for the advocates of nuclear weapons and the great hope for those who unreservedly oppose them is that despite all efforts to either sanctify or popularize these armaments and the attendant ideology of support, these efforts have never been able to gain anywhere near as much ground as its purveyors have wished. This has certainly not been for want of trying. Ever since such weapons were invented, pro-nuclearists have been trying to make them into desirable icons, to build glorious myths, and weave attractive images around them, to routinize and domesticate their meanings. Yet, there is this *relative failure.*

We need both to look at the reasons for failure and to remind ourselves that the failure is only relative. It is relative to the much greater success in implantation that genuine religious systems achieve, and to the much more unequivocal successes that other forms of militarism have secured in the general culture of a mass society. Militarism is the ideology that sustains and promotes the values associated with militarization like violence, aggression, coercion, survival of the fittest, etc. Militarism promotes sexism and sexist stereotypes because it portrays such values as part of a supposedly natural and desirable masculinity. It is hardly surprising then that the discourse justifying nuclear weapons, production and deployment should also be deeply sexist and macho in the most blatant and obvious ways from the loaded, sexual symbolism of 'penetration' of enemy spaces to the 'mating' or 'coupling' of warheads with missiles and other delivery vehicles to the depiction of the nuclear-tipped missile as a phallic symbol of national potency, power, and virility.

Militarism also invades the various forms and practices of mass popular culture: books, comics, music, films, toys, TV programmes, etc. Again, this paves the way for the more specific discourse surrounding nuclear weapons to intrude into all manner of areas. When a society is not just steeped in the ideology of militarism but also in that of commercialism, then the consumerist-advertising world of concocted symbolisms, artificial demand-stimulation, and market strategies will not remain immune. Throughout the nineteen-fifties, advertising and marketing professionals in the US used nuclear and atomic icons and symbols to great effect.[2]

True, the discourse and symbolism justifying, prettifying, and normalizing nuclear weapons has never extended its tentacles into the mass societies of today to anywhere near the same degree as the more standard non-nuclear forms and motifs of militarism. What has been achieved however is disturbing enough. Anti-nuclearists must be constantly on guard to recognize where and how these efforts are made, and then to repeatedly contest them.

So why the relative failure? The two intertwined dimensions of nuclear weapons stimulate two different kinds of discourses. The first is one of power, dominance and impact as the derivative properties of nuclear weapons, and with them, the alluring promise of *control.* The glorification of such attributes (and the promise that they embody) can find a place in a range of activities from strategic studies speculating about pre-emptive use and deterrence efficacy to cigarette advertising to James Bond stories to graphically sexist and masculinist representations in the construction of popular images.

The second kind of discourse emerges out of the recognition of the overwhelming destructive power, and therefore, the *uncontrollability* and irredeemable evil of nuclear weapons. This is a discourse not of acceptance or glorification, but of opposition to the horrific properties and attributes of nuclear weapons. It therefore defends human dignity, decency, the values of community, of caring and sharing. This is a discourse not of power or strategy, vicarious thrill or consumer manipulation, but of ethics and respect for life, peace, harmony and hope—hope in a humane future for the whole world. Arundhati Roy's powerful essay, *The End of Imagination,* featured in the Indian and international media, is an expression of the endurance and importance of just this kind of discourse.

The problem for pro-nuclearists is that there is an irresolvable tension between the two discourses where the second implicitly or explicitly, openly or in subterranean ways, contests and rejects the first kind of discourse. It is an irresolvable tension because it is not possible to fully separate in the minds of most people the awe-inspiring dimension of nuclear weapons from its destructive–repulsive aspect, but all efforts to sanctify and popularize the properties of nuclear weapons aim precisely to carry out this separation and are always only partially successful.

The intrinsic 'power' of nuclear weapons gives them an attribute similar to religion, the capacity to evoke awe, making nuclear weapons suitable candidates for worship. Religious systems use rituals to organize collective forms of worship around the symbol or object that is invested with sacredness, i.e. a certain kind of awe. In doing so, they make religious power and influence quotidian. The transcendental is connected to the everyday and the ordinary. Religious belief and practice is thus both normalized and institutionalized through these rituals which help cement a wider community of believers. However, because sacred power is necessarily nebulous and polysemous, religious élites (those who most strongly control the organization, infrastructure, and interpretation of rituals) can never come near to monopolizing the meaning, purpose, and role of worship. This flexibility and diversity, this possibility for ordinary people to invest sacred power with benign properties appropriate to addressing positively their actually existing human conditions, gives religion a popularity and meaningfulness that the 'religion of nuclear weapons worship' or nuclearism (to give it its more sophisticated label) can never have.[3]

The inseparable connection between the two dimensions of nuclear weapons means they cannot have the 'natural' or popular appeal that genuine religions can at least aspire to. To preserve a system of nuclear weapons worship, a much greater burden of responsibility has to fall on a powerful but also relatively more isolated nuclear–religious élite. It is the ways in which this élite, its apprentices and allies, its acolytes and admirers, organize and control the production, dissemination, and consolidation of the discourse of nuclearism that enables it to have the degree of popular support it has. The nuclear élite comprises people who fulfil two, sometimes overlapping, functions—shaping and making decisions, or shaping and making opinions that endorse the possession, production, or deployment of nuclear weapons.

There are no everyday or truly popular rituals of nuclearism. If the nuclear élite and its supporters are to sanctify nuclearism (a matter to be entrusted to the special priesthood of strategic and security experts) and to popularize it (via the domain of culture), then to do so to whatever extent possible, this élite must rely on two key structures of mass communication. The first is the print media of mass-produced journalism; newspapers and wide-circulation magazines. The second is the audio-visual media of TV news broadcasting and programming, and popular films.

However, cutting across this technical divide is the more important contrast between non-fictional and fictional forms of representation in the discourse and imagery of nuclearism. Non-fictional forms of discourse are deadly serious and quite transparent. Here the nuclear élite has been like the fairy-tale emperor without clothes. For much of the story, the emperor does not know he has no clothes on, and when this reality seeps into his consciousness, he has to pretend that everything is still the same. This is precisely the dilemma of nuclear élites everywhere.

The nuclear mindset is not only immoral but also, intellectually and politically, the *haven of mediocrity*. The chapter in this book on deterrence and the more general style of strategic thinking that lies behind it explains why. In few other professions or areas of so-called expertise is it possible for so many to become so prominent or to get away with so much while knowing and understanding so little! Problems of global and national security and power in today's era of modernity (or 'late' modernity as some would say) are by their very nature so incredibly complex and dynamic in their character, that they are not amenable to easy solutions or to the pretensions of those who would provide easy solutions.

Nuclear élites resemble nothing more than an esoteric, quasi-religious cult who have long convinced themselves that they have the right to 'play God', to gamble with the dice of unimaginable destruction in the name of national security, with themselves as its self-appointed interpreters and guardians. They pretend to know best and most about matters of security and power when they actually know so little, and because they know so little, search most desperately for the 'strategic easy fix'—that symbol of incontestable power which they believe all should acknowledge and worship as they themselves do. The nuclear mindset is not a wise thing, it is a vile and irrational thing whose vileness and irrationality is sought to be made publicly palatable precisely through legitimizing discourses in print and TV, especially in the nuclear weapons states (NWSs) themselves.

Hollywood and the Bomb

The fictional world of popular movies is somewhat different. Here, the United States and Hollywood occupy a distinctive place. No other country has had anywhere near the same resources or the same degree of national self-confidence or as strong a belief in its universal mission that the 'American Way' should also quite naturally be the 'Global Way'; or to put it differently, 'what is good for America is good for the world'! Hollywood has always reflected in the main this real, albeit always contested, common sense. Here however, there are important differences from the world of non-fictional representation of nuclearism. Driven by commercial and entertainment considerations more than strictly ideological ones, pro-nuclear films from the US have generally defended the dominant élite ethos regarding nuclear weapons in indirect ways, and when these élite values have changed over time, the change too has been reflected. Thus nuclear weapons have usually figured as a vital backdrop to the more upfront story of heroic endeavour by American males or governments, or in the genre of Cold War and post-Cold War spy thrillers and dramas.

When films have focused explicitly and centrally on nuclear weapons they have often provided an anti-nuclear message. Such has been the case with films like *Dr Strangelove, The Day After, Failsafe*, and the films and sequels of the *Planet of the Apes* and *Mad Max* respectively. To swim against the tide represented by the dominant élite ethos has always required a strong conviction. This is likely to be found among more politically committed film-makers. To swim with the tide on the issue of nuclear weapons can take many more, and a wider variety of, indirect forms of cinematic and thematic representation.

Naturally, the production and popularity of both kinds of films—explicitly anti-nuclear, implicitly pro-nuclear—is affected by the changing rhythms of popular concern with the issue of nuclear weapons and its associated politics. What is particularly disturbing in this regard is not just the fact that there have always been far too many pro-nuclear films and messages emanating from Hollywood, but that the end of the Cold War and the nineties has not altered this situation. Indeed, now that the American nuclear élite must find new rationales for the retention of nuclear weapons, fresher and stronger life has been given in Hollywood to a genre seeking to resolve just this problem. Since even the 'nasty' Arab or Iranian or Islamic 'fanatic' (common enough hate-figures in recent Hollywood productions) is too weak in real life to warrant a nuclear riposte, the burden of justification for the presence of nuclear weapons has to fall on the genre of movies concerning alien invasion or cosmic threat which is then resolved through their judicious use. Recent films like *Independence Day, Deep Impact,* and *Armageddon* have all carried the dual message of America saving the world and doing so through nuclear weapons.

To leave all this uncontested or uncriticized would be a mistake. Wherever the ugly messages of nuclearism surface, in fictional as well as non-fictional forms, they must be opposed. Indeed, if the battle for the minds and hearts of people is to be consciously fought and fully won then it must be waged as determinedly, consistently, and strongly as possible on the terrain provided by the most popular forms of print and audio-visual media. In the national societies of the nuclear weapons states (NWSs), where the battle must be most strongly enjoined, the achievements on behalf of the anti-nuclear cause have hardly been dramatic. It is in spite of the weaknesses of anti-nuclearists on this score, and not because of their successes, that progress has nonetheless been made.

We can be thankful that in the post-Cold War era, whatever the predilections of Hollywood film-makers, the second discourse of ethics has nevertheless gained ground over the first discourse of power, even in the US. Ordinary people have become more aware of the unacceptably dangerous nature and ultimate futility of nuclear weapons. A clear transition is in evidence: at the end of the century, and at the threshold of a new millennium, the prospect for nuclear abolition appears brighter than at any time since 1945. There is, however, no guarantee that the second discourse will continue to overshadow the first. Much of humanity has overcome in large measure its long-standing fascination with raw power, power divorced from its purposes, and freed of limits. If, however, significant numbers of people still hesitate to go the whole hog to demand unconditional, rapid, nuclear disarmament, it is because they have not committed themselves fully to the second discourse.

What this Book is About

The central argument of this book is that nuclear disarmament is an absolute imperative, that it is eminently desirable and feasible. A transition to the second, ethical, discourse is an overwhelming necessity for all of us. The crossing of the nuclear threshold by India and Pakistan further reinforces, rather than weakens, this proposition or renders it less feasible. Yet, there is a paradox here. People the world over have rarely been horrified by an evil as strongly as they are by nuclear weapons, with their overwhelming power of destruction. Many have opposed such weapons regardless of their general political innocence and inactivity. This evil is not ubiquitous in the ordinary sense of the term: only in about half a dozen states are all the world's nuclear weapons concentrated, yet the danger is, and is considered to be, universal and global. Despite this, however, the nuclear obsession of the ruling élites in a handful of states has proved thoroughly addictive and almost irresistible to change. It is only recently that the obsession has begun to weaken or loosen.

In effect, nuclear weapons have proved far more durable and difficult to eradicate than just about any other kind of evil—at least in relation to the sentiment against them and popular mobilization against them.[4] The contentious terrain of debates over nuclear disarmament has not permitted the free and full expression of popular sentiments. Nuclear élites, comprising experts, strategists and specialists of various kinds, most of them not really accountable to the public, still tend to dominate and try to hijack discussions on the feasibility and desirability of nuclear weapons abolition. This book is a critique of the nuclear élite's mindset and its debased sensibilities. It questions the principal premises underlying nuclearism. It polemicizes against the principal arguments advanced by the NWSs for developing, manufacturing, inducting, stockpiling, refining, deploying, using, or threatening to use, such weapons, and criticizes their reluctance to move rapidly towards the total abolition of nuclear weapons. It is equally critical of states (and their apologists) which wish to emulate the nuclear weapons powers, and deals with some of the artifices they use to delay or obstruct progress towards nuclear abolition.

We as authors have sought to address different kinds of audiences simultaneously—invariably a hazardous endeavour! We hope, therefore, that both informed insiders such as long-time anti-nuclear activists, NGOs, the more open-minded members of decision-making and decision-shaping national élites and the general public will find much of value in these pages. The book has been organized in such a way as to try and take the reader on a particular journey. We start with a wide historical overview of the nuclear age to the present, aiming to situate the more specific politics of nuclearism within the wider framework of Cold War and post-Cold War international politics. It was systemic rivalry between the East and West that dominated nuclear politics in the first period although the real threat of actual use of nuclear weapons emerged mostly in the context of the North–South conflict which was, of course, also connected to the East–West rivalry. In the second post-Cold War period new rationales are having to be found to justify retention of nuclear weapons. If the West is trying to give new meaning to NATO to justify its nuclear activity, Russia sees the possession of such armaments as virtually the sole mechanism for retrieving something of its former 'superpower' status whose loss is lamented by its political élite.

Having brought matters up to date, as it were, the focus shifts to the more specific story of how and why India and Pakistan trod the path of nuclearization till the recent denouement of May of 1998. The justifications for going nuclear are sought to be exposed. There is a description of the official positions and explanations, and the ways in which even these violate the earlier stated official doctrines, certainly in the case of India. By way of rebuttal and critique, the real reasons for the tests are highlighted and there is a comprehensive survey of the various negative consequences of the Indian and Pakistani actions. These range from the diplomatic–political (e.g. Kashmir) to the security-related (the nuclearization of tensions in the India-Pakistan face-off, complications vis-à-vis China) to the domestic (advancement of the Hindu communal and Islamic fundamentalist agendas, the socio-economic wastefulness and burden imposed by the costs of maintaining nuclear weapons systems in both countries) to the international (the damage done to the global momentum for disarmament).

Two central chapters then take up respectively the unique evil of nuclear weapons and their unique danger. The purpose of doing the first is not merely to evoke (fully justified) moral outrage, but to stress the centrality of the generation of controlled moral anger if the effort to bring about a world free forever of nuclear weapons is to ever succeed. Colonialism would not have been overthrown without generating and politically harnessing such moral opposition. The same holds true of bringing a permanent end to nuclearism. We also seek to attack the nuclear mindset not just at its weakest point (its immorality) but also at its supposedly strongest point—its claim to promoting strategic security through reliance on the wondrous powers of nuclear deterrence. The illogicality and fallacies of nuclear deterrence thinking and practice are highlighted with the historical record showing that, far from endorsing the claims of deterrence, reliance upon it led to behaviour, e.g. the arms race, that promoted greater nuclear insecurity and danger. How successful we are in these twin endeavours, readers must judge for themselves, just as they should ask what is left of a pro-nuclear case that cannot adequately or satisfactorily answer criticisms at either or both these levels.

The subsequent chapters look more closely at the combination of intrinsic and extrinsic factors that have shaped not just the political context in which India and Pakistan took their decisions, and the implications this has for the wider gamut of inter-state relations in which the two countries are embedded. We also look at the implications of Pokharan and Chagai on the general character of the post-Cold War nuclear order. The penultimate chapter, in particular, asks and then seeks to address the question of how badly or little damaged (or not at all) the existing global nuclear order is by the efforts of India and Pakistan to join the nuclear club. Here the central conclusion is that it is not the non-proliferation order but the anti-disarmament struggle that has been most seriously damaged—not just by what India and Pakistan have done but by the continuing behaviour of the other existing NWSs.

Finally, we look at what the lessons of the past are on which we must draw to best arm ourselves to rapidly bring about a nuclear weapons free world. We trace the obstacles to this, the most promising lines of pursuit, the combination of comprehensive and partial disarmament perspectives, and so on. Here many issues come up. The question of how to set up some kind of genuine multilateral body empowered to negotiate full and final global nuclear disarmament is explored. Matters like the Comprehensive Test Ban Treaty (CTBT) and the Fissile Materials Cut-off Treaty (FMCT) are investigated. There is a survey of the strengths and weaknesses, the relevance and value of extending the spread of nuclear weapon free zones. And of how transitional measures like de-alerting and No First Use pledges can help lead to more comprehensive reductions and eventually the abolition of nuclear weapons.

It is a question not just of preparing a desirable wish-list but of how to make it achievable.

The General Perspective

We should also clarify our general stand and disposition. We have long been connected with the international peace movement and nuclear disarmament campaigns. We are aware of, and participants in, the debates and arguments that are part of these campaigns' life. At the same time, we are firmly rooted in the realities of South Asia, and are an integral, activist part of the movement for nuclear restraint and disarmament in that part of the world. We have been witnesses to, and critics of, the growing phenomenon in South Asia of a coarsening of the élite's political sensibilities and its moral degradation over the past 30 years, especially in India. This is the period that saw India shift from nuclear abstinence to nuclear ambiguity, and then on to the wholesale embrace of nuclearism with the crossing of the nuclear Rubicon. As witnesses, analysts and activists, we believe the process must be and can be reversed. This book explores ways in which that could be done.

There are no easy solutions to the problem of how states can be impelled to move away from a pathological and misguided reliance on weapons of mass destruction in their search for security. However, two things should be evident. One, the primary impetus towards nuclear weapons abolition cannot simply come from state-level actors and governments. The very nature of the present global nuclear regime is such that those who possess nuclear weapons have no real or immediate stake in getting rid of them, and those who do not possess them lack the leverage and the will necessary to achieve that objective by effectively persuading or compelling the NWSs to undertake cumulative nuclear disarmament. The Nuclear Non-Proliferation Treaty (NPT) is indeed a poor and rusty instrument for this separating as it does the non-proliferation regime from the goal of disarmament. That this should be the case even a decade after the Cold War ended, undermining the fundamental stated rationale of massive military–nuclear preparations under the NATO structure, is both a tragic reality and a deeply unflattering comment on the quality of leadership in some of the most powerful and prosperous nations on earth.

Secondly, no one today has, or can have, a fully worked out blueprint or road map of how to reach the goal of elimination of nuclear weapons from the present starting point. This is quintessentially a case of learning by doing, where the process of progressing towards the final goal, of reaching it, will itself illuminate how we are to permanently sustain the desired end state. This creates, on the one hand, a huge conceptual obstacle, and makes the task of potential agents for disarmament extraordinarily difficult. How indeed can they generate the necessary energies and gather the numbers without a well-defined road map? On the other hand, it presents a truly exciting opportunity to them to bring to their task an amazing range of ideas and imaginative schemes, to be creative in a foundational sense: to produce something, as it were, out of nothing.

We see ourselves as just two participants in this process, as learners along the road to the final destination. We envision our role not just as chroniclers and analysts, nor as publicists and evangelists, leave alone preachers. Above all, we are committed scholar–activists, or activist–scholars, who reject the status quo and who are committed to altering it through conscious public action. Our basic stance is that of *independent* analysts and campaigners, who believe it is important to integrate into the core of their analytical work their moral concerns, and their commitment to universal objectives such as nuclear disarmament, peace, defence of human rights, pluralism, social justice and equality.

We lay claim to another distinctive characteristic as regards our perspective and work. We are from, and belong to, the global South. We believe that it is vital to have a strong Southern input into the global struggle for nuclear disarmament. So far, not just state-level activities and negotiations on the nuclear weapons issue, but even the international peace movement and nuclear disarmament campaigns, have borne a strongly Northern impress. Many of the perspectives, ideas, and debates in that movement have tended to reflect the concerns and predilections of activists from the industrially developed states. This is also true of their methods of organization, of campaigning, of public education, advocacy, and lobbying.[5]

All these need to be enriched with strong inputs from the South, rooted in different sensibilities, experiences and methods. Such pluralism is not just intrinsically worthy and desirable. It is indispensable to the construction and advancement of a truly global momentum and an authentically international movement for nuclear disarmament. Such a movement cannot be a mere aggregate of different national campaigns with their discrete, domestically driven, agendas. It must be truly internationalist in outlook, concerns, reach, and representation. The regrettable fact that the world's nuclear club now features two Southern members should only further underscore the importance of this proposition.

The timing of this book is spurred by the Indian and Pakistani nuclear tests of 1998. The authors have been campaigners against nuclear weapons for many years, but unfortunately we could only produce this volume after the nuclear threshold was crossed in South Asia when we would have preferred to have made an intervention in order to prevent such an outcome from emerging. However, it might perhaps be an even greater pity if the world has begun to recognize the full salience of South Asia's silent race towards nuclearization only because that very undesirable development took place.

This long non-recognition, or slippage from global consciousness, is undoubtedly related to the structure of power distribution in the world and its reflection in the media and hence in the shaping of public awareness globally. In some ways, this is a reminder, even if a grim one, that the struggle to abolish nuclear weapons is integrally connected to the larger agenda to change the world, to alter the distribution of power, to re-evaluate the content, purpose, and meaning of power. This calls for a broad campaigning front and a holistic, inclusive agenda. The fight for nuclear disarmament is thus a fight for more than disarmament alone, although its specific focus must of necessity be narrowed down if it is to be sharp.

Such a struggle, we believe, cannot be left to political leaders, military experts, disarmament and arms control negotiators, diplomats, and other state level actors, however competent, sincere, and well-meaning they might be. It must at its centre involve social movements, non-governmental organizations, and activists—the broadest coalition of civil society groups. It is these collective resources that can generate the moral commitment, the political conviction, the imaginative and practical forms of dissemination of information, coupled with expertise and technical competence, that are necessary for the task.

Perhaps never before was global society called upon to intervene so centrally, so universally, and with such commitment, as it is in this instance. This challenge is part of the broader democratic agenda before humanity: to bring under public scrutiny plans and programmes conceived, designed, and operated by experts and strategic specialists, who claim to guard the public interest and generate security for the people. If the process of democratization involves detaching expertise and specialized knowledge from vast bureaucracies and military machines, and putting it into the public domain, then nothing could serve its aims and objectives better than the rightful appropriation of the supposedly specialized sphere of defence and security by the public whom it is meant to secure, and in whose name it is created and run at massive expense.

The world's denuclearization and its democratization are inseparable processes. As the peace movement has always argued, issues such as security, war and peace, nuclear weapons, and their elimination, are too important to be left to experts and specialists alone. The people of the world must appropriate, or rather recover, these agendas. We can only hope this book makes a modest contribution to that recovery.

Notes

1. The results of the 'Newseum' survey, sponsored by Freedom House in the US were released on 23 February 1999.'Hiroshima comes first, then the moonwalk', *The Pioneer*, New Delhi, 25 February 1999.
2. Half a century later, the image of the mushroom cloud and the icons of Pokharan and Chagai are being turned into the brands and logos of products in India and Pakistan as well as finding their way into the materials used for partisan political propaganda by the Bharatiya Janata Party (BJP) and its cohort organizations in the Sangh Combine.
3. This term, nuclearism, features in Robert Jay Lifton and Richard Falk, *Indefensible Weapons,* Basic Books Inc, New York, 1982, where it is defined as the ideology and doctrines of extreme, pathological dependence on nuclear weapons for a range of goals and objectives, among them security.
4. Recent polls show that 84 per cent of Americans and over 60 per cent of the British population want nuclear disarmament. Seventy three per cent of Indians are against the use of nuclear weapons, '72.8% opposes use of N-weapons, says survey', *The Economic Times*, New Delhi, 24 June 1998.
5. Thus Jonathan Schell in his book, *The Gift of Time* does not even mention, leave alone interview, a single person from the South. All those who figure in it are from the United States, Russia and Europe, barring the half-exception of Merav Datan, an Israeli-American. The book is strong, often excellent, when it deals with the deficiencies of nuclear deterrence and related security perceptions. However, in no way does it challenge standard US liberal assumptions about the general political nature of the Cold War era in which the role of US and Western imperialism is effectively disguised. This could be excused on the grounds that for the most part it is not the voice of Schell that we are hearing but of his interviewees. These are for the most part either prominent liberals or former Cold Warriors who have had some change of heart on the nuclear issue.

   But Schell himself adds no corrective of his own. Indeed, he persistently uses the ideologically loaded and conceptually bankrupt term of "Totalitarianism" to describe the formerly Communist societies of the East. However, the very manner of Communist collapse was itself the most striking confirmation of the theoretical incoherence of the concept which had its origins in rightwing Western Cold War historiography before becoming widely dispersed in liberal mainstream discourse. *The Gift of Time*, Jonathan Schell, Metropolitan Books, Henry Holt and Company, Inc., New York, 1998.

   For an alternative framework and a different discussion of the politics of the Cold War era, see the following chapters 2 and 3.

CHAPTER TWO

The Global Context-I

Bloc Rivalry and the High Noon of Nuclearism

The end of the Cold War and the manner in which this impacted upon the nuclear arms race definitively answered a debate that had raged within the Western anti-nuclear peace movement during the eighties.[1] Despite the horror and terror it evoked, its inertial continuity and irrationality, that arms race did not command or control the politics of the Cold War. On the contrary, the politics of nuclearism was firmly embedded within the wider-ranging politics of general Cold War rivalry and subordinated to it. The nuclear arms race had its distinctive self-reinforcing dynamic emerging out of the degenerative logic of deterrence and from the politics of nuclearism, but it did not have an independent 'life of its own'.

Any survey of the era (1945–87) of strong nuclear rivalry and arms racing thus has to situate it in an understanding of the Cold War's beginning, its subsequent course, and the way it ended. This is a prerequisite for understanding the politics of nuclearism of that period, namely its origins, pattern, and course. This in turn sheds invaluable light on the current politics of nuclearism in the post-Cold War era. In the latter half of the eighties there emerged for the first time since the nuclear age began in 1945, a new and real momentum of actual disarmament and not just arms control. It is this precious outcome that we seek to preserve and strengthen, but the deficiencies of this momentum will not be adequately grasped if we do not also correctly apprehend the way in which the Cold War ended and what the negative consequences of this were.

The General Politics of the Cold War Era

The Cold War confrontation was many things but above everything else it represented a political–ideological systemic rivalry between two blocs led respectively by the US and USSR. This was a conflict between two different social orders. It was not simply a conventional Great Power conflict of the kind which 'balance of power' theorists belonging to the Realist school of International Relations thinking love to go on about. On the one side was a set of nationally structured advanced capitalisms usually taking the political form of perverse democracies. In their internal make-up these countries were, and are, liberal-democratic and thus justifiably attractive to those living under more authoritarian regimes. They nevertheless were (and are) perverse democracies because most such governments repeatedly supported foreign policy positions or carried out practices that were anything but democratic: the pursuit of economic and political imperialism. On the other side were perverse socialisms. Despite often significant national variations in the distribution of popular rights, the countries of what was called the Communist bloc rested on a common foundation of authoritarian–bureaucratic structures denying basic political and civic liberties to their respective populations.

This systemic rivalry was also significantly fed and shaped by intra-bloc and inter-state rivalries and conflicts of various kinds that did not themselves have the same character as the conflict represented by the central fault-line of the overarching Cold War system. Thus even within the advanced capitalist world or between the poorer South and the richer North there were a range of inter-state tensions. Similarly, within the Communist world there were also inter-state and intra-state tensions of various kinds among which the most notable in the post-Second World War period were the Sino-Soviet and China–Vietnam conflicts, the intra-Indochinese wars, and the political eruptions in the Eastern European bloc of countries dominated for decades by Soviet military might. In the last named case the conflicts were not of an inter-state character, but were related much more strongly to popular resentments against both Soviet overlordship and the authoritarian internal practices of what were perceived as client regimes of the USSR.

While responsibility for the perpetuation of the Cold War was shared between both sides, it was not equally distributed. The US emerged out of the Second Word War as the only major participant whose territory was physically unscathed, whose material losses were the least, and whose economy was booming as a result of wartime preparations and activity. The USSR by contrast was devastated, suffering severe physical destruction of its industrial structure and having anywhere between 20 to 25 million dead. Its foreign policy perspectives had to be, and were, of a deeply defensive nature and concerned above all with retrenchment not expansionism. This did not preclude belligerence on its part, nor a fierce determination to hold on to what it had, e.g. control over an East European buffer zone, nor does it mean the USSR did not have some responsibility for the creation of Cold War tensions and hostilities especially through its behaviour in Eastern Europe over subsequent years and decades.

However, the West, and the US in particular, bore greater responsibility for it. It more strongly shaped the general pattern, pace, and course of the Cold War. This simple truth is likely to be increasingly obscured in contemporary and future histories of this period because of the victory of the West in this historic confrontation. The *systemic* character of this conflict was revealed not just by the political collapse of the Soviet bloc but by its acceptance of the fundamental anti-Communist ideological precepts of the winning side and by its determination to establish a capitalist economic system in place of what it earlier had. All this will undoubtedly promote those evaluations most strongly associated with Cold War right-wing Western historiographies. These kinds of history writing have portrayed Western behaviour as being a legitimate moral–political response against Communist evil and expansionism, itself seen as the principal source of Cold War tensions and problems. The West, led by the US, has been portrayed as largely the reactor and defender in this stand-off between the 'Free' and the 'Communist' worlds. Moreover, the final outcome of this confrontation is widely perceived as providing powerful validation for Western practices and behaviour during that period, thereby disguising the objective realities of that time.

With the benefit of hindsight we can see that some kind of Cold War was probably unavoidable even though the weaker side (the East and the USSR) was always more willing to accommodate to, and compromise in the search for, some kind of global status quo arrangement. The inability to arrive at such a modus vivendi was due not so much to a subjective failure, e.g. a misperception on the Western side of Soviet intentions or ambitions, but was an objectively rooted one. Though over time the West came to accept the reality of Europe's division and the satellite status of Eastern Europe, it could never have reconciled itself to the challenges to US imperial power, in particular, that were thrown up by decolonization, national liberation struggles, and anti-capitalist revolutions in the third world. From today's vantage point of comprehensive victory in this historic bloc confrontation, it is easy for many in the West to forget that between 1945 to 1979, there was, on average, one successful anti-capitalist revolution every four years that shifted one country or the other from the capitalist to the non-capitalist so-called Socialist sector!

These victories were not the handiwork of the USSR but for the overwhelming part had independent sources indigenous to the country concerned. The objective fact, however, was that it strengthened one side of the systemic divide at the expense of the other. Any successful long-lasting compromise between the US and USSR that could have avoided the Cold War required what the latter could never have delivered, even if it had wanted to—the elimination of such third world challenges to the US and to Western imperialist power. Furthermore, Cold War hostilities between the two leading countries meant that the USSR could not but seek to exploit, however, half-heartedly or hesitantly or howsoever contradictorily, the opportunities that thereby emerged in the third world for weakening the US's global authority, thus adding further fuel to this systemic face-off. Soviet support to third world challenges to US power was uneven, self-serving, cautious and uncertain but rarely absent.

Throughout the Cold War period the central arena in which it was fought out was not Europe but the third world.[2] To be sure, Europe was an enduring terrain of tension and the most *explicit* site of the politics of nuclearism associated with Cold War hostilities. It was, however, in the third world and over third world issues that nuclear weapons came closest to actually being used. Apart from the definitive moment of the Cuban missile crisis in 1962, the use of nuclear weapons was contemplated on several occasions, ranging from the 1948 Soviet–Iranian Azerbaijan crisis to the 1950 retreat from Chosin reservoir in Korea to the last days of French control in Vietnam (Dien Bien Phu in 1954) to the Formosa Straits crisis of 1959 to the siege of Khe Sanh in Vietnam in 1968 to the 1973 war in the Middle East between Israel and Egypt–Syria.[3]

It was, of course, the US that was tempted to use nuclear weapons on these occasions, and most of the time it was the US that contemplated such use. Though Krushchev did publicly threaten use of such weapons against Israel–UK–France expeditionary forces in the 1956 Suez crisis, he was careful to do so only after the US had come out against the Israel–UK–France combine, and when it was clear the real crisis was over and the latter would have to retreat. The one occasion when the Soviets most seriously contemplated use of their arsenal was in 1969 against China. The 1948 Berlin Airlift crisis was the one exception when the US considered the use of nuclear weapons against the USSR over a Europe-related issue.

Sizeable popular movements against nuclear weapons were always limited to Western Europe, Japan, and the United States. Their absence in the USSR and China can safely be put down to the absence of a democratic civil society, but in Eastern Europe, during the eighties there was widespread and growing public sympathy with the anti-nuclear cause even if this could not be openly expressed in the form of public demonstrations. It was here in Europe and the US that the possibility of a nuclear outbreak was a *popularly felt* danger. This was because it was in Europe and the US that a *constantly looming overhang* of nuclear weapons prevailed as a persistent reminder in public imagination of the reality of the nuclear threat.

In contrast, the stronger likelihood of the use of nuclear weapons in the third world was only sporadically expressed and except in the case of the Cuban missile crisis did not directly portend a US–Soviet nuclear exchange as distinct from a (usually) US threat against a non-nuclear regime. Such possible use did, of course, indirectly raise the prospect of escalating into an eventual US–Soviet exchange but not as an immediate, direct, or 'impossible to avoid' outcome. Moreover, most such threats in the third world were not public knowledge or widely known at the time and have been confirmed post facto, often only by the release in later years of official documents. That the US government was repeatedly tempted to use nuclear weapons in third world conflicts is undeniable, but despite strong pressures on each such occasion their use was eventually not sanctioned. This is not because of any so-called efficacy of deterrence, i.e. fear of possible Soviet retaliation. It is difficult to seriously believe that the US or USSR or any NWS would be prepared to risk nuclear suicide by going into a nuclear war for the sake of some third world ally, no matter how apparently close.

The decisive reasons for the US eventually deciding not to resort to nuclear arms had to do with, (a) the peculiarly *astrategic* character of nuclear weapons as a means of providing general foreign policy support, and (b) fear of domestic and international public horror, opprobrium, and anger. It is not the case that general public opinion in the US was, or is, unequivocally anti-nuclear in all circumstances. Recent poll surveys, however, show that around 84 per cent want the complete elimination of such weapons as rapidly as possible.[4] Also, after Hiroshima and Nagasaki, and increasingly over time, that public opinion has become more and more unwilling to endorse the use of nuclear weapons except in the case of extreme self-defence when territorial US is itself seriously threatened. Throughout the Cold War period no third world-related conflict has ever possessed any such logic or threat dynamic for the US.

Indeed, so many decades have now passed despite innumerable political crises, that an ever stronger, even if not always explicit, public resistance has built up to any 'casual' or 'easy' use of nuclear weapons 'merely' for general foreign policy or so-called strategic purposes and gains. This does not of course guarantee that nuclear élites will never use such arms in pursuit of their foreign policy ambitions. So long as nuclear weapons and nuclear élites exist the possibility of their use exists. The strongest obstacle to their actual use however lies not in the mindset of deterrence or in the fear that such weapons inspire but in the wide and deep public consciousness in, above all, the NWSs themselves, that opposes their use in any circumstances barring the most extreme case when the very survival of the country is called into question by external threats.

This sentiment was no doubt widespread in the USSR and China, and therefore also acted as a powerful barrier. Soviet and Chinese rulers could scarcely have been unaware of it, but the existence of an authoritarian political set-up in the two countries meant that this public sentiment could not exercise the kind of institutionalized pressure that could be expected to operate in the more internally democratic system of the US. In one sense, this left the Soviet and Chinese rulers 'freer' than otherwise to use nuclear weapons if they so desired. Thus the Soviet regime, as pointed out earlier, did in 1969 consider a nuclear strike on China. It tentatively explored the prospect of a joint US–USSR strike but was rebuffed by the US.

Similarly, only the leader of an undemocratically controlled society like Mao Zedong could speculate with callous equanimity about China's ability to 'absorb' a nuclear attack which might kill tens or even hundreds of millions but according to him would still leave tens or hundreds of millions as 'survivors'. This was the partial basis for his famous claim that nuclear weapons were a 'paper tiger'. The other more sensible assumption of the paper tiger claim, that such weapons were strategically useless, was not seriously held by Mao and was effectively belied by Mao's responsibility in leading China into the development and deployment of such weapons.

If overall, during the Cold War, the US leadership behaved with greater nuclear irresponsibility than its Soviet and Chinese counterparts, this was because the greater virtue provided by its internal democratic system was outweighed by the vice of its much stronger imperialist ambition. However, the general lesson to be learnt is undiminished in its importance, and one that is confirmed by the history of the Cold War period. The existence of a democratic polity and of strong popular sentiment does constitute a vital bulwark against any 'easy' use of nuclear weapons.

Nuclearism during the Cold War Era

The dropping of atom bombs over Hiroshima and Nagasaki was also the first act in the nuclearization of post-Second World War politics. It was clearly directed as a symbolic–political warning to the USSR. The bombing was not an act of deterrence—Japan had no warning and the USSR no nuclear weapons then—but a conscious attempt to harness nuclear weapons might for general political and foreign policy purposes in the post-War era.

The early efforts to internationalize control over nuclear weapons—the

Baruch Plan and the Soviet counter-proposal—were, in retrospect, clearly doomed to fail.[5] The general political circumstances of mutual suspicion more or less ensured this. Time and again, this pattern affecting possible arms restraint measures was to be revealed. Not only the prospects for arms restraint but the specific character of arms control/management perspectives would invariably reflect the general character of US–USSR political relations at the time. Shifts in the character of that relationship—what would come to be called the alternating phases of thaw and freeze or detente and deterioration—would witness similar shifts in the nature of arms racing and arms control. Arms control, throughout the Cold War era, should not be seen as something counterposed to arms racing and the ongoing politics of nuclearism but as an integral part of both. However, arms control perspectives did not emerge until the sixties when Soviet nuclear strength reached the point when the United States and Western Europe had to recognize its potential for devastation of their territories in a second strike. Arms control measures became an ever more important part of the general dynamic of arms racing as the USSR reached a rough nuclear parity with the US in the seventies and early eighties.[6]

Every country that went openly nuclear and retained/improved this capacity in the Cold War era did so because it was motivated by a politics of nuclearism that went beyond the issue of nuclear deterrence itself. This is obvious enough in the case of the US which exploded the bombs and produced warheads and delivery systems for reasons intimately related to its general foreign policy ambitions and perspectives. Certainly, once the USSR developed its own nuclear arsenal, then deterrence arguments became an additional and ever more important rationale for both countries in justifying their possession and further development of such weapons.

If for the USSR the initial spur to developing such weapons was US possession and deployment of them, this was not the only purpose behind its subsequent investment in the perpetuation and modernization of a nuclear weapons system. That is why the USSR devoted so much effort and resources to following US behaviour in making their weapons system ever more sophisticated, diverse, and larger; well beyond the needs of any notion of a sensible, let alone minimal, deterrence posture. For the UK and France, matters of national pride and a desire to maintain a supposedly global status, partly to compensate for their unavoidable decline as major colonial powers, were absolutely crucial inputs into their decisions to go nuclear. China too, sought nuclear status not only for purposes of deterrence but as a perceived currency of power for foreign policy and diplomatic projection.

The central axis of Cold War nuclearism was, however, always the US–USSR relationship and dynamic, of which the former was the principal shaper and initiator. That is why it is legitimate to treat a taxonomy of the different phases of Cold War nuclearist politics as effectively synonymous with the different phases of US nuclear politics. There were four such phases. (1) 1945 to around 1960: massive retaliation; (2) early 1960s to the beginning of the 1970s: flexible response; (3) from the early 1970s to the end of that decade: detente and the acceptance of a rough nuclear strategic parity; (4) 1980 to 1987: the quest by the US for nuclear superiority and winnable nuclear wars.

None of these phases should be seen as sharply exclusive of the preceding one. Within the US nuclear establishment, different currents have continually vied for dominant influence and there has been frequent interchange of personnel between these currents so that the same people can have different views at different times. If these categorizations have a meaning it is as a rough description of the dominant policy-shaping trend at the time. The shifts from one phase to the other were decisively determined by two things. The first was the change in general political relations between the US and USSR as systemic and global rivals; a relationship that was itself always subject to changes in a host of factors, both external to, and domestic in, each country and bloc. The emergence of many such factors, and the kind of impact they had, was effectively out of the control of either government.

The second was related to the more narrow assessment of the comparable nuclear capabilities of the two countries. It was here that the degenerative logic of deterrence and arms racing operated. It was here that the problem of limited nuclear war most strongly asserted itself. No matter that the USSR from the sixties to the end of the Cold War period said it only believed in massive nuclear retaliation. Should deterrence break down and a nuclear exchange be initiated, it remained in both countries' interests to restrict the outbreak as much as possible, i.e. to be able to fight a limited nuclear war and to make their respective nuclear preparations accordingly. However, to carry out such preparations, thereby making a limited war more feasible, itself further undermined the credibility deterrence supposedly provided through the presence of a weapons system capable of massive retaliation. What emerged was an insecurity-generating arms race spiral with quantitative and qualitative increases at all levels whether in regard to tactical or strategic weapons/delivery systems.

'Massive Retaliation' to 'Flexible Response'

Thus, the first two phases of US nuclear politics were never counterposed to each other. From the early fifties, Washington was clear about the need to have tactical weapons in Europe not only to counter a possible Soviet conventional threat on that continent but to separate the European battleground from a transcontinental Soviet–US one. Nonetheless, given the great imbalance between the US and Soviet arsenals even after the latter developed the bomb in 1949, the US's early nuclear posture was of (1) how to maintain an overwhelming nuclear superiority both in numbers of warheads and in the range, extent, and spread of delivery systems, e.g. ringing the USSR with air bases from Iceland to Italy to Turkey to Japan and places in-between; and (2) how to translate this superiority into tangible political gains. It was only around 1960 that the USSR developed the capacity to threaten the US mainland through land-based intercontinental ballistic missiles, and really only in the mid-sixties that it had such missiles in sufficient numbers to constitute an assured second-strike capacity.

Massive retaliation in Europe meant deterring any Soviet 'adventurism' of even a conventional kind by creating a fear of the disastrous consequences for the USSR of taking any such decision. Of course, from the Soviet side, interpretation of US and NATO designs was very different. In the event, once the USSR had equipped itself with a sufficiently large, diverse, and sophisticated arsenal to not only threaten the US mainland but also to wreak nuclear damage on Western Europe roughly equivalent to what NATO could do to it, whatever 'political advantages' the US and the West thought they had obtained from the nuclear imbalance in their favour had disappeared even by the peculiar and distinctive logic of nuclearism subscribed to by the Western nuclear establishment.

'Flexible response' was the reaction to the changed nuclear equation in a larger political context marked by a general and continuing Western confidence in its ability to contain Communism worldwide despite increasing unease about growing Soviet influence in the third world and revolutionary successes in certain regions. Krushchev may have talked of the need for 'peaceful coexistence' from the mid-fifties onwards and suggested long-term compromise with the US and the West, but this was still, in Western eyes, the era of 'containment' and 'possible roll-back'. The German question lying at the heart of European politics was still perceived in terms faithful to the immediate post-Second World War reflex. The West was still a decade away from Ostpolitik (1972) and the definitive recognition this would embody of the permanency of the 'post-War settlement' in Europe.

Flexible response was a new way of pursuing an older US aim. Earlier, the nuclear battleground of Europe and Russia was separated from the US mainland by virtue of the sheer inability of Soviet nuclear forces to reach the North American continent in sufficient numbers. In the new situation, flexible response was a way for NATO and the US to pursue three aims. First, such a policy practice would presumably retain some credibility for the NATO tripwire principle, i.e. deterring a Soviet conventional attack across NATO lines through the threat of a nuclear retaliation. By introducing gradations and new possibilities in the form that such a nuclear response by a US-led NATO might take, it no longer had to hang on to the supposedly implausible and less credible option of an all-out nuclear response. Second, for the same reason that nuclear responses could now be more measured and 'limited', there were more chances of it not leading to a direct exchange between the US mainland and the USSR. That is to say, if nuclear war did break out it could more likely be confined to the European battleground. Third, by introducing more gradations and therefore more and newer levels of sophisticated tactical weaponry more rungs were being created in the ladder of possible escalation. If NATO then possessed nuclear superiority at all or most of these rungs, this would be yet another way of achieving political gains through the application of perceived 'nuclear superiority'. This time, superiority would not be of the old kind. It could not come from the threat of massive retaliation by the West in combination with an inability of the USSR to adequately target the US mainland. It would now come about because the West could now better control the 'ladder of escalation'. At the maximum limit (something that would obsess the Reaganite war-fighting hawks of the eighties) NATO might possess not merely 'escalation control' but 'escalation dominance', i.e. 'superiority' at every rung of the ladder of escalation.

The political purpose of the new flexible response strategy was the same as that of the earlier phase: to somehow harness a perceived or hoped-for 'nuclear weapons superiority' to the pursuit of general foreign policy and political ambitions. What forced the Western shift from flexible response to acceptance of arms control and acknowledgement of 'strategic parity' between the US and USSR (the shift into the third phase) were two developments. By the late sixties, Washington was mired down in Vietnam, losing not just the political war but international prestige and its own self-confidence as a global power and policeman. Furthermore, the USSR had by the end of the sixties acquired the capacity to threaten second-strike devastation on the US mainland. As both arsenals proceeded to gross and multiple overkill levels (and formal disparities in numbers was also declining considerably) a strategic parity of sorts became an inescapable fact of life. If a world order amenable to Western interests was still to be maintained, it now seemed to require the establishment of 'responsible' regional powers, that is, pro-Western surrogates, as well as a greater degree of compromise with the USSR with the aim of enlisting its support in containing third world revolutions.

In recognition of the Soviet nuclear advancement, a new era of arms control activity was inaugurated. It is however important to note that this arms control regime was only initiated because of a relative shift in the overall political relationship of forces between the USSR and the US against the latter caused by accumulating Western defeats in the third world. The future course of the arms control regime and of this period of détente politics would also remain hostage to the larger political–global ambitions and perceptions of the West and the US. Détente would not inaugurate, as the Soviets may have hoped, a new era of global political equality between itself and the US or between East and West.

It was seen from one side as a deal to at least sustain under pressure the existing status quo of Western dominance of the global order, albeit a dominance less conspicuous than in the past. The USSR would be offered a more honourable status as a great power but it had to play its part in stemming the tide of challenges emanating mostly from the third world. In return, the West made a concession that represented little more than making a virtue out of necessity: it prepared itself to formally acknowledge the permanency of the post-War European settlement. In August 1968, during the crushing of the Prague Spring, the West had by its reaction acknowledged its impotence in this regard. Except as fodder for ideological–moral rhetoric by the West, Soviet control of Eastern Europe was neither on the agenda of serious disputation between the two sides nor something that the West was much interested in challenging. Willy Brandt's Ostpolitik was largely the formal endorsement of this reality; a carrot offered to the USSR in return for it upholding détente. However, détente was bound to fail, as it eventually did, because what each side understood as its rationale and purpose was different and did not coincide. The crucial condition for its sustenance—the absence of further third world challenges to Western power—simply could not be ensured even if the USSR had wanted to.

On the arms control front during the period of détente, though such negotiations only sought to manage the race, not put an end to it, there did emerge the second great gain in the effort to bring about some restraint in the process of arms racing. This was the 1972 Anti-Ballistic Missile Defence or ABM Treaty. The first important breakthrough in arms restraint measures, which was also in a way a deep disappointment, was the 1963 Partial Test Ban Treaty or PTBT. This became possible because of the Cuban Missile Crisis of October 1962 and the fright it caused in government circles in both the US and USSR as it brought them to a literal hair's breadth from an actual exchange.[7] Furthermore, throughout the fifties and early sixties, public hostility to the environmental effects of atmospheric testing was accumulating to significant proportions. The final draft of the PTBT emerged from side negotiations between Moscow, London and Washington and disappointed other countries which subsequently became signatories. The widespread expectation then was that a comprehensive test ban treaty was in the offing. The non-nuclear weapons states (NNWSs) were putting pressure for this and anticipating it to be the final outcome. Instead, what finally emerged, a PTBT, was, therefore, also seen as a betrayal of universal hopes and an indication of how these three NWSs wanted to contain arms restraint measures within the wider framework of continued arms racing and further quantitative and qualitative development of their arsenals. France and China rejected the PTBT and continued to test in the atmosphere till the early eighties, only then shifting to purely underground testing.

The manner in which the 1972 ABM treaty emerged reflected the impact of various pressures. Domestic factors in the US were as important as external ones even as the former were also influenced by the latter. The success of the Soviet nuclear expansion in the sixties and the emergence of China as a nuclear weapons power after 1964 increased the pressure within the US to construct a nationwide ABM system. On the one hand, growing Soviet might suggested the need for strategic stability and compromise but on the other hand, the standard US reflex of wanting to maintain a strong lead over the USSR was also in play. In 1967, Robert McNamara, the US secretary of state, inaugurated the debate on a possible ABM system by stressing the need for strategic stability and hence the dangers represented by an ABM system. He, however, simultaneously attempted to rationalize the construction of a 'light' nationwide ABM system both to shield the US from a future Chinese arsenal and as a counter of sorts to a Soviet strike.[8]

In short, McNamara was mired in a contradiction forced upon him by fealty to the traditional US desire for one-upmanship over the Soviets (embodied in flexible response doctrines) and growing awareness of the need to promote strategic stability. The Soviets had begun developing an ABM system around Moscow, thus pushing many lobbies in the US to pursue a 'keep-ahead-of-the-Russians' approach. The US thus began developing a Sentinel system of 15 ABM sites near major cities. What was unexpected was the sudden public eruption of concern and debate between 1967 and 1970 over the Sentinel system which subsequently involved scientists and Congressmen in a way that no nuclear weapons-related issue had ever done before. First, the very siting of such proposed systems highlighted the vulnerability of city populations as never before. Second, the instability generated by defence systems, even according to the logic of 'security through deterrence', created further public fears. The Nixon administration sought to reorient the ABM towards a Safeguard system aiming to protect not cities but the newly developing Minuteman missile fields. By now, however, a sophisticated technical opposition had emerged to such attempts to 'destabilize' the terror logic of mutual assured destruction or MAD.

Such domestic opposition, and the general political weakness of the Nixon administration caused by a wealth of domestic and external factors, pushed the government towards the idea of using the ABM as a bargaining chip within the framework of the first Strategic Arms Limitation Talks or SALT-1, then in progress. At the same time, the US view was that it needed to build multiple warhead missile systems or multiple independently targeted re-entry vehicles (MIRVs) to overcome a Soviet ABM system, and that it needed to have an ABM system of its own as protection against Soviet developments of their own MIRVed missiles. The overall result was the enshrinement of the principle that the best way to control arms was also through threatening to build more arms, hence the importance of the ABM as a bargaining counter.

Nonetheless, though the ABM Treaty did not halt MIRVing on both sides nor the development of mobile delivery systems on land, it did halt for some time the quest for the construction of ballistic missile defence (BMD) systems until the Reagan administration changed tack. The Reagan administration put forward a radical reinterpretation of the ABM Treaty's provisions that effectively nullified it. It claimed that the Treaty did not explicitly prevent research, testing, development and deployment of space-based systems or those involving exotic new technologies. Reagan's Strategic Defence Initiative (SDI), better known as the 'Star Wars' project, would have effectively destroyed the relevance of the 1972 ABM Treaty. The latter, however, secured a reprieve because of the demise of the Star Wars project with the end of the Cold War. However, new pressures have emerged in the current phase of the post-Cold War period that are once again threatening the gains of the ABM in the name of constructing theatre (as supposedly opposed to strategic) BMD systems.[9]

Arms Race Management to the Second Cold War

If the seventies, through treaties like SALT-1 and SALT-2 marked an effort at managing the arms race, albeit modestly and insufficiently, why did this break down to be followed by a period of greater nuclear belligerence from roughly 1979 onwards? Why was détente followed by what came to be called the 'Second Cold War'? The basic explanation was not difficult to find. The MPLA (Popular Movement For the Liberation of Angola) triumph in Angola (1975), that of the Sandinistas in Nicaragua (1978), the fall of the Shah in Iran (1979) and the emergence of a succession of pro-Soviet regimes in Afghanistan eventually backed by direct Soviet invasion (1978–80) sounded the death knell of détente. Neither the overall political strategy of the US and the West, nor the nuclear arms control regime as a component in that wider scheme, had succeeded in their larger purpose. Both the general politics of Cold War conflict and the more specific politics of nuclearism entered a new phase.

Its essential direction was again set by the US and the Reagan administration, though the previous Carter administration had already begun moving in that direction. Well before the Soviet invasion of Afghanistan and the fall of the Shah, the Carter government called for an escalation of arms spending, deployment of intermediate range Cruise and Pershing-2 missiles in Europe, and proclaimed the need to set up a Rapid Deployment Force in the Gulf, while SALT-2 was stymied in Congress. Indeed, Presidential Directive (PD) 59 on 25 July 1980, which raised the idea of nuclear warfighting as an official doctrine, was promulgated under Carter.

While the strategic goal—reversal of the global weakening of US-led Western dominance in its systemic rivalry with the USSR and the Socialist bloc—remained the same, the means to be adopted now changed. Given the failure of détente, this was inevitable. The specific politics of nuclearism this gave rise to was embodied in the new Reagan doctrine of preparing to fight and win nuclear wars. In this regard, two key initiatives were pursued—the emplacement of Pershing-2 and Cruise missiles (or Euromissiles) by NATO in Europe and targeted on the USSR; and the 1983 Strategic Defence Initiative or Star Wars programme whose first concrete fruits were anticipated to emerge in the mid-nineties. The first initiative had a history preceding Reagan. The second, although it had a continuity with fears and desires expressed earlier by significant lobbies in the US, was the Reagan government's own decision. Star Wars sought to destroy the spirit, intent, and purpose of the 1972 ABM Treaty and thus introduce a dangerously destabilizing new dimension into the arms race. Both initiatives were part of a new 'nuclear warfighting' perspective.

In the sixties and seventies NATO reduced the vulnerability of its theatre nuclear missiles by making them sea-based (fitted on to Polaris submarines) and made them more devastating by MIRVing them. NATO removed land-based missiles by choice! In the calculus of nuclear accounting this gave it an advantage over the USSR in the field of intermediate range missiles. The central point at issue in the SALT-2 negotiations from 1972 to 1979 was this imbalance in theatre nuclear forces between the two sides. The USSR repeatedly sought to get the issue into the negotiations but was constantly opposed. After 1976 it sought to redress this imbalance somewhat by producing and deploying SS-20s which were mobile and MIRVed but still markedly inferior to NATO's weapons systems which were far less vulnerable and had a longer range.

The SS-20s were not seen as a problem by the US and Western Europe at the time (and were excluded from the SALT-2 negotiations) but their deployment later became the publicly declared justification for deploying Pershing-2 and Cruise missiles. In actual fact, a complex of factors led to the decision to deploy the Euromissiles. These included West Germany's (headed by Chancellor Helmut Schmidt) desire to have a strong symbolic expression of continuing US commitment to NATO and the defence of Western Europe against the USSR. The eruption of the Euromissile controversy which then rocked the West German government and stimulated a huge peace movement, the likes of which had never before been seen, was not expected. It was the nature of these missiles, their relation to a new warfighting strategy, and the growing technical expertise available to anti-nuclear activists and groups, that ensured the subsequent political turmoil.

NATO was now reintroducing, after a prolonged stretch of well over a decade, land-based weapons, siting them in densely populated Western Europe near major cities, making them in effect more attractive targets. Worse still, the Pershing-2s were far and away the most accurate missiles yet produced. They represented a qualitative leap in this respect with the capability of hitting a target within a radius of 100 feet. Their proposed deployment fitted into a new strategy different in one decisive respect from flexible response or earlier strategies for fighting limited or protracted nuclear wars. These were consciously perceived as first-strike weapons par excellence. Cruise missiles (fitted either with conventional or nuclear warheads) undetectable by existing radar facilities or by satellites represented the first breakthrough in stealth technology and delivery systems. They were ideal tools for waging a limited nuclear war and thus powerful complements to the Pershing-2 missiles. What the latter provided the US and NATO with was the new ability to 'decapitate' the political–military leadership of the Soviet weapons system.

Crowning the already imposing arsenal of the West, imposing both in quantity and quality, their introduction made no sense except in providing a much more refined ability than ever before to carry out the decapitation option. Insofar as five to ten per cent of Soviet warheads (400 to 800) might still survive such a decapitating first strike, these were to be countered by the development of a Star Wars system covering the US mainland. Thus Euromissiles and SDI were complementary and integrated parts of a new politics of nuclearism aiming to set the pattern for the next decade and more. Of course, the SDI project was ridden with enormous difficulties. Building a near-impenetrable shield was always something of a chimera, but what is important here, and disturbing, is that large and very influential sections amongst the US nuclear élite believed in the efficacy and feasibility of SDI, and in nuclear warfighting generally, and were preparing accordingly.

The new political and nuclear belligerence brought about by Reagan's doctrines and nuclear preparations was not only deeply provocative to the USSR but obviously raised fears of a pre-emptive strike by the Soviet Union (before such preparations could come into effect) and led to a dramatic increase in nuclear tensions and arms racing. The Euromissiles made Europe particularly vulnerable. Here the peace movement reached hitherto undreamt of heights and led to much more radical demands. In the US, by contrast, the central unifying demand of the growing anti-nuclear peace movement was not for dramatic reductions in arms or an end to the Cold War or for growing European neutrality across its East–West divide, both of which surfaced strongly in the European peace movement. It was simply for a nuclear freeze. This movement was, however, also bigger and wider than anything in the US since 1945, far eclipsing the 1967–70 opposition to the Sentinel and Safeguard ABM systems. This movement of the late seventies and eighties had significant influence on the US's political institutions from the local to the Congressional level.

Because the two major peace movements did not ever succeed in achieving their central demands despite massive and unprecedented popular mobilizations, it is easy to dismiss them as of no ultimate consequence in weakening or halting the arms race. To do this, however, would be to make a fundamental error of assessment regarding the overall impact and relevance of these movements which was very considerable indeed. They helped produce and disseminate a radical and powerful critique of nuclearism. They paved the way for future mobilizations and activities, thereby clearing the ground for sustained NGO interventions in later years. This has now become an institutionalized and important part of the general political scene concerning disarmament negotiations. Governments and officials became accessible and 'answerable' to non-official sources in ways quite different from the pre-peace movements era. A proper evaluation of these peace movements will be taken up in a later chapter. For the moment it will suffice to point out that apart from raising and changing consciousness on a mass scale, they decisively influenced the terms of nuclear discourse and debate.

Advocates of continued arms racing and, worse, of preparing for limited nuclear wars, were pushed onto the defensive having to rely ultimately on their rock-bottom 'trump-card' claim that the Cold War necessitated such measures. Thus when the Cold War began to unwind it was no longer possible for decision-shaping and decision-making élites to avoid going along the new path of actual nuclear restraint and reductions. This shift towards greater sanity would neither have been so easy or so rapid or so widely endorsed without the prior impact of these peace movements. Furthermore, Gorbachev's own efforts to progressively denuclearize East–West relations through his specific proposals banked heavily on the positive internal input into policy making in the US and Western Europe imparted by a mass public opinion made more responsive precisely by these peace movements.

Notes

1. This was a debate about the meaning of the nuclear arms race and the nature of its relationship to Cold War structures. It was sparked off by E. P. Thompson, perhaps the single most representative figure on both sides of the Atlantic of the peace movement of the eighties. His powerful essay, 'Notes on Exterminism, the Last Stage of Civilization' postulated an 'exterminist logic' out of superpower control that overrode the Cold War face-off and subsumed it, thereby posing an even more acute danger than thought. Thompson sought to uncover the 'distinctive' sources (beyond recognized Cold War theorizing of the time) of this terrible logic. For all his many insights, Thompson's basic argument was flawed. The central weakness was to grossly underplay the significance of the *systemic* character of the divide in his effort to understand the nature of the nuclearized world order and its likely future discontents. For a comprehensive survey of various arguments for and against Thompson's thesis at the time, see *Exterminism and the Cold War*, edited by New Left Review, Verso, London, 1982. An even more extreme form of this mistake (from the left) was Noam Chomsky's thesis of a clash of superpowers structurally indistinct from each other. N. Chomsky, *Towards a New Cold War*, Pantheon, New York, 1982.
2. See in particular, the essays by Mike Davis, 'Nuclear Imperialism and Extended Deterrence', Roy and Zhores Medvedev, 'The USSR and the Arms Race', and Fred Halliday, 'The Sources of the New Cold War' in the collection, *Exterminism and the Cold War.*

   Between 1948 and the present time, Russia directly invaded three countries, all of which were on its borders: Hungary (1956), Czechoslovakia (1968), Afghanistan (1979). Over the same period, the US sent troops and bombers to many more countries far from its borders: Korea (1950–3), Iran (1953), Guatemala (1954), Lebanon (1958 and 1984), Vietnam (1960–75), the Congo (1960), Cuba (1961), the Dominican Republic (1965), Laos (1960, 1970s), Kampuchea (1970–5), Grenada (1983), Honduras (1985 onwards), Panama (1989), Iraq (1991), Somalia (1993), Haiti (1995), and Serbia (1999).
3. See M. Kaku and D. Axelrod, *To Win a Nuclear War*, Zed Books, London, 1987, Ch.1, 2, 3 and 7.

4. See results of a poll conducted by Lake Sosin Snell & Associates which asked the question, 'Do you feel safer knowing that the US and other countries have nuclear weapons, or would you feel safer if you knew for sure that no country including the US had nuclear weapons?' Appeared in a leaflet issued by the Global Resource Action Center for the Environment (GRACE), New York, April 1997. Information also available at aslater@igc.apc.org
5. The Baruch Plan (named after a Wall Street financier, Bernard Baruch) called for the creation of an International Atomic Development Authority that would take control of 'all phases of the development and use of atomic energy'. Three aspects of the Plan doomed it in Soviet eyes. This Authority while under the UN would not be subject to the Security Council or otherwise be subjected to a national veto. The USSR, not unreasonably, felt this would ensure US domination through the UN of that time. The Plan also threatened 'condign punishment' for violators. In this case the only potential violator was the USSR and the US the only country in a position to impose punishment. The Plan also assigned obligations to the US which were vague but to the USSR which were clear and harsh. The US would have retained a knowledge monopoly on how to make the bomb.

   The Soviet counter-proposal insisted on the retention of national sovereignty but called for an international convention 'prohibiting the production and employment of weapons based on the use of atomic energy'. All stocks would be destroyed within three months of the convention coming into force. Two other committees would respectively ensure circulation of relevant information so as to eliminate a knowledge monopoly, and devise a system of safeguards against violation. This would emerge in full and institutionalized form only after the stocks were destroyed. The US viewed this Soviet proposal with deep suspicion as aiming to eliminate the US 'advantage' without a prior Soviet sacrifice, while not trusting that the Soviets would not subsequently hide their capabilities.
6. *Perceived Nuclear Balance in 1963*

	US	*USSR*
ICBM launchers	229	44
SLBM launchers	144	97
IRBM launchers	105	20–40 in Cuba (before removal)
Strategic bombers	1300	155+

By 1970

ICBMs	1054	1300
SLBMs	656	240
Strategic bombers	520	140
Total warheads	4000	1800
Megatonnage	4300	3100

By 1980

ICBMs	1050	1398
SLBMs	544	920
Strategic bombers	375	150
Warheads	9900	7800.

For the US, subs carried 57 per cent of total warhead strength, land-based ICBMs carried 22 per cent, and bombers carried 21 per cent. For the USSR, land-based ICBMs carried 68 per cent of warhead strength, subs carried 23 per cent, and bombers 9 per cent.

By 1988

ICBMs	1000	1382
SLBMs	640	922
Strategic bombers	396	155

The US had a total of 23,400 warheads of which 13,012 were strategically deployed; and the USSR had 20,600 warheads of which 11,450 were strategically deployed.

SOURCES: *Living With Nuclear Weapons* by Harvard Nuclear Study Group, Harvard Univ. Press, Cambridge, Mass. 1983, pp. 87, 90 and 120.

SIPRI Yearbook 1988, Oxford Univ. Press, Oxford, 1988; Tables 2.1, 2.2, 2.4 and 2.5; pp. 36, 37, 39 and 40.

7. Information released in 1995 and 1996 revealed that there were three occasions during the three-week Cuban missile crisis when either side could have launched a strike because of system failures and miscalculation compounded by fear. There was a routine missile test flight by the US Navy from Florida into the Atlantic which was not immediately identified. The US thought it might be a launch from Cuba at them, the Soviets thought it might be a launch by the US against Cuba. Ten minutes of high tension passed before the character of the incident became clear. From a secret airbase in North Dakota a false alert was triggered leading to nuclear-equipped planes already instructed to hit targets in Russia almost taking off before being stopped at literally the last minute. From Alaska, a US plane mistakenly intruded deep into Soviet airspace and two Soviet planes equipped with air-to-air missiles were sent to knock it down. Before this could happen, two US planes went after it because tower signals were not reaching it. Fortunately, these US planes reached the offending pilot first and radioed him to turn back and get out of Soviet airspace before the Soviet planes could reach him. It was however a near thing.

All this was quite apart from the pressure exerted on Kennedy by sections of the military and civilian leadership to launch a first strike. In this regard, see the book transcript of *The Kennedy Tapes* by E. R. May and P. D. Zelikow, Belknap Press, Harvard Univ., Cambridge, Mass, 1997; and *One Hell of a Gamble: Krushchev, Castro, and Kennedy 1958–64* by A. Fursenko and T. Naftali, W. W. Norton, 1997.

8. See J. Finney, 'A Historical Perspective' in *The ABM Treaty: To Defend Or Not To Defend*, ed. by W. Stutzle, B. Jasani, and R. Cowen, SIPRI publications, Oxford Univ. Press, Oxford, 1987.
9. The ABM Treaty allows theatre missile defences (TMDs) but places two limits on them. TMDs cannot be given 'capabilities to counter strategic missiles' nor can they be 'tested in an ABM mode', i.e. against targets with the characteristics of strategic missiles. However, since the ABM Treaty does not clearly define the difference between theatre and strategic missiles nor the meaning of 'capabilities to counter', this grey area is currently being exploited by the US through the development and testing of two high altitude wide-area TMD systems: the Army's Theatre High Altitude Area Defence (THAAD) system and the Navy's Upper Tier System.

   Both intend to make intercepts above the atmosphere and appear to have intrinsic strategic capabilities. They raise serious compliance problems with the ABM Treaty. The US is currently seeking modifications in the ABM Treaty through negotiations with Russia in favour of these TMDs. The key issue is to fill the lacuna in regard to TMD demarcation.

CHAPTER THREE

The Global Context–II

Hesitant but New: Disarmament Momentum after the Cold War

Ultimately the single most important reason why the Cold War began to unwind and then ended was because the Gorbachev leadership of the USSR decided to end it by offering, in effect, what can be called a 'global historic compromise'.[1] This was a deeply contradictory political phenomenon with both negative and positive consequences. Its negative aspect was most clearly visible in the third world where the USSR now effectively abandoned all efforts to provide a counterweight to Western and US power. Third world challengers to any Western approved form of the status quo could no longer count on the existence of a systemic rivalry to mean even cautious Soviet support for themselves. From Namibia to Cuba to Somalia to Panama to the anti-Iraq Gulf War, the USSR (and its successor Russian state) since 1987 has either silently acquiesced or explicitly endorsed, or even sought to partner in some way, US initiatives there. Insofar as Russia today has expressed unease and opposition to US and Western political initiatives, these have to do with its concerns in the regions of the ex-USSR and in Europe, e.g. ex-Yugoslavia, but not in regard to US and Western behaviour in the third world except in those parts of Asia closer to home, e.g. Afghanistan, where Russia has been somewhat more critical.

Global historic compromise was a Soviet attempt to rewrite the rules of systemic incommensurability in a way whereby rivalry would be replaced by a longer term acceptance of systemic difference and a more determined search than ever before for convergence to a new status quo stabilized enduringly on the basis of strategic cooperation, if not quite strategic partnership. Gorbachev did not envisage a systemic convergence of the two different social orders. He pursued the chimera of an enduring and stable compatibility between two different social systems to be brought about by changes on both sides. On the Western side it should rest on (1) the emergence of a new non-antagonistic foreign policy towards the USSR and the Soviet bloc of countries; (2) political approval of, and non-interference with, the domestic changes he was preparing to undertake; (3) providing material and economic–financial assistance. On his side it would rest on wider popular legitimacy for the 'socialist system' to be brought about by internal democratization in the USSR and guided but steady democratization in the Eastern European countries, and Soviet economic reorganization in the direction of establishing a vaguely understood and vaguely defined form of market socialism.

Six Renunciations

The ending of the Cold War had its most positive impact in two areas. First, in freeing Eastern Europe from decades of Soviet domination even if its systemic collapse was not foreseen. There was also the reunification of Germany. This was a positive step because it was ultimately desired by the overwhelming majority of Germans on both sides of the former divide. There was, however, also an unfortunate dimension to this historic event because what actually took place was not renunification but the effective annexation by West Germany of the eastern part. Second, the end of the Cold War completely derailed the politics of nuclearism pursued by the US under Reagan. However, any hopes (between 1986–9) that the dismantling of the various structures of the Cold War would be effected somewhat symmetrically and that the decline of Soviet hegemony would be paralleled by a broadly commensurate decline in US-led Western imperialism, would be dashed by the cataclysmic and revolutionary events of 1989 and after.

The systemic collapse of Soviet Socialism, its own political, territorial, economic, and ideological breakdown as a result of the general dynamic let loose (but not controlled) by the specific pattern and pace of the Gorbachev reforms, led to an unexpected 'victory' for the other side. This was an utterly unexpected victory both in its comprehensiveness and in the speed with which it came about. This had to have significant consequences for the new politics of nuclearism that was, and is, slowly emerging after the end of the Cold War. Not all of these consequences have been positive.

The end of the Cold War and the initiation of a process of arms reduction effectively extinguished the felt danger of a nuclear exchange that had been the vital emotional foundation for the existence of an active, anti-nuclear mass movement in Europe and the US. After all, the political basis for fearing an exchange was no longer present and a momentum of sorts involving genuine and substantial arms reductions much beyond the scope of earlier arms management exercises, had been well and truly established. From the 1987 Intermediate Nuclear Forces (INF) Treaty eliminating all land-based theatre missiles to the removal (not formalized by treaties) of tactical missiles from all surface ships of the US and Russia (this began from 1991 onwards) to the negotiation of the Strategic Arms Reduction Talks (START-I and START-II), which cut strategic warheads by more than half, much was seemingly being accomplished, and more was promised.

So far as things go, this judgement was not incorrect. Other restraint and disarmament measures also received a fillip. Three actual NWSs—Belarus, Kazakhstan, and Ukraine—all gave up their NWS status. The first two countries (had they wanted to) would have found it difficult to buck Russian objections to retaining this status based on what Moscow claimed was its missiles. However, they didn't want to keep the weapons systems although they had the sovereign right to do so. Ukraine, with the third largest arsenal in the world, could have done so much more easily had it wanted to, overriding any Russian objections. Again, it chose to trade in its nuclear arsenal to Russia for financial rewards from the West. All three joined the Non-Proliferation Treaty or NPT. Three nuclear capable states, South Africa, Argentina and Brazil, gave up nuclear threshold status, at least in part motivated by the emergence of a new climate of global disarmament and restraint in nuclear matters. Certainly, the white de Klerk regime had begun to dismantle the nuclear arsenal because the end of apartheid was near and this would mean the accession of a black majority government. Or to be put it bluntly, neither they nor their Western protectors wanted a black government to have the bomb. It is, however, necessary to note that the African National Congress (ANC), even during the period of opposition, had always opposed nuclear status for South Africa. When apartheid was overthrown and the Mandela government took over, South Africa also became (under black rule) one of the most active governments anywhere in regard to issues of general and global disarmament.

All the NWSs joined and ratified the South Pacific nuclear weapons free zone (NWFZ) agreement called the Treaty of Rarotonga. Two new NWFZ treaties were drawn up: the African NWFZ or Treaty of Pelindaba, and the Southeast Asian NWFZ or Bangkok Treaty. For the latter to come into formal existence it had to be ratified by the Philippines, which was accomplished in mid-1999. However, the US and China still have reservations about recognizing this Southeast Asian NWFZ because of their objections to its insistence that there be no transit of nuclear weapons in the sea areas they deem should lie outside the Treaty's purview. Moreover, the Treaty of Pelindaba did not demand a real sacrifice on the part of the existing NWFZs especially as the nuclear munitions base of Diego Garcia was excluded from the Treaty. Nevertheless, these NWFZs were valued gains in themselves, besides further promoting the possible creation of more NWFZs some of which would, if established, require dismantlement of existing nuclear placements. In general, the overall disarmament momentum was being strengthened by such developments even though more sacrifices on the part of the NWSs had to be demanded. However, the overall judgement of post-Cold War disarmament possibilities, to be accurate, had to take more into account, and when this was done, excessive optimism guarded against.

The weaknesses inherent in the manner in which the Cold War ended were beginning to surface more clearly. Since West and East shared the blame for initiating and perpetuating the Cold War (albeit unevenly: the West had more of the blame), the long anticipated ending of the Cold War was expected to bring about more changes and improvements than it actually did. Many, if not most, opponents of the Cold War who also did not align themselves with either side, expected both military–nuclear blocs in Europe to be dismantled more or less completely. The drift towards greater European independence from, and neutrality in, bloc politics that had emerged during the eighties was expected to be reinforced by the ending of this bloc conflict. Instead, what emerged was the complete collapse of the Warsaw Pact but not of NATO.

Negative and Positive Consequences

Not only was US ascendancy in Europe retained but strengthened. The earlier pressures for the establishment of a series of European NWFZs, e.g. in the Baltic–Nordic region, the Balkans, and in Central Europe, were actually weakened. The way in which Germany was unified deprived the former Soviet Union of any bargaining capacity whatsoever. So, while the eastern part of Germany would, in deference to Soviet wishes, be kept nuclear free, the same would not apply to the western part where US-controlled NATO missiles would remain. The presumed East–West imbalance of the past would now be reversed. Earlier it had been claimed that the Warsaw Pact countries enjoyed a conventional superiority over their NATO counterparts which had to be countered by NATO's nuclear arsenal. Now the Soviets felt the need to rely more strongly than before on their nuclear might in order to compensate for their conventional inferiority vis-à-vis NATO forces. As it was, the massive collapse of the ex-USSR reinforced the views of those Russians who now felt that a strong nuclear weapons system was the one symbol of great power status that Russia now possessed and should still retain. In a striking reflection of its new strategic reliance on an albeit much reduced arsenal, Russia retracted from its decades-long commitment to No First Use of nuclear weapons. Of the five first NWSs, only China still continues to adhere to this posture.

Many of the former members of the East European Socialist bloc, in the face of their own crises of transition to capitalist democracies, had no other strategic vision beyond a desperate desire to join the European Community as quickly as possible. Insofar as joining NATO could be paraded as an expression of their determined loyalty to the European Union (EU) and to its related Atlantic Alliance, the new East European leaderships had no qualms whatsoever about joining NATO on whatever terms it or the US might propose. Such was the alacrity of countries like Poland, Hungary and Czechia or the Czech Republic in this regard that they unilaterally declared themselves willing to accept NATO nuclear emplacements on their territories without this even being stipulated as a required condition for their membership of this military–political alliance.

With the end of the Cold War the earlier rationale for the existence of NATO had greatly weakened but only one bloc was demilitarized. The other military–nuclear bloc continued, indeed was strengthened politically and territorially and was under no serious public pressure from any direction to dismantle itself. Russian desires in this respect are impotent and incapable of being fulfilled. What NATO has had to do is to find a newer rationale as well as clothe an older one (keeping Russia out, Germany down, and the US in) in an outward public garb that is different from that of the past, which was protecting Europe against the Soviet threat. Only a small dissident minority in the US strategic establishment has rightly seen a historic opportunity arising after the end of the Cold War to completely reorganize US–Soviet and European–Soviet relations on a dramatically newer basis of a 'common' European security in which Russia would be invited to play an honourable and welcome part. This would imply taking rapid and very significant steps towards the steady demilitarization and denuclearization of NATO, as well as a much more dramatic withdrawal of the US military–political presence in Europe.[2] The much larger majority within this establishment have been happier promoting an expanded political–military role for NATO, and as the bombing of Serbia (1999) showed, they have won out.

NATO Enlargement and 'Stockpile Stewardship'

NATO enlargement as a now approved and established policy perspective represents a dangerous continuity with previous policy aspirations. It indicates that the US still seeks to use its 'victory' in the Cold War to institutionalize and consolidate its relative political gains vis-à-vis Russia in a global game the latter is no longer able to play. This policy is dangerous because it continues to treat Russia as a strategic opponent (no matter what other public rationale for NATO expansion is given), and in doing so has all the makings, in a worst-case scenario, of becoming a self-fulfilling prophecy. Even if the worst does not happen, it will still certainly create and sustain avoidable tensions between Russia and the West whose outcome is deeply unpredictable in the longer term. NATO expansion in Europe is also a way for the US to maintain political–strategic–military dominance over a potential capitalist rival—a German-centred Europe should that emerge as a likely possibility in the future.

The specifically nuclear consequences of NATO enlargement are twofold. It virtually guarantees that there will be stronger limits to the extent to which further Russian de-nuclearization will proceed. It is also one of the two most serious blows that have been inflicted on the new global disarmament momentum emerging after 1987, slowing it down and making it more tenuous and uneven well before the Indian and Pakistani tests of May 1998 added their own body blows.

Another consequence of the particular manner in which the Cold War ended was that it effectively gave the US a much freer hand to pursue its imperialist ambitions in the third world. On the level of nuclear politics this means the emergence of a peculiar contradiction. On the one hand, third world challenges no longer imply by proxy a Russian or systemic conflict against the US or West, thus reinforcing the astrategic irrelevance of the nuclear threat for coping with these. The US might feel freer to indulge in such threats without fear of this escalating into a great power nuclear exchange, but it also has much less reason than ever to engage in, or carry out, such threats. On the other hand, this situation of greater flexibility and freedom for US power also reinforces the non-proliferation dimension of US strategic–nuclear thinking and its approach to post-Cold War arms restraint and disarmament proposals and measures. Hence 'counter-proliferation' has become the new code word for a developing policy of preventing at all costs potential opponents in the third world from obtaining such weapons or otherwise trying to pose any kind of strategic threat to the US.

To be sure, after the end of the Cold War, there has been in the US a definite shift in the relationship of forces between arm reducers/moderators and arms racers in favour of the former, but the other side of the picture has not been equally positive. While there is a growing lobby in the opinion-shaping élite that genuinely wants to move towards complete arms elimination, it remains so small as to be literally dwarfed by arms retainers whether of the more moderate or extreme kind. The earlier autonomy of the Arms Control and Disarmament Agency (ACDA) has been ended as it is being merged with the State Department. In the Houses of the Congress, Republican domination has created another major obstacle to pressing the scope and pace, and sometimes even the fact, of arms reductions.

In the US, the basic direction of the new politics of nuclearism is revealed by two important strategic documents: the Nuclear Posture Review or NPR (September 1994) and the Presidential Decision Directive or PDD-60 (November 1997). Recognizing a new post-Cold War reality in which the overall trend will be towards further reductions in the arsenals of the US and Russia, the crucial aim of these documents is to provide a new strategic rationale for the enduring *retention* of nuclear weapons. Thus even though the US establishment is not in its decisive majority willing to buck the current trend of qualitative restraint and quantitative decline in nuclear weapons (unless there is some dramatic change in global politics or a sharp reversal in the existing disarmament momentum), it is determined not to allow that momentum to gather such pace that the US is no longer able to factor it into its overall nuclear strategy and by doing so partly control and direct this momentum.

Thus NPR and PDD-60 attempt to make a smaller number of nuclear weapons do newer and more things like countering biological and chemical weapons. Newer enemies, e.g. 'rogue states', have to be discovered to justify their retention, and newer, yet to be fully articulated, strategic tasks for these weapons, have to be established. With the end of the Cold War, these 'rogue states' are to be found in the third world, especially in places of continuing strategic importance like the Middle East but not only there. The countries which the US has in mind as actual or potential rogue states are Iraq, Libya, Iran, and North Korea, but of course the label can fit any other possible challenger to future US interests. The formulation of a new nuclear–strategic doctrine is obviously connected to the need to formulate a new general ideology of justification for continued US efforts to dominate the world order. Thus the peregrinations of a Samuel Huntington, professor of politics at Harvard University, are also part of this same process of wider and newer ideological and strategic rethinking in the post-Cold War era. His thesis about the 'clash of civilizations' obviously aims at highlighting the possible new challenges to US political dominance by, on the one hand, the 'Islamic' states of the Middle East, and on the other hand, to US and Western economic eminence by the 'Confucian' countries of the Far East, i.e. China and other 'rapid industrializers' in that region.

Since a smaller arsenal must do more things it must last longer, hence the US's science-based stockpile stewardship and management programme or

SBSS & MP. Ostensibly directed at assuring 'safety and reliability' of an ageing stockpile, it is a much more comprehensive programme which, when allied with ongoing subcritical experiments, computer simulation activities, and R&D into direct fusion weapons, clearly aims at continuing the development of new applications of existing weapons designs and designing new weapons to the degree possible within the limits imposed by the ban on explosive testing. The US has already carried out a first series of six subcritical tests with more such series of tests contemplated. Research into direct fusion is, of course, a leap into the unknown, but it is continuing. The point is that there exists a strong pro-nuclear lobby with particularly strong roots in sections of the defence services and especially in the weapons laboratories and their associated bodies and personnel. If they are not decisively weakened these activities will continue.

True, a Comprehensive Test Ban Treaty (CTBT) imposes powerful limits on what can be achieved in qualitative advance through all such activities. Nonetheless, the SBSS & MP violates the general intent and spirit of the CTBT which aims at ending such efforts at qualitative advancement regardless of how successful or unsuccessful they might prove to be. Such activities, even if they fail to achieve their desired ends, preserve much of the software and prepare much of the hardware for a rapid return to major qualitative advances in nuclear weaponry should the US ever break out of the CTBT in the future.

All this then is part of the continuing project of ensuring US global political–military dominance. While there is (after 1987) a significant relative decline in nuclear arsenals and preparations when compared to what was taking place during the Cold War period, it is noteworthy that in regard to conventional weapons preparations and expenditures by the US, there is no such comparative decline over a similar period![3] The post-Cold War era then has seen a distinctive mix of the positive and the negative in its ongoing and contested politics of nuclearism. In contrast to the 1945–87 period when the negative outweighed the positive (despite the PTBT and the ABM Treaty, the overall trajectory of the arms race was upwards), today the positive has so far outweighed the negative. However, even positive measures of significant import like the CTBT and the 'Advisory Opinion' against the legality of nuclear weapons issued by the International Court of Justice or World Court in July 1996, have had their effects weakened by the continued perfidy and hypocrisies of the existing NWSs, most notably but not solely by the US. The US, the one country that is today uniquely placed to lead the world rapidly to complete or near-complete nuclear disarmament, is the country most determined to continue to use the possession of nuclear weapons for the pursuit of general political and foreign policy objectives.

Indefinite Extension of the NPT

If NATO consolidation and expansion was one major assault on the post-Cold War disarmament momentum, the other big blow was dealt by the permanent and indefinite extension of the NPT in April 1995. This symbolized as nothing else the determination of the existing NWSs to maintain their exclusive club and to completely distort the original purpose of the NPT. The NPT should now no longer be lauded as the one living institutionalized commitment of the NWSs to carrying out their own eventual disarmament. The NPT through its permanent and indefinite extension has been finally and fully transformed into little more than the central institutionalized mechanism for ensuring non-proliferation, i.e. the enduring exclusivity of the nuclear club.

The fact that France and China finally joined the NPT regime in the post-Cold War period did not reflect a new found commitment on their part to obey Article VI that calls on the NWSs which are signatories to the Treaty to pursue negotiations 'in good faith' for complete disarmament. Nor did it mean a new-found enthusiasm on their part for promotion of global disarmament. Both countries had earlier repeatedly committed themselves to joining disarmament negotiations if the US and Russia reduced their arsenals by fifty per cent. Once this became feasible and certain in the post-Cold War era, both quite shamelessly resiled from their promises in this regard. France and China (along with the UK) now declared that they would only enter such negotiations when the US and Russia had reduced their arsenals by 95 per cent. It is in keeping with this cynical mentality that China and France joined the NPT. That is to say, they joined the NPT when they correctly perceived it to have been reduced to little more than a collective mechanism for ensuring non-proliferation outside the ranks of the NWSs while also legitimizing their own 'formal' entry and status into the nuclear club.

How did this betrayal of earlier hopes in the NPT entertained by the NNWSs come about? It was due to a combination of factors. At the heart of the NPT lay a bargain: renunciation of the nuclear option by NNWSs in return for a commitment by NWSs which were members of the Treaty to move towards complete global disarmament. The NPT still contains the only legal commitment made by the NWSs to carry out total disarmament, hence its enduring attraction for many NNWSs and anti-nuclear activists and groups that see in this the existence of some minimal point of international diplomatic leverage vis-à-vis the NWSs. Even the ICJ ruling took strength from Article VI and the legal commitment it embodied.

So disillusioned, however, had the NNWSs become with the perfidious behaviour of the NWSs in not obeying this Article that by the time the Treaty's life was ending (25 years after 1970 when it came into force) and the issue of its possible extension arose, the precise fate of the NPT was quite uncertain. It was by no means self-evident that the NPT would survive. Certainly, its permanent and indefinite extension was widely considered to be among the less likely outcomes. The most widespread view was that the NPT would be extended but not indefinitely and that most bargaining would be around the length of time for which it should be extended. The NWSs would want as long a time period as possible while the NNWSs would have to arrive at agreement about what would be a reasonable period. It was obvious to all that as long as the extension was limited, the NNWSs would possess stronger leverage on the NWSs since the NPT's future life could again be made more easily conditional on future behaviour by the NWSs.

Yet the unexpected happened and the NPT was permanently and indefinitely extended, thereby depriving the NNWSs of the earlier leverage they had and could have maintained. Three factors best account for this denouement. First, the NWSs were broadly united in expressing and pressing for this common aim. The US, in particular, carefully played the numbers game exercising enormous behind-the-scenes arm-twisting pressure to get the maximum number of NNWSs lined up in support of its own position. Second, while the NPT was not itself in any way responsible for the reductions in arms that took place after 1987 between the US and Russia, the fact of such reductions and the existence of a new more positive climate of restraint and disarmament in its own way also gave something of a reprieve, a new infusion of life, into the NPT regime. A number of NNWSs were more inclined to believe that in the new improved political context, the NPT could perhaps be made to function as it was earlier expected to, with Article VI being taken more seriously. The fact that certain key NNWSs like South Africa, which were among the most proactive on disarmament, were inclined to support permanent extension also helped to swing matters that way. The single most important factor was however almost certainly the time-bound commitment made by the NWSs (for the first time) to conclude a Comprehensive Test Ban Treaty or CTBT before the end of 1996. This commitment was legally enshrined in the new 'Principles and Objectives' drawn up and appended to the newly extended NPT. Without this commitment to the CTBT the whole NPT regime risked unravelling. The CTBT then was a vital concession; one that the NWSs had to make in order to preserve the NPT as the central pillar in its non-proliferation regime.

The final passage of the CTBT, despite Indian opposition to it, marked one of the more significant gains in the effort to promote arms restraint and a cap on the qualitative nuclear arms race. The political–psychological, health, and environmental effects of a world permanently free of further testing should not be underestimated. Apart from this, the CTBT had other distinctive strengths. Unlike the PTBT or even the NPT (where the penultimate draft was drawn up behind closed doors by the US, USSR, and UK and passed with only minor revisions), the CTBT was the first genuinely multilaterally negotiated nuclear arms related treaty ever. As such, it set a crucial precedent: that global disarmament and restraint measures are too important to be simply left to the NWSs alone. Furthermore, the CTBT, after entering into force would for the first time set up a genuinely international monitoring system of structures, institutions and powers which in key respects would override national authority and sovereignty. Insofar as a world free of nuclear weapons necessarily requires both a mindset that transcends nationalism, and actual institutions and structures that override national sovereignty, all in the interests of a universal humanity, the CTBT in this regard too sets a vital practical–institutional precedent.

However, the CTBT in its final form also suffers from two serious weaknesses. The first pertains to the manner prescribed for its coming into force. This requires states like India and Pakistan, which at the time of writing have not signed the Treaty, to do so before the Treaty enters into force. Not only is this undemocratic and unfair to the countries concerned who have the right (howsoever mistaken it might be to exercise it) to refuse their assent, more importantly it is unfair to the Treaty which should enter into force as quickly as possible and apply to all those countries that have agreed to come under its aegis.

The second major flaw is that the CTBT is important not just in itself but as a step that further strengthens the momentum to more restraint and disarmament measures. Here the linkage of the CTBT to this general process is significant. In order to promote the multilateralization of disarmament negotiations, the CTBT should have been linked to the setting up of an Ad Hoc Committee on global nuclear disarmament in the Conference on Disarmament (CD) with at least a discussion mandate to begin with, striving for a negotiating mandate later. (It is an Ad Hoc Committee because the mandate for it has to be renewed each year in accordance with the CD's special procedures.) Achieving this would have constituted a major breakthrough, and endorsing the setting up of such an Ad Hoc Committee could have been embodied in the preamble of the Treaty.

This is absent from the final Treaty but could have emerged as a very real likelihood if India had been prepared to lead many other NNWSs in fulfilling this demand that they were already pressing hard for. Since India's accession to the CTBT was greatly valued by the NWSs, it could have bargained for this as the price for its assent. New Delhi was, however, never serious about wanting a better or stronger CTBT, but primarily concerned with justifying its rejection not just on 'national security' grounds but on the moral plane as an opponent of a Treaty that was supposedly deceptive, flawed, discriminatory, manipulative, etc.[4] Thus an opportunity to strengthen the link between the CTBT and the wider process of disarmament was lost.

A Spate of New Initiatives and the World Court Verdict

If the various treaties embodying arms reductions, the establishment of more NWFZs, the CTBT, a possible fissiles materials cut-off treaty (FMCT) can all be said to represent the 'hardware' of the new global restraint and disarmament process, then there is also the matter of generating new 'software' products. Changing the 'software' means, above all, attacking the moral legitimacy of nuclear weapons possession, undermining its strategic–political claims, and eroding the appeal and hold of the mindset of deterrence. The credibility and authority of nuclear élites—their 'security managers' and their pro-nuclear opinion-shapers—has to be progressively weakened. In the post-Cold War era, among the most important initiatives in this regard have been the Canberra Commission Report, the public statement by over 60 retired admirals and generals from seventeen countries against nuclear weapons, and the spate of new UN resolutions by NNWSs, e.g. Malaysia, newly motivated to activate themselves and others on the disarmament issue.

On 4 December 1996, the former head of the US Strategic Air Command, George 'Lee' Butler, and former NATO Commander, Andrew J. Goodpaster, issued a statement calling for the eventual elimination of nuclear weapons from the world's arsenals. They were joined by 60 others the following day. It has since become a very important point of reference precisely because so many of its signatories are former advocates of deterrence and have now turned opponents of this doctrine. One of its leading figures, General Butler, has repeatedly declared that far from nuclear deterrence providing security during the Cold War era, the truth was that for the decision-making élite, of which he was so important a part, it did not provide such security and that this élite never felt the US was safe during the whole period of arms racing.[5]

On 26 November1995, the Australian Premier, Paul Keating, announced the formation of a 15-member Canberra Commission to outline 'practical steps towards a nuclear weapons-free world including the related problems of maintaining stability and security during the transitional period and after this goal is accomplished'. Members of the Commission included General George Butler, Field Marshall Lord Carver (UK), Robert McNamara (former President of the World Bank and ex-US Secretary of State), Professor Joseph Rotblat (Nobel Prize Winner), and Michel Rocard (former Premier of France). The Commission submitted its report on 14 August 1996 outlining a phased programme for total disarmament.

The Malaysian-sponsored UN Resolution (A/C.1/51/L.37) of 6 November 1996 called for the 'commencement of negotiations leading to the conclusion of a Nuclear Weapons Convention . . .' It declared that the 'time has now come for the issue of the elimination of nuclear weapons, which is an equally important, indeed integral, part of the NPT process, to be addressed by the international community. Unless this issue is addressed, and addressed promptly, . . . the entire trade-off would be questioned by many non-nuclear weapons States Parties . . . if this trend were to continue, it could only undermine . . . the prospects of its attaining universality.' The Resolution called for sponsorship and support 'of all delegations who share these sentiments and are opposed to the threat or use of nuclear weapons and who would like to ensure that concrete and effective steps are taken now to pave the way for their total elimination within a realistic time frame, in the interest of ensuring the well-being and survival of humanity.' On 10 December 1996, there was a landmark vote in the UN General Assembly with over two-thirds of the 169 voting states supporting the resolution for an NWC.

In late 1998, after an SPD–Greens coalition government was formed in Germany, the new government publicly called for a re-evaluation of NATO's nuclear doctrines. Specifically, Germany called for NATO to reconsider its First Use tripwire perspective and to consider the adoption of a No First Use nuclear weapons pledge. This badly shocked the US, France, and the UK. Under their pressure, the new German government reiterated that it was not questioning the general rationale for NATO's nuclear arsenal but still did not budge on the issue of re-evaluating existing First Use doctrine. Belgium and Canada, also NATO members, did the same. The fact remains that for the first time some NATO members have called for such strategic re-evaluation of NATO nuclear doctrines in the post-Cold War era. In December 1998, seven countries (Sweden, Ireland, Egypt, Mexico, Brazil, New Zealand, South Africa) in, what is called the New Agenda Coalition, pushed an anti-nuclear resolution at the UN which received overwhelming support including abstentions from 12 out of the 16 NATO countries, which defied great pressure from the US, UK, France on them to vote against the resolution. The US, UK, France, Russia, India, and Pakistan voted against this resolution. The new political cracks in NATO regarding the doctrinal basis for the Alliance's retention of nuclear weapons are real and will not go away.

But perhaps the single most significant event was the historic ruling on 8 July 1996 by the International Court of Justice (World Court) at The Hague. The UN General Assembly had put the following question to the World Court: 'Is the threat or use of nuclear weapons in any circumstances permitted under international law?' Through its verdict the ICJ (considered the highest tribunal in the world on matters of international law) provided the first-ever legal determination on the issue. It held that 'the threat or use of nuclear weapons would generally be contrary to the rules of international law applicable in armed conflict and, in particular, the principles and rules of humanitarian law.' The ICJ also unanimously affirmed that Article VI of the NPT obligated the NWSs to move towards rapid disarmament, and called upon them to do so.

The verdict vindicated the principles of international humanitarian law, judging not just the use but the existence and possession of, and the preparations for development of, nuclear weapons a violation in this regard. The phrase 'general incompatibility' indicated both the minimum basis of agreement on the unethicality and indefensibility of nuclear weapons and of nuclear deterrence thinking. It also revealed that there was no collective agreement or ruling among all 14 judges on the narrower and legally problematic issue (which some judges held invalid to begin with) as to whether the use of nuclear weapons might be justified in extreme and exceptional circumstances such as threats to 'the very survival of a state'.

The whole case was considered so weighty that all 14 judges passed separate opinions, some of outstanding quality, like the 87 page document of the Sri Lankan Judge C.G. Weeramantry, which declared that 'the use or threat of use of nuclear weapons is absolutely prohibited by existing law—in all circumstances and without reservation'. Though the appointment of judges to the ICJ is a political choice and they usually vocalize and defend the views of the nominating states, this did not prevent an overall verdict that deeply dismayed the NWSs despite the presence of country judges (e.g. from Germany and Britain) expected to be more favourable to their nuclear concerns. The ICJ verdict did not fully delegitimize nuclear weapons possession but it was a historic step forward in the effort to globally delegitimize nuclear weapons. It was an example of what NGOs and other actors in international civil society can do to strengthen the general disarmament process. It was, after all, a coalition of peace groups that took the initiative known as the World Court Project and got it adopted by the UN system and referred to the ICJ for a ruling.

If we were to sum up the overall trajectory and character of the post-Cold War disarmament momentum up to mid-1998, we could in a single sentence say that it was hesitant, uneven, frequently faltering, fully capable of being reversed, but nonetheless, new, genuine, alive, and significant. It was in this context that the Indian and Pakistan tests erupted in May 1998. That this severely damaged the momentum is beyond doubt, that it might lead to its reversal has yet to be seen or determined. The final outcome depends on what can be done from now on to salvage what has been gained, to preserve and strengthen this momentum through other positive steps. This is the central task of our times.

Notes

1. *Compromesso Storico* or 'Historic Compromise' was a term first coined in the seventies by Enrico Berlinguer, then leader of the Italian Communist Party (PCI) to justify his new strategy of calling for a new partnership of sorts to replace the longstanding and deep-seated historical rivalry between the two major forces in domestic Italian politics: the PCI and the Christian Democrats. This apparently bold venture did not impress the CD and did not provide the hoped for political breakthrough to the PCI. It was part of a developing Eurocommunist strategy in Western Europe. However, Eurocommunism merely paved the way for the rise of Eurosocialism (the eclipse of mass Communist parties in Western Europe by their social democratic rivals) which in turn swung to the right and thereby paved the way for the dominance of a hard right neo-liberalism among its liberal and conservative opposition.
2. A German 'non-paper' had been submitted before the election of the new government of the Social Democratic Party and the Greens which reportedly called for substantial denuclearization of NATO. This report gained credence from the fact that after the elections the new government publicly called for a re-evaluation of NATO's traditional nuclear doctrines and effective scrapping of its First Use of nuclear weapons policy.
3.

	US	*Russia*	*UK*	*France*	*China*
Total operational	8420	10,240	160	449	400
Awaiting dismantling	1350	12,000	220	50	50
Reserve	2300				
Total	12,070	22,500	380	500	450

SOURCE: W.M. Arkin, R.S. Norris, J. Handler, *Taking Stock: Worldwide Nuclear Deployments, 1998*; Natural Resources Defense Council, Washington, March 1998.

4. For a detailed refutation of the criticisms of the CTBT by the Indian government and its supporters, see P. Bidwai and A. Vanaik, 'Why India Should Sign the CTBT: Returning to Our Own Agenda' in *The Economic and Political Weekly*, 19–25 September 1998, Mumbai. See also Appendices 1 and 2 below.
5. The Statement called for the following steps to be taken:
'First, present and planned stockpiles of nuclear weapons are exceedingly large and should now be greatly cut back.

'Second, remaining nuclear weapons should be gradually and transparently taken off alert, and their readiness substantially reduced both in nuclear weapons states and in de facto nuclear weapons states.

'Third, long-term international nuclear policy must be based on the declared principle of continuous, complete, and irrevocable elimination of nuclear weapons.'

CHAPTER FOUR

The Road to Pokharan-II and Chagai

The Fateful Days of May 1998

When the Prime Minister's Office (PMO) in New Delhi announced in the early afternoon of 11 May 1998 that Atal Behari Vajpayee, then having completed only seven weeks in office, would hold a press conference at 5.30 p.m. Indian Standard Time (12 noon GMT that day), few journalists in India could have guessed that he would make the fateful declaration about Indian nuclear test explosions that shocked the world. At that hour, barely 8 a.m. on the East Coast in the United States, the junior officer at the Defence Intelligence Agency (DIA) of the US monitoring images from satellites that periodically fly over north-western India was still to notice that a series of three explosions had actually taken place just two hours earlier at Pokharan, in the desert state of Rajasthan, where India first tested a nuclear explosive device in May 1974, and which had long been suspected to be the site of further nuclear preparations.[1]

It took the world some hours before responding with a mixture of astonishment, shock, anger, disbelief, and disgust to India's announcement. Many Indians were stunned. Some were impressed at what they thought was an act of defiance directed at the world's nuclear hegemons. Some were persuaded that the explosions were a political stunt. A few (especially supporters of the Hindu-chauvinist Bharatiya Janata Party which led the rickety coalition in New Delhi) were overjoyed at this technological 'feat'.

Meanwhile, India's media managers—guided by the handful of journalists and spin doctors who were privy to the information, or at least some of it, of a likely test or some such event at Pokharan—got busy writing, rewriting, and displaying the story, hyping the 'achievement', getting selective accolades and favourable comments from self-styled 'experts', crafting captions and slogans for adulatory editorials and catchy lines: 'Explosion of Self-Esteem', 'Megatonnes of Prestige', an 'India that can Say No', etc.

In the offices of India's major political parties, utter confusion prevailed amidst stunned silences and resentment that the BJP had successfully pulled off what might be a populist trick, which could win it some support and help it outmanoeuvre its alliance partners with whom it had been having serious trouble ever since its coalition was sworn in on 19 March 1998. The resentment was soon overpowered by the impulse to give out what many politicians long thought to be the standard but safe reaction: congratulate the scientists and engineers responsible for the tests, but remain silent on the politicians who directed them and mandated the tests in the first place.

At 10, Janpath, in the heart of New Delhi, where Sonia Gandhi, president of the Indian National Congress, the country's oldest and largest political party, lives, a debate broke out between those who thought the party should strongly condemn the tests as adventurist and unrelated to India's security; and those who believed it would be more expedient not to criticize the tests since the popular mood was pro-nuclear. Gandhi was inclined to be critical. She was soon persuaded to issue a statement questioning the tests' rationale and reiterating India's commitment to global nuclear disarmament, reaffirmed by Rajiv Gandhi in a well-drafted three-stage plan submitted to the United Nations General Assembly's Special Session on Disarmament in 1988.[2] Just as the statement was about to be put out, news came from Madras that Sharad Pawar, former defence minister and a senior Congress leader, had congratulated the scientists responsible for the tests, but expressed reservations about the government's intentions. In particular, he also criticized the BJP for not taking the Congress into confidence over so important a matter as crossing the nuclear threshold. Sonia Gandhi decided to withhold her own statement.

The Congress's intervention was widely taken to mean it had signalled its approval and gone along with 'the current'. But the 'current' was now being defined by the media. Instant television soundbytes were manufactured and recorded, *Ex post* justifications were proffered by India's nuclear 'paid priesthood' (from the state-funded Institute for Defence Studies and Analyses in the Capital). Statistically meaningless and fraudulent telephonic interviews were broadcast as the unalloyed truth: this in a country where less than a tenth of households have a telephone connection! The cameras selectively focused on BJP supporters bursting crackers and dancing with joy in the streets. Much of this contrived scenario in favour of the tests would soon unravel.

The element of surprise in the tests was undeniable despite the BJP election manifesto's (February 1998) statement that if elected, the party's government would 'review India's nuclear policy and exercise the option to induct nuclear weapons', and the common programme of the BJP-led coalition called 'National Agenda for Governance' which too, in March, reiterated that formulation—among the few phrases transported verbatim from the party's manifesto. Many saw nothing new in the formulation. The BJP—beginning with its earlier avatar, the Bharatiya Jana Sangh—had been demanding the Bomb since 1951. This hawkish rhetoric had been stepped up during the Comprehensive Test Ban Treaty (CTBT) debate of 1994–6. A majority of India's strategic 'experts' did not expect the party to move towards a major decision and do something irreversible and controversial within only a few weeks of coming to power.

The BJP also consciously tried to mislead the public on the issue. When asked in April what the phrase 'exercise the option to induct nuclear weapons' meant, Vajpayee said India would cross the threshold only if it was considered absolutely necessary, and hinted at a strategic review prior to such a decision.[3] India's defence minister George Fernandes was explicit on this: No major change in India's nuclear posture would be effected before a proper strategic review and evaluation of the country's security needs.[4] An editorialist in *The Times of India*, citing these very statements, dismissed all talk of a shift in India's defence and nuclear policy, as irresponsible and alarmist.[5]

Washington Misjudges Signals from India

The new government managed to disguise its real intentions and plans from its international interlocutors too. Specifically, it misled Bill Richardson, sent by President Clinton as a special envoy to talk to the new government in April. Richardson came with an entourage consisting of officials of the State Department, including its newly established South Asia desk, and of the US Arms Control and Disarmament Agency (ACDA). After several rounds of discussions with Indian ministers, diplomats, and bureaucrats on a range of issues, the delegation went back convinced that the BJP-led coalition would maintain a high degree of continuity with the core policies of its predecessor regimes. It would do so on the economy, on foreign and security policies, cooperation with the West, on domestic matters such as attitudes towards the religious minorities, especially Muslims, whom the BJP has long regarded with suspicion and hostility, and whom it, along with its cohorts, explicitly confronted by demolishing a sixteenth century mosque at Ayodhya in Uttar Pradesh in December 1992.

'No, we don't expect a major shift; we are convinced that the Vajpayee government is not about to do anything dramatic and alarming', a State Department official told one of us: 'The South Asia desk line is, "expect continuity, and a friendly stance towards the US and Washington's concerns"'.[6]

He accepted distinctions between three different possible postures on the part of the US towards the Vajpayee government. First, in view of the BJP's history of extreme positions on some issues and its right-wing religious–chauvinist character, the US should seek definite answers of 'normal' behaviour before endorsing the Indian government and accepting it as friendly and legitimate. Second, Washington would wait and watch, while maintaining an open and friendly stand, but not rush into giving the government a clean chit. Third, the US would proceed on the assumption that the BJP has already 'reformed' and 'normalized' itself, and that the experience of actually wielding power—with all its presumed responsibilities—would further sober and moderate the party's policies and actions.

'We are clearly inclined to the third view,' the official emphasized. 'We don't believe the BJP is about to do anything radical—like nationalize foreign capital, start a war over Kashmir, or conduct a nuclear blast. We expect them to be sensitive to US concerns; we appreciate the fact that the BJP was among the few parties in India which during the Cold War were strongly anti-Soviet and largely supportive of the US.' Adding to the complacency were the signals that Defence Intelligence Agency personnel read from satellites monitoring activity in and around Pokharan. According to *Newsweek*, they found nothing 'unusual' in the desultory movements at the site which had witnessed a flurry of activity late in 1995.[7] Satellite pictures in 1995 had clearly pointed to the drilling of a hole in the Pokharan test range, similar to that drilled for India's first nuclear test in 1974.[8] In December 1995, intelligence sources leaked the story to *The New York Times*. India first denied the story as 'baseless' and 'speculative'. When, however, US ambassador Frank Wisner confronted Indian foreign minister Pranab Mukherjee with satellite photographs, the government, then led by the Indian National Congress, sheepishly confirmed that there was activity at the site. For Wisner, this was not enough. He asked Mukherjee to declare that New Delhi would not, and was not about to, conduct a test. Mukherjee did.

Later, imagery from commercial satellites too confirmed preparations for a test in late 1995. Analysing the data, US nuclear weapons laboratories were satisfied that such imagery would provide fairly reliable verification of nuclear test preparations and would be a very useful tool in the CTBT verification process in the long run.[9] This was, however, wisdom in retrospect: verification after the event. No analyst even suspected anything much before 4 May. Yes, there was some activity at Pokharan range, but the site had been downgraded in the DIA's list of priorities. Other sites, in Bosnia, Afghanistan, Sudan, and in Russia, were far more important. Only a junior officer had been put in charge of looking at the Rajasthan desert in north-western India, where

Pokharan is situated.[10] The intensity of monitoring too had been reduced: only casually scanned images rather than high-alert frequent monitoring recommended for sites. Fairly crude camouflage methods, such as nets and meshes, further obscured the reality at Pokharan: hectic activity, visits of the top brass of the Department of Atomic Energy (DAE), the Defence Research and Development Organization (DRDO), and the Indian military, actual transportation of explosive assemblies, wiring up of detonation devices, the triple fence with high security erected around the blast site, etc.[11]

It is possible that the level of activity in the weeks preceding 11 May was far lower than in late 1995, and that the preparations made then were never fully dismantled. This time around, the DRDO–DAE–military personnel were of course not starting from scratch. It is also possible that sandstorms in the Rajasthan desert, which are routine, and acquire greater frequency in the hot months of April to July, further complicated the picture, reducing the accuracy of satellite imagery. However, the general complacency in the US administration about the BJP's intentions and the downgrading of the monitoring level were clearly far more important factors.

By conducting the tests on 11 May and then again on 13 May, New Delhi shocked not just the rest of the world, but some of its own policy-makers, past and present. Vajpayee chose to explain the rationale of the tests first not to the Indian public, but to President Clinton. On 11 May, in New Delhi, he only issued a bland technical statement announcing the tests and their purpose: developing nuclear weapons of a diverse range and capabilities, their explosive yield varying from a few hundred tonnes (equivalent of TNT) to a claimed 45 kilotonnes, and encompassing what India claimed was a thermonuclear bomb as well as first-generation fission weapons. India had suddenly crossed the threshold and plunged headlong into weaponization, not just demonstration, of a technological capability.

Although there was a gradual degeneration in India's nuclear policy and practice, especially after the first May 1974 test, there was a far higher measure of continuity at the doctrinal level. Going by its stated policy, New Delhi until 11 May never accepted the view that nuclear weapons are legitimate, strategically rational, or essential to security, whether of a nation or of the world. It had always forcefully rejected the doctrine of nuclear deterrence as 'repugnant' and unworthy. Long ago, it demanded that the manufacture and possession, and use or threat of use of nuclear weapons be declared 'a crime against humanity'. It rightly argued that one great lesson of the Cold War is that reliance on nuclear deterrence can lead to a runaway nuclear arms race, with strategically disastrous and economically ruinous consequences.

True, New Delhi repeatedly and sharply criticized the unequal global nuclear order dominated until recently by the Big Five, and saw its own established nuclear capability as a form of defiance of that order. But until May, that was only a capability, a technological ability, to make nuclear weapons. That is one thing. Making weapons with a finite possibility that they will be used, a possibility always bound up with their existence, is another thing altogether. India executed that doctrinal rupture suddenly, swiftly, without as much as the pretence of a policy review, an analysis of the strategic environment and of new security 'threats', or of the best ways of meeting them. According to highly placed sources, the order to conduct these tests was issued well before Vajpayee's government won the vote of confidence in the Lower House of India's Parliament. Interestingly, a leader of the Rashtriya Swayamsevak Sangh confirmed that the BJP, which had formed a minority government that lasted a mere 13 days in 1996, had ordered a nuclear test, although there was virtually no prospect of the government surviving. The test was planned for the day of the vote of confidence![12]

Clearly, the BJP was bent on crossing the nuclear threshold regardless of India's strategic environment. It conducted the tests simply when it could: that is, when it came to power. The real rationale for the decision had more to do with its long-standing nuclear obsession, than with India's security or foreign policy goals. Two consequences followed. One, it had to invent a plausible sounding rationale for the doctrinal breach it had effected; and two, it had to create a *post facto* regional rationalization for its own tests by goading Pakistan to follow its own footsteps. On the second count, it was successful: Pakistan followed on 28 and 30 May with its own explosions, discussed below. On the first count, New Delhi was more than just a little ham-handed.

Vajpayee's Rationalization

In his letter of 11 May to Clinton, soon leaked to *The New York Times*, Prime Minister Vajpayee cited China and Pakistan, India's old adversaries, and clandestine nuclear collaboration between the two, as the principal justification for crossing the nuclear threshold. So preoccupied was he with naming the two neighbours, and so keen to curry favour with the US, that he even offered 'cooperation' with Washington in its efforts to promote nuclear non-proliferation and 'disarmament'. When this did not wash, and Pakistan accused India of having created a new threat to its security via nuclearization, New Delhi changed its tune and said its nuclear decision was not 'Pakistan-specific' and that it went beyond South Asian or regional considerations. Meanwhile, by the end of the week following 11 May, home minister Lal Krishna Advani had launched a fiercely militant rhetorical attack on Pakistan, linking the new nuclear equation with the Kashmir dispute.[13]

When China reacted with strong words and anger at having been named specifically as a 'threat'—a term Fernandes had repeatedly used in April, without provocation, leave alone reason, even accusing China of having built a helicopter landing pad on its territory—the Indian government hastened to 'clarify' that China was not really a threat. Vajpayee's powerful principal secretary Brajesh Mishra (a former diplomat known for his hardline views), was roped in to mollify Beijing.[14]

As soon as Pakistan conducted its tests—an outcome Indian leaders devoutly prayed for—Vajpayee announced that India's stand was 'vindicated'. The tests only confirmed Pakistan had a hidden bomb as well as every intention to detonate it. New Delhi once again got busy citing the Pakistan 'factor' or 'threat' as a justification for its own nuclearization. By late June–early July, India had again returned to the old, familiar theme of attacking the nuclear 'hegemons' and their refusal to undertake nuclear disarmament.

Ironically, and, contradictorily, this happened after it had colluded and collaborated with these very powers in effectively smashing the unity of the non-aligned Group of 21 (G–21) at the Conference on Disarmament in Geneva (CD) on the conditions under which they would agree to begin negotiations on a fissile material cutoff treaty (FMCT), on which there had been an impasse for several months. The principal condition was that the nuclear weapons states must agree either to negotiate a Nuclear Weapons (Abolition) Convention or to set up a formal committee on the subject of nuclear disarmament in the CD—a proposal they have vetoed for years.

The mutually inconsistent and contradictory explanations and rationalizations at the official level were supplemented by hawkish nuclear lobbies outside the government, often inspired by clandestine official briefings, offering expedient apologia wherever possible for India's nuclearization. The rationalizations varied: India had done nothing new, dramatic or unexpected on 11 and 13 May. It was long known that we had bombs in the basement; we only put them out. What was covert became overt. India's 'compulsions' arose from reliable information that Pakistan was about to conduct its tests. It had to be pre-empted (why?). India lost its patience with the P–5 when the NPT was extended and it became apparent that the prospect for disarmament had receded. (This however, happened in 1995, three years prior to the tests). China may not have been an immediate threat, but it is a long-term threat in the future: did it not go to war with India in 1962? And did it not covertly aid Pakistan (probably even gifted it a fully-made nuclear bomb in 1989)? Sooner or later, India would have to have a credible deterrent against China as well as Pakistan. The BJP only created it sooner rather than later.

Wild imagination, flights of fancy, semi-literacy in strategic affairs, pure prejudice, misinformation, inaccuracies, half-truths, and outright lies were blended in varying proportions to churn out this smorgasbord of apologia to suit different hawkish tasks and cater to various notions of national 'pride' and hubris. In all this, it is just impossible to separate fiction from fact, or to find a thread of consistency in the logic proffered in explanations of India's violent departure from its own stated doctrines and positions.

The Indian attempt to goad Pakistan into testing was equally deplorable. It was probably the first instance of a nuclear weapons state actually instigating its own rival to go nuclear. Islamabad's first reaction to the Indian tests was a mixture of shock and anger. However, Nawaz Sharif, despite severe domestic political pressure, did not rush into conducting a test in retaliation. Indeed, he carefully weighed his options during the week after 11 May, reckoning that the economic consequences of crossing the nuclear threshold would be almost unbearable. There was advantage to be reaped from showing restraint: not only would Pakistan escape attracting opprobrium; it could seek to occupy the moral high ground as a responsible, peace-loving state. This would help it overcome to some extent the stigma that attaches to it owing to its involvement with the Taliban, and support to Kashmiri secessionists in India, as well as the links of Pakistani military agencies with narcotics smuggling. Besides, the US was offering it a $5 billion package of economic aid and military assistance in special negotiations opened by deputy secretary of state Strobe Talbott.

However, the BJP had already decided that the road to Chagai (the nuclear test-site in the Baluchistan mountain ranges) must traverse through Kashmir. Beginning 18 May, home minister Advani consciously started linking India's newly acquired nuclear weapons status to Kashmir. He announced that in the now-changed 'geostrategic' environment, which had rendered Pakistan much weaker in relation to India, New Delhi would follow a 'proactive' policy on Kashmir, resorting to 'hot pursuit' into Pakistan territory of the militants whom it claims, Pakistan infiltrates into the Kashmir valley to foment trouble there.

Advani, and following him, Fernandes, issued statement after militant statement chiding Pakistan, and threatening military action in Kashmir. BJP party functionaries even went a step further. They demanded that Proud New Nuclear India must 'recapture' the part of Kashmir that Pakistan illegitimately annexed in 1948–9, although this would violate the 1972 Shimla Agreement which prohibits either state from unilaterally altering the status quo and which mandates that all differences be resolved through bilateral negotiations alone.

Teased, chided, insulted, threatened, Sharif in the last week of May finally asked army chief, General Jehangir Karamat, to evaluate the Kashmir situation and the impact of India's bellicose rhetoric on the Pakistan army. Karamat was clear: the troops' morale would collapse unless Pakistan conducted retaliatory tests and equalized with India. On 27 May, Pakistan suddenly announced it had definite intelligence reports that India was about to launch an armed incursion into its territory. The following day, five claimed nuclear explosions followed at Chagai. On 30 May, Pakistan announced yet another test—a total of six to get even with India's five earlier that month, in addition to the very first test of 1974.

There was some confusion over the number of tests. On 30 May, the Pakistan foreign secretary was first quoted as saying that two more tests had taken place that day. This was later 'corrected' to one. The claimed yields have also been open to question. (See chapter Annexe 'Willie Rivalry'.) India's assertion that it had conducted a successful 'thermonuclear' explosion (with a yield of 45 kilotonnes) on 11 May has been challenged by a number of scientists both at home and abroad, and there are reasons to doubt the veracity of the Pakistani claim of as many as six fission tests. The two have long engaged in competitive boasts about their scientific and technological prowess, of having mastered complex and difficult processes, and they have rarely missed an opportunity to denigrate and run down each other's nuclear and science and technology establishments.

BOX 1

'Safe' Tests and Popular Doubts

Official Claims and People's Experience don't Match

One of the greatest myths propagated by a section of the Indian media was that the Pokharan tests were hugely popular in the vicinity of the test site in Western Rajasthan. There too, villagers, charged with patriotic fervour, enthusiastically welcomed the explosion of national 'self-esteem'. This was held out as proof that the Bomb found acceptance even in an extremely poor, inhospitable part of Rajasthan, essentially a desert, the best of whose land grows shrubbery and a few hardy millets.

Similar claims have been made about Baluch tribals living close to Chagai Hills in Pakistan. Nothing could be further from the truth.

For the inhabitants of Khetolai, the village closest to the Pokharan

Firing Range, 11 May 1998 was a black day. Around 1 p.m., Khetolai's 1500 residents were rudely herded out of their houses by soldiers of the Indian Army and told: 'there is going to be a big explosion, a big bomb'. They could not leave the village, nor could they stay indoors or seek the shade of trees to escape the scorching sun. (The temperature in the shade that day was 47 degrees Celsius).

They were made to stand out in the open for four hours. The three simultaneous explosions occurred at 3:45 p.m., soon after which they were told they could safely go home. When they entered their homes, they found there were huge cracks in the mud walls and the water had drained out of a number of village wells, whose walls too had cracked.[1]

The people of Khetolai were livid. On 20 May, the day Vajpayee visited the Pokharan test site, they decided to stage a protest against the treatment meted out to them, and more important, against the refusal of their demand for an independent investigation into the health and environmental effects of the tests. Vajpayee was originally meant to stop at Khetolai. On reports of the protest plan, he changed his itinerary.

The people in villages close to Pokharan, including Khetolai, have had grievances against the setting up of the range since 1967. They have registered their protest in a variety of ways. In June 1998, they welcomed a Japanese peace delegation, including a *hibakusha* from Hiroshima, and passed a resolution condemning all nuclear test explosions and calling for a permanent ban. In November, they voted in strength against the BJP in elections to the Rajasthan legislature. In Khetolai, the turnout was a record high of 93 per cent; it is believed everyone cast their vote against the BJP.

The government maintains that the 'perfect tests' posed no risk to the people or to the environment. There was no discharge of radioactivity.[2] However, it refused to divulge details of background radiation, concentration of long-lived radionuclides such as Strontium-90, Cesium-137 or Plutonium-239 in the soil, air, water and vegetation close to the site. It had made a similar claim in the first test of 1974 too.

The residents of villages in the vicinity, such as Khetolai, Loharki, Bhadariya, Mava and Dhauliya, have a different story to tell. They say that the rate of incidence of cancer and numerous physical deformities rose significantly some years after 1974. In Khetolai, for instance, the village headman says, there have been 18 deaths from cancer between the mid-1980s and 1998—indisputably high for a population of 1500.[3] It is known that the fence erected round the tests explosion site in 1974 rotted and disintegrated soon after the site was abandoned by the security forces in the late 1970s. Cattle, sheep, and goats belonging to the villagers, many of them shepherds, would routinely stray into the test range area.

It would thus be surprising if there were no contamination of the food chain with dangerous radionuclides through the shrubbery and grass which the animals browsed. However, the government did not bother to monitor the health of the population living close by. Nor did it regularly check the environment for radioactivity and presence of products of fission and other matter released during the 1974 test.

Some of the suspicions and claims of the villages are corroborated by a group of doctors of S.N. Medical College, Jodhpur, Rajasthan, the nearest teaching hospital. Drs R.G. Sharma, M.S. Maheshwari and S.C. Lodha writing in the *Indian Journal of Cancer* analysed data collected on cases of various kinds of cancer from the records of government hospitals and private clinics in Jodhpur in 1984–8—that is, ten years after Pokharan-I.[4] Since the findings are from non-exhaustive sources and take no account of precisely where the patients came from or who they were demographically, the data cannot be interpreted to say anything about the absolute incidence of cancer. Since no pre–1974 data are available for comparison in the Jodhpur region, in which Pokharan is located, all conclusions must be extremely tentative.

Nevertheless, some results are noteworthy. The Jodhpur region shows a high frequency of cancers of the mouth and throat (in relation to the rest of India, and also to the WHO numbers for developing countries). There were also more frequent cases of ovarian cancer, lymphomas, and leukemias. Ovarian cancers were more frequent by 50 per cent in comparison to the average figures for either developed or developing countries. Lymphomas in men and leukemias in both men and women were more frequent by 50 to 80 per cent. Again, a comparison of the Jodhpur region with the frequencies reported to the National Cancer Registry in 1983 from various cities of India shows a high frequency of cancer of the urinary bladder. Leukemias were higher by a factor of 50 to 150 per cent. Bone and skin tumors were more frequent by a factor of 40 to 300 per cent.

Even in the absence of base-line data, comparison with which alone can permit decisive conclusions, these results constitute a sufficient and strong reason for a transparently designed and conducted *independent* epidemiological survey of the region. Similarly, there is a powerful case for an independent survey and monitoring of the environment for radiation, radionuclides, and other harmful substances.

Much less information is available from near the Chagai site in Pakistan's Baluchistan province. Moreover, the 1998 tests being the first, it is not yet possible to determine their related health effects. However, there was a strong popular protest against Pakistan's tests from that province, which in turn prompted its chief minister to complain to the federal government. In Pakistan too, there is a powerful case for an independent health and environment survey and continuous monitoring.

Notes

1. Personal interview with the authors, June 1998.
2. This claim has been repeated parrot-like by the local administration, the Atomic Energy Commission, and other agencies. On 3 February 1999, AEC chairman R. Chidambaram said the tests were 'perfect' and no radioactivity was released. (See Note 2 in Annexe to Chapter 4).

   Such claims about the 'safety' of nuclear testing have been routinely made by governments all over the world. The truth is radically different, especially as it is recorded in testimonies of victims of nuclear testing, whether in the South Pacific, in Nevada or in Kazakhstan. See International Physicians for the Prevention of Nuclear War, *Radioactive Heaven and Earth*, Zed Books, London, 1991.
3. Personal interview, June 1998.
4. Vol. 29, pp. 126–35, September 1992.

Whatever the truth about the nature and number of the nuclear explosions and their yields, there can be no doubt whatever that the two subcontinental rivals now possess not just a well-established nuclear capability but the wherewithal to manufacture at least first-generation fission weapons (if not boosted or higher yield fission or fusion weapons) which can be delivered by various means, including short-range missiles, to large population centres with devastating effect. In May 1998, the world added two more overt nuclear weapons states to its tally of five, increasing the global nuclear threat.

India, Pakistan under Flak

The crossing of the nuclear Rubicon by India and Pakistan was bound to shock, revolt, and anger the rest of the world. It did, and all the more strongly because their action had no clear, obvious security rationale; and because it appeared to be such a terrible perversion of the real priorities before the two countries, which have among the lowest ranks in human development in the world (hovering around the mid-130 mark among the 174 covered by the UN Development Programme's yearly *Human Development Report*), and which together are home to the largest number of poor and destitute people in the world: nearly half of their over one billion people live in want and suffer from all manner of deprivation.

Following the tests, the United States, Japan and some other states in the industrially developed world imposed sanctions and cut off aid, loans, and credit guarantees to India and Pakistan. The European Union did not. Nor did major individual European states such as Russia, Germany, France, and

Britain. However, the G–8 met to pass a tough resolution reprimanding India and Pakistan, calling upon them to sign nuclear restraint agreements such as the NPT, as well as the CTBT, i.e. to effectively give up their nuclear capability.

The Security Council met in June 1998, and unanimously passed a resolution (number 1172) reprimanding India and Pakistan and urging them to exercise restraint: a number of international/multilateral fora, from the Conference on Disarmament to the European Union, and from the Non-Aligned Movement to ASEAN (Association of Southeast Asian Nations) Regional Forum sharply criticized the two.[15] In November, the First Committee of the United Nations General Assembly passed a resolution by 98 votes to 6 reprimanding India and Pakistan for their tests and asking them to sign the CTBT. India moved a resolution in the General Assembly calling for de-alerting of nuclear weapons, which went through with 68 votes for and 44 against.

This was India's new diplomatic gambit: appear to be responsible in advocating nuclear restraint, but only to the point that India and Pakistan do not explicitly deploy ready-to-use nuclear weapons—with delivery vehicles on hair-trigger alert. The move might be seen to be making a virtue out of necessity—given the relatively low level of Indian and Pakistani nuclear preparations and the alarm that would in all likelihood be generated in the event of the two entering into an eyeball-to-eyeball nuclear confrontation in the form of deployed missiles facing each other. It can, however, scarcely be regarded as amounting to adequate restraint or as reversal of the negative consequences of the May 1998 tests that shattered the global nuclear status quo.

By June, the sanctions had begun to bite. The Pakistani rupee, within three weeks of the tests, plunged from Rs 40 to Rs 56 to the US dollar. The Indian rupee lost 15 per cent of its value. The effects were compounded by the unfolding of the Asian meltdown. Foreign investment flows began to dry up. Withdrawal of state credit for US and Japanese exports and infrastructure projects meant that their costs rose sharply. The cost of borrowing for Indian industry in international markets rose significantly. Most important, the drying up of aid from Japan, the largest donor to India, seriously affected social sector spending, including schemes such as drinking water supply, rural sanitation, literacy and health programmes, in which the poor have the highest stake.

In October, the US Congress gave a special one-year authorization to Clinton to lift sanctions selectively. In November, many prohibitions on multilateral loans and export credit and guarantees were lifted, but 40 Indian 'entities' (companies, laboratories, and institutions) with 200 affiliates or subsidiaries were placed on the US blacklist for trade. Pakistan, virtually on the brink of economic collapse, got a breather in the form of an assurance that Washington would not veto an urgently, desperately, needed IMF loan.

By this time it was plain that neither country was unaffected by the sanctions; their costs could prove onerous if they continued, although it was unlikely that this would happen. Indeed, they were subsequently to be further eased.

There have been differences among India and Pakistan policy-makers over the likely effects of the sanctions and the best ways of coping with them. What is beyond doubt and incontrovertible is that nuclearization has led to India's and Pakistan's isolation in the international community, and a considerable lowering of their stature not only in the eyes of the Global North, but of the Global South. The vast majority of the world's nations and peoples view India and Pakistan in a negative light after May 1998. Few believe they have challenged the unequal global nuclear order in a principled way in order to radically transform it. Rather, they have joined it on the side of the discriminators.

Special Section

Historic Degeneration

Evolution of India's Nuclear Policy

Supporters of nuclear weapons and the 11 and 13 May tests argue that India's decision under the BJP-led coalition to cross the nuclear threshold was in essential continuity with New Delhi's past policies: to the extent there was any change, it happened only in response to the altered situation on the ground, especially in India's neighbourhood.

This is misleading and false. At the doctrinal level, May 1998 marks a violent break with India's past postures and policies. The decision to acquire, and plan to deploy, nuclear weapons is a betrayal of India's past commitments to nuclear disarmament and its repeated promises never to use nuclear energy for military purposes. This does not mean that India's nuclear weapons policy was constant and unchanging for the 51 years since Independence. It went through four distinct phases, culminating in the disastrous decision to test and acquire these weapons of mass destruction.

1947 to the Mid-1960s: Phase I
Abstinence in the Nehru Era

This might be termed the period of voluntary nuclear abstinence. Nehru was not only deeply committed to the complete elimination of all nuclear weapons, but also opposed to their manufacture and possession by any state, including India. He was opposed to nuclear weapons on moral, political and strategic grounds, and demanded that their possession be declared a 'crime against humanity'. He integrated this opposition into India's foreign policy, giving it an activist edge. He was the first world leader to call in 1954 for an end to all nuclear testing following US hydrogen bomb tests in the Pacific, and their disastrous radioactive fallout. However, India's civilian nuclear energy programme also had a 'dual use' or military capacity, of which other major figures like Homi Bhabha (the first chairman of the Atomic Energy Commission) were fully aware, and which they wanted to develop. Bhabha himself was not as categorically opposed to a possible future bomb as was Nehru.

On 24 July 1957, Nehru said in the Lok Sabha, 'We have declared quite clearly that we are not interested in making atom bombs, even if we have the capacity to do so, and that in no event will we use nuclear energy for destructive purposes . . . . I hope that will be the policy of all future governments.' Just months before his death, when reports were pouring in of China's nuclear preparations, Nehru rejected the suggestion that India should follow China and acquire nuclear weapons for 'deterrence'.[16]

A top secret US government document of 1961, declassified in 1995, contains valuable material on the American assessment of Nehru's commitment to opposing nuclear weapons even in the face of Chinese preparations to acquire and detonate such weapons, preparations and plans for which were detected by Western intelligence agencies.[17] The State Department document deals with 'anticipatory action pending Chinese Communist demonstration of a nuclear capability' and considers providing active assistance in nuclear weapons technology to India as a counterweight to a nuclear China. It notes that in US Ambassador John Kenneth Galbraith's assessment, Nehru would reject the idea with a probability of 90 per cent, and, therefore, concludes that other methods, including influencing Homi Bhabha, and launching a 'covertly mounted informational campaign' have become necessary.

The document is devoted to a discussion of the 'early action we might take to minimize the impact on US and free world security interests of a first Chinese Communist explosion of a nuclear device'. It locates the need for such action in the following way: 'If Communist China could detonate a nuclear device as early as 1962, as has been estimated, we should consider now what actions should be taken in anticipation of the event, instead of later in reaction to it. The initial impact will be primarily psychological, with secondary politically and military effects deriving from it. This establishes the psychological field as one deserving immediate attention.'

China, it argues,

> is likely to get at least two types of psychological dividends from its explosion: (1) Many Asians are likely to raise their estimate of Communist China's present and future total military power relative to that of their own countries and the capabilities in the area of the US ; and (2) they are likely to see the accomplishment as vindicating claims that the Communist method of organizing a backward state's resources is demonstrably superior. Both reactions are likely to contribute to feelings that communism is the wave of the future and that Communist China is, or soon will become, too powerful to resist. It will not be possible to prevent the accrual to Communist China of such dividends, but it may be possible by advance action to reduce them.

However, the argument continues:'If another, but non-Communist Asian state detonated a nuclear device first, a subsequent and consequently a somewhat anticlimactic Chinese Communist explosion would not carry a comparable implication of Communist superiority, or make quite as much impact on those who fear China's growing power.'

The document holds that India is the best candidate for this: 'According to one estimate, India's atomic programme is sufficiently advanced so that it could, not many months hence, have accumulated enough fissionable material to produce a nuclear explosion. While we would like to limit the number of nuclear powers, so long as we lack the capability to do so we ought to prefer that the first Asian one be India and not China.'

There is however a catch. Nehru, the document admits, is not willing to play ball:

> Nehru was quoted as saying, upon his arrival in Belgrade on 31 August [1961] and in the context of the Soviet decision to resume weapons tests, 'I am against nuclear tests at any time in any place.' The same day, an official spokesman in Delhi was quoted as making the less categorical statement:'We are against all tests and explosions of nuclear material except for peaceful purposes under controlled conditions.' . . . Given the context and taken together, these statements suggest that it would be difficult to get Nehru to agree to any proposal for an Indian nuclear test in the near future, and that the chances of its acceptance would depend upon the extent to which it met rather narrow criteria.

This is confirmed by Galbraith: 'The idea has also been discussed with Ambassador Galbraith, who is strongly opposed to any US approach to Nehru. He thinks the chances are roughly only one out of fifty that Nehru's reaction would not be the negative one that we are seeking India as an atomic ally.' The document then goes on to evaluate the reservations raised by officers in different sections of the State Department, although 'preliminary exploration within the Department has elicited concurrence with the idea, per se, that it would be desirable if a friendly Asian power beat Communist China to the punch, and it has turned up no likelier candidate than India.'

These reservations and doubts are listed:

> (1) India might require considerable technical assistance in order to explode a nuclear device before Communist China does; (2) there appear to be legal obstacles to the supplying of such assistance by either the British or ourselves; (3) we are not good at keeping such things covert, whereas the explosion could be expected to have utility only in proportion as it appeared to be an Indian accomplishment; (4) there probably would be considerable difficulty in finding a practical peaceful use for such an explosion, and fallout from it would be open to the usual and valid objections, including ones related to the fears which could arise or be created among an ill-informed and partly superstitious populace; (5) alternately meeting the requirement of 'controlled conditions' for an experimental explosion might present problems; (6) Pakistan could be expected to react most adversely to an Indian explosion which might subsequently be exploited against it, and to be highly resentful of any outside instigation and assistance, known or surmised; and (7) an Indian explosion would provide the Chinese Communists basis for urging that the USSR increase its assistance to the Chinese Communist nuclear programme.

Nevertheless, it concludes that an approach should be made to Bhabha, although not to Nehru. Galbraith took a dim view of raising the issue with Nehru: not only did he think the chances of Nehru rejecting a US offer of assistance are 49 out of 50, but 'he sees the calculus of prospective benefit inherent in the one chance as outweighed by the harm implicit in the other forty-nine. He also thinks his British and Canadian colleagues would be unwilling to make such an approach to Nehru'.

The most that Galbraith would be prepared to do is allow, a US nuclear energy official, Dr Wiesner, on a possible future visit to India, to raise in the course of conversations with Dr Bhabha the matter 'of the prospective Chinese Communist nuclear explosion and ask what effect if any it will have on India's programme in the atomic field. Presumably any further initiatives in the matter, if the idea germinated in Dr Bhabha's mind and bore fruit, would have to come from the Government of India, when we could decide what the US response should be within the framework of something more concrete than we now have to work with'.

The document then concludes:

> While nothing else would have so much prophylactic value as a prior atomic explosion by a free-world Asian state, a covertly-conducted information programme might achieve some effect in reducing the psychological impact of the first Chinese Communist nuclear explosion. Assuming as we do that the Chinese Communists are fully committed to acquiring nuclear capabilities, publicity about their programme

probably would not have important effect on their determination or rate of progress. It might provide them with an argument with which to press their Soviet ally to give increased assistance, but this would seem unlikely to weigh heavily among the factors considered by the Soviets in determining where their own interests in the matter lay.

It recommends a 'covertly-mounted informational programme' to drive home some illustrative points:

(a) India (and perhaps Japan) have nuclear-development programmes sufficiently advanced so that they could by now have produced a nuclear explosion; their programmes, however, have been directed rather at peaceful uses of atomic energy.

(b) Observers are puzzled by the failure of the Chinese Communists, who have been engaged in an effort which started in 1950, thus far to explode a nuclear device of their own. Since several other powers pioneered the way, the technological requirements for producing such an explosion have become widely known. Communist China has scientists, including ones trained abroad, of requisite capability; the essential raw materials; and suitable testing areas.

(c) It accordingly can only be speculated that Communist China (1) has organized its effort poorly, or (2) realizes that nuclear weapons are not ones which will contribute to realization of its expansive aims—sincere world opinion, which will condemn all aggression in proportion as it can be identified as such, will tolerate aggression with nuclear weapons even less than aggression by conventional armed forces.

This is also a period during which the idea of a Western 'nuclear umbrella' for India is mooted. The idea acquires some force especially because of India's defeat in the China War of 1962. However, the proposal does not fructify. India continues to fight for nuclear weapons elimination in international fora.

Mid-1960s to 1974: Phase II Preparations for the 1974 Test

This is a period of New Delhi's disenchantment with the prospect for global nuclear disarmament, and its own quiet preparations to acquire a nuclear weapons capability, while retaining a strong opposition to deterrence and weaponization. India's nuclear programme under Homi Bhabha undergoes a significant shift at the ground level. Bhabha in 1964 commissions a plant to reprocess spent fuel from the CIRUS 'research' reactor built in 1960.

CIRUS (Canada–India Research Reactor, US—standing for the United States, which donated the heavy water to start this Canadian-designed 40 MW-thermal reactor) was meant to be operated for 'peaceful' purposes only, although there were no formal 'safeguards' to ensure this. Bhabha took advantage of this, and by 1964, started reprocessing spent fuel from CIRUS to extract plutonium. This was the source of India's 1974 explosion.

There is evidence that Bhabha shifted towards active acquisition of a weapons capability after India's defeat in the China war of 1962. In his speech in October 1964, following China's first nuclear test, he says India too can conduct a test in 18 months. But such changes are not articulated at the policy level. India's nuclear doctrine remains unchanged. Thus, in October 1965, Prime Minister Lal Bahadur Shastri tells Parliament: 'Despite the continued threat of aggression from China which has developed nuclear weapons, the government has continued to adhere to decisions not to go in for nuclear weapons but to work for their elimination instead.'

In April 1968 Prime Minister Indira Gandhi says in Parliament that India's nuclear 'policy is framed after due consideration of the national interest, specifically with regard to national security... we do feel that the events of the last twenty years clearly show that the possession of nuclear weapons have not given any military advantage in situations of bitter armed conflict'. She argues that 'The choices before us involves... engaging in an arms race with sophisticated nuclear warheads and an effective missile delivery system. Such a course, I do not think would strengthen national security... it may well endanger our internal security by imposing a very heavy economic burden....'

Indian policy pronouncements in the post-Nehru period undergo a subtle shift best described as one from a categorical opposition to nuclear weapons, to a 'No Bombs Now' orientation. New uncertainties are reflected in India's role and attitude to the NPT negotiations in which it had initially played a significant role. The final draft of the treaty waters down what India and other non-nuclear weapons states wanted, namely a better balance between the differential obligations of the nuclear weapons states signatories and the non-nuclear weapons states signatories. Despite this watering down, the other non-nuclear weapons states go along with the treaty, but India does not sign it when it is opened for signature in 1968.

The major reasons for India's non-signature were China's decision not to sign the NPT and India's new reluctance to commit itself to complete or permanent future abstinence. Subsequently, however, India's refusal to sign the NPT is invariably and repeatedly stated in terms of 'principled' opposition to the 'discriminatory' character of the NPT, i.e. the very fact of it enshrining differential obligations for the nuclear weapons states and the non-nuclear weapons states. The NPT becomes an exemplar not just of an unequal global nuclear order, but of unequal distribution of power in the world. Behind the curtain of criticism of the NPT from the moral high ground, however, India intensifies nuclear preparations at the ground level.

The ground-level preparations, and accumulation of unsafeguarded plutonium from CIRUS, give Indira Gandhi an opportunity to conduct Pokharan-I in May 1974—a test that Department of Atomic Energy (DAE) scientists had long been demanding. The test, purportedly for 'peaceful' civilian purposes, itself termed a 'peaceful nuclear explosion (PNE)', is carried out for primarily domestic political reasons. The Indian media, briefed by the government, announces the test as signifying the country's entry into the 'Select' Group of 'Technologically Advanced Nations' or the 'Nuclear Club', yet India continues to strongly reject nuclear deterrence or grant any kind of legitimacy to nuclear weapons.

On 22 May 1974, four days after Pokharan-I, Indira Gandhi writes to Bhutto to assure him:

> I am aware that in popular parlance a nuclear explosion evokes an awesome and horrifying picture. However, this is because our minds have been conditioned by the misuse of nuclear energy for the development of weapons and by the use of these weapons in Hiroshima and Nagasaki. We in India have condemned and will continue to condemn military uses of nuclear energy as a threat to humanity.

She emphasised that 'it is strictly in this context that our scientists have launched on this experiment .... There are no political or foreign policy implications of this test.'

1974 to 1995-6: Phase III Ambiguity and its Degradation

Further work on India's nuclear weapons capability is suspended after the adverse fallout of the 1974 PNE, and immediate withdrawal of Canadian assistance, and protests from several other powers the world over, including the India-friendly USSR. A conscious policy of nuclear ambiguity is adopted by New Delhi. This consists in both affirming and denying that India has/could have [a] nuclear weapons/capability. In effect, India becomes a Nuclear Threshold State.

In 1978, under the non-Congress Prime Minister, Morarji Desai, the Indian government distances itself from the 1974 PNE. Desai emphasizes distrust of and opposition to nuclear weapons within a framework of ambiguity while. expressing misgivings about the safety of nuclear power. The DAE's importance within the government is downgraded.

After the mid-1980s, hawkish pressure mounts on New Delhi to respond to Pakistan's reported nuclear preparations by itself going overtly nuclear. During the period 1983–93, India rejects a total of seven proposals by Pakistan for nuclear restraint and regional disarmament. India opposes all regional approaches. It says it will only discuss nuclear disarmament in 'global', 'multilateral' fora, and in a 'non-discriminatory' framework. India's sole strategy of containing what is claimed to be the 'Pakistani threat' is to entreat the US to put pressure on Islamabad, e.g. through the Pressler Amendment to the omnibus US Trade Act, making armaments sales to Pakistan conditional upon annual certification by the US President that Pakistan does not possess, and is not about to make, nuclear weapons. Meanwhile, India's own stockpiling of high-grade plutonium continues, with an estimated 300 to 450 kg accumulated by the mid-1990s—enough for 60 to 90 fission bombs.

However, India joins the Five-Continent Six-Nation Initiative for Nuclear Disarmament in 1986, signs the important 'Delhi Declaration' for a nuclear weapons-free world with Gorbachev in the same year, and puts forward the Rajiv Gandhi Plan for the total elimination of nuclear weapons in the UN General Assembly's Fourth Special Session on Disarmament (SSOD-IV) in 1988. This involves a step-by-step process including restraint at an early stage by the threshold states, including India. This is a serious, well-conceived plan, but it is not energetically pursued after its presentation.

India rejects a number of proposals put forward in the late 1980s and early 1990s for regional nuclear restraint, or for a nuclear dialogue involving either the P–5 and India and Pakistan, or the US, Russia, China, Germany, Japan, and the two South Asian states. Meanwhile, in 1992, India agrees to start a bilateral dialogue on the nuclear weapons issue with the US. Four rounds of talks at the topmost diplomatic (not ministerial) level take place, but to no avail.

In 1993, India and the US co-sponsor a resolution in the UN calling for the early completion of the CTBT in the Conference on Disarmament. As the negotiations for a CTBT, which India had pioneered, enter their final phase, New Delhi begins to stall. In 1995, it makes its signature of the CTBT conditional upon a commitment to disarmament within a 'time-bound' framework by the P–5. It tries to hedge the treaty in with clauses that appear radical, but are meant to delay negotiations and prepare the ground for non-accession and opposition to a test ban agreement whenever one matures.

During this period, there is an operational reorganization of the process of making and articulating India's policy on nuclear weapons. Foreign secretary (chief of diplomatic service) J.N. Dixit creates new structures of policy consultation and formulation, directly involving the hands-on scientists and bureaucrats of the DAE and the Defence Research Development Organization (DRDO) who have been working on nuclear weapons and missiles development programmes. The Indian foreign ministry no longer lays down nuclear policy and determines the strategy and tactics to be adopted in international fora and bilateral or multilateral negotiations. Rather, it asks the DAE and DRDO what their needs are, and how it might best articulate and satisfy them at the diplomatic level through strategic and tactical manoeuvres.

Domestically, New Delhi comes under growing pressure to oppose the CTBT and then 'logically' proceed to conduct test explosions: why reject the CTBT as a 'trap' and 'conspiracy' and then behave as if it were still in place? Why bear the costs of opposition to the treaty without reaping the 'benefits' of nuclearization? In late 1995, before the CTBT 'rolling text' acquires its penultimate form, the Narasimha Rao government launches preparations for a test at Pokharan. The Cabinet is divided, and US military satellites detect preparations for a test in the Rajasthan desert. Publicity, as well as fear of economic sanctions, deters India from testing, but a big shift has occurred at the ground level in India's nuclear preparations and upgradation of its nuclear weapons option.

Yet, at the stated doctrinal level, there is no change. India passionately argues in 1995 before the International Court of Justice that

> use of nuclear weapons in any armed conflict ... even by way of reprisal or retaliation ... is unlawful .... Since the production and manufacture of nuclear weapons can only be with the objective of their use, it must follow that ... their production and manufacture cannot under any circumstances be considered as permitted .... The threat of use of nuclear weapons in any circumstance, whether as a means or method of warfare or otherwise, is illegal and unlawful under international law.

India's foreign secretary Salman Haidar makes a special appearance before the Conference on Disarmament in March 1996, at the height of the CTBT debate, to say:

> We do not believe that the acquisition of nuclear weapons is essential for national security, and we have followed a conscious decision in this regard. We are also convinced that the existence of nuclear weapons diminishes international security. We, therefore, seek their complete elimination. These are fundamental precepts that have been an integral basis of India's foreign and national security policy.

However, slippages are now evident from India's professed commitment to nuclear restraint and global nuclear disarmament. Indian 'ambiguity' degrades significantly. For instance, policy-makers hint that they will oppose other restraint measures too, besides the CTBT, such as a fissile material cut-off treaty.

On 20 June 1996, New Delhi formally announces that it will not sign the CTBT. Soon thereafter, Arundhati Ghose, India's ambassador at the CD, announces that New Delhi will not sign the CTBT 'not now, not ever'. India blocks the CTBT's passage at the CD, but in an unprecedented (and legally questionable) move, the text is taken to the UN General Assembly and signed. Hawks both within and outside the government raise the level of rhetoric in favour of India crossing the threshold, as if in 'retaliation' to this manoeuvre. The BJP and right-wing commentators in the media seize on the anti-CTBT rhetoric, to which there is little organized resistance from the political left and centre.

1996 to May 1998: Phase IV
Collapse of Ambiguity, Slippage into Nuclear Deterrence

Having thus yielded much ground to hawkish positions and stoked jingoistic nationalism over resisting the 'trap' that is the CTBT, New Delhi now becomes a prisoner of its own devious manoeuvres. The nuclear and defence establishments get hyperactive in lobbying for a policy break that will permit full weaponization of the Indian nuclear option through test explosions.

The BJP articulates this point of view most vociferously at the political level. By 1997, it starts getting insistent in asking for overt nuclearization. Its manifesto for the February 1998 national Parliament elections says the party, if voted to power, will 're-evaluate the country's nuclear policy and exercise the option to induct nuclear weapons'.

Until March 1998, the BJP is the sole Indian party to advocate nuclearization. But the situation changes with the BJP-led coalition's 'National Agenda for Governance' which repeats the precise formulation of the BJP manifesto on this issue. The BJP issues orders to the DAE, Defence Research & Development Organization and the armed forces to prepare for and conduct tests without consulting its coalition allies, but the RSS is privy to the decision.

The first statement of the strategic rationale of the tests is offered by Vajpayee not to the people of India, but to the President of the United States, on 11 May, the first day of the tests. This makes no reference whatever to the 'unequal global nuclear order', 'nuclear apartheid' and the failure or reluctance of the P–5 to disarm, which the Bomb's apologists cite as the rationale for crossing the threshold. Instead, it offers 'close cooperation' to Washington to jointly promote with it 'the cause of nuclear disarmament', thus wrongly conceding that the US has such a commitment in the first place. It locates the tests' rationale in the so-called threat from China and Pakistan, heightened by alleged Sino-Pakistani strategic-level nuclear and missile collaboration.

On 27 May, the government makes a feeble but devious attempt to rationalize its reversal of earlier nuclear policies through a paper entitled 'Evolution of India's Nuclear Policy' laid in the Lok Sabha. This strings together half-truths and distortions to claim continuity in the evolution of India's policy. Other *ex post facto* rationalizations follow.

Notes

1. 'Why Only a Bomb Would Do', *Newsweek*, (Asian Edition) 19 October 1998, p. 15.
2. Interview, Praful Bidwai with Mani Shankar Aiyar, a Congress party functionary, August 1998.
3. Vajpayee held out that assurance to Clinton's emissary and former US ambassador to the United Nations Bill Richardson, during his visit to India soon after the new government was sworn in. See *Newsweek*, op. cit., pp. 13–14.
4. Fernandes said at his first press conference after taking ministerial charge: 'We did not say that we are going in for nuclear weapons .... We will re-evaluate policy and to ensure security .... In the light of that, we will decide on the nuclear option. We will not fight shy of induction if that becomes necessary.' Quoted in 'N-option put on hold: Fernandes', *The Hindu*, 21 March 1998.

   On 18 March, after releasing the 'National Agenda' document of the BJP-led coalition, Vajpayee said that India 'will induct nuclear weapons only if necessary.' Answering questions, he said that there was 'no time-frame' to induct atomic weapons. 'The option [to induct nuclear weapons] will be exercised if need be.' Earlier, releasing the BJP's manifesto in February, the party president L.K. Advani had refrained from unqualified advocacy of a nuclear test, saying: 'Nuclear tests may not be necessary for India to induct nuclear weapons.' Quoted in 'N-weapon induction, if necessary', *The Hindu*, New Delhi, 19 March 1998.
5. 'Nuclear Hype', *The Times of India*, 1 April 1998, The editorial not only lambasted Pakistan, but also deplored 'the politicization of the issue by the Indian Opposition, especially after both the Prime Minister and the defence minister have clarified that the option would be considered only if necessary. Whether the BJP could have expressed itself in more sophisticated terms is a different matter. Even if the BJP had opted to abjure nuclear weapons, Islamabad would have denounced it as a cunning plot to disarm Pakistan, take away its nuclear deterrent and assert Indian supremacy in conventional armaments.' It also said: 'Ironically, the chorus against nuclearization is being led by those who have held office in the past and have themselves contributed to building up India's capabilities.'
6. Interview, Praful Bidwai with an official of the South Asia desk who preferred anonymity.
7. *Newsweek*, op. cit., p. 15.
8. Chidanand Rajghatta, 'It walks, squawks like a duck, so it's a duck', *Indian Express*, New Delhi, 21 Dec, 1995. This article quoted a US intelligence officer commenting on satellite pictures of drilling in progress at Pokharan in December 1995.
9. Vipin Gupta and Frank Pabian, 'Investigating the Allegations of Indian Nuclear

Test Preparations in the Rajasthan Desert', *Science & Global Security*, Vol. 6, Overseas Publishers Association, Amsterdam, 1996.

10. *Newsweek,* op. cit., p. 15.
11. See Raj Chengappa's adulatory cover story, 'The Bomb Makers', India Today, New Delhi, 22 June 1998.
12. K.S. Sudarshan of the RSS, quoted in 'PM goes to Opposition for Support', *Indian Express*, New Delhi, 15 May 1998.
13. Advani demanded that Pakistan 'roll back its anti-India policy with regard to Kashmir.' Proceeding on the assumption that India's 'decisive step to become a nuclear weapon state has brought about a qualitatively new stage in Indo-Pak relations, particularly in finding a lasting solution to the Kashmir problem', the Union Home Minister, Mr L.K. Advani, has called upon 'Islamabad to realize the change in the geo-strategic situation in the region and the world.' See 'Pak. told to roll back proxy war', *The Hindu*, New Delhi, 19 May 1998.

    So alarming was this bellicose statement that the US State Department commented sharply on it, accusing India of 'foolishly and dangerously increasing tensions with its neighbours and being indifferent to world opinion . . . ' See 'US takes strong exception to Advani's warning on J–K', *The Hindustan Times,* New Delhi, 21 May 1998.
14. *The Hindu*, New Delhi, 19 May 1998, op. cit.
15. Nelson Mandela, long considered India's friend, delivered India a strong rebuke at the NAM summit in Durban, and said all non-aligned countries remained concerned over the problem in Jammu & Kashmir and 'should be willing to lend all our strength for the peaceful solution of this problem'.

    Vajpayee took strong exception to this and India later claimed that South African deputy president Thabo Mbeki apologized to India for the remark. This was promptly denied by South Africa. 'See South Africa offers an apology to India', *The Asian Age*, New Delhi, 5 September 1998 and 'SA apologizes for J&K remark', *The Pioneer,* New Delhi, 5 September 1998.
16. An overwhelming number of references can be cited to support the view that Nehru was categorically committed to voluntary nuclear weapons abstinence, and to fighting for the elimination of these armaments.

    However, it has also been urged by some that his rejection of nuclear weapons was less than categorical. As their strongest evidence, they quote a 26 June 1946 address at a public rally in Bombay, before India's Independence: 'As long as the world is constituted as it is, every country will have to devise and use the latest scientific devices for its protection. I have no doubt India will develop her scientific researchers and I hope Indian scientists will use the atomic force for constructive purposes. But if India is threatened, she will inevitably try to defend herself by all means at her disposal.'

    It has also been argued that Nehru, when attacked during a heated Parliamentary debate for his insistent distinction between the peaceful and military uses of atomic energy, was reduced to saying: 'I do not know how you are to distinguish between [them] . . . . Of course if we are compelled to use [atomic energy] for other purposes, possibly no pious sentiments of any of us will stop the nation from using it that way. But I do hope that our outlook in regard to this atomic energy is going to be a peaceful one . . . and not one of war and hatred.' (Quoted in I. Abraham, *The Making of the Indian Atomic Bomb,* Orient Longman, New Delhi, 1998, pp. 48–49.)

However, it seems illogical to put inordinately heavy interpretation on such statements to conclude that Nehru was ambivalent about nuclear weapons. The evidence to the contrary, especially from well-considered and carefully enunciated policy formulations, is massive and persuasive. And yet, any inference as regards ambivalence can only be a function of *interpretation,* not explicit, unambivalent, statement. By contrast, Nehru's *actions,* as well as the central thrust of his reflections and pronouncements on the issue, support our premise.

17. 'Top Secret' Note from George C. McGhee on 'Anticipatory Action Pending Chinese Communist Demonstration of a Nuclear Capability', Declassified Authority: NND 959001. dated: 17 February 1995, Reproduced at National Security Archive, Washington.

Willie Rivalry

What is the Truth about the Yields of Indian and Pakistani Tests?

The overt nuclearization of India and Pakistan is inseparable from fierce mutual rivalry and muscle-flexing over assumed technological prowess and claims of military superiority, as well as of greater valour and virility. Nothing illustrates this better than official statements about the character and number of nuclear test explosions carried out in May 1998 and their yields, as well as competitive claims about each other's missile capabilities. These, 'my-bomb-is-bigger' statements have been questioned by independent experts both internationally and in India and Pakistan. It seems very likely that New Delhi and Islamabad grossly exaggerated the tests' yields. In all probability, India's claimed 11 May 'thermonuclear' explosion, by means of which it was supposed to have established decisive nuclear superiority over Pakistan, was a dud. The 'secondary' of this 'hydrogen bomb' probably did not go off.

India's hawkish publicists and strategic analysts have repeatedly asserted that India has unassailable superiority over Pakistan in missile technology too. The only exceptions to such assertions are made when it suits them to make the opposite, perhaps equally poorly substantiated, claim, namely that India is inferior and needs to sink more investment into its 'indigenous' missile programme to compete better with Pakistan's 'import-based' programme.

Pakistan's claims of superiority in missile technology come from the very top. In January 1999, Abdul Qadir Khan, the father of the country's uranium enrichment programme and the *Ghauri* missile, asserted that Pakistan's missiles are 'far superior to what India had in its arsenal and that New Delhi would have to think twice before daring to attack Pakistan.' He said, 'Our missiles can hit any Indian city within 10 to 15 minutes at a speed of three kilometres per second .... Pakistan's missiles [are] far better than *Prithvi* and *Agni* ... they could not be neutralised or destroyed once they were launched.'[1]

These boastful assertions have little to do with hard facts. Rather, they are an integral part of the exchange of bellicose rhetoric that has become a subcontinental routine. India claimed to have simultaneously exploded three nuclear devices: on 11 May 1998, a fission device with a yield of 12 kilotons (a kiloton is the equivalent of 1,000 tonnes of TNT), a thermonuclear device, *Shakti-I,* with a yield of 43 kt, and a third device of less than a kiloton. The last was reported to have a yield of 0.2 kt. The combined total yield was said to be 50 kt. (This was revised upwards to 60 kt in February 1999, according to Rajagopala Chidambaram, chairman of the Atomic Energy Commission.[2]

As for India's two 13 May tests, these were claimed to be of low-yield devices, with yields between 0.2 and 0.6 kt. It is not clear if these involved developing battlefield-usable 'tactical' nuclear weapons (some writers have even suggested that these may be adapted into artillery shells), or if they were 'boosted primaries' (extremely light devices with yields usually in excess of 10 kt, which are particularly useful in setting off high-yield 'secondary' explosion assemblies in a thermonuclear bomb).

The 12-kt device tested on May 11 (Chidambaram later said it had a yield of 15 kt) was reported to have been a lighter, more compact version of the kind of device India tested in 1974. India's claim about the 43 kt *Shakti-I* device came under serious questioning from scientists within a week of the test. Some suggested that *Shakti-I* was a 'boosted fission' weapon, not a thermonuclear one. Thermonuclear weapons usually have an explosive yield in the megaton (1000 kt) range, while boosted fission devices yield something of the order of 30 to 100 kt.

However, Atomic Energy Commission (AEC) chairman Chidambaram insisted at a press conference on 17 May that it was a thermonuclear device. Its yield, he claimed, was kept deliberately low in view of the risk of seismic damage to villages in the vicinity of the site.[3] Officials of the AEC and the Defence Research & Development Organization (DRDO) were categorical that 'weaponization is now complete. We have tested the size, weight, performance, and vibrations for nuclear warheads designed to go on *Prithvi* and *Agni* missiles.'

It was also claimed that 'the tests provided critical data for the validation of our capability in the design of nuclear weapons of different yields for different applications and different delivery systems and significantly enhanced our capability in computer simulations of new designs and taken us to the stage of subcritical experiments in the future, if considered necessary'.

Since then, a number of independent scientists and engineers, including seismologists, nuclear physicists, and weapons designers have collected and analysed data from both AEC sources and seismographs at different locations in the world. (The AEC's disclosures about the measurements of the yields in question have all been based on seismic data; data relevant to other methods, such as assays of radionuclides from the explosion tunnel/hole, have not been released). Terry Wallace, a University of Arizona seismologist, concluded that the total yield of the three 11 May explosions was only 10 to 25 kt, not 50 kt.[4] This is similar to other non-official estimates. For instance, according to data compiled by the Natural Resources Defense Council (NRDC), the expected mid-point of a range of probable yields for all three tests on 11May was only about 12 kt.[5]

However, seven months after the tests, Chidambaram described the Pokharan-II series as 'the perfect tests'. He reiterated that India had conducted its full complement of tests and had 'obtained three robust bomb designs' from the Pokharan explosions. He dismissed all doubts raised by independent experts about the AEC's claims, by saying he was not surprised by their reaction. 'This was expected,' he said, pointing out that 'though the Indian side had presented the yield data along with corroborative proof, the credibility of Indian figures continued to be doubted.' He described the doubts as 'baseless'. 'Though the US had conducted 1,030 tests and China 45, India's tests should be considered equivalent to the several which other nuclear weapon states had conducted because the Pokharan tests were undertaken from a higher technological threshold.'[6]

There are several internal inconsistencies and contradictions in the official claims. For instance, the claimed yield projections for the 1998 tests are based on the assumption that the May 1974 test at the same Pokharan site had a yield of 12 to 14 kt (and there was no significant change in the geology of the area). Independent estimates of the 1974 yield, confirmed by some Indian officials, are, however, as low as 2 to

4 kt.[7] If the lower numbers are used, the combined total yield of the 11 May tests only works out to 10 to 20 kt, not the claimed 45–60 kt. P.K. Iyengar, former AEC chairman and the principal physicist involved in the 1974 test, once said its yield was about 8 kt. However, in a recent interview, he said that, based on radiochemical analysis of samples of bomb debris, the yield of the 1974 blast was closer to 10 kt than 8 kt.[8] While higher than the 2–4 kt estimate, this is still below the originally claimed 12 to 14 kt.

In November 1998, *Nucleonics Week,* the international nuclear industry's trade journal, reported that 'analysts at the Z Division of the Lawrence Livermore National Laboratory, responsible for making estimates of progress in foreign nuclear weapons programmes based on classified data, have now concluded that the second stage of a two-stage Indian hydrogen bomb device failed to ignite as planned.'[9] A hydrogen or thermonuclear bomb is a two-stage weapon in which the principal contribution to the explosive energy results from the fusion of light nuclei, such as deuterium and tritium. The high temperatures required for that reaction, produced in the secondary stage of the device, are initially generated by fission at the primary stage.

Nucleonics Week quoted US analysts as saying they 'strongly believe that, on 11May the primary stage of an Indian H-bomb detonated, but its heat failed to ignite the secondary stage.'

One US official, who was quoted, said: 'if India really wants a thermonuclear capability, they will have to test again and hope they get it right'. As a result of the apparent failure, US official sources said, the Indian government is under pressure by the Department of Atomic Energy (DAE) . . . to test the H-bomb again, in the face of ongoing bilateral talks in which the US seeks to persuade India to agree to a global nuclear test ban.'[10] (The 'pressure', if it did exist, appeared to have eased off by the end of 1998: India in early 1999 seemed all set to move towards signing the CTBT.)

However, Chidambaram once again contended that 'India had indeed tested a thermonuclear bomb. He claimed this was of a 'fusion–fission–fusion' type. A boosted fission device was part of this explosion, making its separate testing redundant.' India, he also said, 'was working on powerful lasers for 'inertial confinement' to produce fusion energy and uranium enrichment.'[11]

He also said that Indian scientists have reason to feel proud since they had achieved a 'perfect three' with the tests: 'mastering the optimum emplacement design' for the nuclear device, getting specific yield calculations, and ensuring zero radioactive contamination.[12] (The optimum emplacement design technology determines how far down to place the nuclear device: deep enough to ensure that there is no nuclear venting and yet not so deep as to incur needless expenditure.) Another boastful AEC claim is that 'India has achieved a world record by conducting five nuclear tests in a span of 48 hours.' However, in the former USSR alone, there is recorded and published data 'on 25 different tests where each test comprised four to eight near-simultaneous explosions. In fact, the USSR conducted a test way back on 23 August 1975 . . . consisting of eight near-simultaneous explosions within several seconds, leave alone 48 hours.'[13]

As for Pakistan, the first tests on 28 May 1998 involved the claimed detonation of five devices, the largest of them yielding, according to A.Q. Khan, 30 to 35 kt. The other four tests were of small, low-yield weapons ideal for missile attack against troops. However, the independently estimated total yield of the five explosions was 9–12 kt. On 30 May, Pakistan first claimed to have detonated two nuclear explosions—foreign minister Gohar Ayub Khan was on record as saying so. Later, however, it was 'clarified' that only one took place. 'Khan explained the next day that two tests were were originally planned, but after the results of the first day's tests were evaluated, it was decided to conduct only one test.'[14] Pakistani officials claimed that the yield of that test was 15 to 18 kt. Some Western seismologists put it at 2 kt (Wallace at 4 to 6 kt).

There are other discrepancies too. For instance, the Pakistan Atomic Energy Commission said that Pakistan tested only fission weapons and categorically stated that 'Pakistan tested no thermonuclear or tactical nuclear device.' But A. Q. Khan held that there were five tests, 'one was a big bomb . . . of about 30–35 kilotons . . . the other four were small tactical weapons of low yield'.[15]

The term 'big' bomb was first used by India's Prime Minister on 15 May 1998, although it was quickly withdrawn.[16]

The discrepancies, dissonances and contradictions highlight divisions within the decision-making establishments and a proclivity to make extravagant claims about scientific and technological 'achievements'. They also raise questions about the authenticity and reliability of official stands and doctrines, and create doubts about India's and Pakistan's real capabilities. Quite simply, even the basic assumptions underlying deterrence—secure knowledge and understanding each other's capabilities, military strengths and weaknesses, and security doctrines, and full appreciation of the adversary's ability to cause 'unacceptable damage'—do not obtain in the Indian subcontinent. Such uncertainty degrades stability, and greatly enlarges the scope for strategic miscalculation. It also encourages knee-jerk or panic responses in situations of crisis.

Given that weapons of mass destruction are involved, uncertainty has potentially devastating consequences. This phenomenon of dubious claims and uncertainty is not confined to nuclear test explosions or weapons alone, but extends to missiles too. India and Pakistan have both challenged, or mocked at, each other's claims about the origins, character, range and other parameters pertaining to their missiles. Both contend that their missile development programmes are basically, if not fully, indigenous and self-reliant, although the truth appears to be more complex. India obtained some rocketry technology from France and the former USSR, and various components for its *Prithvi* and *Agni* missile series from these and other sources too. Pakistan is believed to have obtained M–11 *(Hatf–3)* missiles and other missile technology components/sub-assemblies from China and North Korea.[17]

However, few Indian or Pakistani leaders have any hesitation in pointing fingers at one another. For instance, India's defence minister George Fernandes in April 1998 named China as 'the mother of the *Ghauri*'. However, many independent researchers are inclined to think that the *Ghauri's* source is North Korea. (Among the more prominent of them is S. Chandrasekhar, formerly with the Indian Space Research Organization, who believes, on the basis of published information and images of the *Ghauri,* that it is a single-stage liquid-fuelled vehicle like North Korea's *Nodong* missile.[18]

Tall claims have been made about conventional weaponry and the domestic arms industries of India and Pakistan too. They have little to do with reality. For instance, the output of India's military industry has dropped by 57 per cent since 1990–1. And Pakistan's military production fell by 33 per cent between 1973–4 and 1996–7.[19]

India's Defence Research and Development Organization (DRDO) claims a budget equivalent to about 6.5 per cent of total military expenditure (a proportion exceeded only by the UK, France, Sweden, and the US). Its biggest projects are nevertheless in extremely poor shape. The worst examples are the Main Battle Tank (MBT), a plan to develop a nuclear power plant for a submarine, codenamed 'Advanced Technology Vessel', and the Light Combat Aircraft (LCA).

For example the *Arjun* tank has repeatedly failed to meet service requirement tests. The MBT–*Arjun* project was launched in 1974. The first prototype was planned for 1980. 'The design, however, was finalized only in July 1996 and the earliest the MBT can enter service is 2002.'[20] The *Arjun* engine has failed to come up to the mark. Strangely enough, the *Arjun* was accepted by the army for limited duty on condition that it would be allowed to purchase more Russian tanks. (A controversy now rages over the T–90 Russian tank, with former Prime Minister H.D. Deve Gowda pleading against its procurement.)[21]

The nuclear submarine–ATV project, launched in 1975, has claimed an R&D expenditure of Rs 2500 crores ($600 million) without substantial results. According to Buddhi Kota Subba Rao—a former Navy captain who worked on the project in the 1970s and was victimized by the DAE for having criticized its functioning, even falsely charged and detained for 'espionage'—the project may be unviable. Its basic pressurized water reactor design is badly flawed.[22]

The LCA project was launched in 1983, with a view to replacing the MiG–21 fleet by the mid-1990s, is in the doldrums. Its first flight has been repeatedly postponed 'and the most optimistic date for its entry into service is between 2005 and 2007'.[23] After its indigenous *Kaveri* engine repeatedly failed tests, India decided to get it redesigned by Lockheed Martin, but the agreement was put on hold after the nuclear tests. The job is now being contracted out to a Russian company.

In Pakistan's case, the military R&D infrastructure is far weaker and the planning less ambitious. For instance, military R&D claims only Rs 130 million (less than one-hundredth of India's).[24]

Given the budgetary constraints of both India and Pakistan, their ambitious military programmes often compromise on quality, reliability, and safety. This adds further to uncertainties and raises the probability of conflicts getting out of hand, military leaders making disastrous miscalculations, and accidental wars being triggered off.

Notes

1. 'Pak claims nuclear superiority over India', *The Telegraph,* Calcutta, 1 February 1999.
2. R. Chidambaram, during a two hour-long briefing for the Indian Science Writers' Association on 3 February 1999, made a series of claims about the 'perfect' character of India's tests and the country's 'high technological threshold'. Cited in 'Further nuclear tests unnecessary', *The Hindu,* New Delhi, 4 February 1999 and 'No more N-tests needed: AEC', *Indian Express,* New Delhi, 4 February 1999.
3. *Joint Press Note* issued by the DAE and DRDO, New Delhi, 17 May 1998, p. 3.
4. T. Wallace, *Seismological Research Letters,* September-October 1998, B. Barker, et. al. *Science,* 25 September 1998, estimate the yields at 9–16 kt.
5. Cited in David Albright, 'The Shots Heard Round The World', *The Bulletin of the Atomic Scientists,* Chicago, July–August 1998, pp. 21–25.
6. Cited in *The Hindu,* op. cit.
7. September 1987 interview by the authors with P.N. Haksar, former Principal Secretary to the Prime Minister in 1974. Also confirmed by George Perkovich, cited in *The New York Times,* 18 May 1998.
8. Cited in Albright, op. cit., p. 22.
9. Mark Hibbs, 'India May Test Again Because H-Bomb Failed, US Believes', *Nucleonics Week,* 26 November 1998.
10. Ibid.
11. *The Hindu,* op. cit.
12. *Indian Express,* op. cit.
13. A. Gopalakrishnan, 'Margins of Error: Verifying Claims on Nuclear Tests', *The Times of India,* New Delhi, 20 November 1998. Gopalakrishnan is a former chairman of India's Atomic Energy Regulatory Board.
14. Albright, op. cit.
15. Cited in Zia Mian, 'Pakistan's Nuclear Descent', *INESAP Bulletin,* Darmstadt, November 1998, p. 11.
16. 'We have the capacity for a big bomb now for which necessary command and control system is also in place.' 'India is now a N-weapons state: PM,' *The Times of India,* New Delhi, 16 May 1998. Also in 'Nuclear weapons only for self-defence, says PM' *The Hindu,* New Delhi, 16 May 1998: 'India is now a nuclear weapons state, and . . . India has a big bomb.'
17. For detailed accounts, see W. Potter and H. Jencks (eds.), *The International Missile Bazaar: The New Supplier Network,* Westview Press, Boulder, 1994,

pp. 201–3. Also Andrew Koch, W.P.S. Sidhu, 'South Asia goes ballistic, then nuclear', in *Jane's Intelligence Review,* June 1998, S. 36–7, p.19.

18. See excerpts from Ashutosh Misra, 'The Pakistani Ghauri Missile', *INESAP Bulletin,* Darmstadt, November 1998, p.14.
19. Eric Arnett, 'Big Science, Small Results', *The Bulletin of the Atomic Scientists,* Chicago, July–August 1998, p. 46–7.
20. W.P.S. Sidhu, op. cit.
21. See Kanwar Sandhu, 'Virtues of the indigenous tank', in *Indian Express,* New Delhi, 26 January 1999.
22. Interview with Subba Rao, 5 February 1999.
23. Sidhu, op. cit.
24. Arnett, op. cit.

CHAPTER FIVE

South Asia in the Nuclear Trap

The Causes and Consequences of Crossing the Threshold

On 11 May 1998, India crossed the nuclear Rubicon, embarking on a journey that can only bring greater insecurity, tension, and maldevelopment even as it represents another crucial phase in the ongoing efforts of the Sangh Combine to totally transform the character of Indian society and to impose its version of what constitutes the Indian nation and nationalism.[1] What is at stake for them is not simply institutionalizing their version of the cultural essence of India but of imposing their versions of what constitutes Indian greatness, national security, national interests, etc. Overnight, a ruthless political force of great evil and determination totally transformed the parameters of debate and struggle on so vital an issue as nuclear security and insecurity, as well as on related concerns such as India's relationship with its neighbours and the world. The horror and strategic stupidity, and the political danger of allowing the Sangh to get away with what it has done, will hopefully sink in amongst an ever widening public, Indian and international, for only then can one hope to successfully reverse the journey directions, internal and external, on which India is now embarked.

False Explanations

Three kinds of arguments can be put forward to explain why the Indian government embarked on this course. The first has to do with supposed changes in the external security environment, or perceptions about such changes, i.e. Pakistan and/or China have become more nuclearly threatening and belligerent. The second kind claims that the nuclear hypocrisies of existing NWSs and their reluctance to move rapidly to full nuclear disarmament has finally 'driven' India out of frustration/impatience to try and gatecrash into their club. The third set of arguments focuses on changed self-perceptions and the domestic factors behind such changes. Such an understanding will naturally focus much more strongly on the changing character of élite Indian nationalism and the role of the Sangh Combine in bringing about such changes as well as in pushing its own distinctive agenda.

Those who support the tests and the logic they unveil of moving towards weaponization and deployment, will distribute their explanations for the testing between the first two kinds of arguments. To an extent, anti-nuclearists in the other NWSs (notably in the West), given their anger against the enduring hypocrisies of their governments, their lack of knowledge or interest in Indian domestic matters, and the existence of a certain moral capital built on India's past record as a country seriously committed to global disarmament, have also done the same. It should, however, be obvious to anyone situated in India at this time and prepared to think objectively, that neither changing threat perceptions nor the enduring hypocrisies of the existing NWSs explain the Indian decision. Decisive weight has to be given to the third factor of changed élite self-perceptions and the role of the Sangh Combine in bringing this about.

The external threats most commonly cited by India's pro-nuclearists to justify the Pokharan-II tests have been Pakistan and China, both separately and in presumed concert. The citation of the Pakistan nuclear threat has always had the great advantage of being publicly highly saleable. Its great disadvantage has, however, been that in more informed circles the argument has had little weight for the simple and powerful reason that Pakistan's nuclear diplomacy (though not its nuclear preparations) has always been strongly *reactive* to India's. It would never be the first to test nor the first to go openly nuclear but would follow an Indian decision in both cases, as eventually proved to be the case.[2]

Although there has always been a small but significant lobby in Pakistan which has argued that Pakistan should go nuclear in order to compensate for the imbalance in conventional forces in favour of India, they have always been outweighed by those in Pakistan who believed that non-nuclear parity between the two countries was to be greatly preferred. Thus Pakistan throughout the last decade and a half repeatedly put forward on the official governmental level a variety of proposals for the denuclearization of the South Asian region. Of several such proposals, the three most important and comprehensive were the following: Islamabad repeatedly offered joint and simultaneous signature by both countries of the NPT; bilateral renunciation of nuclear weapons; or the establishment of a South Asian NWFZ. In each and every case, on each and every occasion, India and its supporters provided no serious counter-proposals but rejected these initiatives, invariably citing the Chinese nuclear threat to it as well as claiming that these selective, regional measures were inappropriate and a diversion from the task of securing global disarmament. This argument has, however, not prevented India from supporting, or at least not opposing, NWFZs proposed, or set up, elsewhere in the world.

The reference to an utterly abstract, never exercised or articulated, 'Chinese threat' then has been quite central to the Indian armoury of justifications for first, its position of maintaining ambiguity, and now, for having gone openly nuclear. The meaning of the Sino-Indian border conflict has therefore been asymmetrically interpreted. For China this has always been (especially since it got the territory it more or less wanted during the 1962 war) a distant and minor affair. For India, militarily humiliated during that war, the border defeat has always been something of a running political sore which many in the foreign policy establishment have periodically found useful to scratch and revive.

There has, however, also been a widespread recognition within the same establishment that, despite, and regardless of, this border dispute, there has always been a basic open-endedness and room for flexibility in India–China relations. India's casualties in the border conflict were less than half of those suffered during its 1987 military intervention in Sri Lanka. China quickly returned all Indian POWs and imposed no punitive measures despite its victory. Indeed, although the Indian army was in complete rout, the Chinese unilaterally withdrew to the present Line of Actual Control to indicate that they had no designs beyond the border dispute. That is to say, Sino-Indian relations have always hitherto (before the Pokharan-II tests) lain between the two poles of strategic friendship and strategic hostility, comfortably distant from either. In fact, they have also been distant from the point represented on this spectrum by the posture of strategic rivalry that is obviously considerably closer to the 'hostility' rather than to the 'friendship' end. Although some Indian strategists have repeatedly talked of an inevitable strategic rivalry between the two, this too has always been much more a matter of occasional speculation than of concrete reality.

Thus, the mainstream discourse in India on China has had a character quite distinct from that on Pakistan where strategic hostility has been the defining fulcrum. Indian foreign policy and nuclear strategists, for the most part, have never been quite able to define a consistent or strongly felt position on China. On the one hand, to justify India's nuclear posture it has been necessary to cite the 'Chinese threat', i.e. treat it as at least a nuclear–strategic rival of sorts. On the other hand, there has always been a certain unease that to do so risks making relations with China much worse than they need be given the more open-ended character of relational possibilities between the two. Both aspects were visible in the aftermath of the Indian tests. The Indian defence minister, George Fernandes, personally a longstanding and notorious China-baiter, waxed eloquent about the Chinese threat just before the tests, a ploy used by the BJP-led government to subsequently rationalize them. After the tests, the Indian Prime Minister, Atal Bihari Vajpayee, in his first attempt at public explanation of the reasons for the tests (which was not given to Indians) wrote a letter to President Clinton of the US in which the Chinese threat was referred to.[3] To compound matters, letters were sent to all other NWSs except China. However, subsequently, not only did a very large number of pro-nuclearists from the unofficial sector of the nuclear–strategic establishment criticize the unnecessary provocation to China, but the government officially repeatedly announced that the tests were not directed against China ('not country-specific' has been the official term used) and that it did not consider the Chinese to be a strategic opponent.

This was not simple dissimulation. Rather, it reflected the long ongoing difficulty and uncertainty that the 'China question' has posed for India's pro-nuclearists. The idea that the 'Chinese threat' necessitated the May tests was always false. Over the last two decades, especially since the end of the Cold War, relations between India and China steadily improved. So much so, that in 1996, Jiang Zemin, the President of China, on his visit to both New Delhi and Islamabad, shocked his Pakistani hosts by publicly stating in Islamabad that Kashmir should be bilaterally resolved between Pakistan and India. This was correctly perceived (in Islamabad) as a revision of earlier Chinese policy indicating a shift away from Pakistan and towards an exploration of better ties with India.

This was not surprising. Sino-Pakistan and Sino-Indian ties were always situated in a wider context of Cold War relationships, more specifically, Sino-Soviet, Sino-US and US–Soviet ties. Here the crucial axis for most of the three decades of the sixties, seventies, and eighties was Sino-Soviet hostility. Not only was Pakistan a crucial conduit at the turn of the seventies to forging a Sino-US entente directed against the USSR, but Soviet attempts to bring India into an alliance (the Asian Collective Security System) directed against China were clearly noted. On its part, India valued Soviet diplomatic support on Kashmir, its military supplies and economic assistance, and in the context of the 1971 Bangladesh War for independence, the strategic counterweight the Indo-Soviet Treaty of that year provided against the Sino–Pakistan–US axis then emerging. The US and China were both opposed to the dismemberment of Pakistan although the cause of Bangladeshi independence was entirely justified.

However, what was noteworthy then and after, was the refusal of China to provide anything more than rhetorical political support for Pakistan against

India when it was literally being dismembered, and India's parallel refusal to allow the Indo-Soviet Treaty to be interpreted as an expression of its strategic opposition to China. Where the Soviets saw the Treaty as a part of its China containment strategy, India saw it as a one-off treaty necessitated by the political exigencies of the time. Both China and India were determined not to allow either Pakistani or Soviet concerns respectively, to decisively determine their postures vis-a-vis each other. By the late seventies the Chinese ended their support to rebel insurgents against Indian rule in the north-eastern states of the country. The Sino-Pakistan relationship has always meant much more to Pakistan than to China. By the end of the Cold War, and after the cessation of Sino-Soviet hostilities, the Sino-Pakistan connection simply could not carry the same (limited) strategic–political weight that it had in the past. For fifteen years before Pokharan-II and right up to these tests, Sino-Indian relations on the political, diplomatic, military (border dispositions and atmospherics), cultural and trade fronts were steadily improving. There was simply no way that anyone could logically or convincingly argue that the 'strategic situation' between India and China (nuclear or otherwise) had worsened over the last few years thereby necessitating a change in India's strategic posture, leave alone in its nuclear response.

A Sino-Pakistan 'Axis'?

Yet some such claim about some form of Chinese and/or Pakistani 'culpability' had to be found to justify Indian behaviour! It is in this respect that the Sino-Pakistan nuclear-related connection served an important purpose. This was (and continues to be) played up for much more than it was, or is, worth. That there has been such a connection is undeniable. Yet in the weight of its contribution to Pakistan's development of a nuclear capability, it has been very much a secondary factor in comparison to Islambad's own clandestine efforts at equipping itself with the necessary hardware and software. Technologically, building a simple atomic bomb is really no big deal. Iraq, purely through purchases on the private markets of the West (especially in Germany) had made, despite the bombing of the Osirak reactor in 1981, very significant advances in its efforts to build the bomb.[4] Pakistan developed its capacity sometime in the mid-or perhaps early eighties.

Perhaps the best way of situating the Sino-Pakistan relationship is to recognize that there have been basically three kinds of nuclear-related relationships between countries. The first can be called a nuclear alliance or near-alliance relationship. The closest historical approximations to this kind of relationship have been the US–UK connection and the Sino-Soviet connection of the fifties. Of course, the US–UK relationship was of a closer and stronger order than the Sino-Soviet one, but in neither case did the senior partner give its most advanced secrets to the other. Indeed, eventual Soviet refusal to give the secret of the bomb was one of the key reasons for the Sino-Soviet break-up from the late fifties onwards. The second kind of relationship can be called a patron–client nuclear relationship. The closest historical approximation here is the US–Israel relationship. The third, and far and away the most common form, is that of cooperation in nuclear-related and dual-use materials for mutual political, economic, technological, and commercial purposes. This has characterized (in milder or stronger versions) not only Sino-Pakistan nuclear ties but the kind of support in nuclear and dual-use technologies and equipment that China has given to Algeria and Libya; Germany to Argentina; France to Brazil. France even wanted to supply a plutonium reprocessing plant to Pakistan in 1974, something China has never sought to do. France was prevented from doing so by the US. Then there is the fact of missile supplies by Russia to Cyprus, Iran, and even to China; China to Iran, Saudi Arabia, etc; and, of course, the US supplied dual-use materials to a number of countries.

Russia has supplied SS–20s, SS–18s, and cruise missiles to China in the nineties, but to read into this some 'strategic relationship' directed against a third country would be utterly mistaken. China and Russia have been particularly keen in recent years to maximize the commercial benefits of arms and technology sales of various kinds even while claiming to be adhering to international norms regarding such transfers. China may or may not be violating such norms, but the important point to note is that these transfers should not be constituted as signifying a strategic alliance. Insofar as the Sino-Pakistan connection has had a political dimension, the political import of such cooperation should be seen as obeying the general rhythms of the political ties between the two: more important during the Cold War, far less so after its ending.

To further put Indian objections on this count into a proper perspective, we need only ask what the Indian reaction would be if China were to announce that it was supplying two complete nuclear reactors to Pakistan, its most advanced fighter aircraft, and the signing of a 10-year military supply commitment to be known as a 'Strategic Accord'? It is hardly difficult to imagine what the reaction would be: there would be an uproar in India. Yet this is exactly what the Russians have committed themselves to doing with India! Nevertheless, the Pakistani hawk who sees in this connection a strategic alliance of sorts (nuclear-related or otherwise) between Russia and India against

Pakistan is as seriously mistaken as any Indian hawk who sees in the Sino-Pakistan nuclear connection today a similar alliance or threat against India.

In 1995, an official Indian delegation headed by the then Indian defence minister, Sharad Pawar of the then ruling Congress party, at a meeting with their Chinese counterparts officially raised this issue. The Chinese reply was striking. The Indian side was politely informed that China was in the business of undertaking commercial transactions and would be willing to supply on Indian request each and every item they believed China had supplied to Pakistan! These matters are not unknown to many a pro-nuclearist inside or outside the Indian government. If in spite of this, so much has been made out of the Sino-Pakistan nuclear-related connection, then it is essentially because of the need to rationalize through 'external considerations' the May tests of 1998.

Hypocrisy and the Bomb

In this regard, Indian anti-nuclearists have to be somewhat disappointed with those Western anti-nuclearists who have given so much credence to the 'China threat' as a factor supposedly provoking India to go nuclear, or indeed to the claim that the hypocrisies of the existing NWSs 'finally drove' India to take this route. Location matters. Anti-nuclearists in the West have a constant responsibility to remind the world of the culpability of the existing NWSs, and that the biggest among them, most notably the US, are the greatest culprits. India was not, however, driven by 'frustration' or the hypocrisies of the NWSs to do what it did. After all, what is new about such hypocrisies? Indeed, these hypocrisies have more recently operated within a context of greater hope and optimism about the prospects of global nuclear disarmament precisely because of the existence of a new disarmament momentum. India's decision and its excuses for it reflected utter contempt even for the existence of such a momentum! That its past record on disarmament issues has (justifiably) found considerable sympathy and support from Western anti-nuclear advocates should not be allowed to obscure the reality that the India of the nineties and after May 1998 has become much more cynical than that of the past.

Hypocrisy never drove any country to go in for the bomb. That argument, by its very nature, does not describe an objective cause for proliferation but describes a 'useful' justification after a decision to proliferate, motivated by other, more fundamental reasons, is taken. Hypocrisy arguments are to be tackled at the level of ideology, and ideological rationales offered and resisted, not at the level of 'real' or 'true' causes or explanations of causes for going nuclear. It is one thing for anti-nuclear activists and others to resent the hypocrisies of NWSs and to sympathize with the resentment of NNWSs regarding these hypocrisies. It is altogether another thing to believe that such resentments serve as major, let alone crucial, motivations for other countries to actually go nuclear. Between 1964 and 1987, despite the persistence of such hypocrisies on a stronger, deeper, and wider scale than after 1987, there was still no addition to the ranks of the nuclear club.

In a post-Cold War context, when a more positive situation emerges and when these hypocritical NWSs make some positive movement of a kind that they did not make before, are the opponents of nuclear weapons suddenly to give more credence to India's self-serving claim that it was motivated to act as it did because of the hypocrisy of the NWSs? Indeed, there is every reason to appreciate that the overwhelming number of not just NNWSs but of nuclear capable NNWSs are sensible enough to keep the hypocrisy issue in proper perspective and not to let its persistence or even its institutionalization 'lead' them to break out into open nuclear status. What this persistent hypocrisy can more strongly, and likely, lead to is a break-out from the NPT and to greater suspicion of disarmament and restraint measures endorsed by the NWSs. It can also lead to a more despairing 'well, what did you expect' attitude if some newer countries (like India) do go nuclear which will of course never be because of 'frustration' with hypocrisy but will be based on much more basic reasons related to deterrence or currency of power perceptions.

That is to say, it is external threat perceptions and élite self-perceptions, and changes in these two, that constitute the basic grid of explanation for why countries go nuclear. Indeed, the NWSs realize that their hypocrisies are not the reason for proliferation and this makes it more difficult to get them to renounce hypocritical nuclear behaviour precisely because it doesn't cost them so much. Ironically, anti-nuclearists justly angered by such hypocrisy tend to wish the culprits were in some way 'paid back' for continuing to be hypocritical, and so look for self-confirmation of their righteous anger and of the validity of their implicit or explicit belief/claim/hope that such persistent hypocrisy poses a 'danger' and hence some kind of an eventual 'comeuppance' or 'lesson' even to the NWSs. Unfortunately, this is not the way the world is, nor is it the way to understand the processes of proliferation and non-proliferation, nuclear armament or disarmament.

The existence of hypocrisy does not pose a serious problem to its perpetrators because it does not lead to more countries wanting membership in the nuclear club out of some ever-growing frustration. It can represent a comeuppance for the NWSs in one way only: that those who are against nuclear weapons harness the reality of the existence of such hypocrisies to mobilize emotional and intellectual anger and opposition by ever wider sections of society who, being ordinarily moral, are or can be nauseated by such hypocrisy. This is to use moral anger to generate changes in mass consciousness and thus various practical forms of resistance against the NWSs.

Western anti-nuclear advocates willing to take the hypocrisy or the 'China threat' arguments seriously as explanations for Indian behaviour are making a mistake. For a number of reasons, they are tempted to 'respect' the China factor argument much more than they should. Most anti-nuclearists are not anti-Realists. They tend to give, as a general rule, serious weight to Realist arguments about external security threats motivating countries to go nuclear. This is reinforced by the fact that in the cases of the USSR and China, this was certainly a very important though not the sole motivating factor. It is not so in India's case but is obviously so for Pakistan. Moreover, the implicit Realism of so much of anti-nuclear thinking about global politics also reinforces the tendency to separate the domestic from the external as explanatory factors and to concentrate on the latter. It is also convenient to do so because it then obviates the need seriously to familiarize oneself with the complexities of domestic politics in a country like India. Most anti-nuclear champions in the West and outside India, for understandable and not unworthy reasons, have neither the time nor the inclination to develop such a familiarization. It is here, however, on the domestic terrain of Indian politics, general and nuclear, that the crucial explanations for India going nuclear must be sought.

Nuclear Nationalism: the Sangh Factor

There are both fundamental reasons, and more proximate causes, for India's going nuclear when it did. To understand the foundational factor it is necessary to recognize that for at least fifteen years there has been an ongoing battle for the 'soul of Indian nationalism'. One side has been trying with ruthless determination, belligerence, and deceit to impose its version of what this must mean, both internally and externally. It has advanced its cause considerably, winning major support within the Indian élite and so-called middle-classes. In a context where this élite's sense of nationalism is frustrated, tension-filled, and insecure, the Sangh's message of an aggressive, belligerent. and essentialist–exclusivist nationalism, of 'blaming the others' (be they Muslims, China, Western hypocrisy, or whatever) has found powerful resonance. The very fact that the RSS was clearly privy to knowledge of these blasts while the BJP's coalition partners in government were not should indicate not only how deeply authoritarian and contemptuous of democracy the Sangh Combine is, but how determined it is to carry out a total transformation of Indian society towards the establishment of a Hindu *rashtra*.[5]

The Sangh meant what it said (deliberately contradictory signals and all) on Ayodhya and it meant what it said on the Bomb.[6] The BJP (or its earlier incarnations) it should be remembered, is the only political party which officially said it wanted India to be a nuclear weapons power. It has been saying this consistently since 1951, well before there was any issue of the Pakistan and Chinese bombs! To be sure, previous Congress and UF governments in the nineties speculated about the possibility of testing but eventually resiled from taking such a decision at least in part because it would (in contrast to the BJP) have been such a sharp break from their own declared party positions without their making any public or even private preparation for such a dramatic turnaround. The fact that this becomes a serious possibility only in the last few years itself reflects precisely the point we are seeking to make about the change in the élite's nationalist self-perceptions and how this process of change is linked to what has been happening to India internally ever since the rise of Hindutva![7]

It cannot of course be the aim here to provide a disquisition about the transformation of Indian society over the past fifteen years or more. Only a very brief survey will be attempted. From the early seventies onwards, in most countries of the third world (partially excepting East and Southeast Asia whose plunge into economic crisis is of more recent nineties vintage) there has been a deepening crisis of capitalist developmentalism; a failure of the post-Independence promise. In most countries it has been a many-sided failure of growing socio-economic inadequacy, serious political–democratic limitations and weaknesses, ideological disarray and confusion. One consequence has been the dramatic rise of culturally exclusivist political movements, currents, forces, and parties everywhere in the third world. These have invariably been pivoted on issues of ethnicity, religion, and nation, either singly or in some combination. When the latter, the nation has had the capacity to subsume the other two themes in a way that cannot be reciprocated on their part. Thus, an exclusivist (often viciously so) form of nationalism has emerged and gathered strength in many countries. We have in mind here not merely Islamic nationalisms of various kinds, usually misleadingly placed for convenience under the single rubric of Islamic fundamentalism, but also Hindu nationalism, Buddhist revanchisms and nationalisms, and irredentist nationalisms of other kinds, e.g. those in the ex-USSR and ex-Yugoslavia.

India has not escaped this trend. The specific form taken by its crisis of capitalist developmentalism has been the collapse of what was called the

Nehruvian Model or Consensus, itself the legacy of the National Movement for independence before 1947. This had four central components, all of which have come under assault: socialism (a Fabian-influenced, social democratic notion of welfarism and social justice within the framework of a capitalist economy), democracy, secularism, and non-alignment. Whatever the deficiencies in the particular understandings and elaborations of these four basic principles, they represented for twenty-five years after 1947, a relatively humane notion of Indian development internally and of its behaviour and ambitions externally. What is now under attack is not the failure of these principles to be realized or institutionalized effectively, *but the very principles themselves.*

For decades, the incredible plurality and diversity of Indian society, its enormous cross-cutting of communities of all kinds, its great social disparities between richer and poorer, literate and illiterate, meant that its integrating form of nationalism was a centrist, secular–populist one with progressivist pretensions to securing greater prosperity and social justice for the majority, namely those oppressed and exploited in one way or other. The failure to make enough such progress, symbolized by the political failure and historical decline of the Congress, coupled with the dramatic increase in social polarization between the well-off and the rest, the greater hedonism and arrogant insularity of an élite which in numbers is very large (10 per cent of 950 million) and misleadingly calls itself a middle-class, has created both a political–ideological vacuum and a shift in the character of élite nationalist inclinations. It is into this vacuum that the forces of Hindu communalism and nationalism, relatively marginal throughout the National Movement and for decades after Independence, have stepped in with alarming consequences. The basis for an explicitly right wing party of mass proportions now exists, and has been taken advantage of, in a way decisively different from the political past of the country.

It is not the case that what the Sangh Combine has to say is new. Far from it. It has been saying the same thing for decades, but before the eighties it was never seriously heard even by the élite. What is new is the much greater élite *receptivity* to an old message because it at least promises a way out of the current morass. The promise is illusory and the way disastrous for the preservation of democracy and decency in the country. It is, however, a coherent perspective of sorts in a context where the opposing forces and ideologies are in some disarray. The central motif of this Hindutva ideology is the idea of a 'strong India'. To become strong, India must be united culturally and politically. This in turn requires recognition and acceptance of its cultural foundations, which are supposedly unambiguously Hindu, and a complete transformation of society. The construction of this new social anatomy is to be carried out on the basis of the existing skeleton established by the RSS's three million-odd dedicated activists, its 50,000 plus *shakhas* (branches), and their associated structures of operation. The practices of the government and state apparatuses must also express a new determination and 'virility', for India can only secure its proper civilizational role as a major world power if it follows the prescription of the Sangh. The classic statement of Hindutva from virtually the birth of the RSS in 1925 has been 'Unite Hindus and Militarize Hinduism'.

No one should underestimate the extent to which the Sangh Combine has extended its influence, especially amongst the élite and 'middle-classes' of cities and towns. In three areas, the centre of gravity of Indian politics has swung sharply to the right over the last decade. Regarding the economy, a right-wing neo-liberalism holds sway. Regarding secularism and democracy, both have been reinterpreted to mean something other than they should mean or once meant. Therefore, whereas once secularism at least meant a wide public commitment to the maintenance of a non-denominationalist state independent of religious affiliations, it has now come to mean in many more eyes, a religiously tolerant state where the false self-image of Hinduism as uniquely tolerant becomes the implicit justification for having a Hindu state as the correct or best embodiment of 'true' secularism. Democracy has come to be seen as majoritarianism within which the 'majority' who are Hindus should have their voices and interests preferred.

Finally, in the domain of world politics, with the collapse of the Cold War and the growing irrelevance of old-styled non-alignment, India must ruthlessly pursue its global ambitions to become a Great Power, breaking away from a past marred by a namby-pamby third worldism and excessive moral posturing especially on the nuclear issue. It should come as no surprise that amongst the great admirers of Samuel Huntington's thesis of the 'clash of civilizations' (where civilizations are understood as cultural–religious entities of a sort) are a number of top leaders of the Sangh Combine. For them the identification of a supposedly unified 'Islamic civilization' is vital not only as a counterpoint for the purposes of identifying a unified 'Hindu community' in opposition to Islam and Muslims, but also to promote a perspective that might be attractive to Western right-wingers—of a possible civilizational alliance between a strong Hindu world with a Christian one against Islam certainly, and the Sinic world possibly.[8]

On the nuclear front specifically, this is tantamount to suggesting to the US that it see merit in a potential Indian nuclear ally against its other civilizational rivals. That the Indian Prime Minister, Atal Behari Vajpayee should therefore send feelers of this kind need not occasion surprise to anyone familiar with the Sangh's fundamental ideology. Thus A. B. Vajpayee not only sent a letter to President Clinton immediately after the May tests hinting at such a China-directed alliance, but again sent a feeler in his speech to the Asia Society in New York during his Autumn 1998 UN visit. In an astonishing display of outrageously grandiose ambition, he declared, in effect, that not only were the US and India 'natural allies' but that the cornerstone of a new and better twenty-first century would be this alliance.[9]

At this point, to sum up the basic argument: it was not changes in the 'external security environment' or even changes in threat perceptions that was the principal cause of India's decision to go nuclear. It was changes in élite self-perceptions and the fact that the Sangh was in power, albeit in a coalition government. Self-perceptions, unlike threat perceptions, are far more susceptible to alteration as a result of significant changes in domestic politics and dominant ideologies. Élite frustrations have risen in tandem with external ambitions and also been fed by the lack of adequate fulfilment of these aspirations. Things have not turned out the way this élite expected or hoped. If at the time of independence there was an easier self-confidence that India would in time 'naturally' take its place at the high table of the great nations or obviously enough become a great Asian power, this has clearly not happened. India's own search for regional eminence has been so uneven and the outcome so uncertain that this too has left its mark on the frustrated ambitions of this more callous and self-serving élite. If the 1987 Indo-Sri Lanka Accord was the high water mark of India's post-Independence foreign policy ambitions, its collapse the following year revealed how difficult it was to realize these aspirations in a world becoming ever more complex.[10]

There is another way of recognizing the accuracy of this explanation. Unequivocating anti-nuclearists in India have for years said that not only is nuclear ambiguity unstable, but that of the three states practising such ambiguity—Pakistan, Israel and India—it was always India that would go publicly nuclear first if any of them did. It is important to understand why this judgement was made and why it proved correct.[11] In the cases of both Pakistan and Israel their retention of nuclear weapons capability was always much more strongly linked to an identifiable and explicit externally perceived threat. It was India for Pakistan, and, for Israel, its Middle East opponents. India, on the other hand, could not seriously point to Pakistan, whose policies were reactive, nor with much conviction or consistency to China, though of course, it repeatedly played on both these themes.

Thus both Pakistan and Israel could pursue a coherent nuclear diplomacy which India was never able to do. Having clearly identified their external threats they could also clearly spell out the conditions under which they would be willing to give up ambiguity for non-nuclear status, as well as clearly establish the conditions under which they would not end their ambiguity, i.e. clarify what made their ambiguity more stable. For Israel, ambiguity would be given up for non-nuclear status in the framework of an overall and permanent Middle Eastern settlement extending to acceptance by countries like Iran and Iraq as well as the other Arab states. Certainly, it would be better for Israel not to have insisted on an overall political settlement as a precondition for giving up its nuclear option and to have endorsed the idea of a Middle Eastern NWFZ or WMDFZ (weapons of mass destruction free zone) instead, but at least its diplomatic posture was clear. Similarly, Pakistan could spell out the conditions under which it would give up its option and those under which it would not break with ambiguity. It would give up the option if India did so, and it would not break with ambiguity unless India did so too. India, alone of these three countries, would be most prone to ending ambiguity in favour of the exercise of the nuclear option because it alone had a posture that was most strongly connected to the issue of élite self-perceptions and changes in this.

Hardliners' Muscle-flexing

It is in this general context that the more proximate causes for the Indian tests should be situated. Here the three most important factors were the pressures imposed by the nuclear–scientific community, the consolidation over the last decade of an unofficial lobby of hardline strategic hawks positioned in various think tanks, in influential academic institutions and in the national print media, and, of course, the impact of the CTBT debate between 1994 and 1996. The nuclear–scientific establishment headed by key scientocrats (more bureaucrats–administrators than practising scientists) in the Atomic Energy Department, at its upper echelons, has always been inclined to preserve the option, and then later on, to exercise it. They have seen their own professional prestige, importance, and bureaucratic power as connected to this. The Indian civilian nuclear programme is almost certainly the most inefficient in the world. It is a standing disgrace by all indices, whether of production or safety. Of the nine worst performing reactors in the world, four are in India. In the world's list of the fifty worst, figure nine out of India's ten power reactors. After over 50 years and one of the earliest programmes to be initiated in the third world, and that too on a large scale, India's atomic energy establishment works at roughly half its installed capacity, and contributes between 1 per cent to 1.5 per cent to total electricity generation. At full capacity this would be 2.5 per cent to 3 per cent. Its safety record is also shameful.[12]

By maintaining the military dimension of the nuclear programme, and even more by extending it, this scientific establishment is able to maintain its position of self-importance and to sustain some credibility for itself. For some years now its top scientocrats have been pressing to carry out tests. It was, however, the CTBT issue that really brought things to a head. The decades-long posture of ambiguity obviously raised the question of what to do about the technological upgradation of this option. From 1974 and the first Pokharan test, all Indian governments took the policy decision that while ambiguity would not be broken, technological upgradation should continue so that if the option were ever to be exercised in the future, it should be at an appropriately higher level than in the past. As a part of this policy, delivery systems potentially capable of being nuclearly fitted were also being continuously upgraded.

So long as the prospects of a CTBT was a distant eventuality, various Indian governments could occupy the moral high ground and endorse it. The moment, however, that it became an imminent and real possibility, it raised a decisive problem and dilemma for India which had to be addressed. If India acceded to a CTBT it would effectively end its capacity to upgrade its option, thereby putting severe limits on any future nuclear arsenal it might have even if it decided subsequently to go nuclear. Thus the CTBT issue focused attention as never before on the peculiar incoherence that always underlay Indian ambiguity. Should India give up forever the option of testing? Should it test and then sign the CTBT? That may well have been the purpose when in April 1995, while CTBT negotiations were going on, India began initial military logistical preparations to carry out a possible test in December 1995. That the US detected it and pressurized New Delhi not to do so partly accounted for the then Congress government's decision to deny that it had any such intention.

In 1996, when the government finally decided that it would not go along with a CTBT, it for the first time officially cited 'national security' considerations for keeping the bomb option and invoked the relevance of 'deterrence', something that it had never done before. Indeed, it had always hitherto officially held that nuclear deterrence was 'abhorrent'. But this was not all. Indian rejection of the CTBT was couched not only in terms of national interest or security but also as a morally grand posture in support of 'genuine' disarmament and in defiance of nuclear hegemony, especially by the US. That many an anti-nuclear activist in the West was taken in by this posturing by the Indian government and the wider strategic establishment in the country instead of seeing in this a new, cynical India carrying out something of a stall, was a real disappointment. This can, however, be attributed in large measure to the moral capital that India had in the past built up on global disarmament issues leading to widespread trust in its disarmament bona fides.

The very terms of the Indian debate on the CTBT were so shameful, dishonest and deceitful that this was even more dangerous than the Indian rejection of the Treaty itself. In the generation and sustenance of this discourse, the unofficial lobby of strategic hardliners played a particularly significant role. All political parties, including those of the left, and virtually the entire electronic and print media, bought into the claims that India must not sign the CTBT—not only in its national interest but to avoid the 'trap' that it represented for countries like India in particular. The CTBT, it was claimed (to virtually total élite agreement) was utterly flawed because it permitted subcritical tests and computer simulation. It was no restraint on the US but was aimed at restraining India. This then raised an obvious question. What was the point of India formally avoiding the 'trap' by not signing the CTBT but afterwards acting in practice as if it was still going to remain permanently in the trap by not testing? Thus a powerful logic had been created by the distortion of the whole terms of debate on the CTBT issue encouraging further movement towards testing. Moreover, such had been the (albeit manipulated) public acclaim and approval for India's stand on the CTBT that any future government deciding to test could, with a great deal of confidence, expect widespread public approval for that decision.

When in the election manifesto of the BJP in 1998, the party promised to 'exercise the option to induct nuclear weapons', the writing was clearly on the wall for all who cared to see it. When it came to power, the Sangh, literally overnight, destroyed the dominant position which still was to maintain the option without exercising it. In effect, the Sangh in power carried out a dramatic, undemocratic, sudden, political coup, decisively shifting the direction of India on the nuclear question in actual defiance of what till then still remained the dominant perspective. The Sangh had done the same on the issue of secularism when on 6 December 1992, it defied the Indian Constitution and calculatedly and deliberately destroyed the Babri Masjid at Ayodhya. The tragedy that has befallen India can be summed up in a single sentence. 'In a little over a decade, secularism has become an increasingly dirty word and the bomb an increasingly glorious one'!

Nuclearization's Horrendous Costs

Among the various ill effects of this decision to go nuclear through these tests, five will be highlighted here. One of these, the internal social and economic opportunity costs of nuclearization–weaponization will be taken up separately. It needs to be noted, however, that such a form of argument is not in principle a critique of nuclearization per se but of any form of wasteful military or militaristic expenditure. This is also the case with those concerns about the negative effects of militarization (in any form, nuclear or otherwise) on the ideologies and practices of everyday life. Both are very powerful forms of argument against going nuclear and must, of course, be a major part of the brief of those opposing nuclearism. It is, however, those effects caused by the specificity of nuclearization and not by the more general issue of militarization that will be concentrated upon here.

Also, the question of economic sanctions and India's international political isolation will not be addressed here since it is a consequence that is both the most immediate and obvious, and the one most likely to prove ephemeral in a longer time span. Pakistan, too, faces such sanctions and isolation but as the reactor to India, it does not share anywhere near the same opprobrium. Both the sanctions and the isolation are likely to end if India (followed or even preceded by Pakistan) signs the CTBT. It is clear that this is the minimum price India will have to pay to overcome sanctions, end isolation internationally, and pose semi-successfully as a 'responsible' nuclear power concerned about strengthening international arms control regimes. It was earlier quite possible that before September 1999, when a review conference of the CTBT is scheduled to take place, India would have signed the CTBT, especially since doing so would not prevent it from further weaponizing and deploying nuclearized delivery systems. Certainly, a growing lobby within the government and outside it amongst the opinion-shaping élite and media now wants India to do this for precisely the reasons just pointed out. After losing the confidence vote in April 1999, the BJP led government being a caretaker regime could not risk such a decision before the September–October 1999 general elections. Indian signing is not thereby precluded but may well be postponed till after a new government is formed.

Even doing this, however, has to overcome significant domestic opposition from various quarters. These range from opposing parties out to embarrass any incumbent government, especially in view of the earlier élite consensus against the Treaty; from super-hawks whose conception of a 'minimum deterrent capability' requires more advanced weaponry which a CTBT would still prevent India from developing; and from those who continue to believe that the CTBT is a worthless restraint measure on the NWSs, particularly the US, and therefore is nothing more than an instrument of their 'nuclear hegemony'. Large sections of the Indian left continue to hold this last position. The Indian government is also looking for some kind of behind-the-scenes deal with the US regarding future supplies of dual-use technologies, as well as some form of *de facto* acceptance of India's new status as an NWS if it cannot bring itself around to formal acknowledgement of this. In any case, the four principal effects that are elaborated below are all of a more enduring and serious nature.

(1) The Kashmir question has now been nuclearized and therefore internationalized. For some three decades India had more or less successfully established Kashmir as a bilateral issue.[13] In winter 1996, when Jiang Zemin, the President of China, visited Islamabad after his trip to Delhi, he shook his hosts badly when he declared that Kashmir was a bilateral issue to be sorted out between India and Pakistan. This was a major shift away from China's earlier more supportive stand for Islamabad. All this is now over. It is a new ball game. It is one thing to claim that non-nuclear tensions, or even a conventional conflict, is a purely bilateral or South Asian issue. It is absurd and laughable to claim that a nuclear exchange or the possibility of a nuclear conflict arising from tensions or escalation from an initial conventional conflict is purely a bilateral or South Asian affair!

From now on the discourse over Kashmir will be internationalized and it will be a question of how best to intervene in this internationalized discourse, not how to insist that it remain enclosed within a purely bilateral framework. The nuclearists of India will, of course, argue that India and Pakistan must now establish proper mechanisms of political and military control so that the Kashmir dispute is never allowed to escalate to the nuclear level and that therefore the dispute can remain bilateral in character. Such efforts will, however, fail completely for three reasons. First, Pakistan has no reason to let it remain enclosed within a bilateral framework but will make every effort, now more legitimate and convincing than ever before, to internationalize the issue.

Second, establishing control mechanisms that will reduce the danger of escalation to a possible nuclear level, is certainly desirable and something to be sought after, if further weaponization/deployment by either or both sides can no longer be prevented. The danger of such escalation cannot, however, be eliminated. Whatever the confidence-building measures or procedures to prevent such a nuclear outbreak, they cannot be a guarantee against such escalation because the political foundations for the persistence of mutual suspicion and hostility remain intact and such hostilities and suspicions have themselves been deepened by the nuclearization of the Kashmir issue. Putting into place a stable and enduring 'firebreak' between conventional hostilities over Kashmir and the possible use of nuclear weapons is not possible when Pakistan has officially rejected India's proposal of both sides agreeing to a No First Use of nuclear weapons posture.

Before becoming overly critical of Pakistan's stand on this issue, one needs to go into Indian motivations more seriously. India has taken a unilateral position of No First Use against any NWS and of No Use against any NNWS. This is similar to China's No First Use and No Use declarations. It is, however, important to understand that so far, and for some time to come, India has not deployed and may not even be able to 'hardwire' its planes to carry simple gravity nuclear bombs. Thus its declaration of No First Use when it doesn't yet have the capacity to use a weapons system, whether first or second, is really a clever, pre-emptive diplomatic ploy on its part to indirectly *legitimize* going in the direction of having a properly fitted and deployed weapons system. Therefore, for anti-nuclearists opposed to India proceeding in this direction, it would be a disastrous political mistake, *at this juncture*, to endorse such a declaration.

A crucial distinction must be drawn here. The importance of continuing to press for a No First Use pledge by all five recognized NWSs is undeniable. This is a vital step that will significantly strengthen the disarmament momentum. This position should not, however, be confused with the stand that India has currently taken of a unilateral pledge about its own nuclear behaviour. Its unilateral pledge must *not* be endorsed by nuclear disarmament activists now, even as they continue to press for a similar pledge by the five NWSs. The Indian No First Use proposal and pledge is part of its ongoing efforts at constructing itself as a 'moderate' and 'responsible' power after it has shamelessly behaved in the most immoderate and irresponsible manner by going openly nuclear! The pledge is also a cover to enable India to go ahead and put a nuclear weapons system in place. At this point of time, those opposed to nuclear weapons must pursue all efforts not to let such a weapons system emerge.

Further weaponization by India, induction of nuclear weapons, deployment of them, building a command, control, communications, intelligence infrastructure—i.e. pursuing the building of all the components that together make up a viable nuclear weapons system—must all be strongly opposed. To endorse India's unilateral pledge now is to fall into a major political trap. India has so far only tested and declared itself to be a nuclear weapons power. It does not have a viable nuclear weapons system yet and it will take some time for it to establish this and put it into place. Therefore, to endorse or applaud its pledge of No First Use does not arise. Indeed, the pledge must be exposed and attacked for what it is—a clever ploy at pre-emptive justification for going along a path it should abhor! It is only if (and after) anti-nuclear opposition fails to stop India from establishing a viable nuclear weapons system or a meaningful capacity to actually launch a first strike (which, of course, in time is quite possible) that the question of endorsing such an Indian pledge arises.

Third, the very fact of the nuclearization of the Kashmir issue has legitimized its internationalization. It is now correct and necessary that this issue be internationalized. The possibility of a nuclearized level of conflict now exists whereas it did not before, and this inescapable reality means the Kashmir issue has become too important and too frightening in its potential trajectory and implications (extra-regionally and globally) to be left to only India and Pakistan or even to the people of Kashmir on both sides of the border. It is characteristic of the casualness of most supposedly strategic thinking that this fact of internationalizing Kashmir by nuclearizing it was not foreseen by the Indian hawks. The political–diplomatic defeat for India over the Kashmir issue is as decisive as it was unexpected.

(2) The second effect is on the India–Pakistan–China axis. Can anyone doubt that matters here have taken a qualitative turn for the worse and that once again it is an entirely new ball game? Yes, the pro-nuclearists will claim that India–Pakistan and India–China relations will improve sooner or later to become better than they were in the pre-nuclear period. Never underestimate either the arrogance or stupidity of the nuclear élite, whether of India or of other NWSs. For the first time ever, a qualitatively new dimension, the nuclear one, has been added to the pre-existing level of tensions between India and Pakistan. The pro-nuclearists who say that nuclearization will actually improve relations between the countries have an inverted logic. The causes of the underlying hostility are political, not military or nuclear. Military and nuclear preparations express the existing political hostility and add to them. They can never be the methods or mechanisms for the resolution of such political tensions. To put it in the form of an historical analogy: the Cold War arms race between two politically hostile countries, the USA and USSR, in its nuclear dimension was not reversed because of nuclear weapons. Nuclear weapons preparations did not lead to a reduction of Cold War political tensions but the other way around. It was Gorbachev's determination and effort to end the political Cold War that led to reductions in nuclear arms and a reversal of that arms race! South Asia is the only region in the world that has had a continuous hot-cold war for 50 years. Only if the political foundations of this situation are first undermined can we hope to decrease nuclear tensions, not the other way around.

As for the India–China relationship, this has now embarked on a different trajectory. From now on, no matter what the fluctuations in China's official declarations and statements on India-China relations, if India further weaponizes and deploys, as is most likely, (unless somehow prevented by domestic opposition), China must factor India in as a nuclear–political rival and make its nuclear preparations accordingly. The more India seeks to establish what it believes will be a minimum credible deterrent against China, the more China must go along this route. Defence minister George Fernandes says China is a potential rival and threat. However, his government moved a very long way down the road to making China not a potential but an actual nuclear threat and political rival to India—when this need not ever have been the case. In short, the spectrum within which India–China relations will now operate has, after Pokharan-II, decisively narrowed. Its two ends are no longer strategic friendship and strategic hostility but strategic hostility as one pole, and as the other, a position hovering close to strategic rivalry. That India's pro-nuclearists should not have perceived this outcome once again testifies to their strategic bankruptcy.

When China went nuclear it did so substantially because of its perceived fears regarding the USA and USSR in a context that everyone recognized was one of clear strategic hostility between China and the other two. China explicitly stated as much. It did not have to try and make a case that there was such a hostility, let alone rivalry. This was obvious. The USSR and USA were not potential strategic opponents to guard against in the future, but actual present opponents, although the later entente between China and USA changed this picture at least for these two countries. In the case of India, there has never been such clarity or obviousness in respect of characterization of the nature of the India–China political relationship. Hence the constant need to make out a case that there is a such a situation of strategic rivalry or hostility or opposition if not now then in the future. Moreover, China never cited India as the reason for going nuclear or perpetuating its nuclear status for the simple reason that India has never been the reason nor ever perceived to be one by China. To put it another way, the larger web of hostile relationships in which China decided to go nuclear is not comparable to the political context in which India has decided to do so.

That is why the constant harping on China as a nuclear threat to India was so dangerous. It has now led to a denouement which is a classic case of a self-fulfilling prophecy. China has now become or is very close to becoming (once India weaponizes and openly deploys) a nuclear opponent and threat with actual, as distinct from conceivable, nuclear targeting and preparations vis-à-vis India.

But what about the Sino-Pakistan link? Not only was the nature of the Sino-Pakistan nuclear link misrepresented, the loosening of these ties in favour of a Chinese exploration of better ties with India has now been halted. Chinese pragmatism means that it is not axiomatic that Beijing will want a closer relationship with Islamabad against New Delhi. However, the likelihood of China reversing the trajectory of improving mutual relations, has now become greater, not less. Certainly, the more India in practice treats the Chinese arsenal as a threat and prepares accordingly, the more likely a closer Chinese–Pakistani nuclear relationship in the future can become. No matter how much India talks about its nuclear preparations not being aimed at China (interspersed, of course, with statements about China's more strategic and longer-term threat), the Chinese have to be much more inclined than ever before to operate on the opposite premises. However, our community of 'strategic experts' who support the tests and going nuclear tell us that Indian security will be greatly enhanced by what has happened!

The Domestic Fallout

(3) The third effect of going nuclear has already been referred to, and in some ways is the most dangerous. This is the domestic political consequence. The Sangh Combine has moved a decisive step forward in its overall programme to transform this country and to fulfil its hegemonic project of defining what India and Indian nationalism should be. Unless this force's general ideological and political vision of nationalism is effectively confronted at the level of nationalist discourse itself, the fight to prevent them from destroying the democratic, tolerant, civilized and humane fabric of India can be lost. Indeed, when the RSS–BJP decided to go nuclear they made much more careful calculations as to the likely consequences internally than they ever did about its external ramifications. That much should be obvious now. It is also indicative of how much more important to them is their longer term domestic agenda and of this decision's purpose and place within that agenda. The by-election results that took place after the May tests did not show that they had gained much in terms of votes but that is to miss the issue. The fact is that once again, they have decisively determined the direction that this country is taking and have organized to their overall advantage the parameters of future discourse on the issue of national security.

It is truly extraordinary how swiftly and comprehensively they have destroyed the 'middle ground' on the nuclear issue. That was, as has been pointed out earlier, the posture of nuclear ambiguity which until 10 May 1998 was still the position of all non-BJP parties and of the overwhelming bulk of the 'strategic community' of opinion shapers, and of the leaders of the civilian and military bureaucracies. The Sangh did not seek to adjust its perspectives to suit this last community of so-called experts. On the contrary, it accurately assessed the specific moral–political character of this important section of the Indian élite and recognized that it had nothing to worry about from them. They would adjust their perspectives to suit the Sangh's politics! That is exactly what happened. Overnight, the middle ground was destroyed leaving the opposition parties and the members of the 'security establishment' with either the option of directly or indirectly endorsing the crossing of the nuclear Rubicon, or of opposing it.

Of the political parties, only the left came out (after initial hesitation and confusion) against the tests. All other mainstream parties, regional and national, took no such unambiguous stand. Some Congress leaders tried to make political capital by questioning the timing of the tests. Some like the Janata Dal (a key component in the United Front government prior to the BJP-led coalition government) sought to take the credit for themselves by claiming that they had made the first preparations for the tests and were themselves contemplating them. Most political parties will probably not reverse the trajectory now set, though the pace and manner in which it is followed will certainly be influenced by which parties are in power at the Centre. Only the main left parties, the Communist Party of India (CPI) and the Communist party of India-Marxist (CPM), can be expected to reverse this trajectory. However, not only is there no prospect of their heading a central government and being powerful enough to do this in the near future, but they also continue to pursue the chimera of restoring ambiguity rather than committing themselves to complete denuclearization of India or of the South Asian region regardless of what the five other NWSs do.

As for the 'strategic experts', their volte face was almost total. Most (whether active or retired) are drawn from the bureaucratic, military and diplomatic services, journalism, think tanks concerned with security matters, and academic disciplines like International Relations and Area Studies. They busied themselves trying to justify the Indian decision and to explaining why the tests were inevitable.[14] In a display that would be laughable if it was not so ironically tragic, the *very same people* who had for years used arguments to explain why India must hold on to the nuclear option, yet not exercise it openly, now used the *very same arguments* to explain why India had to go openly nuclear! Interestingly, it was only among academics of the social sciences other than International Relations that a much larger proportion of former ambiguists came out clearly against the tests. No doubt their greater sensitivity than conventional Realists to the moral dimension of human affairs must have been part of the reason for this.

(4) The fourth effect is on the general momentum towards global nuclear restraint and disarmament that has existed ever since the Cold War began running down and then ended. This momentum, whose existence is testified to in so many ways, is halting, hesitant, uneven, and also incorporates negative and dampening developments. It is nonetheless real and new, and its overall direction has been positive. In short, there has been a concrete basis for a real

hope that we can and are making progress, howsoever difficult and slow, towards the final goal of total nuclear disarmament. This momentum has been severely damaged by what has now happened in South Asia. It is still too early to say whether it has even been reversed, but the damage is grave with the chances of other countries following suit having become greater. If other countries, particularly what the US likes to call 'rogue states' (when it is itself the biggest and most dangerous nuclear 'rogue state'), get the bomb or are preparing for it, it will not become more likely that the US (and other NWSs) will move more seriously towards denuclearization. The opposite will be the case and those within these NWSs pushing for meaningful reductions, restraint, and eventually total disarmament will not be strengthened politically, but rather weakened by such developments.

Concomitant with this adverse impact on the global disarmament process is the great damage done to India's standing in the world. Its diplomatic stature is greatly diminished. The decision to go nuclear was the search for a political 'easy fix'. In truth, even within the nuclear club, membership is graded and India and Pakistan are third class members with the UK, France and China occupying the second rung. The so-called diplomatic or 'prestige' benefits that India's nuclear hawks have assumed would fall to the country are not just ephemeral but mostly nonexistent. Thus India's prospects for a Security Council seat in the UN have greatly diminished, not increased. Neither India nor Pakistan will be 'rewarded' in this way for going nuclear for that would set a terrible precedent. Of course, the very existence of a Security Council of 'special nations' which is not democratically subordinated to the General Assembly is itself an affront to the struggle to democratize international diplomatic institutions, but that is a separate issue.

In general, most NNWSs will come to realize that this is a new more cynical India that talks now for the most part like all the other NWSs, with a forked tongue. As such India's capacity to play a valued world role in pushing for disarmament has lessened greatly. New Delhi will find that a junior and very subordinate status in the nuclear club, accompanied by the ongoing reality of being a poverty-stricken country whose internal 'successes' are few and unimpressive beyond the preservation of a vibrant democracy (now itself under threat as never before), will be no diplomatic compensation for what it has now squandered, namely its decades long legacy of being an important moral–political actor in pursuit of global nuclear disarmament.

A more detailed survey of what the prospects for global restraint and disarmament are after the May tests will be taken up later, but before going on let us take a briefer look at both the causes and consequences of Pakistan's decision to go nuclear.

Pakistan in Imitation Mode

An earlier single line summary of Pakistan's decades long nuclear policy bears repetition. Islamabad's nuclear preparations have been carried out independently of New Delhi, but once having come close to achieving nuclear weapons capability, successive governments have uniformly shaped their nuclear diplomacy with India as their central point of reference. In this sense Pakistan's nuclear policy has been strongly reactive to India. Despite internal pressures from sections of the 'nuclear establishment', Islamabad has never seriously wavered from the policy of not being the first to go openly nuclear. Indeed, Islamabad has always shown willingness to abandon the carefully constructed nuclear option if New Delhi was also prepared to do the same.

The earliest speculations about a possible Pakistani nuclear bomb appear to have surfaced around 1960 when the US was pushing its 'Atoms for Peace' programme worldwide.[15] Pakistan was then a faithful ally of the US, keen to ingratiate itself with that country. The idea of a possible Pakistani nuclear deterrent against, ironically enough, China (a US bugbear at the time) was then mooted. At this initial stage, developing a minimal level of theoretical expertise and some basic understanding of how to run a (dual-use) programme of power and research reactors was essential for laying down the minimal foundations upon which serious thinking could then be devoted to whether or not a nuclear weapons capability should be sought and constructed. Through the sixties and seventies, the US trained at its various institutions over a thousand Pakistani, and over a hundred Indian, scientists and technicians in nuclear physics, chemistry, engineering, etc. and their practical applications.

In both countries, the scientists' lobby has ever since been a significant pressure group urging further upward movement on the ladder of nuclear weapons preparations. In Pakistan, the actual decision to go ahead with building a weapons capability even though no civilian nuclear energy infrastructure of serious note existed, came after the defeat and dismemberment of Pakistan in 1971–2 when Bangladesh was formed. Bomb designing though may well have been explored even earlier in the late sixties. After the second (1965) and third (1971–2) Indo-Pakistan wars with their continuing tensions throughout the seventies, the Sino-Indian border conflict of 1962, and the secret preparations at the end of the sixties for entente between the US and China (via the good offices of Islamabad), the political rationale for a Pakistan bomb was obviously India, and India alone. Indeed, China had come to be seen as a Pakistani political ally (especially after its strongly pro-Islamabad and anti-liberation stand during the Bangladesh war) and a source of possible support in the development of such a nuclear weapons capability.

It was at the famous Spring 1972 meeting in the northern city of Multan between the then Prime Minister, Zulfikar Ali Bhutto and a gathering of the country's top nuclear scientists and bureaucrats that the formal decision was taken to develop a weapons capability. This was two years before Pokharan-I in India although that event clearly stimulated Pakistan to press more aggressively than ever for such a bomb-making capacity. Over the next decade, Pakistan clandestinely acquired the necessary supplies and equipment to build a gas centrifuge uranium enrichment facility at Kahuta. The key figure in organizing this venture was Abdul Qadir Khan, a metallurgist by profession who has been called, in many circles, the 'father of the Pakistan bomb'. It was he who, before returning to Pakistan, copied the all-important list of private suppliers of crucial components for building a gas centrifuge plant when working at the centrifuge enrichment plant operated by Urenco at Almelo in The Netherlands.[16] He was appointed head of the Kahuta project which was separated from the Pakistan Atomic Energy Commission. This was a clear indication of the secrecy and urgency attached to the project.

Pakistan in all probability developed its capacity some time in the early to mid-eighties. In 1987, Abdul Qadir Khan gave his famous interview to Indian journalist Kuldip Nayar, when he publicly declared that Pakistan had the bomb, or to be more precise, could assemble it immediately if required. That is to say, by the mid-eighties both India and Pakistan could be said to have secured 'bombs in the basement with the last wires unconnected'.[17] Between then and 28 May 1998 when Pakistan first tested, the Islamabad government consciously played the ambiguist card of sending mixed signals. There would be different kinds of declarations (sometimes simultaneous) to the effect that Pakistan had the capacity but no current intention to build the bomb, but that this might or might not change in the future.

Indeed, Islamabad was always careful never to formally or officially assert in any written statement or declaration that it had this capacity! Thus it rejected all Indian diplomatic overtures in the nineties for a bilateral declaration on non-use of each country's nuclear weapons capability. It was one thing for different officials, even very senior leaders, to verbally assert that Pakistan had this capacity. However, given the various Congressional laws and amendments in the US forbidding military assistance, and indeed calling for imposition of US sanctions on countries pursuing nuclear weapons, Islamabad was always careful never to acknowledge in the form of any treaty or written statement that it had such a capacity. That would have been to greatly complicate for the worse its relationship with the US government.

Given that Pakistan secured its capacity through the clandestine route, relying for the most part on private suppliers, how important was Chinese assistance? Clearly, it is Chinese assistance before the early eighties and not subsequently that should be considered of greater value. Certain kinds of speculation can be safely discarded. There is no evidence that Pakistan ever tested a bomb of its making at China's Lop Nor test site. Similarly, for all the talk of an 'Islamic Bomb', there is no evidence that other states in West Asia or northern Africa (e.g. Libya, Iran, or Iraq) secured significant, let alone decisive, Pakistan support of any kind in this regard. Although the US–Israel relationship is a partial exception, in general, NWSs have imposed strong self-limits on the extent to which they would go beyond provision of certain dual-use technologies, certain forms of information exchange, to help another country secure such capabilities. Perhaps the best way to sum up the level of Chinese assistance to Pakistan is to point out that, (1) it was more important in the seventies and early eighties than in the late eighties and nineties. (2) That its major contribution was at the level of information (much of which was available in the public domain) than at the level of technology or equipment supplies. (3) That such assistance was significant but not decisive in Pakistan's quest. At best it accelerated the pace at which Pakistan reached its goal.[18]

Islamabad's Search for Parity

From the mid-eighties, the community of nuclear scientists exerted continuous pressure on the government to go ahead and test, citing the first Indian test of 1974 as political justification. They were joined by a small section of so-called strategic and military experts who repeatedly argued that Pakistan needed the bomb to compensate for the claimed 2:1 or 3:1 imbalance in conventional military forces between itself and India. However, despite such constant pressure, there was never any sign or fear that Pakistan would be the first to cross the threshold in South Asia. The nuclear hawks were always considerably outweighed by others within the 'national security establishment' who clearly and sensibly recognized that the negative consequences of precipitating a nuclear arms race with India were much greater than any presumed benefits. The socio-economic burden of carrying on a continuous nuclear arms race with India would be much greater on Pakistan. Being much smaller in size, Pakistan lacked strategic depth of the kind that might lead some Indians to believe they could 'absorb' a small nuclear exchange.

Thus the quest for non-nuclear parity between Pakistan and India always made much more political and diplomatic sense and remained the pivotal basis of Islamabad's nuclear diplomacy. Pakistan was never seriously tempted to even 'match' India's first test in 1974 by carrying out its own for fear that this would be read as a provocation and excuse for India to break out into open nuclear status. Even for Pakistani hawks, whose first preference was for a Pakistan openly equipped with nuclear weapons, the quest for a non-nuclear parity made sense as a 'second best option'. Thus Pakistan repeatedly proposed to India a variety of measures for bilateral or regional renunciation of such weapons. These were not in the nature of a 'bluff' as Indians, embarrassed by such proposals, falsely insinuated. They were seriously meant, though Islamabad was aware that India would be very unlikely to give up its option, in which event Pakistan would at least gain in terms of diplomatic one-upmanship. Even on the CTBT, Pakistan's position during the 1994–6 negotiations was pegged to Indian behaviour: if the latter signed the CTBT so too would Pakistan.

However, since Pakistan carried out the tests, the position and influence of its hawks has become much stronger. Pakistan will continue to endorse and be open to proposals for regional and bilateral denuclearization but this appears even further away and more unrealistic now than it did earlier. Thus the new 'common sense' that prevails is that Pakistan having become a nuclear weapons power, must now keep these weapons to compensate for the conventional military disadvantage it has with regard to India. To be sure, Islamabad continues to say (and there is no good reason to doubt it) that it will not be the first to deploy such weapons but will only do so after India first deploys its arsenal. However, the form of justification for possessing nuclear weapons, which did not enjoy much public (or even élite) resonance earlier has now gathered stronger support and will influence in dangerous ways Pakistan's future nuclear–strategic thinking and practice.

Was it inevitable that once India tested and went openly nuclear that Pakistan would have to do the same? The answer would seem to be 'No'. Pakistan waited for two weeks before responding with its own tests although Abdul Qadir Khan informed the top civilian and military leadership that Pakistan needed at most three days to carry out its own tests. In between, especially during the first week, the government did not state that it would definitely respond in kind but sought strong political reassurances as well as significant material help from outside countries, particularly from the US. There were sound reasons for Islamabad being cautious. It was clear that Pakistan would be subject to economic sanctions (as were imposed on India after its tests) by some important countries and international institutions and the Pakistan economy was in a far more parlous and externally dependent a state than India's at the time. Indeed, Pakistan had been in the throes of a serious economic crisis from mid-1997 onwards and has remained immersed in it to date.

Furthermore, there was also something to be gained in terms of international prestige and political sympathy by not following India. Pakistan could hope more successfully than ever to mount a collective diplomatic campaign against India and thus broaden its own international support base on the Kashmir issue as well with regard to its own demands for security now newly imperilled by the Indian action. In short, there was something to be said for Pakistan refraining from testing and milking the international community, particularly the US, for what it could get on the economic, military, and political–diplomatic levels. Thus the Pakistan government did seek to bargain with the US for compensatory support. If, nonetheless. Pakistan decided to eventually duplicate the Indian action, this was determined by a combination of external and internal factors.

On the external front, Pakistan was disappointed that the opposition to the Indian action was not as sharp as it had hoped. Even the NWSs did not unite to impose sanctions on India, with Russia and France explicitly refusing to do so. Pakistan was further disappointed that the US did not declare its willingness to provide a nuclear umbrella to it. Nor did the financial–economic–military package offered to Pakistan by the US measure up to its expectations. More significant in shaping the final decision, however, were domestic factors. Two considerations were particularly crucial: one political, and the other, more directly military.

The position of the Pakistan Prime Minister, Nawaz Sharif, was unenviable. His political support had been steadily falling. His party, the Pakistan Muslim League (PML) was under pressure not only from the opposition Pakistan's People's Party headed by Benazir Bhutto, daughter of former premier Zulfikar Ali Bhutto, but also, more seriously, from an array of explicitly fundamentalist, right-wing Islamic forces that had been immeasurably strengthened by the recent successes of the Taliban in Aghanistan. Since the early eighties the nexus between Afghanistan and Pakistan had become very strong with events in the former country having a major impact on Pakistan's social and military life besides exacting heavy domestic sacrifices as the price to be paid for sustained Pakistani support to the Taliban militias. Without sufficiently powerful incentives or strong, visible benefits to justify a Pakistani refusal to emulate Indian action, the Sharif government found it very difficult to confront such internal pressures that had secured majority public support for retaliatory tests.

The second factor was the sentiment within the armed forces, especially within its officer ranks. The military services, dominated by the army, have always exercised enormous influence in Pakistan's polity despite the steps made in recent years towards stabilizing a civilian regime of 'controlled democracy'. To begin with, the head of the army, Gen. Jehangir Karamat, was not inclined to endorse retaliatory tests for all the reasons outlined earlier. It was only after visiting the Pakistan controlled part of Kashmir to assess military morale that he was persuaded to change his mind. He discovered not only that morale was low after the Indian tests but that sentiment among the officer corps was strongly in favour of an equivalent Pakistani response to the Indian action. He then advised the Sharif government accordingly.

Precisely in order to fulfil the widespread popular belief that Pakistan could 'match' India's nuclear capabilities, Islamabad carried out its own tests on 28 and 30 May, claiming six tests in all in order to balance the six that India had undertaken—one in 1974 and five in 1998. However, the technical data released by both countries and evidence from monitoring stations in other countries do not substantiate either Pakistan's claim to have carried out six tests or India's claim to have carried out a thermonuclear explosion or hydrogen bomb test. (See Annexe 1).

Inviting Ruin

(1) Because Pakistan was near-universally seen as being 'forced' to follow India, political opprobrium internationally was never as great. A reluctant Pakistan was seen as having been pressurized into following an adamant and belligerent India. Nonetheless, it too had to face economic sanctions that affected it much more adversely than was the case for India. Its foreign debt is over $30 billion and the country has been effectively in default. Such was the extent of its immediate balance of payments crisis that the US, recognizing the possibility of internal chaos and the fillip this might give to pro-Taliban and anti-US Islamic forces, decided subsequently, in November 1998, to ease the sanctions it had earlier imposed. These had to do largely with agriculture-related and aid-related activities but restrictions on trade relating to high technology acquisitions remained. Since it had to appear even-handed, sanctions on India were also eased, but the primary motivation was alleviating Pakistan's desperate plight.

Nor is it at all coincidental that towards the end of 1998, when Pakistan had to make a major repayment of its external debt and was simply unable to find the wherewithal to do so, the US finally decided (after over a year's delay) to release the amount Pakistan had earlier paid for F-16 fighter planes whose shipment had subsequently been cancelled by Congressional rejection of the deal. However, quite apart from the immediate debt and financial crisis, the general state of the Pakistan economy is such that the actual, and opportunity costs, of building an 'adequate' nuclear weapons system will impose an enormous burden. Only if the current firebreak between testing and not yet deploying is maintained can Pakistan hope to avoid paying this huge price. For an economy and civil society already devastated by the effects of the Afghan imbroglio, further nuclearization and the initiation of an arms race with India will only plunge the economy and civil society into deeper crisis.

(2) In no way can it be argued that Indo-Pakistan security has been enhanced. This was discussed earlier. A specifically Pakistani perspective would recognize that Pakistan is well behind India in the size of its stockpile of weapons-grade fissile material as well as in the range, numbers, and types of delivery vehicles (missiles, submarines as platforms) that it can deploy. It has a real problem in coping with the possibility of a decapitating first strike, i.e. one that would target and destroy the headquarters, as it were, from which command, control, communications and intelligence functions ultimately flow. Moreover, unlike the US-USSR nuclear face-off, neither India nor Pakistan has the capacity to establish a highly sophisticated and expensive 'early warning system'—whatever use such a system could be given that missile flight time between the two countries is as little as three to four minutes.

Possessing neither the geographical depth nor the numbers of bombs or a meaningful warning system to be able to cope with this problem, Pakistan will be under great pressure to disperse its nuclear missiles and planes and to decentralize their command and control, for only then can they hope to 'credibly deter' India from a decisive and debilitating first strike. Whether India ever has or does not have such intentions is beside the point. Once the logic of nuclear deterrence for security operates, Pakistani nuclearists have to prepare for such contingencies. Once such dispersal and decentralization of command and control takes place, the possibilities of launching or using nuclear weapons through miscalculation or accident become considerably higher. Thus, for systemic reasons, the likelihood of pre-emptive use is greater on the Pakistani side not because of a greater belligerence on Islamabad's part but simply because of the inescapable problems posed by asymmetry between the two countries and their respective nuclear weapons systems.

Pakistan's rejection of India's No First Use proposal might appear to make sense because a missile flight time of three to four minutes does not give much technical–practical value to such an assurance. Moreover, keeping things uncertain by refusing adherence to the No First Use principle maintains Kashmir as a nuclear flashpoint that could erupt by an escalation of conventional military conflict. This suits Pakistani diplomatic efforts to internationalize the Kashmir issue. Nevertheless, a major reason (and stated as such) for Islamabad's decision to reject India's No First Use proposal is that it wants its future nuclear arsenal to compensate for the imbalance between the conventional military strengths between the two countries. That is to say, the last thing Pakistan wants to do is to introduce any kind of firebreak between conventional conflict and its possible escalation into a nuclear exchange.[19]

Such an approach is not only dangerous and irresponsible in itself, but is also based on yet another false premise—that Pakistan can use nuclear deterrence not only to avoid a nuclear conflict but also to deter or control a conventional outbreak to its advantage. The logic of pursuing such an approach must be a retention of the willingness to use nuclear weapons first if the conventional conflict on the ground is somehow 'perceived' to be reaching some point of supposedly decisive disadvantage to Pakistan. Not a few Pakistani anti-nuclear activists have serious reservations about the sense of maturity and responsibility of some Pakistani hawks in entertaining such a logic. Rejection of the principle of No First Use is here linked to a conscious perspective (in at least some Pakistani leading circles) of possible pre-emptive use of nuclear weapons against the 'enemy'.

Of course, Pakistani hawks can also see value in having some bilaterally agreed restraint measures to reduce the risk of accidental or miscalculated use by either side of their respective arsenals. It will be no surprise, therefore, if both countries, once they have openly deployed, were to arrive at limited bilateral confidence-building measures (CBMs) and mechanisms: hot lines, regular high-level meetings of senior military personnel, etc. However, the basic factors that ensure the sustenance of political distrust and differences in nuclear doctrines/strategies/perspectives, will remain.

(3) The internationalization of the Kashmir issue as a result of the nuclearization path followed by the two countries has been a diplomatic gain for Pakistan, but its value should not be exaggerated. The very fact of such internationalization (unavoidable once deployment of nuclear arsenals in both countries take place) is a setback for India. For this to be a *lasting* gain for Pakistan, however the issue has not merely to be internationalized but done so in such a way as to bring Pakistani aspirations closer to fulfilment. This is in no way assured. It can only be a matter of time before the Indian government, recognizing that earlier forms of diplomacy are now untenable, adjusts to the new circumstances and itself begins to intervene in an internationalized framework of diplomatic activity in ways that would suit its own interests. What the future outcomes of such Indian and Pakistani interventions in the now wider arena would be is an open question.

Setback to Democratization

(4) Finally, what are the likely domestic political consequences of Pakistan's going nuclear? In subsequent historical retrospect, this might well be seen as the final act that precipitated a decisive historical transformation of the Pakistan polity, dramatically reversing for a long time to come the difficult process of democratic consolidation. One hopes this will not be the case, but it could be. Over the past fifteen years there has been a striking contrast in the general political trajectories of India and Pakistan. Whatever the ups and downs and its enduring strengths, India's polity has drifted in a more anti-democratic and authoritarian direction. For Pakistan, whatever its ups and downs over the same period, the direction of its polity has been towards a less authoritarian and militarily controlled system to that of a civilian regime although one in which the army plays a disproportionately large role.

This is not the only contrast. Whereas the Indian state is officially secular and secularism is its legitimizing ideology, religio-political forces of a very negative and dangerous kind, or what are called communal organizations and parties, have made dramatic inroads into the Indian polity. At the national electoral level, such communal forces have acquired 25 per cent of the popular vote. In Pakistan, the state is not secular but confessional, and its legitimizing ideology is Islam. As such, it is not a liberal democratic state nor does it preside over a properly democratic society with a minimum of constitutionally guaranteed freedoms. However, the national electoral vote of all the explicitly Islamic and fundamentalist parties put together has for almost five decades never crossed seven per cent and was as low as three per cent in the 1990s.

In India, where matters have been worsening over the years, a decisive transformation of the character of the whole country has been a growing and looming threat. The threat has come from Hindu communal forces. Incidentally, all communal forces feed off one another. Advances for the cause of Hindu nationalism strengthen the cause of Islamic nationalism, and vice versa, yet something of an equilibrium between state and civil society has so far been preserved. India has not yet tilted beyond the critical point when a weakened democratic polity becomes a qualitatively different entity, i.e. some form of authoritarian political rule, however mild or strong.

In Pakistan, where over recent years matters had seemed to be improving, the threat posed by Islamic fundamentalist forces has nonetheless been a constant and steady one. Insofar as here too there has been an equilibrium of sorts, it has been of a different kind where communal forces have not so far been able to capture state power and more actively try and suborn its apparatuses to carry out the wholesale transformation of Pakistani polity and society in the way that these forces are wont to, and can. This equilibrium is now being threatened more seriously than ever before. Islamic fundamentalist forces are currently poised to make the kind of dramatic political breakthrough hitherto denied to them for decades. The scale of this threat can be gauged by the extent to which the Sharif government *after the nuclear tests* has had to go along with their agenda. Through the Fifteenth Amendment to the Constitution, a major effort at Islamization of the polity is proceeding apace. The Shariat bill, which will completely alter the character of state jurisprudence, has been passed in the Lower House of Parliament. A majority in the Upper House, the Senate, opposes it and it will take the Prime Minister, Nawaz Sharif, much skill to get his way. The fact that a beleaguered and desperate government has sought to steal the fundamentalist thunder in this way testifies to its plight.

There is a deeper pathology at work here, which is centred on a grim, systemically rooted crisis of legitimacy facing the Pakistan state. This crisis, which has deepened, especially since the mid-nineties, was further aggravated by the post-1997 economic recession—growing fiscal crisis of the state, declining production and economic malfunctioning—as well as the disintegration of a number of institutions of the state under the impact of corruption, cronyism, Machiavellian political manoeuvres, and exacerbation of ethnic tensions and breakdown of law and order in city after city, epitomized above all by the current state of its principal commercial–industrial centre, Karachi. Thus, analysts and even some foreign diplomats started in 1996–7 to describe Pakistan as a 'failing' or 'failed state'. The systemic crisis of legitimacy, the increasing loss of the state's moral purpose, the inability of Islam to provide the foundations of a viable modern state, have all contributed to the growing failure of the Pakistani political system.

Overt nuclearization, which invited sanctions, further aggravated the crisis. If Pakistan proceeds to manufacture and deploy nuclear weapons and missiles, the economic consequences could become unbearable. The state could literally disintegrate and Pakistan become what has been described by some commentators as a 'nuclear Somalia'. The Nawaz Sharif government has tried to use Pakistan's newly acquired weapons status to bargain for help from the US to help stave off this possibility but has so far had only limited success in this effort. If the Pakistan People's Party (PPP) of Benazir Bhutto was a united and respected force, then as the major opposition party it would have benefited most from the deep public disillusionment with the present government. The PPP, however, with two recent stints in power has a serious credibility problem of its own, and it is indeed in great disarray. Thus the real beneficiaries of governmental unpopularity are a variety of Islamic groups that can play the card of being an 'untested alternative' that should now be given a 'chance to rule'. Though the nuclear tests were popular, they also had been strongly demanded both by the PPP and the Islamic opposition to the Sharif government. When the government eventually decided to carry out the tests, this did not provide it with any distinctive dividends but simply reinforced the growing swell of sympathy for the Islamic opposition.

Had the Sharif government not tested, it would in effect have frontally challenged these most dangerous internal forces. Sharif could scarcely have hoped to defeat them simply by succumbing to their pressures. Admittedly, given the Indian action, it would have been very difficult for any Pakistan government to resist emulation, but decisive political conjunctures always call for statesmanship of the highest order if the threatened negative momentum is to be stemmed and reversed. In May 1998, and after, neither the Indian nor the Pakistani governments nor their respective 'national security establishments' have shown that they possess such qualities of statesmanship. This judgement was only confirmed by the symbolically much touted, but in terms of practical value, quite pedestrian and empty, prime ministerial summit meeting between Vajpayee and Sharif in Lahore in late February 1999.

Notes

1. The Sangh Combine is the name given to the collective comprising the Rashtriya Swayamsevak Sangh or RSS (National Volunteer Corps), the Vishwa Hindu Parishad or VHP (World Hindu Council), the Bajrang Dal (Lord Hanuman's troopers), and the Bharatiya Janata Party or BJP (People's Party of India). The RSS is the 'father' of this collective. It is the single, dominant and guiding force. It is a cadre organization run on internally undemocratic lines with top-down selection of its key full time officials and committed to an anti-Muslim ideology of Hindu nationalism and right-wing authoritarianism. It has definite fascist characteristics in its ideology and organizational structure. Its key founding figures were open admirers of Hitler and the way he sought to make Germany strong. The RSS had its birth in 1925. The RSS has decisive control and influence over the BJP although the former claims to be only a cultural organization. It is in no way democratically accountable to the people of India nor even to the ordinary member of the BJP.

   The VHP was set up by the RSS in the early sixties to serve as an explicitly religious–cultural front. It also participates in communal and political activities of various sorts and operates worldwide amongst the Hindu diaspora. The Bajrang Dal are a modern day equivalent of lumpen storm-troopers resorting to physical violence to intimidate the opponents of the Sangh Combine. The RSS also engages (more subtly) in physical violence and when necessary promotes communal riots. It also involves itself in positive rehabilitation work and gains support in that way. The BJP is the parliamentary and electoral wing of the Sangh Combine. It has achieved phenomenal success over the past fifteen years. From having only two members in 1984 in the Lok Sabha or Lower House of the national Parliament, comprising 545 MPs, the BJP has over a little more than a decade become the single largest party with about 180 MPs today, i. e. before the scheduled elections in September–October 1999.

2. Immediately after the 11 and 13 May tests, top Indian officials by their public statements literally goaded Pakistan into testing. The Prime Minister, A. B. Vajpayee, made no distinction between nuclear and non-nuclear conflicts, implying that nuclear weapons would be used by India for 'defensive' purposes i.e. even in conflicts of a conventional kind. The home minister, L. K. Advani, talked of changes in 'geo-political circumstances' and 'hot pursuit' (See Chapter 4). The Parliamentary Affairs Minister, M. L. Khurana, challenged Pakistan to a fourth war between the two countries at 'any time, any place'. At the time all the three leaders belonged to the BJP. Whatever chances Pakistan had of avoiding a like response to India's tests were almost certainly destroyed by such statements.
3. Vajpayee referred to China as 'an overt nuclear weapon state on our borders, a state which committed armed aggression against India in 1962'. He accused China of having 'materially helped' Pakistan, a 'bitter neighbour' at the hands of which 'we have suffered three aggressions', 'to become a covert nuclear weapons state'. Letter sent on 11 May and published first in *The New York Times*, quoted as 'Text of Vajpayee's Letter to Clinton' in *The Hindu*, Delhi, 14 May1998.
4. Seven thousand technicians and 20,000 assistants worked on the programme, 'Petrochemical Project Three' at a cost of $10 billion. Iraq had built up to 10,000 centrifuges for uranium enrichment with components and designs secured largely from German companies. The uranium came from Portugal and Nigeria. Iraq probably retains the theoretical capacity to produce nuclear weapons. See, the paper by K. R. Timmerman, 'The Poison Gas Connection: Western Suppliers of Unconventional Weapons and Technologies to Iraq and Libya', Simon Wiesenthal Centre, Los Angeles, 1990; *Der Spiegel*, 'Ideale Verstecke', 7/1998; *Der Spiegel*, 'Palaste um Fadenkrenz', 6/1998.
5. Hindu *rashtra* means 'Hindu nation'. Less than an hour after Prime Minister Vajpayee's public announcement of a test in the afternoon of Monday, 11 May, the English language mouthpiece of the RSS, *The Organiser*, usually released till then on Wednesdays, hit the stands with a special issue commemorating Pokharan-I. The issue carried stories with captions like 'Time to Tame Pakistan' and information that could only have been obtained privately from official sources. The timing and content of the issue was no coincidence. This is a judgement that gets, but needs no, reinforcement, from the well-known fact that the Cabinet list of appointees of the BJP-led coalition government was first vetted by the RSS, just as the draft of the founding document of the coalition, the 'National Agenda for Governance' was first shown for corrections to the RSS before being

shown to the other coalition partners. The RSS, incidentally, claims to be a non-political, purely 'cultural' organization!

6. On 6 December 1992, the Sangh Combine calculatedly destroyed the Babri Masjid (mosque) at the north Indian town of Ayodhya. It did this despite all earlier assurances that it would not violate Supreme Court orders in this regard. It deceitfully claimed that the destruction was a spontaneous expression of uncontrollable and mass Hindu anger. For years before this culminating act, the Sangh had systematically carried out a nationwide, hate-filled, anti-Muslim campaign claiming that a temple commemorating the birth of the mythical God-king Rama had been constructed at this site in Ayodhya before allegedly being destroyed on the orders of the first Mughal Emperor, Babar, in the sixteenth century and replaced by a mosque. This campaign represented the atavistic politics of a cultivated historical grievance and revenge. No proper archaeological or historical evidence to substantiate this claim has ever been produced. Indeed, there is no real evidence of any temple, whether devoted to the worship of Rama or to any other deity, being razed to make way for a mosque at this site.

   Currently, there exists a makeshift temple erected after the mosque was destroyed with the Sangh promising to eventually construct (once current legal disputes are over) a magnificent Ram temple. Incidentally, preparations for the construction of such a Ram Mandir (temple) began in 1990 or two years before the act of destruction which the Sangh said was unplanned and unforeseen.

7. Hindutva or 'Hinduness' is the name given to the general ideology of the Sangh Combine. It represents the most pernicious form of Hindu nationalism. It was first systematically articulated by the Hindu nationalist ideologue, V.D. Savarkar in the twenties followed by further 'refinements' introduced by the second supremo of the RSS, M. S. Golwalkar.

   The *Panchjanya* (a Hindi weekly journal brought out by the Sangh) of 30 August 1998 featured a cover story called 'Ye Kaise Hindustani?' (roughly translated as 'What Kind of Indians Are These?') attacking in the name of nationalism and national loyalty, a number of public opponents of the bomb. These included Jyoti Basu, senior leader of the Communist Party of India (Marxist), Kuldip Nayar, long time advocate of friendship between India and Pakistan, prominent novelist and film-maker Arundhati Roy and writer and activist Praful Bidwai. The connection between nuclear glorification and the Sangh's version of Indian nationalism could hardly be more clearly or crudely displayed.

8. BJP ideologues have always looked upon Israel and Zionism with a considerable measure of sympathy. The BJP strongly endorsed the formal diplomatic recognition of Israel carried out by a previous Congress government. However, while the BJP is all for closer ties with Israel, it recognizes that the latter is a regional power that can only play a minor supportive role to the US in confronting the supposed global challenge of 'Islamic civilization'. In the larger 'civilizational' scheme of things, Judaism counts for little and a Hindu–Christian 'civilizational alliance' of a kind attractive to Western right-wingers will more or less automatically bring Israel along in tow. However, the internationally publicized

assaults on the Christian minority carried out by the BJP and its Sangh partners during its coalition's term of office have damaged the prospects that some such alliance might emerge in the future.

9. Vajpayee said, 'I have argued for restructuring of Indo-US relations not just because this will help India—but also because this will help the US itself...Indo–US ties based on equality and mutuality of interest is going to be the mainstay of tomorrow's stable, democratic world order'. Excerpt from the text of the speech distributed to the media by the Prime Minister's Office, 28 September 1998, p. 8.
10. The Indo-Sri Lanka Accord effectively endorsed India's right to be the principal arbiter in Sri Lanka's internal civil war between the Sinhalese dominated central government and the Sri Lankan Tamils of the northern Jaffna region. From being the protector of the Tamils, India effectively became their 'hunter', exactly the claim then correctly made by the Sri Lankan premier of the time, R. Premadasa, in justification of the Accord. That this Accord was accepted by other countries like the US only further enhanced the sense of self-importance of the Indian élite which overwhelmingly supported it and the Indian intervention as the expression of the country's new-found stature as the globally acknowledged regional hegemon. The Accord collapsed when India could not fulfil its end of the bargain. It had been given this status by Colombo in return for sending an expeditionary force to hunt down and crush the Sri Lankan Tamil insurgency. This, the cynically named, Indian Peace keeping Force (IPKF) was unable to do. With its presence in Sri Lanka becoming an ever greater political liability to the incumbent government in Colombo, the latter broke off the Agreement.
11. See A. Vanaik, *India in a Changing World*, Orient Longman, New Delhi, 1995, pp. 83–8 and p.123.
12. The former chairman of India's Atomic Energy Regulatory Board (AERB), A. Gopalakrishnan, not only provided a list of safety and construction failures but also pointed out the absurdity of a situation where the body (the AERB) empowered to monitor the functioning and performance of the Department of Atomic Energy (DAE) is not itself autonomous of the DAE but comes under its authority. For his pains, Gopalakrishnan was publicly vilified and his tenure as chairman not renewed. The performance of India's civilian nuclear programme remains a sacred cow rarely criticized by the 'strategic community'.
13. In October 1947, the Hindu ruler of the Muslim majority province of Kashmir, Maharaja Hari Singh had yet to decide whether to accede to India or Pakistan. Troops from Pakistan suddenly attacked Kashmir. Hari Singh desperately sought Indian help to expel these attackers. New Delhi promised support only if Hari Singh formally agreed to accede to the Indian Union which is what he hurriedly agreed to do. This accession is the legal basis for India's claim that the whole of Kashmir belongs to it. Indian troops moved in and halted the Pakistani advance and under UN auspices a ceasefire line was agreed to in 1948 to bring the war to an end. To this day, Kashmir remains territorially divided along the ceasefire line or line of control largely established in 1948.

India holds the Kashmir valley and the regions of Jammu and Ladakh. Pakistan holds the regions of Gilgit, Baltistan, and Muzzaferabad which together make up what it calls Azad or 'free' Kashmir.

In 1954, Prime Minister Jawaharlal Nehru agreed to the idea of a UN organized plebiscite to ascertain the wishes of the Kashmiri people after Pakistan withdrew its troops. At the time he made the offer, Nehru had every reason to believe that such a plebiscite would favour India. Later this was no longer the case, and Nehru withdrew the offer. Nonetheless, that offer became something of a diplomatic millstone around India's neck. Pakistan made as much as it could out of it but the offer was also contingent on Pakistani troop withdrawal from the regions occupied in 1948, something that no Pakistan government has ever been willing to countenance. Moreover, the offer was restricted to a choice between India and Pakistan and precluded the third alternative of Kashmiri independence in part or whole.

After the 1971 war when India defeated Pakistan decisively, the then Indian Prime Minister Indira Gandhi offered to make the existing ceasefire line a permanent border. This was not accepted by Pakistan. That is to say, on the Kashmir issue, India is the status quo power content with the existing division. Only the BJP, of India's principal Indian political parties, entertains aims of getting the whole of Kashmir for India. It is Pakistan that is most committed to changing the status quo, and as the weaker power, is constantly seeking to internationalize the Kashmir issue.

14. Four books, two of which are edited collections, coming out after May 1998, carry virtually the whole gamut of views and arguments of the pro-nuclearists though the odd anti-nuclear contributor is also featured. The only two prominent hawks not covered in the two edited volumes are C. Raja Mohan and B. Chellaney but their views are widely known and circulated as they are both prolific contributors to 'national' English language dailies. The four books are A. Mattoo (ed), *India's Nuclear Deterrent: Pokhran II and Beyond,* Har Anand, New Delhi, 1999; Jasjit Singh (ed), *Nuclear India,* Knowledge World in association with IDSA (Institute of Defence Studies and Analyses), New Delhi, 1998; J. N. Dixit, *Across Borders: Fifty Years of Indian Foreign Policy*, Picus, New Delhi, 1998; Jaswant Singh, *Defending India,* St. Martin's Press, London, 1999.

All the pro-nuclear advocates follow a set pattern of arguments concerning the causes and consequences of India going nuclear. They are all unproblematic subscribers to a very conventional form of Realist thinking as their operative framework. As such they make no attempt to connect the rising influence/popularity of, and propensity towards, a politics of nuclearism with the rise and impact of the politics of Hindutva. They all seek to justify the decision to go nuclear as some kind of inevitable and 'logical' culmination of an evolving Indian nuclear policy refusing to recognize or accept that the decision to test and go openly nuclear represented a decisive rupture with India's past policy of ambiguity. Were they to concede the fact of rupture they would then have to explain it, and this would push them in the direction of doing what they do not want to do—namely, relating such a dramatic shift to matters like the relationship between the domestic politics of Hindutva and changes in the character of élite nationalism. All of them claim the hypocrisy of existing NWSs in part 'drove' India to act as it did. This is more of a common thread than the claim which not all are prepared to make—that a deteriorating external security environment, namely a supposedly growing 'China threat' and/or a China–Pakistan nexus 'forced' India to go nuclear. Amitabh Mattoo and Jaswant Singh, however, are among those who do put more weight on the China factor.

All the pro-nuclearists claim Indian security has improved or will soon enough do so as a result of this decision. All claim that Indo-Pakistan relations will improve and some that Sino-Indian relations will also become better. All are inclined to favour the notion that in the long run Indo-US relations can improve and that they should do so. That is to say, any rhetoric about the deceits of US nuclear policy or its role as a 'nuclear hegemon' is just that. It does not indicate a principled or consistent opposition to the US in the name of constructing a better world order. Nor does it indicate any serious unwillingness on their part to promote better bilateral relations provided 'sobriety'—namely, acceptance of nuclear India and of the 'possibilities for strategic cooperation' now opening up—prevails in Washington. Some pro-nuclearists are more inclined than others to promote the prospect of a future India–US tie up of sorts vis-à-vis China. After all, the RSS once called the USA's Vietnam war a 'dharm yudh' or holy war and the Sangh is ideologically by no means anti-US. All believe India's going nuclear will improve prospects of eventual global disarmament. All believe in having a 'minimum deterrent' but there exist very substantial differences on what this would actually mean by way of required warhead strength, patterns of deployment and attitudes to restraint measures/treaties regarding testing, missile development/proliferation, fissile materials stocks, etc. At an extreme end people like Bharat Karnad in the Mattoo volume want thermonuclear bombs, 350 to 400 warheads and a well developed triadic pattern of deployment vis-à-vis China. Most of what Jaswant Singh (foreign affairs minister in the BJP-led coalition government) has to say is utterly pedestrian stuff said by many other prisoners of conventional Realism. His most distinctive chapter concerns India's supposed lack of a strategic culture. Here a Hindutva-inspired reading of history, replete with motifs like India's susceptibility to external invasions throughout the centuries, its internal weaknesses, its unrealistic and moral–sentimental attitudes to the exercise of power, etc. are on parade. Again, such views claiming the existence of a historically-rooted and evident Indian weakness are hardly surprising coming as they do from a leader of the Sangh which sees itself as *the* principal instrument for the resurrection of a 'strong India'. More disturbing is the echoing of such themes by some other 'strategic experts' not otherwise noted for being Hindutva inspired. One such example is provided by K. Subrahmanyam even before the Jaswant Singh volume came out. See his 'India's Lotus Eaters' in *The Times of India*, 20 April 1998.

Our text has, of course, anticipated and addressed the general set of such arguments and claims by the pro-nuclearists. This Indian nuclear élite really has nothing new to say after May 1998.

15. Private conversation with Dr Zia Mian. Dr Mian, of Pakistani origin, is a nuclear physicist and long-time disarmament campaigner currently teaching and researching at Princeton University. He is preparing a major study of Pakistan's post-Independence nuclear preparations and policies.
16. The most detailed study of Pakistan's preparations for making the bomb remains the book by S.R. Weisman and H. Krosney, *The Islamic Bomb*, Times Books, New York, 1981. See also, L.S. Spector, *The Undeclared Bomb*, Ballinger Publishing Co., Cambridge, Mass., 1988.
17. One source says Pakistan had achieved nuclear capability by 1983. See Zahid Hussain. 'The Bomb Controversy' in *Newsline*, Karachi, November 1991. Given the secrecy surrounding the Pakistani and Indian nuclear establishments, estimates of stockpiles and possible numbers of bombs that could be assembled have to be guesswork of sorts. A SIPRI study, *World Inventory of Plutonium and Highly Enriched Uranium 1992* Oxford Univ. Press, Oxford, 1992, gave plausible estimates for what might be the numbers available to India at the end of 1995. This was equivalent to roughly 60 bombs. For Pakistan the figure was around 10. Given the problems that both countries have had with their reactors, it would not be surprising if at the end of 1998, they had stockpiles not markedly higher than these 1995 estimates. Thus India may now possess materials to assemble between 60 and 80 bombs and Pakistan with enough for 10 to 15 bombs.
18. It is in bomb designing that Chinese assistance was probably most significant. Here too, it is not in the field of theoretical physics or calculations but in regard to arriving at appropriate engineering calculations that the Chinese may have passed on useful information. In many ways, this parallels the assistance some US experts provided to the French in regard to engineering problems the latter had over their hydrogen bomb. (Private conversations with Dr Mian and Dr Pervez Hoodbhoy. Dr. Hoodbhoy is Professor of nuclear physics at Qaid-e-Azam University in Islamabad and a well-known disarmament campaigner.)
19. Indeed, it is reluctant to concede that the one significant nuclear-related confidence-building measure (CBM) negotiated between India and Pakistan, on non-attack of each other's nuclear facilities, will have any validity in a weaponized environment. This was stated by the Pakistan foreign secretary, Shamshad Ahmad, at a breakfast meeting at the Asia Society, New York, 7 July 1998, cited by W.P.S. Sidhu, Brian Cloughley, et al. in *Nuclear Risk-Reduction Measures in Southern Asia*, Report No. 26, November 1998, The Henry L. Stimson Center, Washington, p.41.

CHAPTER SIX

Indefensible Arms

The Ethics of War and Nuclear Weapons

Uniquely Immoral

Nuclear weapons are quite unlike any other armaments. Their uniqueness lies in their truly awesome power of destruction on a scale unimaginable until rather recently in human history. Nuclear weapons alone have the potential to cause *total destruction*, exterminate humanity, destroy all life on earth. No other class of armaments can possibly cause that kind of havoc through an unstoppable chain of destructive events—including the release of vast amounts of energy through heat blasts, X-rays, and a range of radioactive poisons, some of which will remain lethal for millions of years. There is not, and cannot be, any defence against nuclear weapons, whether military, civilian, or medical. The totality of destruction wreaked by, and the unending lethality of, nuclear weapons gives them a singularly horrible quality, which is incomparable with any other instrument of war. They are unique even within the category of 'weapons of mass destruction'.

Thus even the horrific fire-bombing of Dresden between 1942 and 1945 (which killed 100,000) or the massive US incendiary raid on Tokyo in March 1945 (which set off a firestorm that claimed 100,000 lives) pale into the shade beside Hiroshima, where a new kind of war took place. In place of the 350 warplanes that bombed Tokyo, there was only one—the B-29 bomber *Enola Gay*. In place of thousands of bombs and other kinds of munitions, there was just one bomb. What began at 8:15 a.m. on 6 August 1945, was vast indefinite butchery, horrible in its indiscriminate character. Hiroshima, then, revealed the reality of the ultimate weapon, of a new kind of war, where potentially there may be no survivors. Even today, half a century later, victims of the 1945 bombing continue to perish in Hiroshima and Nagasaki.

Ten years after the Cold War ended, the world still has enough firepower in its 30,000-plus nuclear weapons arsenal to cause a million Hiroshimas;

indeed, wipe out the human race altogether. At least half of these weapons are in a state of alert or are deployed so as to be ready to be launched in a matter of minutes or hours. It is this sheer awesomeness, this vast, virtually infinite, limitless, destructive power of nuclear weapons that has radically altered the condition of human existence, indeed its very possibility, as never before.

Associated with nuclear weapons is not just a highly evolved sophisticated military infrastructure: command, control, communications and intelligence (C^3I) systems, as well as delivery vehicles, production units and storage facilities. Equally important are elaborate strategic doctrines and political premises: from 'massive retaliation' to 'mutually assured destruction' and from 'minimum deterrence' to 'limited nuclear war'. Equally vital is what has been called 'nuclearism' or 'psychological, political, and military dependence on nuclear weapons, the embrace of the weapons as a solution to a wide variety of human dilemmas, most ironically that of "security".'[1].

At no time in the past has the world experienced such an obsession with a particular type of weaponry, nor has another class of armaments so fundamentally transformed, distorted, and in other ways affected, the way millions of human beings look at security and defence, experience mortal fear and vulnerability, or feel anxiety and uncertainty of the most profound kind. Nuclear weapons have the potential to terminate human culture, end history, murder the human imagination as we know it. Nuclearism is based upon a series of illusions. One illusion holds that security can be derived from insecurity, itself rooted in the capacity of adversaries to inflict limitless violence upon each other. Another is that responsible leadership structures exist at the military and political level which can prudently and effectively 'manage' nuclear weapons, and that the citizen can be reliably protected against the enemy's nuclear weapons. One of the greater illusions is that nuclear deterrence can, and will always, work dependably, enhancing mutual confidence and security.

Nuclear weapons posit, as Robert Jay Lifton puts it, a strain or break in the 'great chain of being', a 'potentially terminal revolution', leading to a 'radical futurelessness'. They are not just weapons. They are something much greater. Henry L. Stimson, Secretary of War, who oversaw the Manhattan Project during its critical phase, expressed this acutely when he said (on 31 May 1945) that 'this project should not be considered simply in terms of military weapons, but as a new relationship of man to the universe.' Similarly, when Harry S. Truman said, 'This is the greatest thing in the world', referring to the first atomic bomb, he was not merely describing the awesome power of this new weapon; he was also acknowledging and articulating the unique mystique that is associated with it, and its transformative potential well beyond its military use.

The epochal fear, deep anxiety about futurelessness, and the all-consuming sense of helplessness that millions of men and women have experienced in regard to nuclear weapons and nuclear war—at one time, more than half the American people thought that a nuclear war was imminent—are only one aspect of the moral, political and psychological problems that these weapons pose. The central issue is the morality or immorality of the use or threat of use. This has been the subject of deep and serious discussion, and of philosophical, legal, and strategic arguments for a long time, indeed, even before the Manhattan project was launched and ever since the possibility of development of a nuclear fission-based weapon began to unfold in the 1930s. Physicists such as Einstein and Niels Bohr were among the first to question the ethics of developing nuclear weapons.

Just and Unjust Wars

The acute problem posed by nuclear weapons is this: are they legitimate weapons of war? and are they compatible with the notion of just wars? This notion has two components going back to St Augustine and the ethics of the use of violence: *jus ad bellum* (justice through war, or the justness of war itself) and *jus in bello* (justice in war, or in the conduct of war).[2] For our purposes, it should be evident that the second is more important than the first. The first aspect is relatively simple to deal with only because nuclear weapons are quintessentially offensive weapons calculated to wreak devastation on an indiscriminate scale. They can have no function in a war waged in self-defence, or to vacate an aggression.

The use of nuclear weapons is simply inconceivable in, say, a war of national liberation, or one waged to defend values of decency, or of democracy and worthy political systems or cultures. Wars are just only insofar as they are waged in self-defence or in pursuit of causes that are noble, and oppose injustice and tyranny. Wars involve the deliberate use of lethal violence, which can be justified only because we recognize '*two* orders of fact, each of them compelling, each of them terrible'.[3]

Wars are indeed 'destructive to the peace of the world' but they may nevertheless be necessary and just under certain circumstances. John Locke argued by analogy against the categorical pacifist view: 'They may as well say, upon the same ground, that honest men may not oppose robbers or pirates, because this may occasion disorder or bloodshed . . . If any mischief come in such cases, it is not to be charged upon him who defends his own right.'

It is virtually impossible to countenance the possibility that a nuclear war could meet any elementary criterion underlying the notion of *jus ad bellum*. How can epochal, apocalyptic forms of mass destruction and insensate violence possibly promote a cause that is noble? The nature of any struggle against tyranny and injustice, however grave, is undermined by the greater tyranny of nuclear destruction. Indeed, even the creation of the wherewithal to wage nuclear war, a gigantic military apparatus ready and willing, and in a state of alert, to wreak devastation upon the earth, itself involves disregard for values such as sobriety, caution, democracy, and transparency, and an obsession with paranoid and jingoistic notions of national security.

BOX 2

Toys for the Boys
How Nuclearism Works against Women

'A nuclear bomb does not discriminate. Nuclearization does.'[1] It discriminates with particular vengeance against women and feminist values and principles. India's and Pakistan's nuclearization took place amidst yet another explosion—of aggressive, bellicose, male-supremacist, tub-thumping, jingoistic nationalism, itself closely tied to religious sectarianism. The images and symbols used to describe the tests, and the terms in which the nuclear triumph of India and Pakistan was announced—'we have a Big Bomb'—were strongly phallic and deeply rooted in the discourse of raw power, aggression, and penetration.

Thus, Indian Prime Minister Vajpayee openly declared: 'We have a big Bomb.' Picking up the same sexual imagery, a cartoon in a leading newspaper depicted Vajpayee propping up his rickety coalition government with a nuclear bomb. 'Made with Viagra' the caption read. Pakistan's Prime Minister Nawaz Sharif was clear that he was 'matching' India in the nuclear competition; he had to. The Vishwa Hindu Parishad, a militant super-patriarchal affiliate of the BJP, was even more categorical. It announced that with the nuclear tests India had finally demonstrated its 'manhood'. Earlier, for decades, India had been 'ruled by a bunch of *hijras* [eunuchs].'[2] (The Shiv Sena, a fascistic ally of the BJP in Maharashtra, echoed the same sentiment.) For the VHP, India had now become all powerful. It could take on any force on earth. India must now be declared a 'Hindu state' through a constitutional amendment.

The connections between nuclearization, aggression, intolerance towards neighbours, male-supremacism, religious chauvinism, and bellicose nationalism were starkly obvious from the very outset in both India and Pakistan. That itself should cause concern and worry among women everywhere. There is, however, an even stronger case why women should want to oppose nuclear weapons. This derives from the likely consequences for women, and for areas of special concern to them, of programmes to manufacture and deploy such weapons.

At least three such areas are important. First, nuclearization will impose a *heavy economic burden* upon India's and Pakistan's already stretched resources. Their governments are themselves deeply in debt, with huge fiscal deficits (see Chapter 7, 'Unaffordable Arsenals'). In India's case the costs of creating even a so-called 'minimum credible deterrent'—a fifth the size of China's arsenal, or smaller—have been estimated to be the same as the costs of providing free primary education to all children between the ages of 6 and 14. Nuclear weapons are liable to claim greater resources than India or Pakistan spend on public health.

Given the fact that the 'committed' expenditures of the Indian and Pakistani governments, on account of foreign and domestic debt servicing, salaries, the conventional military budget, and subsidies and doles for the well-off are over 80 per cent of their total revenue, the *additional* outlays that nuclear weapons and missiles programmes will claim can only come from *deep cuts* in the already meagre and shrinking public budgets for health, sanitation, literacy, primary education, nutrition, drinking water supply, shelter, social security and welfare, and other social sector programmes that are of particular relevance to women. It is well established that in India and Pakistan, girl children and women have the least access to these services although they need them the most. Such cuts spell a further degradation of public services, an increase in the burden of work placed upon women, and further deprivation and want for large numbers of them.

India and Pakistan have long been notorious for high levels of deprivation amongst women, reflected in extraordinarily low sex ratios (in India's case 927 women for 1000 males), high levels of malnutrition—as a proportion higher than in sub-Saharan Africa—and abysmally low levels of female literacy (38 and 24 per cent respectively). Their Gender-related Development Indices, computed by the UN Development Programme, are among the lowest in the world, their rankings oscillating between 125 and 140, from a total of 175 countries. Any reduction in state spending on programmes meant to redress the situation will therefore directly affect women in extremely harmful ways.

Since women carry a disproportionate share of the responsibility for housework, fetching water (in villages usually from long distances), supervising children's nutrition and education, and caring for the sick, cutbacks in social spending, and decline or collapse of services, are liable to affect them particularly grievously. In the event of a nuclear emergency, it is primarily the women who survive who will be called upon to be the prime care-givers and counsellors to the victims and affected families.

Secondly, nuclearization is liable to influence and *change social values* in a perverse manner. The ideology of nuclearism not only sidelines moral questions but genders them. Within its discourse, the policy-making élite is represented as rational, scientific, modern and of course masculine, while ethical questions, questions about social and environmental costs, are made to appear emotional, effeminate, regressive, and pre-modern. This falsely implies that questions about human life and welfare are somehow neither modern nor masculine, and that men have no capacity for peace and morality. This can have disastrous consequences for both men and women.

Nuclearism trivializes human suffering. It pejoratively sees human caring as a sign of weakness or effeminacy, as a concern simply of the oppressed. It downgrades non-nuclear countries as 'backward' and as unequipped to step into the twenty-first century. Nuclearism breeds a politics based on the relegation of the weak to the margins and a neo-Darwinian survival-of-the-fittest mindset.

That is not all. Nuclearization requires secrecy. It demands obedience and conformity. It is repressive and intolerant of dissent. It condemns democratic protest as anti-national. Nuclearization is not a matter of military and technological activities alone. 'Nuclearized India and Pakistan will need to construct a cultural and educational environment that promotes a preference for aggression, violence and revenge.'[3]

To rationalize these priorities, the proponents of nuclearization will feed people with images of militaristic heroism, of brutality, of relentless pursuit of aggrandizement. Contrariwise, they will denigrate images that grow out of peaceability, tolerance, and universal goodwill. Nuclearism denies the possibility of drawing upon humane values and life-affirming and -sustaining attitudes and methods. All this, and the desire to secure public consent for nuclear weapons, will entail the promotion of a mindset that enhances what are *conventionally* known as masculine values: violence, eagerness to retaliate, and brutality, which discriminate against women.

The third effect of nuclearization, particularly in India and Pakistan, pertains to *virulent religion-based nationalism* which is strongly masculinist and patriarchal in orientation, and which legitimizes the subordination of women, reducing them to passive actors without agency. The ideologies of aggression associated with this variety of nationalism are themselves rooted in rationalization of the capacity for insensate violence. Once the idea that massive, limitless, violence against 'the enemy' is legitimate and necessary is rendered acceptable and 'normal', it can be used to rationalize everyday violence against women, and more generally, the underprivileged. Violence is a 'part of life'. More, it gets the imprimatur of religion too. For, the construction of Hindu sectarian nationalism in India or Islamicism in Pakistan is deeply rooted in, and inseparable from, the diminution of women to mere repositories and reproducers of culture, who then embody the Hindu or Islamic 'nation'.

Religion-based nationalism is deeply authoritarian and militarist. In the India–Pakistan context, it has involved recruitment of women into militant outfits, or their systematic brainwashing. For instance, recruits into RSS women's fronts are given daily ideological instruction on the evils of Islam and taught to hate all Muslims. They are trained to translate that hatred into martial action. Such outfits not only glorify women as mothers of soldiers but attempt 'to perfect a formidable machine for producing an ideal-type woman who is herself a fully militarized being. She is, besides, further exhorted, in their training programme, to pass all this on to her children.'[4]

Such militarism and aggressive male-supremacism are profoundly undemocratic and violative of women's rights. A militaristic culture feeds into increased levels of violence against women. Nuclearism allows such violations to be rationalized and 'normalized' in the name of 'national security' and the 'supreme national interest'. Women, then, have a special stake in opposing nuclearization. Feminist groups recognize this. In both India and Pakistan, they have been at the forefront of the struggle against nuclear weapons and for nuclear disarmament.

Notes

1. Kumkum Sangari, Neeraj Malik, Sheba Chhachhi, and Tanika Sarkar in 'Why Women Must Reject the Bomb', *Out of Nuclear Darkness: The Indian Case for Disarmament*, MIND (Movement in India for Nuclear Disarmament), New Delhi, 1998. This box draws upon this essay, and upon the work of other South Asian feminists.
2. Ashok Singhal, president of the VHP, quoted at Patna, India, in 'Test an assertion of Hindu pride: Singhal', *The Pioneer*, New Delhi, 24 May 1998.
3. Sangari, et al. op. cit. p.53.
4. Sangari, et al. op. cit. p.54.

At best, a rather wishful case could be made out in favour of the *threat* of use of nuclear weapons: the idea that through active preparation and readiness to use such weapons, one might be effectively and reliably able to deter an adversary from using his own nuclear armaments or other weapons of mass destruction (WMDs). This, however, really pertains to the issue of nuclear deterrence, its morality and its strategic value, not to the morality of the actual use of such weapons. Nuclear deterrence is discussed separately below.

There are several criteria of *jus in bello*, which have evolved over the past centuries through debates on ethics. Some of these have been incorporated into jurisprudence and bodies of international law and international humanitarian law. War and methods of warfare cannot be divorced from rational strategic considerations. The use of force must be *proportionate* to the threat that it is meant to contain. Excessive force or violence is not permissible. Non-combatants must not be targeted. The use of cruel or inhuman methods with pitiless disregard for basic human values is forbidden. For instance, you cannot mass-poison civilians or starve prisoners of war. Prisoners of war have rights, just as combatants, even guerrillas, have rights. Wars must be fought well and scrupulously. Certain methods of warfare are totally prohibited no matter how admirable and desirable the end they might achieve. There are rules about sieges and blockades, and about reprisals and retribution.

There is a multiplicity of rules that have evolved over the past centuries, but especially since the eighteenth century, that determine the conduct of warfare. Of them there are two principal types or varieties that are of critical and special importance in regard to nuclear weapons. The first concerns the category of agents or persons against whom violence can be directed. These define *who* can be legitimate targets of attack, or can be killed in war. The second relates to the *manner of exercise* of force: with what methods they can be legitimately attacked or killed. That places limits upon how those targeted are dealt with.

The first type of rules draws a strict distinction between combatants and non-combatants, and essentially upholds the principle of immunity for the latter. Non-combatants cannot be the principal target of attack. The use of more or less random violence against whole populations is impermissible. Basically, you cannot wage war against those who are not themselves making war. In war, there is a broad distinction between soldiers, on the one hand, and 'innocent' civilians on the other. The notion of 'innocence' here is a special one. It has nothing to do with personal intention, choice, or culpability. For instance, a reluctant conscript is a legitimate target by virtue of being a soldier, whereas an ordinary civilian, however enthusiastic about the war effort, is not. (Political and administrative decision-makers are of course another category.) In general, soldiers, qua soldiers, constitute a threat. Warriors and soldiers are legitimately subject to violence.

Over the past decades, the category of combatants has been extended to include those who work in munitions factories, but only insofar as their role as workers and their actual location in such factories goes. However, those processing soldiers' food rations are not combatants. There is a distinction between those contributing to the role of soldiers directly as combatants, and those enabling them to survive as human beings, independently of their military role.

Again, different categories of personnel have their own rights. For instance, a soldier who surrenders to the enemy is considered to have been granted 'benevolent quarantine'. Prisoners of war, thus, have a right to try and escape and they cannot be prosecuted for that. However, if, in the process, they kill a guard, then that is not considered an act of war. It is treated as murder: for by surrendering, the soldier had allegedly committed himself to stop fighting, albeit under duress. Such rules have evolved over the years as part of a minimal consensus that humanity has reached over a long period of time, based on some shared criteria.

Indiscriminate Destruction

Nuclear weapons fail each of these criteria. They kill massively, indiscriminately, without distinguishing between combatant soldiers and non-combatant civilians. Indeed, they are quintessentially indiscriminate and acquire their particularly horrifying character precisely because they kill massively and indiscriminately. The manner in which nuclear weapons kill and maim are horrendously cruel—incinerating life-forms within a radius of several (e.g. 20 or more) kilometres at dizzying temperatures, flattening all buildings and structures through ultra-powerful blast- and shock-waves, setting off huge firestorms, releasing blinding light, and spewing out enormous quantities of radiation, with a mix of slow- and fast-acting poisons, some of which will remain in significant quantities in the environment for centuries, even millennia. (For instance, the half-life of plutonium-239 is 24,400 years.)

Studies of the victims of Hiroshima and Nagasaki validate the proposition that the use of nuclear weapons is fraught with the cruellest possible forms of death and long-lasting injury and health damage that make 'life a living hell' for people and where the description about the 'living envying the dead' is not hyperbole. Morally, it is simply impermissible to use weapons that are so destructive. If the world could outlaw chemical and biological weapons, and even agree to an anti-personnel landmines ban, then surely the case for eliminating nuclear weapons—which are incalculably more destructive and more indiscriminate in the damage they cause—is even stronger.

The case extends even to nuclear deterrence, the doctrine that holds that an adversary can and should be effectively deterred from attack by virtue of being threatened with the infliction of 'unacceptable' damage. Nuclear deterrence not only legitimizes horror weapons but entails a willingness to use them, whether in anticipation, to pre-empt an enemy attack, or in retaliation or reprisal. Without such willingness, indeed a firm commitment, to use them, deterrence loses its sting, becomes meaningless. Every established nuclear weapons power has well-formulated, elaborate plans to *use* nuclear weapons. Whatever the difference in the details of their strategic doctrines—whether they profess a policy of No First Use, and of No Use against a non-nuclear adversary, or are wedded to 'extended deterrence' and pre-emptive use of nuclear weapons even against non-nuclear states—each of the P-5 has well-developed plans for the *actual* use of such weapons. These go well beyond mere *intentions,* themselves highly objectionable. They involve *actual* preparations, the creation of extremely expensive command, control, communications, and intelligence infrastructures (which in the US alone have cost over $ 4000 billion), and *credible* war-fighting schemes to which nuclear weapons are central.[4]

Thus, even Britain, among the least advanced of the nuclear states, it has now been disclosed, had a fully-fledged underground shelter, with a virtual replica of Whitehall, and various ministry buildings, and a 'Main Street', and so on. The former USSR's underground cities are as well-known as the US's preparations for nuclear war-fighting in 'nuclear environments' that entail 'hardening' the war machine, and the weapons themselves, to withstand extreme conditions, including scorching heat and radiation and the breakdown of normal telecommunications as a result of the electromagnetic pulse released by a nuclear explosion.

Nuclear deterrence is not just an idea or an abstract strategic doctrine. It entails seeking security through the creation of a threat of mass destruction, a threat that must appear credible and realisable. For it to be *credible*, it must involve the *demonstration* of a military capacity and preparations for a nuclear strike—preparations usually constantly upgraded under a technology-driven regime—as well as the *willingness* to strike. In moral terms, then, your adherence to nuclear deterrence means that you have already crossed the Rubicon, so to speak. You have prepared yourself mentally, politically, and militarily to wreak mass destruction upon the enemy. Indeed, you have made the attainment of security and peace *conditional* upon the highest conceivable level of war-preparedness at the maximal level of damage—much like a modern-day Genghis Khan.

Ethically, that makes nuclear deterrence highly questionable: repugnant, abhorrent, unworthy of respect from a civilized mind. Those who advocate nuclear deterrence seek security through the ability and readiness to inflict unconscionable suffering upon innocent civilians in the 'adversary' state, wherever that may be. They legitimize and make the use of such weapons respectable and 'normal' as a *cornerstone* of military strategy and security policy.

Why Nuclear Deterrence is 'Abhorrent'

Nuclear deterrence marks a moral firebreak, it is akin to endorsing torture. Once you rationalize the use of torture there is simply no limit that you can rationally place on human rights abuses, on the violation of fundamental entitlements and rights, including the right to life. Similarly, once you embrace nuclear deterrence, you have set your face against all accepted criteria of *jus in bello.* You cannot place any restraint on the *magnitude* of violence that is considered permissible. Not just decimation of the military command apparatus, but wholesale massacres, and barbaric forms of butchery, all get rationalized.

It is wrong to invoke the idea of a 'sliding scale' of moral standards in defence of nuclear deterrence. This involves a rejection of the notion of the moral equality of soldiers (combatant equality) and of non-combatant or civilian immunity, in favour of the view that the juster one's cause within the *jus ad bellum* paradigm, the greater right one has to violate *jus in bello* rules that are part of any reasonable war convention.

Even John Rawls is tempted to advance this line of argument. He says: 'Even in a just war, certain forms of violence are strictly inadmissible; and when a country's right to war is questionable and uncertain, the constraints on the means it can use are all the more severe. Acts permissible in a war of legitimate self-defence, when these are necessary, may be flatly excluded in a more doubtful situation.'[5] An extreme version of this reasoning is 'war is hell': the Sherman view that the rights of the just are total, they can do anything to win the war so long as it has been waged in a just cause. This means that the only kind of justice that matters is *jus ad bellum.*

Michael Walzer has dealt with this in his *Just and Unjust Wars* by questioning the 'sliding scale' concept.[6] He argues that there is an alternative to this, besides a position of moral absolutism: *'Fiat justicia ruat coelumn,*(do justice even if the heavens fall), is not for most people a plausible moral doctrine.' This alternative is summed up in the maxim: 'do justice unless the heavens are [really] about to fall'. This, Walzer says,

> is the utilitarianism of extremity, for it concedes that in certain very special cases, though never as a matter of course even in just wars, the only restraints upon military action are those of usefulness and proportionality. Throughout my discussion of the rules of war, I have been resisting this view and denying its force. I have argued, for example, against the notion that civilians can be locked into a besieged city or reprisals taken against innocent people 'in extreme cases'. For the idea of extremity has no place in the making of the war convention—or if it is said that combat is always extreme, then the idea is naturalized within the convention.

Walzer holds that

> the sliding scale erodes the convention bit by bit, and so it eases the way for the decision-maker who believes himself 'forced' to violate human rights. The argument from extremity permits (or requires) a more sudden breach of the convention, but only after holding out for a long time against the process of erosion. The reasons for holding out have to do with the nature of the rights at issue and the status of the men and women who hold them. These rights, I shall argue, cannot be eroded or undercut: nothing diminishes them; they are still standing at the very moment they are overridden: that is why they have to be *overridden*. Hence breaking the rules is always a hard matter, and the soldier or statesman who does so must be prepared to accept the moral consequences and the burden of guilt that his action entails.[7]

Walzer's position, however, is also less than satisfactory. He says:

> The tension between the rules of war and the theory of aggression, between *jus in bello* and *jus ad bellum*, can be dealt with in four different ways: 1) the war convention is simply set aside (derided as 'asinine ethics') under the pressure of utilitarian argument; 2) the convention yields slowly to the moral urgency of the cause: the rights of the righteous are enhanced, and those of their enemies devalued; 3) the convention holds and rights are strictly respected, whatever the consequences; and 4) the convention is overridden, but only in the face of an imminent catastrophe.
>
> The second and fourth of these are the most interesting and the most important. They explain how it is that morally serious men and women, who have some sense of what rights are, come nevertheless to violate the rules of war, escalate its brutality and extend its tyranny. The fourth seems to me the right argument. It provides the best account of the two kinds of justice and most fully recognizes the force of each.[8]

It is, however, difficult even to conceive of 'an imminent catastrophe' that would be of such magnitude as to justify the use of nuclear weapons, that will kill millions of non-combatant civilians. Indeed, what cause can be so sacred as to *necessitate* the deliberate snuffing out of life on such a scale, while brutalizing our own consciousness on a mass scale and cause it to accept unbounded cruelty as 'normal', or at least as necessary. In terms of the mere physical effects of nuclear violence, it is hard to distinguish the use of nuclear weapons from an 'imminent catastrophe'. To most people, such use would *be the catastrophe*: the two are basically tautogical.

At any rate, the moral argument against nuclear deterrence is basically as strong as the argument against the use of nuclear weapons and the complete inadmissibility of nuclear war. Whatever is wrong to do is wrong to threaten, especially if threatening involves the intention as well as preparations to use nuclear weapons. Walzer convincingly argues against the Protestant theologian Paul Ramsey that deterrence is 'a bad way' to try to prevent nuclear war.

Nuclear war 'is and will remain morally unacceptable, and there is no case for its rehabilitation. Because it is unacceptable, we must seek out ways to prevent it, and because deterrence is a bad way, we must seek out others.'[9] The only reliable, and the most reasonable, way of preventing nuclear war would seem to be to abolish nuclear weapons altogether. If there is one cardinal lesson to be drawn from the 50 year-long history of nuclearism, of the nuclear arms race, and from the persistent reliance on nuclear deterrence for security even after the end of the Cold War, it is this: abolition is the only way out. There is no substitute for the complete elimination of nuclear weapons. There is no other option.

Is it possible to reconcile a commitment to nuclear disarmament as the ultimate goal, with some kind of conditional acceptance of nuclear deterrence? Two lines of argument have been advanced, besides Ramsey's (which depends heavily on the intention to use nuclear weapons and whose weakness has been adequately demonstrated by Walzer). The first of these is that while the objective of complete elimination of nuclear weapons is unexceptionable, indeed is the only morally worthy objective possible in the circumstances, there is nevertheless a case for interim reliance on nuclear deterrence: complete disarmament is unlikely to come about in a short period of time, especially because the P–5, in particular the US and Russia—and many variations of the theme are possible—are extremely reluctant to undertake qualitative nuclear disarmament; in the interim, nuclear weapons can serve as useful instruments of national sovereignty, as a 'hedge against [the] hegemony' of the great powers, as a means of preventing 'nuclear blackmail' by them, and so on.[10]

The second argument, that of Pope John Paul II and various Catholic Churches, articulated most explicitly by Catholic Bishops of the US and members of Pax Christi, USA, held (until recently) that although the use of nuclear weapons is morally unjustifiable, 'possession of these weapons as a deterrent against the use of nuclear weapons by others could be morally acceptable, but acceptable only as an interim measure and only if deterrence were combined with clear steps toward progressive disarmament.'[11]

The Pax Christi Bishops' Argument

This was the position of the US National Conference of Catholic Bishops, as stated in its *Pastoral Letter: The Challenge of Peace: God's Promise and Our Response*. They have now revised their evaluation: 'For the past fifteen years, and particularly in the context of the Cold War, we, the Catholic Bishops of the United States, have reluctantly acknowledged the possibility that nuclear weapons could have some moral legitimacy, but only if the goal was nuclear disarmament. It is our present, prayerful judgment that this legitimacy is now lacking.'

The Pax Christi Bishops earlier made their moral acceptance of nuclear deterrence conditional upon 'three criteria: a) a reliance on deterrent strategies must be an interim policy only. As we stated then, "We cannot consider it adequate as a long-term basis for peace": b) the purpose of maintaining nuclear weapons in the interim was only "to prevent the use of nuclear weapons by others"; and c) a reliance on deterrence must be used "not as an end in itself but as a step on the way toward a progressive disarmament".'[12]

Both lines of argument are flawed, although it must be conceded that the second is less deeply so, which is why the Pax Christi Bishops have moved towards rejecting nuclear deterrence itself as immoral, while adherents of the first have ended up as apologists for nuclear proliferation and of India and Pakistan crossing the nuclear threshold. The first argument is based on the premise that nuclear weapons are a central determinant of the admittedly skewed world order and maldistribution of power globally, and that the defence of national sovereignty in the face of hegemonic pressures requires the possession of nuclear weapons, especially by third world states. Nuclear deterrence can prevent nuclear 'blackmail' of the third world by the hegemonic P–5, especially the three Western nuclear weapons states, with their tainted record as bullies who have practised coercive interventions in so many states of the global South.

These premises are open to question. Nuclear weapons today are hardly the central determinant of the distribution of power across the globe. That nature of power has itself changed towards 'softer' forms than purely military ones. However, even insofar as the military aspect is considered important, nuclear weapons are only one attribute of it. The great imbalances and divergences between the North and South are social, economic, environmental, in access to resources, in unequal trade patterns, in maldistributed capital flows, etc. They cannot possibly be redressed militarily, leave alone through the possession of nuclear weapons by the states of the South.

Nor can the possession of nuclear weapons by itself give a state effective power and prestige to influence the course of events. For instance, it is inconceivable that Pakistan's nuclearization will enhance its bargaining power vis-à-vis the international financial institutions and banks on whose subventions its tottering economy has become helplessly dependent, especially after May 1998. Ironically, the harder Pakistan tries to acquire a fully-fledged nuclear arsenal, and the more it invests in manufacturing warheads and fitting them on to delivery vehicles, the more vulnerable it is likely to become.

The possession of nuclear weapons has not prevented the UK's progressive marginalization as a European or world power. Non-nuclear Germany and Japan are more important global players than nuclear France or the UK. There is no convincing evidence that 'Nuclear blackmail' has ever really worked. Nuclear America could not prevent China's entry into the Korean War. The former USSR's nuclear arsenal did not help it avert a humiliating defeat in Afghanistan, nor did nuclear weapons enable the US to change the military balance in Vietnam. Nuclear weapons, then, are not a valuable or reliable currency of power. Whatever the claim made for what they might do for the already powerful states, they do nothing for the powerless or the not-so-powerful. They are not instruments for the promotion or safeguarding of the defence of national sovereignty or a state's freedom of action or independent manoeuvre.

The second line of argument is based on a number of ahistorical premises. It wrongly and quite unrealistically demands that 'reliance on strategic deterrence must be an interim policy only' when it is established at least with regard to the Western nuclear states, especially the US, that the policy is anything but interim. Nuclear deterrence has long been, and remains, a cornerstone of the security architecture that the US defines for itself. For all intents and purposes, US reliance on deterrence is 'an end in itself' and *certainly* not 'a *step* on the way towards progressive disarmament'. Deterrence has never had a 'progressive' character, not even remotely. Besides, the process of its establishment itself strengthens forces and institutions such as the military–industrial complex, that have a stake in opposing the very goal of nuclear disarmament, not just specific steps leading towards that goal.

The Pax Christi bishops are right to note:

> a) The policy of nuclear deterrence is being institutionalized. It is no longer considered an interim policy but rather has become the very 'long-term basis for peace' that we rejected in 1983. b) The role of nuclear deterrence has been expanded in the post Cold War era well beyond the narrow role of deterring the use of nuclear weapons by others. The role to be played now by nuclear weapons includes a whole range of contingencies on a global scale including countering biological and chemical weapons and the protection of vital national interests abroad. c) Although the United States and the republics that made up the former Soviet Union have in recent years eliminated some of their huge, superfluous stockpiles of nuclear weapons, our country, at least, has no intention, or policy position of eliminating these weapons entirely. Rather, the US intends to retain its nuclear deterrent into the indefinite future ....[13]

They, however, fail to see that it is the logic of deterrence as a security doctrine, not just the particular circumstances in which it is practised, and even its location in the Cold War context, that has driven the US towards institutionalizing its claimed value and expanding the role of deterrence several years after the Cold War ended. Once you accept that logic, then extending it into space and time, and adorning it with different purposes and functions, is but a small step. As I.F. Stone remarked, 'the finely spun concepts of deterrence give a rational appearance to an irrational process'.[14]

The logic concedes in the first place that nuclear weapons are legitimate at least as an effective threat; but the threat does not become credible unless you are prepared to use them; there is only a thin line of demarcation between threat and use, and it can easily be crossed. There is a gross inconsistency involved in legitimating an illegimate threat, one that is backed by elaborate preparations for its *translation into practice*, but not actual *use*, which the bishops hold to be totally immoral. The wielders of nuclear weapons and the practitioners of deterrence of course *mean* to use them—reluctantly, in emergencies, under unusual circumstances—but use them nevertheless. By granting moral acceptability to *some function* of nuclear weapons means at the least, bestowing legitimacy upon their existence. This, as argued earlier, is akin to accepting that torture is legitimate under certain circumstances and when linked to certain functions or objectives. Once the goal posts of what is strictly impermissible or inadmissible are thus shifted, there is no telling when and where the 'sliding scale' effect will stop. The impermissible becomes acceptable. Wisely, the Pax Christi bishops have drawn back from the brink, but they should, logically, question the morality of the very concept of nuclear deterrence. A commitment to nuclear disarmament is not compatible with adherence to nuclear deterrence. Even if it is conceded for the sake of argument that there is some 'uncertainty' about the moral status of nuclear deterrence, there is no moral uncertainty whatsoever about all the other justifications given for having these weapons—be they claims that they symbolize power or sovereignty, or are useful as tools of 'foreign policy support'. These other incontestably immoral arguments have been used by all nuclear élites, including those of India and Pakistan.

The Gandhi–Nehru Legacy and Its Degradation

Ever since Mahatma Gandhi declared that nuclear weapons 'represent the most sinful and diabolical use of science', India's leaders have forcefully characterized (until recently, that is) nuclear deterrence as an 'abhorrent' and 'morally repugnant' doctrine. Indeed, India's classical position, officially stated by its first Prime Minister, Jawaharlal Nehru, insisted that not only the use or threat of use of nuclear weapons, but even their manufacture and possession, be 'declared a crime against humanity'. India's diplomats, spokespersons and ministers until 1998 energetically argued that nuclear deterrence is simply impermissible and morally unacceptable: you cannot achieve security by creating the deepest insecurity, by threatening to kill millions of innocent civilians. As a former permanent representative of India to the United Nations said it: 'They [the nuclear weapons-states] are trying to prevent nuclear war by threatening it—a perilous paradox of prophylaxis.'[15]

Thus, it was not an aberration that India in 1995 pleaded before the World Court that nuclear weapons are illegal and incompatible with international law and international humanitarian law, and advanced an elaborate set of arguments for outlawing their use, threat of use, manufacture or possession. The written statement of the Government of India before the International Court of Justice contends, on the basis of Article 2(4) of the UN Charter, that 'any use of nuclear weapons as a measure of use of force to promote national policy objectives would be unlawful' and the 'use of nuclear weapons in any armed conflict as a first attack would be unlawful under international law'. Further, it argued that the use of nuclear weapons 'by way of reprisal or retaliation would violate the principle of proportionality and humanitarian law'; therefore, the 'prohibition of the use of a nuclear weapon in an armed conflict is an absolute one, compliance with which is not dependent on corresponding compliance by others'; it is a 'requisite in all circumstances'.

The Indian official statement reads:

> This brings us to the question as to the legality of the use of nuclear weapons in an armed conflict on the ground that it is open as a measure of last resort under limited conditions as a matter of military necessity. A basic principle of the law of armed conflict and particularly the international humanitarian law, which is contained in Article 22 of the Hague Convention IV (1907) states that 'the right of belligerents to adopt means of injuring the enemy is not unlimited'. Their right in particular is conditioned by Article 23 of the Hague Regulations prohibiting the use of poison or poisoned weapons; the 1925 Geneva Protocol prohibiting projectiles, axphyxiating, poisonous and other gases which incidentally prohibits also the use of weapons which could cause genetic disorders and illness which is likely to prolong for a considerable amount of time; and by the basic principle enshrined in the Declaration of St. Petersburg of 1868 prohibiting any weapon 'which uselessly aggravates the sufferings of disabled men or render their death inevitable'.[16]

Therefore,

> the use of nuclear weapons in response to attack by a conventional weapon would patently violate the principle of proportionality; but also a nuclear response to nuclear

attack, would violate the principle of discrimination, humanity, environmental security and probably the principle of neutrality as such an attack would not distinguish between combatants and non-combatants, causing civilian casualties, ravaging the natural environment and contaminating the territory of neighbouring and distant neutral countries. Nuclear deterrence had been considered to be abhorrent to human sentiment since it implies that a state if required to defend its own existence will act with pitiless disregard for the consequences to its own and adversary's people.

This was not all. India also pleaded:

Since the production and manufacture of nuclear weapons can only be with the objective of their use, it must follow that if the use of such weapons itself is illegal under international law, then their production and manufacture cannot under any circumstances be considered as permitted. Besides, the manufacture and stockpiling of nuclear weapons would constitute as a threat of their eventual use.

Thus, the statement concluded: 'In view of the above, it is submitted that the threat or use of nuclear weapons in any circumstances, whether as a means or method of warfare or otherwise, is illegal or unlawful under international law.'[17]

Similarly, it was the long-standing doctrinal continuity in India's radical and categorical rejection of nuclear weapons that led Foreign Secretary Salman Haidar to state at the Conference on Disarmament in Geneva in March 1996 that India remains committed to the complete elimination of nuclear weapons and wants to locate the CTBT 'as an instrument of disarmament'. He recalled that India had put forward

a formal proposal calling for the establishment of an Ad-hoc Committee on Nuclear Disarmament to commence negotiations on a phased programme of nuclear disarmament for the eventual elimination of nuclear weapons . . . . Nuclear disarmament is not the concern of one group of countries alone but is of universal relevance. We realize that nuclear weapons cannot be eliminated overnight. But surely, in today's world, conditions exist to begin negotiations on this primary disarmament objective.[18]

Most important, Haidar said:

India's objectives are different. We do not believe that the acquisition of nuclear weapons is essential for national security, and we have followed a conscious decision in this regard. We are also convinced that the existence of nuclear weapons diminishes international security. We therefore, seek their complete elimination. These are fundamental precepts that have been an integral basis of India's foreign and national security policy. It shall, therefore, remain our endeavour in the coming months to try to ensure that the disarmament agenda is not lost in a purely non-proliferation agenda.[19]

New Delhi's embrace of this 'abhorrent' doctrine barely two years later, without as much as a figleaf of an attempt at a rational explanation of a change of stance, signifies not so much a change in ground realities or the regional situation, as the moral debasement of the Indian élite and a coarsening of the quality of public discourse in the country. The degeneration of the Indian élite is a long drawn out process, but it has become particularly stark and obvious over the past two decades. It is itself related to the evolution of domestic politics since the early 1980s: a combination of an ascendant Hindu communal ideology, growing alienation of the élite from the people, its militaristic obsession with India becoming a great power, and the spread of profoundly cynical political ideas.

The BJP's lasting gain since the Ayodhya mosque agitation beginning in the mid-1980s has been not so much in its electoral support as its success in influencing substantial sections of India's social and economic élite—typically upper caste and urban—and ideologically penetrating the higher bureaucracy, judiciary, and the professions. This ideology is based on a toxic, belligerent, paranoid, and sectarian nationalism, which sees Hindus as the classical victims of invasion and conquest, who must now settle scores with the 'invaders' (principally Muslims) by 'uniting' and 'militarizing' themselves, and creating an awe-inspiring Hindu state. This framework regards peace, non-violence and justice as effete, and secular Gandhi as a villain out to emasculate Hindu 'manhood'—someone to be eliminated, as he indeed was by a fanatic inspired by the ideology of the Rashtriya Swayamsevak Sangh, the BJP's progenitor, ideological mentor and organizational master.

Militarist Nationalism in India

With the collapse of the Nehruvian paradigm, consisting of democracy, secularism, non-alignment, and 'socialism', the top 10 to 15 per cent Indians, the upper crust of society, have set their face against the rest, especially the poor. Culturally, economically, and in political attitudes they are closer to Northern élites and their own kin in North America and Europe. Strongly influenced by social-Darwinist ideas, they see the poor as a drag on 'their' India. They want a short cut to high global stature. What better route than the military one? Greatness here is defined purely in terms of power, narrowly understood and untempered by civilized conduct or compassion.

The growing importance of militaristic nationalism in politics is reflected in the duality of India's public discourse. At the grass-roots, there is the moral, liberating discourse of rights, justice, self-assertion by the hitherto disenfranchised and underprivileged. Amongst the élite, as if in opposition to this, there is the discourse of power and privilege. This assumes society to be in a sort of primitive, quasi-Hobbesian state, irredeemably immoral. Within this framework, the real becomes the rational. There is a separation between science and ethics, between technology and social responsibility. Developing instruments of mass destruction is seen as an 'achievement' enabling Indians to show the world that they are as *good* as anyone else.

In some ways, the élite's degeneration precedes the rise of virulent Hindu nationalism and is traceable to the growing crisis of legitimacy of the Indian state since the 1970s. Nuclear nationalism has been an undercurrent in the Indian policy debate since the 1960s, especially after India's debacle in the China War of 1962. Thus, there was at best relatively feeble resistance to the change in the official nuclear policy from 'No Bombs Ever' to 'No Bombs Now' in the late 1960s, and to a position of ambiguity (itself shifting and unstable) during the 1970s, especially after India's demonstration of a nuclear weapons capability at Pokharan in May 1974.

Far too many Indians belonging to the opinion-making and -shaping category slid into the comfortable cocoon of ambiguity and nuclear deception. For instance, in 1974, hardly any scientists or even peace-minded Gandhians questioned the dubious official claim that India's first test was in fact a 'peaceful nuclear explosion', and even fewer challenged the additional, even more ludicrous and crude claim, that what took place at Pokharan was not an explosion at all, but an 'implosion'—referring to the *technique* of suddenly bringing together two or more subcritical pieces of machined plutonium to form a critical mass which rapidly undergoes nuclear fission and explodes or disassembles. A large number among élite groups polled soon thereafter thought that the test explosions—based on a well-established body of physics, much of it long available in the public domain—was a 'major scientific achievement' and a 'breakthrough' for a third world country. They felt too that it was also an assertion of national sovereignty and independent decision-making in security-related matters.[20]

In reality, what took place at Pokharan in May 1974 was not a 'peaceful nuclear explosion', but the test explosion, it was subsequently revealed, of a 'Bomb'. Former Atomic Energy Commission (AEC) chairman, and the top physicist responsible for the test, Raja Ramanna, disclosed as much, on 9 October 1997.[21] Theoretically, 'peaceful' explosive devices are possible, but the term refers to the *intention* behind their use—e.g. creation of huge reservoirs or stimulating oil recovery—not to the physical principles involved which are identical with the principles used in a nuclear weapon explosion.

India's insistence that the explosions were 'peaceful' had less to do with intentions or actual plans to put that technology to civilian use than with demonstrating formal compliance with an agreement signed with Canada in 1956 for assistance to build the CIRUS reactor (from which the plutonium used in the Pokharan test was derived), which committed India to 'ensure that the reactor and any products resulting from its use will be employed for peaceful purposes only'. (A similar agreement was signed with the US which provided 21 tonnes of heavy water for CIRUS.) The fact is that India in 1974 consciously adopted nuclear ambiguity as a policy, after the active pursuit and demonstration of a nuclear weapons capability. It stopped short of actual weapons development, but a great psychological and moral barrier had been crossed.

It is difficult to say whether New Delhi would have gone on soon towards full weaponization, preceded by some more tests, had there been less of an outcry the world over regarding Pokharan-I, and had the political costs of conducting the test—especially a sharp decline in India's moral stature, a certain amount of antagonism from the West and from a close friend, the then USSR, and withdrawal of Canadian and American assistance in civilian nuclear technology on which the DAE was dependent to run its rickety power programme—not proved to be higher than anticipated. It appears likely that India's transition to Pokharan-II might have been a little faster in the absence of a fear of international isolation.

Indian nuclear ambiguity, as it evolved, meant different things to different people. To those on the extreme right, it was only a temporary pause, far too prolonged for some, on the road to full nuclearization. For some, it was an assertion of sovereignty, no more, not to be pursued by any further action: it was only a way of warning the world, especially the P–5, that they should not be too complacent about the effectiveness of the global non-proliferation regime and the NPT, or about lack of progress towards global nuclear disarmament. For some others, India's ambiguity reflected nothing more than its policy-makers' indecision at the threshold. However, the option to cross the threshold was open and could be implemented under certain circumstances.

For yet others, the 'option' needed to be expanded through technological upgradation, and ambiguity was eminently amenable to that interpretation. For a good chunk of people on the Left, ambiguity was expedient. Acquiescing in it permitted a passive response to official policy and activity. It was a good hold-all, combining protest against the existing unequal global nuclear order, with some preparation to create a 'defensive' nuclear shield (just in case), and a symbol of sovereignty, which must not be 'surrendered' under coercion or pressure of the hegemonic powers; India must *not* give up or foreclose the option unless the P–5 moved in the same direction.

Few Indians, barring a tiny fringe of nuclear disarmament activists called for closing, circumscribing, or limiting the option even by making this conditional upon the pursuit of pro-active disarmament diplomacy, leave alone unilaterally. Such initiatives in favour of nuclear restraint and disarmament as were taken by the Indian government through the late 1970s, throughout the 1980s (especially the Five Continent Initiative, the Rajiv Gandhi Plan of 1988, and the Delhi Declaration Gandhi signed with Mikhail Gorbachev) came 'from above,' not as a result of advocacy and lobbying from outside the government.

What the broadly 'consensual' position on the issue—keep the option open, but don't exercise it—accepted, at least implicitly if not explicitly, was India's 'right' to have and develop its nuclear weapons capability, and create and refine the nuclear weapons option, although it drew the line at exercising it. This meant investing nuclear armaments with a respectable role as repositories of national sovereignty, itself a positive virtue, however separated such sovereignty might be from the people and from democratic accountability. It also meant implicitly granting the Indian government the 'right' to acquire at least *the ability to commit murder on a mass scale*—merely, or at least largely, because other states possessed such instruments of mass destruction and were reluctant to give them up. Or to put it another way: if possessing nuclear weapons is threatening mass murder, then having a weapons capability is to insist on having the 'right' to threaten mass murder even if there is no insistence that this 'right' be exercised. Not only is possessing such weapons immoral; so too is claiming the right to do so!

The assertion of India's 'right' to a weapons capability sat extremely uncomfortably with India's own advocacy of opposition to the use, threat of use, manufacture or possession of nuclear weapons, to the point of declaring all this 'a crime against humanity'. Thus, Indian nuclear ambiguity was morally premised upon highly dubious foundations: revanchism, and matching vice with vice following the endless logic of retribution. It was sustained by a false sense of national pride, and a vacuous Third Worldism—vacuous because it was elitist and desperately dependent on approbation for India as a major world power from the First World. As a Bharatiya Janata Party spokesperson said in 1993, and this is by no means a rare sentiment: 'we don't want to be blackmailed or treated as oriental blackies'.[22] Ergo, we *need* a nuclear weapons capability, if not these horror weapons themselves.

Even someone like Amartya Sen, despite being a moral philosopher, chose not to comment on the anomalies, antinomies, and paradoxes of Indian nuclear ambiguity until after May 1998. In an interview in December 1998, he said, while criticizing the tests as a 'big moral mistake', that

We are thinking of a world in which nuclear weapons are unlikely to be used, so that the moral quality of it is partly a matter of our self-discipline. And the discipline of having the ability to blast nuclear bombs and not doing so has a certain moral quality to it. So this old position India had, whereby it acknowledged that it could make the bomb but nevertheless did not want to pursue a nuclear programme, could be described as having an ethical characteristic, which is now completely lost.[23]

As a factual description, this is not inaccurate. India's stature in the world has indeed declined after May 1998. What is, however, surprising about this, coming as it does from an Indian thinker and moral philosopher as distinguished as Sen, is its not questioning India's 'ability to blast nuclear bombs'—almost as if this were a mere technical attribute, itself socially neutral, and morally value-free. Implicit in that ability is India's descent into the abyss of nuclear-deterrence thinking and her preparedness to visit mass-destruction upon the people of a supposedly adversary state. Surely, the *virtue* of 'discipline'—stopping short of manufacturing the Bomb—is here far less than the vice of launching such preparations, and building the physical and technological foundations for acquiring nuclear weapons!

The Anomalies of Ambiguity

A large number of supporters of Indian nuclear ambiguity emphasized (until the May tests) only one of the two propositions underlying the dual-faced policy. Ambiguity, on the one hand, meant the acquisition (and perhaps further development and upgradation) of a nuclear weapons capability. On the other, it also meant *not* exercising the option by making the weapons *because* such weapons are evil and must not be made, leave alone used. Indian ambiguists tended to stress the first proposition, and that too, often within a framework of militant nationalism. They would routinely interrogate the government in power on whether it had 'surrendered' or 'capitulated' to the American pressure to 'cap, roll back and eventually eliminate' India's capability. They would however rarely urge nuclear restraint, or ask for a solemn pledge that India would never cross the threshold. Thus in 1994, when a newspaper disclosed that an Indian delegation was about to start the fourth round of bilateral talks on the nuclear issue with the Americans in London, there was an uproar in Parliament. Deeply embarrassed, the government all but cancelled the talks. The diplomatic exchange in London was reduced to tokenist, formal, statements and restatements of known positions. What few ambiguists did, even when the hawkish turn on the debate over the Comprehensive Test Ban Treaty became glaringly obvious in 1996, was to *state* the second proposition (that India should *not* exercise the nuclear option), leave alone articulate the strong moral and political arguments underlying that stance. It was convenient to assume that India would *not* cross the threshold. (Many in the élite would say the government of the day would not 'have the guts' to do so.)

Since the logic of stopping at the threshold was never stated, a moral vacuum developed and grew, which was quickly filled by assertive hawks, both within and outside the government, for whom 'defying' the unequal global nuclear order by blocking the CTBT, refusing all proposals, including eminently persuasive and reasonable ones in favour of nuclear restraint, and pushing for an Indian nuclear deterrent against imagined potential threats, became a talisman of national sovereignty and independent policy-making. The BJP, with its own toxic, aggressive nationalism, and its long-standing obsessive fascination with nuclear weapons, seized on this, much to the hawks' delight.

Apologists for India's nuclear weapons, and for the violent shift in New Delhi's stated nuclear doctrine that took place in May 1998 have advanced a range of *ex post facto* rationalizations on the government's behalf. Most of them are as hollow, unconvincing and mutually contradictory as the different arguments emanating from officialdom: that nuclearization was the 'logical' response to the Chinese/Pakistani threat (or a combined one from both Beijing and Islamabad), that it was India's protest against the unequal global nuclear order and the reluctance of the P–5 to give up their dependence on nuclear weapons, etc. The only difference was that the non-official apologists went to absurd lengths to invent fanciful reasons: e.g. Pakistan was about to test, so India did it; the tests were only a means of reshaping the global nuclear order; and that India's nuclearization was the consequence of the end of the Cold War and the loss of a reliable ally in the shape of the USSR, etc. (So much for non-alignment and the pursuit of an *independent* foreign and security policy!)

Some of the hawkish arguments are morally perverse and distinguished by a peculiar depravity: they cite Gandhi in justification for the utterly cynical and wholly immoral decision to cross the threshold. K. Subrahmanyam, one of India's most committed nuclear hawks, who has called periodically for the Bomb since the early 1960s, provides a prime example of such perversity. It is worth mentioning this not so much for the persuasive power of his arguments, which is feeble, but only because he is an important member, and convenor, of the Advisory Board of India's newly constituted National Security Council, and a prolific writer long in the service of nuclear weapons. Subrahmanyam tries to extend the Gandhian notion of non-violence and non-violent resistance, not just to conventional military conflict—which it would be hard to do—but to nuclear weapons. He actually claims that it is possible to derive a justification for India's Bombs from Gandhian premises about the justness of the struggle against the 'unjust hegemonic and racist [nuclear] status quo'. Because nuclear weapons are used 'as a currency of power, nuclear proliferation has become an instrumentality [sic] of hegemony and the present nuclear security paradigm and nuclear apartheid are patently unjust.'[24]

Gandhi's 'Second Assassination'

Subrahmanyam even invents the wholly ludicrous notion of 'non-violent nuclear resistance'—as chilling an oxymoron as there ever was. The idea of 'turning the other cheek', of satyagraha, of winning the opponent over by demonstrating exceptional moral courage and determination, is here transformed into nuclear muscle-flexing, tit-for-tat retribution, demonstration of the arrogance of the militantly strong, but morally weak and cowardly. If the key element in Gandhi's 'non-violent resistance' lies in the refusal of the oppressed to use the weapons of the oppressor, and instead forge an altogether new instrument of resistance, Subrahmanyam's scheme rests on *imitating* the perpetrators of 'nuclear apartheid' by mimicking with slavish loyalty their doctrines and nuclear theology.

That is bad enough. What is worse, Subrahmanyam is wholly unmindful of the blatant contradiction entailed in speaking of non-violence and nuclear weapons—the ultimate instruments of violence and annihilation—in the same breath. This marriage between the two opposites is facilitated by so slight and flimsy a factor—'a hedge against hegemony' of the P–5, and the 'imposition' upon India of the CTBT—that it barely bears mention. But then, Subrahmanyam, like most hawkish devotees of nuclearism, is unburdened by logical consistency: he blithely uses expressions such as Gandhi's successful use of 'non-violence in its offensive mode to compel the British to quit India.' Positions like these would be worth arguing against if they were based at least on an attempt to explain what is meant by *non-violence in its offensive mode* through historical illustrations or even by analogy, if not rational analysis and argument. Alas, they entail no more than pure assertion, a stringing together of words; mere phrases meant to rationalize the rise of nuclear belligerence in India.

Subrahmanyam's procedure is typical of the petty, insecure, middle class Indian mind that longs for recognition of the Indian élite as something more than a bunch of 'oriental blackies'. He selectively cites certain passages from Gandhi, in particular from a short monograph by Dieter Rothermund, a German scholar, to 'show' that Gandhi refrained from severe criticism of the US using nuclear weapons since he feared that the power of the bomb could be used to dominate the world and impose a mandate on developing countries. He correctly anticipated that big powers could join together to dominate the world—which is today seen in the legitimization of nuclear weapons and imposition of the non-proliferation treaty. Dr Dieter Rothermund infers that Gandhiji came out strongly against nuclear weapons only when it became clear that India would become independent.[25]

The first half of this argument is based on a non sequitur. Why should Gandhi not have criticized the US action in Hiroshima, especially if he feared that the Bomb would be used in pursuit of world domination? He would have done so *a fortiori*. As for the second statement, even if it is assumed that Gandhi saw nuclear weapons as instruments of hegemony, it scarcely follows that he would make his own pronouncements on the Bomb conditional upon India's progress towards Independence. By July 1945, it had become adundantly clear that Indian independence was only a matter of time, and it is therefore difficult to see the link between Independence and Gandhi's view of nuclear weapons.

It appears even less plausible that Gandhi would have even countenanced the thought that resistance to injustice, however grave, is justified in all forms, however violent, unethical and destructive such resistance might be. If modern India had one stickler for the justice of *means* as well as *ends*, it was Gandhi. Subrahmanyam's forays into morally defending the morally indefensible, and doing so through such a distorted use of Gandhi only reveals his own utter moral cynicism about nuclear weapons, and his casual contempt for the *seriousness* of the moral dimension associated with the issue of nuclearism.

Serious scholars of Gandhi who, unlike Subrahmanyam, have read the Mahatma, have an altogether different perception. Gandhi was so stunned by the bombing of Hiroshima and Nagasaki that he did not comment on the event for two weeks. He recognized that nuclear weapons had transformed not just the nature of war, but also of peace. Whenever he spoke on the issue—and he spoke a great deal—he was clear, categorical, and unambiguous about the uniquely evil nature of nuclear weapons and their complete moral unacceptability. He was emphatic about atomic bombs 'deadening the finest feelings that have sustained mankind for centuries' and even described the Allies' victory over the Axis powers as 'empty' on account of the use of nuclear weapons in August 1945.

Y.P. Anand, director of the National Gandhi Museum in Delhi, has compiled 28 references in Gandhi's writings and speeches pertaining to nuclear weapons.[26] A summary of his views reads: Truth and non-violence are more powerful than the atom bomb. The atom bomb is the weapon of ultimate brute force and destruction. Development of the atom bomb represents the most sinful and diabolical use of science. The atom bomb 'mentality' is immoral, unethical, addictive; only evil can come of it. The atom bomb only aggravates violence and never protects anyone against it. It symbolizes the futility of violence. Non-violence is the only antidote against the atom bomb and the only way to canalize hatred and resolve conflicts. It is the duty of large nations, and all other nations, in the interest of world peace, to give up the atom bomb. Gandhi made perhaps his most extensive and articulate statement on the issue in Poona (Pune) in July 1946, on the eve of the first anniversary of the bombing of Hiroshima. This should set at rest all doubts about Gandhi's alleged moral 'ambivalence' regarding nuclear weapons.[27]

The wisdom and humanist passion of the Mahatma on this issue contrasts very sharply with the cynicism, witlessness, illogic, moral chicanery, and intellectual dishonesty of the Bomb's apologists. As an anti-Bomb critic has said: 'They assassinated Gandhi twice, the first time in January 1948, and for the second time in May 1998.' It was not quite an accident that the assassins belonged to the same current: extremist, bellicose, anti-secular Hindu nationalism. It is over Gandhi's dead body—and the body of all the moral ideas he stood for—that the Indian nuclear deterrent was built.

A Distinctive Moral Insensitivity

Perhaps the single most disturbing fact that emerged after the Indian tests (followed by the tests in Pakistan) was the moral insensitivity of India's policy-makers in regard to nuclearism. In no country that had previously gone nuclear was the crossing of the threshold made into such an issue of national pride. The nuclear bombing of Hiroshima and Nagasaki is to this day supported by a majority of US citizens. This is shameful, but the Bombs were viewed with a sense of relief, not pride. They were widely (though incorrectly) seen as helping to bring the Second World War to a rapid end. The Russian and Chinese Bombs were seen internally as necessary responses to the US and there was, of course, the officially organized drumming up of 'patriotic sentiment' typical of the authoritarian undemocratic regimes that existed at the time the first Bombs were developed and exploded in the two countries. In Britain, the public response was far more muted. Indeed, of all the NWSs, in Britain there emerged in the fifties a major anti-nuclear mass movement and sentiment. In France, a significant 'patriotic' sentiment did emerge around nuclear weapons, but there was no euphoria.

In none of the first five NWSs was there anything to parallel or approximate the kind of nationalist euphoria and near-hysterical response that was characteristic of significant sections of upper-caste, upper-class Indian urbanites. The kind of celebratory scenes that were portrayed in the international media gave a misleading impression about the size and depth of popular support to the Indian tests. However, although small, the celebrations were real and disturbing in themselves. If similar behaviour was to be found in Pakistan after their government tested, this is more easily explicable as resulting from the popular belief that Pakistan could now match India. It is the insecurity, immaturity and moral insensitivity of the pro-nuclear Indian élite that is most striking. No one in Pakistan talked of building a mosque in commemoration of the 'grand act', but Hindu nationalist organizations like the VHP declared their determination to build just such a temple to worship Shakti, the goddess of power, in commemoration of the Pokharan-II blasts!

At one level, it is not difficult to understand (without ever condoning) this new élite sense of pride. After all, what else has the Indian élite helped accomplish over the last 20 years that could be a source of national pride? Poverty, illiteracy, institutionalized injustices of all kinds continue to haunt Indian society. To take pride in the possession of what even Indian hawks once used to admit was a 'necessary evil' testified to the existence of a profound moral sclerosis. However necessary one might consider an evil, the fact that it is an evil should preclude celebration or pride at its arrival. But it did not. Equally disturbing was the fact that not a single strategic expert, politician, or media-person among all those who supported the tests criticized the praise (official and non-official) that was showered upon Indian science and scientists following the tests. This was truly extraordinary.

Not one prominent supporter of the Bomb found the intelligence or integrity to say what could easily have been said: That even as he or she supported the tests and India's newly declared status as a nuclear weapons power, he or she lamented the fact that Indian science had to be *misused* and that the skills of 'our wonderful pool of scientists' had to be *abused* to produce these evil weapons (when we would have preferred to use their skills for so much more worthwhile ends) because India felt compelled for security reasons to follow the path of other NWSs which had similarly abused science and the skills of their own scientific community. To have said as much, even while supporting Indian nuclearization, would have at least shown a recognition of the proper relationship between science and ethics. That no prominent pro-Bomb person stated this obvious truth was a striking testimony to the collective absence of a reasonable level of moral sobriety, balance and sensitivity.[28]

Influential sections of the Indian and Pakistani media selectively played up the 'popularity' of the Bomb. Based on no more than a few casual phone calls, one of them reported that 91 per cent of Indians support India's nuclear weapons. The DAE and DRDO scientists and engineers responsible for Pokharan-II were instantly turned into heroes and glamour figures. The circumstance that they disguised their identities, misled their families on their whereabouts, and wore military fatigues, was celebrated as a great achievement. Awards and prizes were showered upon them even as they openly advocated the creation of a 'military–industrial complex' and 'defence-based development'.

Celebrating Mass Destruction

This explosion of national chauvinism and celebration of the militarization of science was of course unprecedented. Its foundations had, however, been laid earlier. Raja Ramanna, who headed the 'research' team responsible for the first Pokharan test, was similarly lionized in 1974. And A.P.J. Abdul Kalam, who was in large measure responsible for the success of India's Integrated Guided Missile Development Programme, which produced the *Prithvi* and *Agni* missiles, was awarded India's highest official honour, the Bharat Ratna, in 1992. This puts him in the same league as India's Nobel Prize winners such as Amartya Sen (Economics, 1998) and C.V. Raman (Physics, 1930). The bestowal of such exceptional honour and status emboldened many practitioners of defence-related science and technology to become more assertive and demand a higher allocation of funds to their projects. The militarization of India's science is a distressing trend. Space, nuclear energy and the DRDO account for two-thirds of all public spending on research and development.

Even the President of India, K.R. Narayanan, a man of the 'old Nehruvian school', and justly and widely respected as a person of political integrity and decency, joined in this shameful burst of chauvinistic euphoria without recognizing the deep contradiction entailed. Narayanan, a former diplomat has, of course, always had a weak spot for nuclear deterrence-based thinking. He earlier supported ambiguity and in May 1998 the tests. There is no reason to believe this was not also his personal view, asserted again in the course of a TV interview to N. Ram, editor of *Frontline*, on the eve of the 15 August 1998 Independence Day celebrations.

It would be facile but false to claim that those who support deterrence and nuclearism in some fashion are more immoral than those who oppose it. What is argued is not that indecent and immoral people uphold nuclearism while moral people (who can also have terribly immoral positions and attitudes on a host of other issues) do not, but that acceptance of the discourse of nuclearism morally desensitizes and benumbs otherwise humane and decent people. Each human being has a moral personality, and this includes even the hardcore Realist who believes that international politics is an amoral affair. (Incidentally, this is also a moral position or claim!). Supporting the immoral always diminishes us in some way, small or large; it deforms our moral personalities. The most common reaction of those who so diminish their moral stature is to deny the diminution altogether or at least to minimize its import.

Indian supporters of the Bomb failed to stress the proper relationship between science and ethics because it did not really occur to them that by showering praise upon the Bomb and its makers they were guilty of a serious moral lapse. They lost, or hid from themselves, the moral sensitivity and balance on the nuclear issue that should have been retained at least in some small measure.

This raises a central point about the nature of the discourse of evil. Primo Levi, one of the wisest witnesses to the Holocaust, himself a survivor of Hitler's concentration camps, explained the way ordinary Germans, at least an overwhelming number of them, aware of the horrific manner in which Jews were being treated, nonetheless did not allow this to affect them seriously. Levi talked of the 'banality of evil', of how the sheer frequency, regularity and repetition of evil violence, as well as the persistent and routine rationalization and justification of its sources, mechanisms and effects in 'normal' political and intellectual discourse—that is to say, the processes by which such violence is made banal—serves to utterly dilute, even disguise the evil in question. To this end the medium of so much of human thought—language—is itself manipulated to fulfil this function! Language is used to make the human seem inhuman and to humanize the inhuman. In wartime, the 'enemy' is called dehumanizing names, e.g. 'Gooks' and 'Charlies' in Vietnam, to help make their 'elimination' more morally palatable. The same phenomenon exists in the everyday language of racism and sexism.

The language and discourse of nuclearism is not only inescapably masculinist, aggressive and morally callous but also deceptive, euphemistic and misleading. The nuclearist discourse embodies both these dehumanizing and falsely humanizing dimensions, hence all the talk of 'collateral damage', 'acceptable levels of damage', 'atomic diplomacy', etc. US scientists called the first explosive device (July 1945) the 'Gadget', while the first bombs dropped on Japan were named 'Little Boy' and 'Fat Man'. The Soviets called their first bomb 'The Article'. Britain called its first nuclear explosion 'Hurricane', France the 'Blue Mouse', while China called its first nuclear weapon 'Device 596'.

India code-named the successful conduct of the 1974 explosion 'The Smiling Buddha', while the 1998 tests were simply called 'Shakti' or power.

The general discourse of nuclearism helps make the morally unthinkable thinkable. It does more. It helps routinize and make banal the evil nature of nuclear weapons and nuclear deterrence. When we support or oppose the possession or use or threat or capability of having nuclear weapons (just as when we support or oppose slavery and its justifications), we are, each one of us, making a moral statement that helps shape our own personalities and lives. This affects in howsoever small a way other lives and the structures around us.

Opposing nuclear weapons is not merely a personal matter. There are certain universal evils that must be recognized as such. They debase all of humanity: those that seek to benefit from them as well as those who are their purported or actual victims. Such is the case with evils like apartheid, colonialism, and nuclearism, all of which involve insensate violence. They are often justified in the name of 'national security', 'the national interest', 'national greatness', etc. We cannot create a sustainable and durable nuclear-free world unless we value our common humanity and sustain a shared anger for such universal evils as nuclearism. It is only on the basis of this shared but controlled anger and passion whose wellsprings are our individual moral capacities that we can hope to build a wider consciousness across national boundaries. That alone can help bring about the goal of complete and global nuclear disarmament.

To forget the horror and shame of what happened at Hiroshima and Nagasaki, and to fail to draw moral as well as political lessons from it, is to debase and degrade our common and universal humanity.

Notes

1. Robert Jay Lifton and Richard Falk, *Indefensible Weapons,* Basic Books, New York, 1982, p. ix.
2. This discussion owes a great deal to the moral argument developed by Michael Walzer in his very useful *Just and Unjust Wars,* Basic Books, New York, 1977.
3. Ted Honderich, *Violence for Equality*, Penguin Books, Harmondsworth, 1980, p.35.
4. See Stephen I. Schwartz (ed), *Atomic Audit: The Costs and Consequences of U.S. Nuclear Weapons since 1940,* The Brookings Institution, New York, 1998.
5. Rawls, *A Theory of Justice*, quoted in Walzer, op. cit., p. 229.
6. Walzer, op. cit., pp. 228–32.
7. ibid. p. 231.
8. ibid. p. 283.

9. ibid. p. 283.
10. See, for example, K. Subrahmanyam, 'Hedging Against Hegemony: Gandhi's Logic in the Nuclear Age', *The Times of India*, New Delhi, 16 June 1998.
11. Excerpted in 'The Morality of Nuclear Deterrence: An Evaluation by Pax Christi Bishops in the U.S.', *INESAP Bulletin*, No. 16, Darmstadt, November 1998, pp. 53–4. Flawed as it is, this is one of the few serious arguments about the morality of nuclear weapons to emerge from any religious tradition. Most theological schools have not confronted the moral issue of nuclear weapons at all.
12. ibid. p. 53.
13. ibid. p. 53.
14. Cited in Rikhi Jaipal, *Nuclear Arms and the Human Race*, Allied Publishers, New Delhi, 1986, p. 61.
15. ibid.
16. Written Statement of the Government of India, 'Status of Nuclear Weapons in International Law: Request for Advisory Opinion of the International Court of Justice', mimeo, Ministry of External Affairs, Government of India, New Delhi, 1995, p. 3.
17. ibid. p. 7.
18. 'Statement' by Salman Haidar, Foreign Secretary of India, at the Plenary Meeting of the Conference on Disarmament, Geneva, 21 March 1996, p. 2.
19. ibid. p. 3.
20. Aqueil Ahmed and Falguni Sen, 'Scientists & Science Policy Formulation: Indian Scientists' View of the Indian Nuclear Explosion', *Journal of Scientific and Industrial Research*, vol. 35, August 1976, pp. 497–501.
21. Ramanna confirmed that the Pokharan-I device 'was a bomb. I can tell you now', cited in A.G. Noorani, 'Many Questions, Few Answers', *Frontline*, Chennai, 20 November 1998, p. 79.
22. Cited in George Perkovich, 'Nuclear Proliferation', *Foreign Policy*, New York, Fall 1998, p. 15. Statements of this kind, often even stronger in tone, are commonly heard in élite circles in India and Pakistan.
23. Quoted in interview with *Frontline*, Chennai, 15 January 1999, p. 50.
24. K. Subrahmanyam, op. cit.
25. ibid.
26. Y.P. Anand, *What Mahatma Gandhi Said About the Atom Bomb*, National Gandhi Museum, New Delhi, 1998, p. 6.
27. Cited in 'The Atom Bomb and Ahimsa' in Kai Bird and Lawrence Lifschultz (eds), *Hiroshima's Shadow*, The Pamphleteer's Press, Story Creek, Conn., 1998 pp. 258–59.
28. Even the two early public statements that were signed by Indian scientists (the first carried 74 signatures, the second over two hundred) opposing the tests and released to the national media, missed this crucial point. While these statements correctly pointed out that the supposed technological achievement was nothing of the sort (first generation bomb-making is a dated, fairly low- level technology),

they did not point out the vital and obvious relationship between science and ethics and therefore the obscenity of showering praise on Indian science or scientists. Just as disappointing was the fact that the two mainstream Left parties, the CPI and the CPM, while opposing the tests, nonetheless found it neccesary in their initial official statements condemning the tests, to implicitly endorse Indian science and the scientists for their technological achievement.

CHAPTER SEVEN

An Unaffordable Arsenal

The Likely Costs of a 'Credible Minimum Deterrent'

Apart from the intrinsic, generic, indefensibility and immorality of nuclear weapons as instruments of war, they pose yet another serious ethical problem. This is the consequential immorality involved in the wholesale distortion of social, economic, and political priorities in the states that acquire, deploy, and stockpile nuclear weapons. All the five countries that went overtly nuclear between 1945 and 1964 spent enormous sums of money on the production, deployment, targeting, defence, supervision, and control of their nuclear weapons and delivery systems, as well as on building the infrastructure that would generate the fissile material, warheads, aircraft, missiles, and command and control systems necessary for their nuclear programmes. These expenditures acquired truly awesome proportions during the late 1960s, and then again during the Second Cold War, inaugurated by President Ronald Reagan in the 1980s. Ironically, although expenditures on nuclear weapons acquisition, maintenance, upgradation, and modernization have (expectedly) fallen from the peaks of the 1980s, they still remain extremely high in absolute terms a decade *after* the end of the Cold War.

Nuclear arsenals have tended to defy all rational calculation of security risks and ways of meeting them. At the heart of their persistence is hostility, enmity or distrust between powerful states, and competitive confrontation between them, driven by technology, mercantile interests, powerful bureaucracies, and mighty military apparatuses. E.P. Thompson described the process of sustaining this enmity and confrontation: 'the armourers excite the other's armourers, the hawks feed the hawks, the ideologists rant at each other like rival auctioneers, and the missiles copulate with each other, and breed on each other's foul bodies the next generation of missiles'.

The distortions of nuclearism—obsessive reliance on these weapons of mass annihilation—are not confined to the economic sphere alone. They extend to the environment, public health, and to political processes, through the subversion of democratic principles and institutions. The production and stockpiling of nuclear weapons over the past five decades has posed serious security risks to all of humanity. More, it has meant unleashing 'a kind of secret low-intensity radioactive warfare ... against unsuspecting populations', as Bernard Lown, co-founder and emeritus co-chair of International Physicians for the Prevention of Nuclear War, has put it.

Nuclear programmes everywhere have involved secrecy and deception, centralization of enormous power and authority (including managerial, investigative, quasi-judicial, and quasi-executive powers) in small élite groups and institutions, such as atomic energy commissions, the military top brass, weapons laboratories, and operators of facilities related to the entire 'nuclear fuel cycle', with very little or no public scrutiny. This violates the democratic principles of transparency and the public's right to know what decisions are taken on its behalf, by whom and why. Nuclear weapons programmes have also been associated with chauvinism, militarism, extreme intolerance, and jingoism. Nuclearism is inseparable from male-supremacist sexism.

Nuclear weapons production has had a terrible impact on the health of ocupational workers in nuclear facilities, people living near nuclear industry installations and test sites, and unsuspecting victims of experimentation on human beings with radioactive materials. Nuclear weapons production has also seriously affected the environment through the deliberate dumping of highly radioactive wastes, accidental releases of harmful nuclear materials and toxic chemicals, contamination of water bodies, acquifers, vegetation and animal life in different parts of the world well outside the boundaries of the nuclear weapons states. In the US alone, a Department of Energy study estimates, the costs of cleaning up the mess left by nuclear weapons production will be $260 billion. This figure is roughly four-fifths of, i.e. of the same order of magnitude, as the entire annual gross national product of India, home to nearly a billion people.

The consequential immorality of nuclear weapons appears particularly stark in India and Pakistan, because they are two of the world's poorest countries, whose rulers have comprehensively failed to provide even a modicum of real security to the vast majority of their peoples. Yet policy-makers in the subcontinent, as well as many opinion-shapers, have indulged in the delusion that nuclear weapons are relatively inexpensive, and in any case, will not be a heavy burden on their economies. Bomb lobbies in India and Pakistan have consciously played down the costs of nuclear weapons programmes. We argue that these would be unconscionably high; they would entail a huge diversion of scarce resources away from the need-based priorities of development; and they could prove economically ruinous to both economies.

Nuclear weapons programmes have proved extremely expensive in the P–5 states, where they tended to do add anything between 20 and 50 per cent to the existing military budget. Secrecy about the exact size of nuclear weapons arsenals and missile programmes, as well as scarcity of facts about the sharing of military infrastructures between nuclear and conventional armaments, makes it difficult to put a precise figure on each item of expenditure in all the five nuclear weapons programmes. However, there are some excellent, detailed, estimates of expenditures by the US, in a landmark study by the Brookings Institution, *Atomic Audit*, and some hard numbers about the other NWSs, especially Britain and France.[1]

Blowing Up $5500 billion

Atomic Audit estimates that between 1940 and 1996, the US spent (at 1996 values) $5500 billion on its nuclear weapons programme. If the (future) costs of dismantling nuclear bombs and environmental remediation are added, the programme's bill jumps to $5821 billion. The per capita expenditure in the US till 1996 works out to $21,646. This is over *four times* the world's average per capita annual income in 1998. To visualize what this astronomical sum means, it would take 184,579 years to count to this amount if $1 was counted off every second. If bricks were made of 200 one dollar notes per inch, and stacked on top of one another, the $5821 billion would stretch all the way to the Moon and nearly all the way back.

Some of the astounding conclusions of the Brookings study are:

- The US spent 'only' $409 billion to build Bombs, or seven per cent of the total cost of the nuclear weapons programme.
- As much as $3,241 billion was spent on the delivery systems (55.7 per cent of the programme cost).
- A hefty $831.1 billion was claimed by the command, control, communications, and intelligence infrastructure (14.3 per cent of the total cost).
- An absurdly high $937.2 billion was spent on 'defending the bomb', by means such as creating vast physical structures including 1500 underground shelters.

This $5500 billion expenditure accounted for 29 per cent of America's total military budget. In other words, the Bomb represented an addition of 40.8 per cent *over and above* conventional military spending. The cost of the nuclear programme exceeded the total expenditure by the US government on all other categories of spending barring 'non-nuclear national defence' and 'social security'. It also exceeded that government's spending on six important sectors put together, including health, education, the environment, space research, and law enforcement. The opportunity cost is truly staggering. Had the US spent even half of the $98 billion that it committed to the Bomb each year on an average between 1940 and 1996, it would have wiped out every trace of poverty and deprivation in that highly dualistic and unequal society.

At the other end of the spectrum within the P–5, China, the weakest nuclear power of the five, has already spent over $100 billion on its modest arsenal. In the decade that *preceded* the 1964 test, China's spending on its nuclear weapons *preparations* alone, was the equivalent of $28 billion (at 1996 prices). In France, expenditure on nuclear weapons ran at between 0.4 and 1.2 per cent of GDP between 1964 and 1992. At its height, weaponization in a single year (1967) alone claimed $1.9 billion (in 1987 dollars) or today's equivalent of $2.6 billion. The UK programme has not only been poorly audited, but according to the Campaign for Nuclear Disarmament (CND), it would have to spend something of the order of £1.5 billion ($2.5 billion) a year to operate the small, now pruned, 'Trident' nuclear deterrent comprising only four submarines.

What would an Indian nuclear weapons programme cost? Assuming that India is to build only a 'minimum deterrent'—i.e. one that is not a fully-fledged nuclear arsenal geared to win in an actual war-fighting situation, or one that remotely aspires to match China in its firepower, the costs will be formidable, if not ruinous, even if there is a great deal of technological leapfrogging and saving on many items of spending. At the very least, in the absence of a nuclear arms race, the costs would work out to about $10 billion spread over five to seven years. This would mean *raising* India's already high *military spending by 20 to 50 per cent a year*, depending on how fast a so-called 'minimum deterrent' is put in place. These estimates are for a bare-bones, no-frills nuclear weapons programmes: 'a poor man's deterrent', with relatively low reliability, very little back-up, and deep uncertainty about survivability.

Although $10 billion appears puny in absolute terms, it corresponds to about three per cent of India's GDP—the equivalent of what the entire country annually spends on such a basic need as primary education. As it happens, the sum also corresponds to what it would cost to provide universal access to primary education to all children between 6 and 14 years of age. No wonder then that after the May 1998 tests, India's education ministry quietly decided to slow down the 'universalization of primary education' programme, even as the government raised the military spending allocation by 14 per cent.

How much will Indian Nuclear Weapons Cost: Conservative Estimates

The $10 billion figure has been arrived at on the basis of a number of extremely conservative assumptions made by nuclear hawks and government agencies that have a stake in 'sweetening' the bitter nuclear pill by underestimating the real costs of a so-called 'credible minimum deterrent'. Although the Indian government has refused to spell out the size of such a force, various military sources, most notably the late General Krishnaswamy Sundarji, former army chief, took this to mean roughly 150 nuclear fission bombs, with a yield of 15-20 kiloton (kt) equivalent of TNT, similar to the ones dropped on Hiroshima and Nagasaki.

This assumes that India would need to develop the ability to destroy five cities in Pakistan and 10 population centres in China with three bombs each, and a small second strike capability. The number of warheads/bombs assumed here corresponds to 'the former AEC official Sethna's own figure of 150 bombs for a credible deterrent' mentioned in a recently declassified US state department telegram to the US embassy in New Delhi of 1966.

This is a truly modest nuclear strike force by P–5 standards. It represents just about one-third to one-fifth of the number of warheads in China's nuclear arsenal. The costs of each of these no-frills bombs are assumed to be just $1 million each, although the Brookings study puts the range at $1 to 2 million. Similarly, the costs of production of plutonium (of which roughly 800 kg will be needed in addition to existing holdings) are assumed to be very low: Rs 700 crores (or $170 million) for a dedicated reactor (capital cost).

The 'minimum deterrent' is also assumed to have triadic delivery systems: aircraft, ground-based missiles, and submarine-launched missiles. This means refitting a squadron of 24 aircraft to carry nuclear bombs, procuring three to five nuclear-powered submarines, 50–60 *Prithvi* missiles, 50–60 *Agni,* and an extended-range *Agni* version, still in the preliminary stage of development, and 15–20 *Sagarikas,* a 300 km cruise missile under development for launch from the sea.

There are no reliable estimates in the Indian case of the next most expensive component of a nuclear weapons programme, namely a command, control, communications and intelligence (C^3I) infrastructure. Typically, this alone accounts for the equivalent of a fifth to a seventh of what the rest of the nuclear programme costs. Even assuming that the fairly arbitrary and probably low estimate made by a nuclear weapons advocate, Brigadier Vijai Nair in 1992, is correct, a C^3I system will cost the equivalent of $1 billion.

This does appear to be a gross underestimate. A 1985 exercise undertaken by a group set up by the Indian defence ministry, comprising senior military personnel and nuclear establishment heads, projected the cost of a nuclear programme with a few hundred missiles and warheads (but apparently without a significant C^3I system). It turned up an estimate of Rs 7000 crores ($1.7 billion). In 1998 rupees, this would amount to Rs 20,000 crores ($5 billion) today. Assuming that a C^3I system, with a relatively large import component—much larger than in the case of missiles or warheads—will cost about the same, the cost of the nuclear weapons programme as a whole would work out to $10 billion.

Even on the lowest possible estimates for the C^3I system and for a defence system for the nuclear arsenal (with phased array radars and anti-missile and -aircraft batteries), research and development, etc, the figure for a 'credible deterrent' works out to Rs 40,000 to Rs 50,000 crores ($10 to 12 billion) (See Table 1), according to Ram Manohar Reddy, an economist and journalist. This table below lists some of the costs.

TABLE 1

Investment Costs of Nuclear Weaponization

	Rs. (in millions)
1. One reactor to produce plutonium	7,000
2. One missile production facility	5,000
3. Cost of a 150-bomb arsenal	6,000
4. Cost of missiles	40,250
55 *Prithvis*	3,850
30 *Agnis*	15,000
25 *Agni*-IIs	15,000
16 *Sagarikas*	6,400
5. Cost of fitting one IAF squadron	600
6. Cost of 3 n-submarines	120,000
7. Cost of C^3I	35,250+
8. Cost of two satellites	20,000
9. Cost of radar, missiles, etc. to protect airbases/launch sites	50,000
Total	280,000

SOURCE: C. Ram Manohar Reddy, *The Hindu*, 2 September 1998.

On an annualized basis, this would be the equivalent of 0.5 per cent to 1 per cent of India's GDP, or a rise of 25 to 40 per cent over India's current military spending.

All this assumes, quite unrealistically, that there will be no nuclear arms racing, and that the additional costs of operating and maintaining the nuclear arsenal will be more or less negligible because they will be accommodated within the existing military budget with minor systems modifications. However, whether there is an arms race or not cannot be determined by India alone, but would also depend on India's adversaries. If China revives its Dong Feng-25 development programme and actively targets Indian cities, New Delhi would come under enormous pressure to speed up and raise the level of nuclear deployment. The history of the Nuclear Age is nothing if not the sequence of competitive rivalry, of one adversary raising the level of preparation and threat, 'provoking' the rival to do the same; a vicious spiral leading to ever-increasing accumulation of weapons. If India gets sucked into this spiral, it could end up spending, like the former USSR did, over 1.5 per cent of its GDP on nuclear weapons alone. This could be ruinous. India cannot possibly match China in the size or firepower of its nuclear arsenal in the immediate future: China has a 30 year lead as a nuclear and missile power, and an economy that is three times larger in absolute size.

As the full costs of deployment unfold, the Indian government, with its meagre resources, will be tempted to cut corners on the accuracy, safety, reliability and eventually, the size of its nuclear programme, especially of the costly C^3I system. This will effectively degrade the strength of the Indian deterrent, and especially its second-strike capability. This could become a case of 'ramshackle deterrence', which makes the country vulnerable to a nuclear strike without being able effectively and reliably to deter an adversary power. Deployment could thus be a Faustian bargain in every sense of the term, including from the conventional military point of view.

Missed Opportunities

The Indian government, with a fiscal deficit of the order of six per cent of the GDP and with a falling ratio of total taxes to GDP, can ill-afford any increase in military spending. Already, the national government's spending on the military is more than double its expenditure on health, education, and other social sectors put together. Indeed, as Amartya Sen has argued, there is a strong case for *reducing* India's existing military expenditures. The opportunity costs of a nuclear weapons programme must not be underrated. The cost of each nuclear bomb corresponds to the cost of building 3200 modest houses under Indian conditions. The expenditure on each *Agni* missile can finance the running of 13,000 primary health centres, which are in a state of advanced decay in the country. There is a straight trade-off between a 'minimal nuclear deterrent', on the one hand, and universalization of primary education or an improved public health programme, on the other.

The costs of a programme of manufacturing and deploying nuclear weapons and missiles would prove even more onerous in Pakistan, which has had persistent budget deficits of 6 to 9 per cent over the past decade. Pakistan currently spends about 5 per cent of its GDP on the military, more than it does on *all* development programmes *put together*. According to Zia Mian, 'In fact, 1990 was the last year when military spending equalled the allocation for the annual development programme. Since then, development spending has fallen as compared to military spending.'[2] Pakistan's foreign debt today is $32 billion, well over one-half of its GDP, and the annual debt servicing burden runs at $5 billion.

India and Pakistan rank among the lowest of the 174 countries listed by the UN Development Programme's Human Development Index: Pakistan's rank in the human development index fell from 120 in 1992 to 138 in 1999, while India's rank has hovered in the 130s from 1995 to 1999. This is not a function of poverty alone, but involves horrendous neglect and callousness towards basic human needs as well as distorted public spending priorities. Nuclearization will further distort these priorities, reducing the people's real security.

TABLE 2

Human Development Indicators for India and Pakistan

	India	Pakistan
Life expectancy, years	61.6	62.8
Infant mortality rate, per 1,000 births	73	95
Child (under 5 years old) morality, per 1,000 births	111	136
Malnourished children, %	53	38
Without access to safe water, %	19	26
Without access to sanitation, %	71	53
Literacy rate (%)	52	38

SOURCE: *Human Development Report, 1998,* Oxford University Press, Delhi.

Notes

1. Stephen I. Schwartz (ed), *Atomic Audit: The Costs and Consequences of US Nuclear Weapons since 1940'*, Brookings Institution, Washington, DC, 1998.
2. Zia Mian, 'The South Asian Bomb: The Politics of South Asia's Nuclear Crisis' *Medicine & Global Survival*, Cambridge, USA, October 1998, Vol 5, Issue 2, p. 78.

CHAPTER EIGHT

The Deterrence Delusion

Why Nuclear Weapons Do Not Generate Security

There is no moral justification for the possession, deployment, production or use of nuclear weapons. Only the most ruthless, arrogant or foolhardy of pro-nuclearists would even attempt to provide some kind of moral justification for their use. Most avoid contestation on this terrain, even to the point of conceding 'victory' to the anti-nuclearist case on this score. Instead, they are content to make the supposed efficacy of nuclear deterrence the centrepiece of their intellectual–strategic–political case for why their country or any country should produce and possess nuclear weapons. There are other arguments that are also advanced. One particular favourite is that nuclear weapons are a currency or symbol of power and as such politically and diplomatically useful in the world we live in. However, since ensuring 'national security' is the principal purpose for having such weapons, the most fundamental and enduring justification remains the stock of arguments centred on deterrence. Indeed, the case for nuclear weapons is so strongly pivoted on this issue that it stands or falls with the strengths or weaknesses of the arguments for or against deterrence.

This much is so well-understood by advocates of nuclear disarmament that the literature uncovering the weaknesses of nuclear deterrence thinking and practice is truly enormous. This is the most common and standard terrain of critique. What is less clearly recognized, however, is that there is a more comprehensive level of critique that rarely makes its way into the anti-nuclear discourse. This is for the simple reason that most people opposed to nuclear weapons nonetheless operate within the same general framework or paradigm of thinking about national security matters as pro-nuclearists do. Where they differ is in rejecting the view that nuclear weapons enhance security because they dispute the proposition that nuclear deterrence has the effectiveness attributed to it.

This chapter will certainly explore the familiar ground of arguments for and against deterrence because this is where the case against nuclear weapons can achieve the widest resonance, influence, and agreement. But it will also, albeit briefly, explore the other, deeper level of criticism.

The Problem of Realism

Votaries of nuclear deterrence think the way they do largely because they think about national security and its relationship to the world order in a certain way. This way of thinking has a name in the academic literature on International Relations. It is called Political Realism.[1] The spread of this kind of thinking is so wide amongst those who do think about international political, strategic or security issues that only a few among the more academically inclined even recognize that it is just one paradigm amongst others, and as such its value should be judged only after comparison with the merits and demerits of other ways or paradigms of understanding the global system, international relations, collective security, etc. Most adherents to Realism simply see it as 'universal common sense'.

The basic postulates that make up this 'vision' are as follows:

The global system is anarchic since the absence of an acknowledged world authority or government means there is no supreme seat of power (the role played by the apparatuses of the state within a country) which can maintain order or arbitrate between conflicting interests, values and aims. Thus the world order is a self-help system in which states are the primary actors. They are also to be considered as unitary and rational actors. In effect, the world system is an inter-state system where each state must pursue its own national interest and security objectives, above all (territorial) survival. In order to successfully do this, a state must accumulate power. Power is so important a means for achieving the goals of security or national interests that it can be seen virtually as an end in itself. However, the distribution of power between different states is extremely uneven and therefore the general shape or contours of the world system is determined by only a few states which are 'Great Powers'.

Thus the world can be described as unipolar, bipolar, or multipolar depending on the number of Great Powers where multipolarity should be understood as only meaning more than two or three Great Powers but not that many more. It is essentially the interaction between existing Great Powers that gives the world system its shape. The more stable this interaction the more stable the world system. Thus Great Powers necessarily have 'global responsibilities' thrust upon them. Longer term historical changes in this global system are related to the fall of Great Powers and the rise of new ones. Within this inescapable inter-state system which has endured for centuries, ultimately the most important form of power is military power because war is the last resort attempt at decisive arbitration and is itself a recurring human and political phenomenon from which no state or part of the world system can ever finally escape.

The most important way in which relatively weaker states cope with the others having more power than themselves is through the diplomatic game of seeking and establishing alliances with other states, alliances which themselves will shift as relations of power between different states shift. Thus the key priorities for any country involved in this game of 'competitive power politics' or 'realpolitik' must be, above all, two things—maintain and enhance strong military power, and play the diplomatic game of shifting alliances as skilfully as possible. Obviously, the central mechanism for maintaining stability, security and maximum influence in this anarchic global system is to secure and maintain the appropriate 'balances of power'. The balance of power, then, is the organizing principle which should guide the behaviour of the 'national security establishments' of the main state-actors in this world arena of the competitive power game.[2]

After adding whatever qualifications or nuances one might wish to this set of assumptions, this constitutes the dominant common sense of the strategic community in all the nuclear weapons states. Belief in the efficacy and importance of nuclear deterrence flows almost naturally from such a Realist perspective. In the nuclear age, security must be sought in the achievement of *nuclearized* balances of power through reliance on 'stable deterrence'. Insofar as nuclear rivalry between countries introduces elements of great uncertainty and arms escalation, the answer to this problem is not to be found in abandoning the trust placed in deterrence and nuclear weapons but in ensuring that this rivalry takes a controlled, predictable, and stable pattern. Diplomatic activity to organize arms control between nuclear rivals is thus a necessary part of the logic imposed by the existence of more than one nuclear regime. Pro-nuclearists then, will simultaneously pursue, (1) the steady upgradation of weapons production; (2) institutionalized arms control between nuclearly equipped rivals; and (3) formal and meaningless assurances of their continuing commitment to the goal of eventual global disarmament.

This is not the place for a comprehensive critique of the Realist paradigm.[3] It will suffice for our purposes to point out some of its basic flaws in the hope that many who are otherwise opposed to nuclear weapons might be stimulated to question and reject the mind-set that constitutes its deepest port of anchorage. Among the conceptual flaws that lie at the heart of the Realist paradigm are its mistaken understandings of state, power, and the global system though these three are the central concepts on which it constructs its 'world view'. Indeed, hardcore Realists who come mostly from the six or seven professions which make up the 'national security establishment'—soldier, diplomat, politician, bureaucrat, scientocrat (active or retired), policy-oriented academic and journalist—pride themselves on their hard-headed understanding of 'state power'. In general, they are blissfully and complacently unaware (or if aware, unconcerned) of their profound inadequacies in this regard. Realism understands the state as a 'national territorial totality', a cartographic notion of the space the state occupies. This effectively eliminates the distinction between the state (understood in the more sociological and narrow sense of being a set of distinct apparatuses) and the national society in which it is located.[4]

This paves the way almost automatically for the global system to be seen as overwhelmingly a set of inter-state relationships when it is actually much more than this. What we call the global system is a complex web of intersecting, overlapping, and interweaving relations of various kinds involving a vast array of actors. These are not just governments or their representative structures and personnel. They are, or can be, transnational corporations (TNCs), markets, religious organizations, banks, media-barons, criminal mafias, insurgency groups, social collectivities like classes and popular movements, and many more. In different contexts, at different times, different actors are primary! International relations are not just about wars, conflicts, and what happens *between* states but also about what happens *within* and *across* states; and between, within, and across *societies*. Relations are between government and government, state and state, (the state is not coterminus with the government), government and state, society and society, government and society, state and society. International relations is not just about inter-state or international relations but about the internationalization of domestic conflicts and the domesticization of international conflicts. It is also about the same processes of internationalization and domesticization in regard to social and economic aspirations, cultures, and ideologies.

The global system is better envisioned as an incredibly complex, multi-level, and multi-dimensional terrain in which, as the twentieth century draws to a close, the *capitalist* world economy is more than ever before in its history, the force-field of all politics.[5] What emerges for the most part on the international political arena is not the fulfilment of great power ambitions or even the compromises associated with supposed balances of power, but the *unanticipated consequences and unintended outcomes* of a complex array of intersecting forces.

Realism's assumption that the state is a unitary and rational actor is of course, quite untenable. Such assumptions help to gloss over the actual dangers that exist when a country goes openly nuclear. Decisions pertaining to the perpetuation of a nuclear regime and the politics associated with it are not the result of straightforward, cool, rational thinking by some supposedly unitary state actor but are, like all other state decisions, partly hostage to the interplay of a variety of domestic forces arising from state–society, intra-state, and intragovernment tensions and conflicts. The assumption that state decision-makers act rationally not only ignores the reality of internal tensions of all kinds but also ignores the fact that irrational decisions become more likely in conditions of intense hostility between countries, and therefore in circumstances where there are possible or serious war threats. The conditions of hostility that supposedly give rise to the need for nuclear deterrence are precisely those in which irrationality is most likely to surface.[6]

The belief that the state, for all the practical purposes related to international relations, can be treated as a unitary and rational actor stems from a failure to give adequate conceptual attention to the fact that the state is not just an actor but also a place or site. As such, domestic politics *must* always intrude via the state into the terrain of foreign policy and international politics because the state cannot escape being the site of internally contending political and social forces. The temporary resultant of such contestations has a definite bearing on the definition of national interest or national security.

For the most part, there is no such thing as an 'objective national interest'. Barring rare exceptions, such as the struggle against colonialism or external fascism, the state hardly ever expresses a truly national popular will or interest. Most of the time, what the national interest is said to be depends on who is doing the defining, and how and why they are doing so. It is definite social forces, groups, or sets of individuals, usually the decision-makers and decision-shapers of the foreign policy or national security 'establishment', who are engaging in this exercise.

The Social-Neutrality Myth

Realism rests on the standard liberal myth that the state is 'socially neutral' when, of course, it has no such property. All states have a distinct social character or at the very least powerfully institutionalized social (class) biases. Most state élites/managers have, unsurprisingly, a highly *state-centric, élitist* and *outward-oriented* conception of national security. Thus state security, when it is not treated as simply synonymous with national security, is nonetheless seen as its central element. The preservaton of state security is seen as something 'above' the domestic interplay of politics requiring that its authority, writ and prestige remains undiminished no matter which political force occupies government or oversees state functions. As for its outward orientation or assumption that national security is largely a matter of foreign policy, this is unavoidable given the theoretical conflation of the state with a national society, as embodied in the map notion of the state so basic to Realism. Insofar as there is allowance for the 'internal dimension' of security, it is usually taken as referring to the need to preserve (against threats from 'subversive' forces) 'law and order' and the 'unity and integrity' of the state, i.e. maintaining the internal writ and authority of the state and preserving the inviolability of the demarcated boundaries that make up the national territorial totality of the state.

If the notion of national security is to be at all serviceable in a meaningful way, it must express the aspirations and needs of the large majority of a country's population. The second half of the twentieth century has been, with all its ups and downs, the Age of Democratization. More than ever before, state élites have had to pay attention to popular aspirations if only to legitimize and thus stabilize their own élite position and authority. This public pressure goes well beyond what Realists mean when they acknowledge, somewhat patronizingly, that 'public opinion' has some noteworthy influence. In fact, precisely because popular legitimation of élite rule has become far more important than ever in human history, understandings of national security have had to change. Such understandings have become less elitist and more *popular,* less state-centred and more *society-centred*, less outward-oriented and more *inward-oriented*.

Everywhere, the newer and more relevant goals of national security are ecologically sustainable economic prosperity for all; social cohesion; establishing, preserving and strengthening the institutions of political liberty; moving progressively towards ever more egalitarian forms of democratization and popular empowerment; reducing, and where possible, eliminating external threats (the domain of traditional foreign policy and security thinking). If the reality of contemporary processes is pushing for such a broadening and deepening of the notion of national security as reflected in its goals, Realism is increasingly an intellectual–political barrier to the proper recognition and appreciation of these changing security needs. To put it more starkly, Realism, more than ever before, is a barrier to the recognition of reality and to the effort to shape it in more humane ways.

Furthermore, Realism's obsession with a one-sided and inadequate conception of power precludes it from charting a course to the achievement of these security goals even if it could acknowledge them as its primary goals. Realism has an ahistorical and aggregative concept of power as means or resources abstracted from any particular ends. It never situates the issue of power where it must *always* be situated: in specific contexts. The crucial question to ask is 'power to do what?' Once this question is borne in mind, the 'means of power' so routinely valued by Realists can also be evaluated as enormously 'powerless'. Once we ask: to the pursuit of what various ends, economic, political, cultural, ideological can nuclear weapons be the means? we can easily see the enormous barrenness and powerlessness of these weapons.

While there are disciplines such as historical sociology and political science which have addressed the issue of power with depth and sophistication, conventional International Relations or Realism is not one of them. There are different *kinds* of power—different in their mechanisms, agencies and effects—and the relationship between them is not necessarily cumulative or reinforcing. All that Realism, Neo-Realism, and Neo-Liberalism can offer are superficial distinctions between 'hard power' and 'soft power', e.g. matters of ideology, legitimacy, popular sentiment, and élite or public morale. The very distinction between hard and soft power carries forward the standard Realist bias that precludes the possibility of grappling with the true complexity of the notion of power.[7]

Realism's big crime is that it effectively reduces the understanding and pursuit of security to the understandings and activities of a very traditional–conventional form of *statecraft*. Precisely because Realism has a flawed conception of the kind of entities states are, it simultaneously overestimates and underestimates what states can do.[8] Realism is essentially a manual comprised of two parts. One part provides the language of apologetics and justification for the arrogances and abuses of power carried out by more powerful countries against others in the global arena in the name of stability, order, security, etc. The second part comprises a series of practical guidelines: the dos and don'ts of a very conventionally understood form of statecraft. This is useful certainly (up to a point) but should never be mistaken for being what it claims to be: a manual of serious security thinking and practice. This Realist manual was originally produced, refined, and finalized in the US in the fairly short period beginning just before the Second World War and ending after the Cold War had more or less been institutionalized.[9]

Its apologetic function was obvious. It provided a discourse in which US imperialism could be presented as the expression or manifestation of the compulsions that the existence of an anarchic and disorderly world system imposed on the more powerful countries to try and provide 'world order'. The US was perhaps an imperial power like many before it in history, but not an imperialist one. Where imperialism implied a conceptual focus on the abusive use of power, imperial or great power or 'major power' status implied a conceptual focus on the 'responsibilities' of power. So certainly the US might sometimes abuse its power but this was, and is, to be understood as an avoidable failure to behave sufficiently responsibly rather than as a structural feature or one intrinsic to US behaviour.

Though this Realist manual was originally produced in the US it has become popular in other countries like India because its value is obviously not restricted to the US alone. It is of very limited use to smaller and supposedly weaker countries but has a stronger justificatory and practical value for countries with ambitions to become 'major global actors'. It is a minor but amusing point that Indian Realists who have often prided themselves on their frequent 'anti-Americanness' are simply unaware how fundamentally Americanized in origin and character is their mode of strategic or security thinking.[10]

Since it is the United States that will have to take the lead in nuclear disarmament if the goal of a nuclear-free world is finally to be realized, a special responsibility devolves on disarmament activists and advocates in that country. In the broad spectrum of those who call for nuclear disarmament and reject deterrence there are different kinds of Realists. There are those who remain ardent imperialists, deeply committed to the preservation of US power and its quest for global hegemony. Realism rationalizes this quest. George (Lee) Butler, former head of the Strategic Air Command (SAC), and Robert McNamara, former US Secretary of state, belong to just this category of Realists–imperialists, however 'liberally' they might word or understand their own patriotic aspirations. After full careers dedicated to the pursuit of such imperialism, they suffered what might be called the 'retirement syndrome' that afflicts some former nuclearists. They have recognized that not only are nuclear weapons potentially catastrophic and immoral, but that they are utterly irrelevant and inconsequential for the pursuit of US global hegemony. Indeed, Butler has explicitly argued that one major reason why he wants a nuclear-free world is that in such a world the US's comparative power advantages over other rivals, actual and potential, will actually become greater than it is now! Such a cynical justification for nuclear weapons abolition can be expected to raise many hackles amongst the nuclear hawks of other countries and to make some of them more reluctant to abandon nuclear weapons even if the US were eventually to do so.

Advocates of nuclear disarmament who do not share such views of a Butler or a McNamara have to present a deeper critique of that mindset. This cannot be done without questioning Realist common sense. A constant balancing act is therefore required in the effort to generate the widest possible anti-nuclear sentiment and movement. The very fact that the Butlers and the McNamaras belong to the circle of 'insiders' who have disproportionate influence on official nuclear policies means their voices against nuclearism are valuable and welcome. The *dominant* thrust in any mass anti-nuclear movement has to be anti-nuclearism and anti-deterrence, not anti-Realism. However, because the struggle against nuclear weapons also requires us to struggle against more than just nuclear weapons, i.e. against an unjust world order and those who wish to preserve it as such, there is always a necessary and important place for a critique of the deeper sources of nuclearism, oppression, and unjustified militarism.

The Fallacies of Nuclear Deterrence

The advent of nuclear weapons poses a terrible dilemma for humanity. Is security—real and enduring—possible in the nuclear age? On one side are those who say we have no choice but to 'live with nuclear weapons' and that it is possible to do so with confidence. Just as we have lived with other kinds of weapons and continue to strive more or less successfully for security, especially national security, we can do the same with nuclear weapons. On the other side are those who insist there can never be enduring or adequate security except by 'living without nuclear weapons' and that therefore there is no choice other than to bring about complete, universal, and permanent nuclear disarmament. What has been done by humans, can be undone, indeed, *must* be undone. Moreover, we must do this as rapidly as possible. The longer nuclear weapons exist, the greater the chances of their being used, and the greater the possibility of a nuclear holocaust.

To understand why genuine, authentic security is possible only in a world without nuclear weapons, it is essential to grasp the fundamental difference between conventional and nuclear weapons. In the case of conventional weapons, even if peace breaks down, they can be used to protect oneself or one's country. Nuclear weapons on the other hand can never actually be used to directly protect a country or achieve security. One can only hope that possessing nuclear weapons will frighten a national rival (which possesses them) into not using its nuclear arsenal except on pain of having 'unacceptable' damage inflicted on it in return. This hope is justified by deterrence thinking.

A state of deterrence is simply a 'state of mind', a psychological condition. That is all it is. To believe that deterrence will always hold or to believe it will hold for whenever or whomever you want, is to believe in a myth. It is to believe that the people you want deterred, such as the 'enemy' nuclear élite—the people in and out of government who shape or make the decisions regarding nuclear weapons-related activity (including the pressing of the nuclear button)—will always behave as the deterrer (your own national nuclear élite) will want them to behave, although this opposing élite is subject to a whole host of military, economic, social, political, cultural factors and pressures as well as a variety of external and internal tensions and confusions whose effects are never under the control of the supposed deterrer.

Nuclear weapons may deter because of their frightening character, but they can *never* deter *certainly, confidently or enduringly*. Those who believe we must always live with nuclear weapons (perhaps because we can never again become technologically innocent of how to make them) are even prepared to claim that nuclear weapons can deter permanently. Deterrence advocates make any or all these claims. To deter is not the same as deterrence which is a *conceptualization*, a *rationalization* or *theorization* about what nuclear weapons are supposed to be capable of achieving. Nuclear weapons did not create a reality of deterrence. It was deterrence that was created, or rather, invented, to cope with the reality of nuclear weapons! The spread of nuclear weapons does not lead to the spread of deterrence-based security but only to the spread of rationalizations and claims that security has increased! Deterrence doctrines legitimize the existence of nuclear weapons and de-sensitize the public to the reality and dangers of nuclear competition. Deterrence makes nuclear weapons both perdition and salvation, peril and hope. The peril is real, the hope an illusion.

To rely on deterrence of any sort is to seek peace or stability by threatening, i.e., generating fear and hostility, in the opponent. This heightens mutual tensions. It is not an attempt to bring about greater peace through cooperation or reduction of mutual threats or hostilities, but through the very opposite route. That is why such efforts at deterring so often break down. The contradiction inherent in deterrence—of tying war avoidance to war preparation, of seeking security through promotion of hostility—is not necessarily fatal in the case of conventional weapons and warfare. One can sometimes use conventional weapons to protect oneself and one's country, but security can never be generated if nuclear deterrence breaks down and a nuclear attack or exchange takes place. If the country that suffers a first nuclear strike decides to launch a retaliatory nuclear attack on the aggressor country this can only be an act of revenge, not of security. It can even push the initiator to launch further attacks.

Whatever security value nuclear weapons may be said to possess resides in the threat of their use, not in their actual use. The contradiction inherent in deterrence always raises the prospect of a breakdown and of actual use of nuclear weapons. To rely on nuclear deterrence is thus to place a burden of expectations and hope on nuclear weapons and their possession that is never similarly placed on conventional weapons. It is to believe that nuclear deterrence will always hold for as long as one wants it to, although one can *never fully control* the conditions in which deterrence is supposed to successfully operate. That is why to subscribe to nuclear deterrence as a doctrine or belief system and to pin one's hopes for security on it, is nothing but an *irrational act of faith*.

Pro-nuclearists come in two stripes. There are the crude deterrence thinkers and the sophisticated deterrence thinkers. The first lot simply adhere to nuclear deterrence as a security doctrine without any self-troubled awareness of its inherent illogicality and incoherence. The second group has a clear awareness of the fallacy contained within the effort to rest security on nuclear deterrence. However, in spite of this they believe that nuclear deterrence does work at least reliably enough to make the pursuit of security through its operation strategically sensible and desirable. Thus these sophisticated 'deterrence worshippers' try impossibly to square the circle. 'No, nuclear deterrence deep down doesn't work and we must not rely on it and indeed we must work to achieve global disarmament as quickly as possible. But yes, deterrence does work with enough confidence and for enough time, so we should rely on it. But true, we cannot fully ensure that it will work and not break down, nor can we specify the time scale for when it will work and after which it will not work!'

Instability of Nuclear Deterrence

Unsurprisingly, deterrence enthusiasts, especially the sophisticated variant, are repeatedly seeking to assure the wider public that it is possible to achieve a 'stable deterrent posture' vis-à-vis rivals, or in the case of lesser NWSs like India, a 'stable minimum deterrent posture'. To believe this is to fail to understand that once security is sought through the production, possession, and deployment of nuclear weapons, a degenerative dynamic is put into place which makes a mockery of any idea that insecurity will not increase, that there can be a stable deterrent posture, or that a country's nuclear weapons system will remain static once some supposed minimum is reached. There are a number of reasons for this. We will list eight.

1. There is the irrationality that lies at the heart of deterrence and this gives rise to what has been called the security–insecurity paradox, or how the search for security through hostility generation is so often counter-productive. Nuclear deterrence has of course a distinctive and frightening irrationality all its own, which distinguishes it from the lesser problems of non-nuclear deterrence. In both cases, however, the same principle operates. The existence of a prior hostility that is rooted in political differences of a very serious nature is what pushes one or both sides to decide on military–nuclear deterrence as the way to enhance their own security. Such military–nuclear preparations are however themselves the symptoms and expressions of the dismal state of hostility. They should be seen as its insufficiently controlled or handled effects.

Moreover, opting in for such military–nuclear preparations and for deterrence as the way to achieve peace and security is to seek and obtain one's own security by threatening the other side with greater insecurity and a greater level of physical and material damage. This can hardly be expected to lessen hostilities that either remain just as strong or become stronger. When a country goes nuclear, thereby enormously raising the level of damage and violence it can inflict on its opponent, a new kind of tension is being created because the political statement that is now being made, is that the other side is considered so serious an enemy as to warrant equipping itself with the ability to inflict a qualitatively more horrible kind, and scale, of damage on it. Stable peace and security between erstwhile opponents comes from eradicating the political causes behind the tensions and hostilities, not by sustaining tensions and hostilities (or even raising them) through quantitative and qualitative increases in the punishment they can inflict on each other. Deterrence operates at the level of effects, not at the level of causes and as such cannot be the basis for a genuinely stable situation of peace or security between countries!

2. Part of the irrationality of nuclear deterrence lies in the very high, almost faultless, degree of predictability it demands about an opponent's behaviour. This is a demand for repeated, regular, institutionalized predictability and symmetry in the whole chain of moves and counter-moves in the ensuing politics of nuclearism by each nuclear 'player' vis-à-vis the other. What can assure this in the real world in which we live? The answer is self-evident: there cannot be such an assurance.

However, as long as one nuclear player or the other does seek to establish what it thinks can be the conditions in which such assured, predictable behaviour by the other side will follow, seemingly as a matter of course, then it can easily slide into the pursuit of 'compellence'. That is to say, the side pursuing such a strategy involving certain kinds of nuclear preparations and their associated political implications and signals, believes the other side is 'compelled' to follow a pattern set by, and therefore more 'controlled' by the first player. Not only is nuclear arms escalation written into this 'compellence' script, but nuclear tensions are even more heightened than otherwise. The 'certainties' of 'compellence' are substituted for the 'uncertain certainties' of 'normal deterrence'. Something like this actually happened with the US pursuing such a compellence strategy as part of its efforts to 'stabilize' and 'control' (to its own 'advantage', of course) the nuclear arms race of the late seventies and eighties.

Either way, of course, there is no certainty that deterrence will hold but compellence is a more aggressive form of nuclear behaviour in which the search for 'political advantage' is more pronounced and systematic and where the likelihood of brinkmanship politics is greater. There is no natural firebreak between the dangerous enough instability of deterrence-based nuclear behaviour and the more dangerous instability of compellence-based nuclear behaviour.

3. Once a country seeks security through nuclear deterrence, for this to be effective, it must be *credible*. If the possession of nuclear weapons is to act as a deterrent then the possibility of its use must be real! An opponent will not be deterred if he believes that the deterrer will never use his nuclear weapons. Thus the *capability* and the *will* of the deterring country must not be doubted. The 'enemy' should be certain that his nuclear opponent will use nuclear weapons if pushed to the brink, or at least uncertain whether or not the opponent will use them, but never certain that he will not. This capability and will cannot be shown once and left at that. In the face of all kinds of challenges and uncertainties—technological, military, political, etc.—the capability must be constantly updated and the will must be periodically displayed, i.e. regularly 'fine-tuned' and available for showing in a variety of circumstances. This creates powerful pressure for the generation and sustenance of both an enduring politics of nuclear-related hostility—including nuclear brandishing and brinkmanship—and of arms racing between nuclearly equipped rivals or opponents.

4. Since deterrence is a concept applied to conflictual situations whose sources of distrust are not nuclear weapons themselves (which of course exacerbate these tensions), these weapons leave untouched the basic sources of that hostility. Political instability is built into the rivalry and confrontation. This also reinforces the pressure for arms racing which in turn sustains nuclear tensions at higher levels of danger and mutual devastation should there be a nuclear breakdown. What happened in Europe between the US and USSR was a classic example of this. The West argued that NATO's stockpile and willingness to use nuclear weapons deterred the USSR from attacking Western Europe. Between 1945 and 1954, it was a few atomic bombs that were said to have done the deterring. By the sixties, the same result was supposedly being achieved by the deployment of dozens of ICBMs and submarine launched ballistic missiles (SLBMs). In the seventies and eighties, the same goal of deterring the USSR had to be achieved through deployment of thousands of warheads.

The Western perception of a Russian danger to Europe changed in the late eighties and especially after 1990 not because of the success of deterrence but because of a transformation in the political relationship between East and West. Nuclear deterrence did not reduce mutual distrust and fears. Mutual distrust and fears first reduced and thus rendered deterrence less relevant. The classic paradox in seeking stable deterrence is this: 'the conditions which are thought to make it necessary to apply deterrence guarantee that it will be unstable. The extent to which deterrence is genuinely stable is the extent to which it is unnecessary'. Britain and France can have a stable deterrent equation between themselves precisely because it is unnecessary to have such an equation between themselves!

5. The first principle of effective nuclear deterrence is survivability of a retaliatory force, its measure of invulnerability to a first strike by a nuclearly armed adversary. This is called establishing a 'credible second-strike capacity'. Unfortunately, survivability of one's nuclear weapons system is not a stable affair. It is affected by the size and quality of an enemy's nuclear forces, the size and quality of an initial attack. In order to counter this, one's own weapons system and its controllers push for 'survivability-enhancing practices' such as high alert deployment, launch-on-warning, hardened silos, constantly airborne bomb/missile-carrying planes, etc. One extreme version of this is thinking based on the 'use them or lose them' principle.

As it is, technology advances in either delivery systems (range and accuracy), in warhead capabilities, in surveillance and detection, targeting and intelligence gathering, all add their own degenerative pressures to promote quantitative and qualitative arms racing. Fear of possible technological advances by one's rival reinforces the tendency to opt for a certain level of redundancy in one's own production levels as compensation for this unforeseeable, but possible, comparative 'disadvantage'. The tendency towards redundant levels of production is further reinforced by the fact that within a country's nuclear élite there will never be a consensus or agreement on what constitutes a country's 'adequate' or 'minimum' deterrent capacity. Thus the safest way out is to go along with the 'extreme' nuclearists because if they are satisfied then, as it were, the lesser demands of the 'moderate' nuclearists are more than covered in passing,

Precisely because one's own 'minimum' is contingent on the opponent's level of preparations, there is no such thing as a 'stable minimum posture'. This is always a moving, not a fixed, position. This is confirmed by the whole history of the arms race between the US and former USSR, between East and West. It is only after the end of the Cold War and the likely eventual emergence of universal arms restraint measures like the CTBT and FMCT that there may now be upper limits to the quantitative and qualitative nuclear arms race which might circumscribe nuclear ambitions in countries like India and Pakistan. There is, however, still space left for them, even after acceding to such treaties, to carry on a dangerous enough arms race. Moreover, unless the existing momentum is significantly strengthened, there is always the danger of a collapse of the restraint regime.

6. For deterrence to hold, one has to be confident that one can inflict what is called 'unacceptable damage' on the adversary in a second strike. The question of whether one will be able to retain an adequate second-strike capacity after a devastating first strike by the opponent is a deeply troubling one. There is also the uncertainty and doubt about whether one's adversary will feel that the damage that can be inflicted upon it is indeed unacceptable and therefore a deterring factor. Given this problem, there was a morally debased but nonetheless very serious debate about what could constitute 'unacceptable damage' for the adversary. Did authoritarian regimes like the USSR and China have higher levels of willingness to suffer than democratic regimes like the US, Britain and France? Did this then not require asymmetrically higher levels of nuclear arms on one side of the Cold War face-off? Would this not cause problems in mutual perceptions/suspicions about intentions and capabilities as well as complicating arms control efforts?

To arrive at some figure of what might constitute 'acceptable' or 'bearable' damage for the USSR in a nuclear conflict, the nuclear élite of the US noted that the USSR had suffered 20–25 million dead in the Second World War and had three-fourths of its industrial capacity destroyed. This then became a kind of benchmark so that unacceptable damage to the USSR was calculated as destruction of at least three-fourths of its industrial capacity and perhaps one-third of its population as nuclear war casualties. This, however, was still only conjecture. France and the UK also had to make calculations of what might deter the Soviets from a nuclear attack on them for there was always a doubt about US willingness to wage a nuclear war or even threaten nuclear war for their sake. France's President Charles De Gaulle, as justification for constructing an independent nuclear arsenal, once openly declared that the US would not sacrifice New York for the sake of Paris.

Proportional deterrence notions thus came into play or the 'tear-off-your-arm' theory of deterrence. Maybe the UK and France couldn't really inflict unacceptable damage to the USSR in a second strike, but it was still worthwhile for them to go in for nuclear weapons as a deterrent because 'tearing-an-arm' off the USSR was good enough. But if this was good enough then wasn't this a capacity for inflicting unacceptable damage? In which case what was the point of the US or USSR having so much stronger an arsenal? In reality, the question what constituted 'unacceptable damage', so supposedly central to 'sensible' discussion about the supposed value of nuclear deterrence, has no real answer. Having first decided that nuclear deterrence works and therefore nuclear weapons must be acquired, the respective nuclear élites then had to answer the question how much of a nuclear arsenal was enough? They found they could not really answer it! They kept on trying and kept on worrying.

Of course, the UK and France couldn't be sure, just as the US, Russia, and China couldn't be sure what was the level of unacceptable damage for the adversary. It was thus safest to keep on trying to expand their destructive capacity! All such uncertainties throughout the Cold War fed the degenerative dynamic of nuclear arms racing in all the nuclear weapons states. No country was certain whether they would retain a credible second-strike capacity if the adversary launched a massive first strike. No country was certain that what it could then inflict would be unacceptable damage to its principal rival(s) and therefore whether it could confidently rely on the nuclear deterrent.

7. Once nuclear weapons become tools of foreign policy, there is enormous difficulty in restricting the range of goals that these 'deterrent-producing weapons' should be used for. The Realist mindset only encourages such a slide. Once upon a time, pro-nuclearists only justified the possession of nuclear weapons because they claimed this would deter a nuclear attack or nuclear blackmail by another country. They did not remain satisfied with merely this goal or justification. Other goals and justifications emerged and were sought to be popularized. Sometimes, new concepts of deterrence to be associated with new goals, such as 'extended deterrence', were forged.

Now, nuclear weapons are required not just to deter attack or blackmail but as a general tool providing 'foreign policy support', 'damage-limitation capability', 'escalation control', 'prevention of conventional war', 'global prestige', even 'promotion of eventual nuclear disarmament'. Before one knows it, nuclear weapons are credited with multiple capacities of many kinds. Such an enormous burden of responsibility and expectations has been placed on what nuclear weapons can achieve, that they have been contemptuously referred to by anti-nuclearists as the new Gods of realpolitik, and 'nuclear strategists' are termed the new 'God worshippers!'

During the Cold War arms race, the absurd sophistry of simulation studies, computer gaming, and systems analysis applied to arms procurement and deployment, did nothing to cover up the basic moral and intellectual vacuity at the heart of it all. The supposed sophistication of nuclear strategic thinking is really the search for a foreign policy Holy Grail; the indulgence in a 'strategic easy fix' whose drugging effect on the mind and heart is sought to be disguised by complicated levels of argument (gaming scenarios) at more abstracted levels.

8. Every country that goes in for nuclear weapons in the belief that deterrence will work, has to ask itself an unavoidable question. What if deterrence breaks down? In that case, a nuclear exchange or war has to be brought to an end as quickly as possible. That is to say, the capacity to fight a 'limited nuclear war' must be established. However, building such a capacity for

nuclear warfighting by making 'limited nuclear war' more feasible itself undermines the efficacy of deterrence. This 'what if' question haunts and shadows all nuclear strategic thinking: it has no satisfactory answer. Since it is supposedly hard-headed lack of sentimentality that led to the 'advocacy of nuclear weapons production and deployment' in the first place, the hard-headed, unsentimental 'what if' question cannot be ignored or left unasked, yet it simply has no good answer. Moreover, the absence of an adequate answer here only highlights the deficiency of another kind of answer to another kind of question. *What are nuclear weapons useful for?* This is not answered by saying 'deterrence'!

How Reliable? Has Deterrence Really Worked?

What has traditionally been called strategic discourse is always strongly speculative in character, yet nuclear strategic discourse is even more strongly speculative. This is because there has so far (thankfully) been no nuclear war and therefore there is no foundational data in existence by which one can cross-check and decisively adjudicate between arguments about the claimed efficacy or inefficacy of nuclear weapons and deterrence. This highly speculative and counterfactual character of the arguments put forward in support of deterrence claims means it is often impossible to prove or disprove such claims. This speculative character enables both sides in the strategic nuclear debate to hold on to their original positions with a fair degree of complacency.

However, this does not mean that an overall judgement on the basis of a 'balance of plausibility' cannot be arrived at or that both sides have an equally plausible case. They do not. There are more sensible and less sensible ways of speculating! What is it that distinguishes undisciplined, fanciful and irresponsible forms of strategic speculation on nuclear security from more sober, informed and disciplined forms of speculation? At least two things, and this is partly why the anti-nuclear position is much stronger and sensible. When there is no accepted external criteria or data by which one can adjudicate between arguments and counter-arguments, then an even higher premium must be placed on the internal coherence and consistency of an argument. Here the pro-nuclearists confront a fatal and inescapable dilemma. They cannot get away from the ingrained incoherence and irrationality of nuclear deterrence as a security doctrine. They can, of course, claim that logic isn't everything. Their losing the logical argument or case does not mean they have lost the political argument. Politics, they might say, is about power, not logic. They should, however, at the very least acknowledge that since (in true Realist fashion) they argue that it is *politically rational* to go in for nuclear weapons, the existence of a logical irrationality lodged within their foundational concept of deterrence greatly weakens this claim.

The second factor that helps distinguish the plausibility or reasonableness of one case against the other are the controls provided by historical evidence. Here too, it is the anti-nuclearist position that rejects deterrence which has shown itself to be the stronger. However, this is not conceded by pro-nuclearists for whom the supposed refutation provided by the 'long peace' argument is central. This is the historically counterfactual claim that the existence of nuclear weapons is what assured the long post-war peace across the political–ideological divide in Europe since 1945.

Generally, three claims are made in this regard. First, that nuclear deterrence prevented the outbreak of nuclear war between the US and USSR in Europe and elsewhere. Second, that nuclear deterrence also prevented the outbreak of conventional war in Europe between East and West. Since such a war, given the awesome power, reach, and ambitions of the two principal protagonists, would have been tantamount to a Third World War, nuclear weapons prevented the outbreak of such a world war with or without nuclear exchanges as part of it. Third, there was not even a local or regional war in Europe and this too can be attributed to the efficacy of the nuclear stand-off.

There is, of course, no way of decisively refuting these claims. There are, however, plausible ways of arguing to show that what is a correlation or coexistence of events—the existence of nuclear weapons and the absence of a Third World War, or of a nuclear exchange or of a local or regional war—should not be mistaken for being a relationship of cause and effect. On the issue of the long peace, there are basically three explanatory perspectives. First, there are those who would give enormous weight to the effect of nuclear deterrence in securing this peace. Here nuclear weapons were not only necessary but also sufficient to bring about this peace. Second, there are those who argue that nuclear weapons were among a set of factors that ensured the long peace. That is to say, nuclear weapons were a necessary but not sufficient condition. Third, there are those who argue that nuclear weapons and its deterrence capacity were irrelevant to procuring the long peace which was over-determined by a whole set of non-nuclear factors.

It is this third position that is far and away the most plausible. The first two arguments suffer from a grave flaw. Having made the presence of nuclear weapons 'necessary' for the avoidance of a Third World War, it must follow that in their absence, the long peace breaks down and a Third World War takes place. In effect, they have made nuclear weapons a crucial hinge in explaining the absence of war. This is a *single-factor* explanation of why world wars take place, even if the second position would also ascribe similar explanatory and causal status to some other 'necessary' factors taken separately and individually. This is an absurdly implausible explanation for why world wars take place. World wars neither 'happen' nor are they 'avoided' because of the presence or absence of a single factor such as nuclear weapons. World wars take place because of a whole *complex* of factors operating in an extremely turbulent wider context. The processes that can lead to a world war depend on a *combination* of structural and contingent factors and causes. This notwithstanding, so desperate are the champions of nuclear deterrence to prove its worth that they perforce resort to sloppy, superficial, and dubious forms of historical explanation and argument.

As for the claim that nuclear weapons prevented local/regional wars in Europe, this came about not because of the presence of nuclear weapons but because of the freezing of the political status quo during the Cold War era. This glacis was itself the consequence of all the *multiple* factors and causes that in complex combination were behind the making and sustenance of Cold War structures. This is precisely why, when the Cold War glacis melted, bitter conventional warfare broke out in the former USSR and former Yugoslavia although the overhang of nuclear weapons (albeit smaller in size) in Europe, remains very much in place. If there has never been any serious threat of internecine warfare in the western part of Europe, this is again attributable not to the presumed potency of nuclear deterrence but to the dramatic changes in Western Europe after 1945—the emergence of the European Economic Community (EEC) and then the European Union (EU)—whereby this has become the one part of the world that is probably moving into a historic post-Clausewitzian era where major war becomes a thing of the past.

Pro-nuclearists irresponsibly cite the historical fact of the absence of nuclear war since 1945 as evidence that deterrence works, but when the historical record does not provide latitude for such self-comforting interpretations, they ignore or downplay it. Thus, it is a historical fact that during the Cold War both sides engaged in an arms race that led to the accumulation of enormous overkill arsenals and capacities, enough to destroy the world 30 or 40 times over. This was utterly irrational behaviour! Is there any *sensible* notion of deterrence or security that can explain such insanity? In the face of this actual historical evidence that directly challenges the rationality claims of deterrence-related behaviour, what do pro-nuclearists have to say? The last thing they admit is that this arms race revealed, particularly starkly, the *degenerative and unstable dynamic* ecapsulated in deterrence as a security doctrine with its associated preparations and practices.

The Myth of 'Nuclear Blackmail'

There is more historical evidence, and little of it can be said to have bolstered the case of the pro-nuclearists. There is no convincing evidence to show that even a single case of attempted nuclear blackmail ever succeeded in its aims.[11] So much for the supposed efficacy of nuclear weapons as a foreign policy tool! This testifies, of course, to the remarkably astrategic character of such weapons. However, the fact that certain nuclear élites have repeatedly attempted such blackmail, and that on various occasions the actual use of nuclear weapons has been seriously contemplated, itself greatly weakens the claims made for the effectiveness of deterrence.[12]

From Afghanistan to Vietnam to Suez to Algeria to the Malvinas, nuclear weapons have not deterred non-nuclear countries from fighting and often succeeding against NWSs. Nor, as the Ussuri River border conflict between China and the USSR showed, did the possession of nuclear weapons prevent conventional military conflict between two nuclearly equipped rivals. This is a point that Indian and Pakistani policy-makers would do well to take note of. There is no reason to believe that some level of insurgency and conventional military strife between the two countries will not continue regardless of the nuclear weapons each of them possesses.

The irresponsible and manipulative manner in which the Indian nuclear élite treats the question of historical controls on strategic speculation reflects, of course, a general disease amongst nuclear élites everywhere, but is nonetheless worth noting. What after all is the historical record of nuclear threats to India that might justify it going nuclear? Those who seek to construct such a case have to stress the China threat, but herein lies the rub. They cannot take recourse to the *actual* historical record to cite examples of belligerent nuclear behaviour by China against India because there are no such examples. Indeed, China, unlike the US or Russia, has never attempted nuclear blackmail against any country. Indian nuclearists cannot deny this historical fact, nor that India lived comfortably with the Chinese bomb for 34 years. They cannot deny the historical record of the ineffectiveness of all nuclear blackmail attempts nor of military–political defeats of NWSs by NNWSs.

All they can do to justify Indian acquisition of nuclear weapons is to refer to *abstract possibilities* such as of China winning a future conventional war by employing nuclear blackmail, or seekling diplomatic leverage against India through its nuclear arsenal. In other words, justification is sought through historically undisciplined speculation about future possibilities which have no foundation in actually existing trends or patterns of Chinese behaviour.

Perhaps the most striking example of the contempt that Indian hawks show for historically grounded possibilities and probabilities, is the way they tackle the following question: What about a possible Chinese nuclear attack on India after it has declared itself to be an NWS, but has not yet produced or deployed a credible second-strike capacity against China?

Here, the standard answer is that the historical record indicates that China will not engage in any such attack if India does not provoke it by threatening Tibet, which New Delhi has no intention of ever doing. China is a cautious, pragmatic country and has shown itself to be so in regard to its nuclear behaviour. This judgement is quite correct, but the irony of the argument is stark. The actual historical record is cited to explain away the fear that China might launch a pre-emptive nuclear attack even when India most provokes China by going ahead and builds a weapons system in part directed against that country. However, the actual historical record of Chinese nuclear non-belligerence is contemptuously disregarded in order to explain why, when India does not have a weapons system and is therefore far less provocative to China, New Delhi must go nuclear for fear of the abstract possibility that China might in future attack or blackmail it! These jumps between the use of arguments that are historically grounded in some serious way and those that are not so grounded, as and when it suits the bomb lobby, is a standard technique and trope of pro-nuclearists everywhere.

If the history of nuclear brandishing, brinkmanship and near-use by some NWSs was not warning enough, there is also a long history of nuclear weapons-related accidents, which is, or should also be, frightening enough. Pro-nuclearists have, unsurprisingly, always made light of such matters. Is it not still the case that there has been after 1945 no nuclear outbreak, whether by design, miscalculation or accident? It appears that nothing will convince such diehard believers in the 'magic' of deterrence except when a disaster occurs. This is not an unusual reflex. Before the Three Mile Island accident, nuclear energy power lobbyists and advocates were repeatedly assuring the public that the chances of a reactor catastrophe were negligible and that nuclear power generation had been made safe. Before the 1985 *Challenger* shuttle accident, similar extravagant reassurances were given about space launch safety.

It is really only after the Three Mile Island, Bhopal, and Chernobyl tragedies that serious study and theorization began about the dilemmas and dangers involved in the organization of hazardous technologies. Those in control, and supportive, of the development and maintenance of nuclear weapons systems have always had strong reasons to deny that accidents pose a serious problem. The cumulative evidence of 50 years has, however, seriously damaged the credibility of their safety claims. Contemporary 'organization theory' argues that organizations (and it is organizations not statespeople or states that actually control nuclear weapons systems) function within a severely bounded or limited form of rationality. They have three characteristics.[13] They show 'interactive complexity' or numerous interrelated but unplanned interactions not easily comprehensible. This is because the organization's various units operate according to routines and standard procedures and rules, not according to individually reasoned decisions. They have 'tight coupling' systems that are very time-dependent and have invariant production sequences. The system has little slack or flexibility. Add to these two structural properties the third trait that there will always be conflicting objectives within an organization and you have a recipe for the 'normality of accidents' and the 'limits of safety'. Indeed, even the ability of organizations to learn from their mistakes is limited.

Whatever one's views about the strengths and weaknesses of such theories, the physical record of accidents is deeply disturbing. Shaun Gregory details 224 accidents of various types concerning nuclear weapons systems. He classifies them in four ways. In Group 1 were accidental, unauthorized or possible detonations of a weapon. Group 2 covers accidental detonation without war risk but radioactive contamination. Group 3 refers to accidents to vehicles carrying nuclear weapons. Group 4 refers to other significant accidents. In Group 1, Gregory says there were at least 10 such accidents. This does not include the event in 1954 in North Carolina when a nuclear bomb accidentally fell off a plane and five of its six safety mechanisms against detonation failed.[14]

Most such knowledge of accidents comes from declassified information from the US, the most open and democratic of the NWSs in this regard. Russia has had its share of accidents as well. On the night of 26 September 1983, a Russian army officer, a software engineer, Stanislav Petrov, was on duty at a surveillance centre near Moscow. 'Suddenly the screen in front of me turned bright red . . . . An alarm went off . . . . The computer showed that the Americans had launched a nuclear strike against us.' Petrov's orders were to pass on the information up the chain of command to the then General Secretary, Yuri Andropov. Within minutes, a massive counter-attack could have been launched. Petrov disobeyed procedure and reported a false alarm. A computer error was later discovered. However, Petrov lost his job for disobedience![15]

On 25 January 1995, a Norwegian scientific rocket to study the Aurora Borealis was mistaken for Trident sea-launched warheads. The mistake lasted for eight minutes, only two minutes away from the launch of a nuclear missile. The Russian ambassador in Oslo had been told of the rocket launch but this information did not make its way up to the top Soviet leadership, military or civilian. If this has been the record of the nuclear superpowers what reason is there to believe that the 'accident factor' or 'miscalculation factor' will not be as serious, if not more so, in countries like India and Pakistan which are technically less sophisticated and whose organizational structures are, if not less sophisticated, at least as unsophisticated? Frankly, none!

The India–Pakistan Face-Off

Apart from technical weaknesses, both the Indian and Pakistani nuclear programmes are even less subject to public scrutiny and criticism than those of the US, Russia, the UK, and France. In the absence of public monitoring of safety, the chances are greater that bureaucratic and military interests will dominate. In Pakistan there is the additional worry that the weight of the military in nuclear decision-making will be greater and less constrained by a more safety-conscious civilian authority. As it is, militaries have stronger organizational biases in favour not so much of war, as for preventive war. In Pakistan, many things combine to put a higher premium on the possibility of miscalculation or accident. Pakistan is much more likely to disperse deployment of warheads and decentralize control, thus raising the chances in particular of unauthorized use. There is the unfavourable asymmetry of its weapons system vis-à-vis India and therefore, a greater fear of an Indian first strike. Then there is Pakistan's rejection of the No First Use principle and relatively greater military dominance in its politics.

BOX 3

Ramshackle Deterrence?

There is Little that is Reliable in the Disaster-Prone Subcontinent

On 11 January 1999, an Avro transport aircraft belonging to India's Defence Research & Development Organization (DRDO) crashed 60 km from Chennai, killing all eight men on board. This was a major setback to India's effort at fabricating an Airborne Surveillance Platform (ASP), itself part of the country's programme to develop an Airborne Early Warning (AEW) system (or eye-in-the-sky).[1] The airplane, which crashed during a 'radar-checking exercise', was a 'technology demonstrator', fitted with a rotodome containing sophisticated radars and other surveillance equipment. It was to act as a major 'force multiplier' for the Indian Air Force (IAF), giving its fighter pilots 20 minutes' warning to take off and intercept any intruding enemy aircraft—in place of the present three minutes.

The ASP, to be the centrepiece of the AEW, was developed as an indispensable part of the effort at 'credible nuclear weapons delivery' by combat aircraft, and at creating a command and control centre which a future nuclear strike force would use. Four of the eight killed were the DRDO's early warning system experts. The crash was a body blow to their project.

The accident, caused by the unhinging and collapse of the rotodome, epitomizes in some ways the disaster-prone character of a good deal of Indian (and Pakistani) military as well as civilian physical infrastructure and hardware, marked as it is by frequent accidents, component failures, substandard designs, poor maintenance and unsafe operational practices. This raises disturbing questions about the operation of any kind of mutual deterrence equation, indeed the viability of an Indian and Pakistani deterrent posture itself.[2]

The subcontinent is notorious for poor engineering capabilities even in areas where the science has been mastered. Substandard manufacturing practices, which lead to a high occurrence of defects, are rampant in Indian and Pakistani industries, especially in defence production factories which are shielded from public scrutiny and safety audits. India and Pakistan have among the lowest indices in physical infrastructure development. There are over 100 prolonged power failures or brownouts a year in virtually every district of India's capital, one of the world's four most polluted and mismanaged cities.

In general, industry and services in India and Pakistan are afflicted by mismanagement and poor maintenance practices, leading to mishaps and failures. India's military hardware is not immune from this. For instance, between April 1991 and March 1997, the Indian Air Force (IAF) witnessed 187 accidents and 2729 'incidents' in which 147 aircraft were destroyed and 63 pilots, most of them young, lost their lives. The IAF lost close to eight squadrons. In financial terms, this loss exceeds over Rs 4000 crores.[3] This works out to about $1 billion or a tenth of India's annual military budget, and *roughly four-fifths* of the IAF's annual budget! Of the 187 accidents during this period, 130 involved fighter jets, most of them in the MiG series.

Among the most accident-prone planes flown by the IAF is the MiG-21, known as the IAF's 'workhorse'. 'I pray for him every time he takes off,' a MiG-21 test pilot's wife is quoted as saying about her husband.[4] Over 40 per cent of IAF accidents are caused by technical defects which, officials say, are primarily attributable to substandard spares. In the past six years, for instance, 17 helicopters and seven transport planes were lost in accidents.[5]

There is little quality control on spares in the Indian military. Many are bought from dubious arms dealers and firms that are blacklisted. Newspapers have reported 'a major racket' in the purchase of spares, 'especially for transport planes and helicopters, compromising flight safety and operational readiness'.[6] Often, the armed services are unable to obtain basic design data from the manufacturer and hence cannot do enough modification, repairs, or retrofitting. The services lack a developed system for reporting and analyzing accidents and failures. They do hold courts of inquiry when major accidents occur, but these are usually manned by non-experts.[7]

In the past, a number of shady arms deals were foisted upon the Indian armed forces by corrupt politicians and bureaucrats. For instance, in the 1960s, *Vijayanta* tanks were bought, which could not be taken to the battlefront because they were defective. In the 1980s, the Indian army procured supposedly new and expensive Combat Engineering Tractors, only to discover these were second-hand British army rejects. The notorious Westland helicopters, considered unfit to fly, were similarly imposed upon the IAF as part of a (political) deal between Margaret Thatcher and Rajiv Gandhi. These had to be junked.[8]

Stories abound in India and Pakistan of non-performance of military assets, subversion of quality standards, breach of contracts, peddling and abuse of influence, vast magnitudes of bribery, etc. It appears reasonable to assume that in an extremely corrupt society and government, levels of graft would be especially high in those sectors that are largely exempt from parliamentary and citizens' scrutiny.

An instance of the Indian armed services' violation of their own performance standards is a 1996 directive from Air Headquarters saying that 'performance of the squadrons in actual flying aspects would not be assessed.' This meant that IAF aircraft's war-preparedness tests would be bypassed, leading experts to comment: 'Had a war broken out in 1997, most Indian Air Force aircraft would have taken to the skies without having undergone a prior inspection for war preparedness throughout the previous year.'[9]

Besides, there are generic problems arising from a poor culture of safety in India and Pakistan. Both are disaster-prone societies, marked by high rates of accidents and mishaps, sloppy precautionary design and planning, little disaster forecasting, poor emergency procedures, and undeveloped relief-provision infrastructures. Large numbers of Indians and Pakistanis routinely die in stampedes, train collisions, road accidents, sinking of ferries, or in construction mishaps.

India and Pakistan are among the world's largest recipients of toxic waste, junked ships (for shipbreaking), and unsafe technologies and products. They have among the lowest standards on food safety, environmental quality, occupational safety and public health anywhere.

The frequency of industrial accidents in India is estimated to be four times higher than, say, in the US. Fatalities in road accidents in India (as a proportion of the number of vehicles on the road) are 10 times higher than in the OECD countries, and in Pakistan 13 times higher.[10] The important point about a generally poor safety culture is simply that if Indian and Pakistani engineers fail to control and reduce the frequency of mishaps in relatively less complex and loosely 'coupled' systems such as road traffic, then they cannot inspire much confidence in being able to ensure that highly complex, 'tightly coupled' systems such as nuclear weapons and C^3I structures can work safely.

Both India and Pakistan have witnessed major accidents in military installations and ordnance depots. In April 1988, a huge ammunition depot at Ojhri, near Islamabad, blew up, killing over a thousand people and injuring many more.

India's nuclear power programme, run by the same agency—DAE (Department of Atomic Energy)—that is responsible for making nuclear bombs, has a remarkably poor safety record. One of its worst accidents involved the collapse of a safety system, no less: the containment dome of a nuclear reactor under construction in 1994. (The dome is supposed to prevent radioactivity releases into the atmosphere in case of a reactor accident.)

Poor safety culture is bound to affect the working of all the hardware and software involved in any possible command, control, communications, and intelligence systems India and Pakistan may build in the future. Their present warning and detection technology is grossly inefficient and unreliable.

For instance, in December 1995, a large transport aircraft carrying firearms entered Indian airspace across the western border without authorization or warning. Not only was it not intercepted; it was not even properly detected. There was no coordination between the civilian and military authorities involved. The plane crashlanded at Purulia, in West Bengal, over 1000 km from the western border, before its crew were apprehended.

In late May 1997, an IAF MiG-25 fighter plane was reported to have intruded into Pakistani airspace at an altitude of 65,000 feet and a speed of Mach 2. The Pakistan government believed that the breaking of the sound barrier by the MiG was deliberate: its own air force has no aircraft that can reach such a high cruising altitude.

Indian and Pakistani missiles and warheads too pose their own safety problems. Many of these were not resolved, and are unlikely to be resolved, given the clandestine nature of nuclear and missile programmes, and official anxiety to avoid detection and publicity (especially as regards technical details). For instance, the *Prithvi* missile, as well as the second stage of the *Agni* missile, use highly corrosive liquid fuel. This is extremely difficult to handle, and highly inflammable.

Again, it is far from clear if India conducted, or was in a position to conduct, 'one-point safety' tests for nuclear warheads. (Pakistan probably lacks the capacity.) In the absence of such tests, the likelihood of accidental detonation of a nuclear bomb during fabrication, transportation, installation or flight must be presumed to be relatively high.

If there ever was a case of 'ramshackle deterrence', or deterrence breaking down under the weight of incompetence of its own practitioners, then it is more likely to be found in India and Pakistan. The problem is aggravated by the total absence of public scrutiny of military, in particular nuclear, programmes.

Notes

1. See '8 killed as defence plane crashes', *The Hindu*, New Delhi, 12 January 1999. Also '8 die as Avro aircraft crashes near Chennai: DRDO project suffers major setback', *The Hindustan Times*, New Delhi, 12 January 1999.
2. For a detailed discussion of the problem with nuclear deterrence, see Chapter 8 of this book.
3. Wilson John, 'Air Force fighters turn pilot-killers', *The Pioneer*, New Delhi, 10 November 1998.
4. ibid.
5. Wilson John, 'Dubious deals imperil IAF fighters', *The Pioneer*, New Delhi, 9 December 1998.
6. ibid.
7. Wilson John, 'Kalam file nails engine malaise', *The Pioneer*, New Delhi, 11 November 1998.
8. Rajesh Ramachandran, 'Serve and Lobby: how the Deals are Swung', *The Hindustan Times*, New Delhi, 10 January 1999.
9. Reported by Dinesh Kumar, 'IAF planes skipped war preparedness tests', *The Times of India*, New Delhi, 8 February 1999.
10. Compiled from *World Road Statistics 1998*, International Road Federation, Geneva, 1998. Also interview with Dinesh Mohan, professor of biomedical engineering at the Indian Institute of Technology, Delhi, 6 February 1999.

Neither India nor Pakistan has either the geographical distance that the US and USSR had from each other, nor the prolonged period of time they had to learn from their experience of innumerable false warnings. At the beginning of the Cold War, the superpowers had many hours to determine the truth and falsity of warnings. In the sixties, their ICBMs flight time still allowed for 25–30 minutes to react to alarms. When in the eighties, some missiles were deployed off each other's coasts allowing 10 minutes flight time, both countries had accumulated years of experience in dealing with each other's arsenals and with deficiencies in their own warning systems. They had agreed to dozens of CBMs, crisis-handling protocols and procedures. However, once missiles are deployed, India and Pakistan will from the beginning have much smaller time margins for correcting errors. India, Pakistan, and China all have contiguous borders. Flight times are short, especially between India and Pakistan. Finally, domestic unrest can produce detonations, accidental or otherwise, in a variety of scenarios from faction fighting within the military to civil strife in the country.[16]

If there is one obvious lesson to be learnt from the Cold War stand-off, it is that the likelihood of use of nuclear weapons is always greatest between adversaries in a wartime or near-wartime situation. The Cold War remained a Cold War, and for reasons, some of which have been detailed earlier, which made a direct confrontation or joining of hostilities unlikely. Even so, it was a close call. It is between rivals where the likelihood of a 'hot' war is the greatest, that the chances of use are the greatest. If the country that has nuclear weapons feels its national–territorial survival is endangered even by opponents who do not have nuclear weapons, the possibility of use also becomes greater.[17] In any such face-off between nuclear rivals, which also have a history of hot wars between themselves, matters become even more fragilely poised when one side perceives itself to be strongly 'disadvantaged' in regard to the mutual nuclear and military balance. This is precisely what Pakistan feels with regard to India.

This is an asymmetry which India's talk of a 'minimum deterrent' does nothing to alter. This is a 'minimum' that will be calculated and pursued with regard to China—not Pakistan. Besides, there is the fact that India is not able to quantify this minimum. Both Indian strategists and the BJP-led government ruling at the turn of 1999 have stated as much in reaction to the US government's call that India declare precisely what it means by 'minimum'. This is not possible to quantify once and for all for reasons already given; that it is a moving position whose point of temporary rest depends on what China's nuclear capacities at any time are. Of all the NWSs, China is the only one that has not significantly reduced the size of its arsenal over the last decade, and has left open the prospect of its quantitative expansion, if it believes that changed circumstances require this.[18]

Such a state of affairs does not bode well for the prospect of establishing a 'stable minimum' deterrent equation for India. Even without a submarine-based nuclear-tipped missile force, India may over the next decade develop missiles with the range to hit some of China's population centres.[19] This is, however, still well short of having an assured second-strike capability against China. However, any notion of an Indian minimum, even a conservatively estimated one, will still be far in excess of the Pakistan arsenal. Insofar as a Pakistani capacity to produce a survivable second-strike capacity against a massive Indian first strike is concerned, this is more than fifteen, if not twenty, years away. Pakistan will be for all this time presented with a 'use them or lose them' scenario regarding its own missile strength in the face of India's capacity to 'decapitate' Pakistan or launch a massive first strike at its military–nuclear infrastructure. Once the two countries openly deploy their weapons, they will let themselves into a zone of considerable nuclear tension and danger.

Moreover, no Chinese leadership can remain sanguine in the face of determined Indian efforts to eventually have a triadic pattern of deployment even if it falls short of building a credible second-strike capacity. All recent accounts indicate that this is what New Delhi currently has in mind. Once India has missiles that can hit China, then the latter has to factor India into its nuclear operational and targeting strategy. It is at this point that China will explore the issue of a closer nuclear relationship with Pakistan, especially if Pakistan has developed a nuclear capacity that can do great damage to India.

Thus the most likely scenarios to emerge in the medium and long term indicate that severe political tensions will remain in South Asia and the India–Pakistan face-off will be the dominant and most dangerous form of confrontation. Insofar as Pakistan seeks to deploy missiles and India attempts a triadic pattern of nuclear deployment, the chances of accidental detonations and miscalculated launches will remain high. The India–Pakistan security equation is very volatile and unstable. The only reasonable assurance that a nuclear confrontation does not break out between them can come, not through so-called stable deterrence, whether with or without open deployment, but through non-manufacture and non-induction of nuclear weapons and missiles.[20]

Notes

1. There is today a very rich debate between Realism and its different categories of critics, from very mild ones like Liberal Internationalism to more radically critical currents influenced by Marxism, feminism, neo-Weberian historical sociology, post-modernism, world systems theory, and ecology. However, even where this exists—in the US—Realism dominates mainstream thinking. In India, this debate is virtually non-existent. The overwhelming majority of the members of the 'national security establishment' are blissfully unaware of its existence. Liberal Internationalism shares so many of Realism's basic assumptions that it is not a serious critique of it.

   These influences (in an unsystematized form) do exist among some Indian security thinkers because insofar as nonalignment was seen as a moral–political alternative to Realist bloc politics and 'balance of power' gaming, it encouraged ways of thinking about international relations that share many perspectives with Liberal Intenationalism. However, with the end of the Cold War and with the Non-aligned Movement now in disarray, conventional Realism dominates Indian security thinking. The principal contemporary legatee of Liberal Internationalism in the West is the school of Neo-Liberalism (not to be confused with the most conservative form of neoclassical economics also going by that label) and its greater emphasis on economic global integration and 'complex interdependence' between states.

2. Conventional Realism is descriptive and normative but often bemoans the fact that leaders of states do not behave as they should. Thus, among the ranks of Realists it is possible to find those who would happily endorse the practice of nuclear deterrence in an 'ideal world' but are fearful of what might happen to nuclear weapons in the real world. Neo-Realism, by contrast, claims not to be merely descriptive but to provide a scientific–structural theoretical foundation to Realism and its normative injunctions. Neo-Realism emphasizes more starkly the supposedly compulsive effects and constraints that the anarchic world system imposes on states and inter-state behaviour, regardless of the internal composition of these states—whether they are democratic or dictatorial, capitalist or not.

   Neo-Realism is thus prepared to arrive at prescriptive conclusions for policy that conventional Realists in the West would not agree with or approve of. Thus Kenneth N. Waltz, the premier theorist of Neo-Realism (he prefers to call it Structural Realism) not only argues that deterrence works and that we should rely on it, but that it works so well that gradual proliferation of nuclear weapons to other states is better than rapid proliferation or no proliferation! Indian nuclearists thus have every reason to welcome Waltz's views even if few properly understand his attempts at more rigorously theorizing international relations. See *The Spread of Nuclear Weapons: a Debate*, the polemic between its two authors, Scott D. Sagan and Kenneth N. Waltz; W.W. Norton & Co., New York, 1995. The key texts of Neo-Realism are K.N. Waltz, *Man, State and War*, New York, 1959 and his *The Theory of International Politics*, Reading, Mass., 1979.

3. For a representative list of comprehensive critiques of Realism/Neo-Realism from a variety of vantage points, see F. Halliday, *Rethinking International Relations*, Macmillan, London, 1994 and J. Rosenberg, *The Empire of Civil Society: a Critique of the Realist Theory of International Relations,* Verso, London, 1994. The above two are Marxists. From the direction of historical sociology, there is A. Giddens, *The Nation-State and Violence,* Polity Press, Cambridge, 1985, and M. Mann, *The Sources of Social Power,* vol. II, Cambridge Univ. Press, Cambridge, 1983. From the direction of feminism, see C. Enloe, *Bananas, Bases and Beaches: Making Feminist Sense of International Relations,* Pandora, London, 1989. From the direction of international political economy, there is S. Strange, The Retreat of the State: *The Diffusion of Power in the World Economy,* Cambridge Univ. Press, Cambridge, 1996. From world systems theory, see I. Wallerstein, *Geopolitics and Geoculture: Essays in a Changing World System,* Cambridge Univ. Press, Cambridge, 1991.

From a post-modernist angle, see R.B.J. Walker, *Inside/Outside: International Relations as Political Theory*, Cambridge Univ. Press, Cambridge,1993.

In contrast to the ferocity of these varied assaults on Realism/Neo-Realism, the contemporary debate between Realists/Neo-Realists and Neo-Liberalism in US academia is very much like two bald men fighting over a comb!

4. 'National Territorial Totality' is the felicitous phrase used by F. Halliday, one of the most measured and insistent critics of Realism, op. cit. Sometimes Realists in certain contexts do refer to the state in the narrow, sociological sense and can provide sensible enough studies of specific regions, countries, and wars, but this is in spite of their theoretical weakness, not because of their framework or paradigm of understanding. This central weakness, nonetheless, exacts its heavy price disqualifying Realism from any serious purchase on human reality in modern times.
5. The period of existence of Communism as a serious systemic rival also meant the more or less successful challenge to the imperatives of the world capitalist economic and political system.
6. So self-consciously committed is Waltz to the structural–compulsive character of the global system as he understands it, that he dismisses all fears of nuclear deterrence ever breaking down. Indeed, he says the possibility of its use is nearly zero. (*The Spread of Nuclear Weapons*, op. cit., p. 50), but this quantified probability assessment of his has no evidential basis whatsoever and simply comes out of his head. To claim that the probability of something happening is very low is different from the more categorical claim that it is nearly zero. Waltz relies extremely heavily on the most extreme form of the 'long peace' argument in which nuclear weapons are deemed necessary and sufficient for bringing it about. Waltz effectively ignores recent revelations about the history of 'near-misses' regarding contemplated and accidental use of nuclear weapons.

   Insofar as he does have to address the 'near zero' possibility of deterrence breakdown, Waltz, with breathtaking self-confidence, reassures all and sundry that 'should deterrence fail, a few judiciously delivered warheads are likely to produce sobriety in the leaders of all the countries involved and thus bring about rapid de-escalation'. (*The Spread of Nuclear Weapons*, op. cit., p.131). Again, there is no serious evidence (how can there be?) or even argumentative basis for this claim, just the Waltzian assumption of high rationality-guiding behaviour among leaders of states even though the Neo-Realist rationality which insists that a nuclear exchange will not take place has broken down in this scenario! Moral issues concerning nuclear deterrence have no place in Neo-Realism.
7. No empire in human history collapsed as comprehensively, as rapidly, and as bloodlessly as did the 'Soviet Empire'. By all conventional indices of 'hard power' this is simply inexplicable. The fact is that even the ruling élite which most benefited from the existing system had long since lost any ideological commitment to the Soviet system and no longer possessed the will to preserve it. The break-up was precipitated not by some supposedly unbearable outside pressure, nor by powerful rebellion from below, but by unexpected political–moral collapse from

above. One would have thought that the manner in which this extraordinary event unfolded—which flies in the face of all Realist common sense about the importance of balance of power, hard power, or security understood as the territorial survival of a state—might lead to serious self-questioning by Realists. Especially since Soviet collapse followed a decades-long history during which there have been numerous political-military defeats of the great powers by weaker and smaller ones from decolonizing wars of liberation to Vietnam and Afghanistan. By all Realist indices of hard power, this too had no business to be happening. Unfortunately, there is no sign whatsoever that Realists will engage in such rethinking.

8. If instances of Realist overestimation of the power and importance of the state and of what statecraft can accomplish in international affairs are obvious and numerous, a classic example of Realist underestimation of the importance of the state and what new forms of statecraft appropriate to a changing world order can do, is to be found on the issue of economic globalization. If a more humane life for the mass of citizens in a country is to be secured, then the state must intervene to regulate and shape market forces. Instead, Realists simply assume that the world capitalist economy is what it was centuries ago and therefore still basically follows a mercantilist pattern, or that it must be left alone in fealty to current neo-liberal economic perspectives on how globalization should proceed. In both cases, the relationship between states and markets, between states and the world economy is seen as unproblematic and requiring the state to do nothing either because it cannot intervene effectively or because it need not, since the world system has not changed in its fundamentals from what it was a few centuries ago. Capitalism is conceptually irrelevant for Realism, so there is no question of seeing its own evolution in the latter half of the twentieth century has having that serious a bearing on the study of international relations.

9. E.H. Carr, *The Twenty Years' Crisis* (Harper Torchbook edition, New York, 1964) sometimes called the founding text of Realism, portrays an understanding of Realism very different from later US versions. Carr's work showed an acute awareness of the limitations of Realism, the necessity for sensible Realist thinking to connect strongly to Liberal Internationalist and highly ethical thinking. He refused to make Realism into an overarching ahistorical model of how the global system is supposed to work. Carr, after all, was himself a great historian as well as a former diplomat.

The English school of Realism has always been at somewhat of a tangent to the dominant US tradition. It has increasingly separated itself from the needs of the British to act as an imperial power (progressively on the wane after 1945) and has generally produced more sensitive and intelligent insights into what it calls 'international society' (as distinct from what US Realists call the 'international system') than its Atlantic counterpart. See the works of its two most famous representatives, Martin Wight and Hedley Bull: M. Wight in G. Wight and B. Porter (eds.) *International Theory: The Three Traditions*, Leicester Univ. Press, Leicester, 1991. H. Bull, *The Anarchical Society: a Study on the. Order of World*

Politics, Macmillan, London, 1977. This English school continues to flourish in the work of Adam Watson and James Mayall, among others.

10. For decades, Indian Realists supported the Indo-USSR relationship on political-strategic grounds, but they remained effectively immune to the conceptual language of Soviet strategic thought. This Soviet thinking was filtered through an extremely crude and highly distorted version of Marxism, but even so, it promoted the use of a superior conceptual alternative to the notion of balance of power. This was the notion of 'correlation of forces'. The concept was superior in the era of systemic rivalry precisely because it was broader, more flexible, not pivoted so centrally on the military dimension, but allowed for the incorporation of other economic, cultural, political-ideological dimensions. That was why it was possible for Soviet strategic thinkers to talk, not inaccurately, of the 'world correlation of forces' vis-à-vis the West and the US as moving in its favour during the nineteen-fifties, sixties and much of the seventies despite the military balance not being weighted in its favour and at most stable between the two blocs.

    In the eighties, when it became increasingly clear that when judged by the other dimensions incorporated in the notion of correlation of forces—the economic, cultural, political-ideological—it was the West that was running way ahead, Soviet strategists increasingly began to prefer the use of concepts like balance of power and 'mutual parity' precisely because these notions were more strongly pivoted on that dimension—the military—in which the USSR could reassure itself that it had not lost ground in relation to the US and the West. The Soviets thus used the superior concept of correlation of forces in a self-serving and manipulative way, but the important point that needs to be stressed here is not this but something else. Indian Realists, despite the prolonged importance of the Indo-Soviet relationship in the post-war history of India, have rarely been inclined to learn anything from the conceptual baggage of Soviet strategic thought but have been so 'Americanized' in their thinking that they have preferred to use the inferior concept of balance of power as their primary conceptual tool throughout.

11. See Chapter 2, p. 17 and refer to Note 3, p. 30.

12. ibid. Recent declassified material confirms what a 1994 article claimed. In a 20 July 1961 National Security Council meeting in Washington, the US military had drawn up a plan for a nuclear first strike on the USSR which was more than a contingency plan. General Lemnitzer, chairman of the Joint Chiefs of Staff, proposed such a strike in late 1963 and proposed a justification for it by suggesting that tensions be deliberately heightened in the period preceding the sudden assault. See Heather A. Purcell and James K. Galbraith, 'Did the US Military Plan a Nuclear First Strike for 1963', in *The American Prospect*, no. 19, Fall 1994, p. 92.

13. Charles Perrow, *Normal Accidents: Living With High-Risk Technologies*, Basic Books New York, 1984; Scott D. Sagan, *The Limits of Safety: Organisations, Accidents and Nuclear Weapons*, Princeton Univ. Press, Princeton, 1993.

14. See Bruce G. Blair, *The Logic of Accidental Nuclear War*, Washington D.C., Brookings Institution, 1993; Paul Bracken, *Command and Control of Nuclear Forces*, Yale Univ. Press, New Haven, 1983; Peter Douglas Feaver, *Guarding the Guardians:*

Civilian Control of Nuclear Weapons in the United States, Cornell Univ. Press, Ithaca,1992; Scott D. Sagan, op. cit.; Shaun Gregory, *The Hidden Cost of Deterrence: Nuclear Weapons Accidents,* Brassey's, London,1990. Gregory's account could not take account of declassified material since publication.

15. A BBC Online television programme of 21 October 1998.
16. The most dramatic example of risky behaviour in a domestic crisis comes from China. In October 1966, in the midst of the Cultural Revolution, Marshall Nie Rongzhen launched a test missile 800 kilometres across China to pre-empt radical interference in the nuclear programme by behaving radically in a dramatic and public gesture of support to the Mao faction. John W. Lewis and Xue Litai, *China Builds the Bomb,* Stanford Univ. Press, Stanford,1988, pp.202–203. See also Scott D. Sagan and K. N. Waltz, op. cit., pp. 80-85.
17. In the Yom Kippur war of October 1973, Israel had reportedly started putting nuclear weapons on its fighter-bomber planes. See Seymour M. Hersh, *The Samson Option: Israel's Nuclear Arsenal and American Foreign Policy,* Random House, New York,1991, p.231. In the Gulf War of 1991, there are reports of Israel placing nuclear-tipped Jericho missiles on high alert readiness. See S.M. Hersh, op. cit., and Bill Gertz, 'Israel Deploys Missiles for a Possible Strike at Iraq' in *The Washington Times,* 28 January 1991.
18. China is very worried about the watering down of the ABM Treaty by the US and current Japan-US discussions about a joint Theatre Missile defence (TMD) programme. This would adversely affect China's capacity to hit the US mainland with its twenty or less land-based long range ballistic missiles in a second strike. Should the ABM Treaty unravel or be perceived in Chinese eyes to have done so, then Beijing will try and compensate itself by expanding the numbers of land-based long-range missiles it has, as well as developing a more sophisticated and expanded submarine arm. At the moment, this is very weak.
19. India is expanding the range of its intermediate *Agni* missiles. It hopes to push this to 2500 kilometres as well as develop even longer range *Surya* missiles. A 'technology demonstrator' will not worry China much. But if over the next five years or so India can carry out a series of missile tests over the requisite range, then this will alarm China and lead to major changes in its strategic planning even though New Delhi will still be far from having an assured second-strike capacity against China. The revival of the *Agni* programme was signalled by the test firing of *Agni-II,* on 12 April 1999. Though the testing partly reflected internal political considerations—the BJP-led coalition was in deep trouble and fighting for survival at the time—it was also a statement of clear intent regarding the government's determination to build a fully fledged and triadic nuclear weapons delivery system. Supporters of the tests called for extending the range so that the missile could more confidently target China.
20. Accidents and miscalculations are less likely if only one form of deployment (sea-based submarine platforms) is resorted to. France and the UK are in fact moving towards just such a singular pattern of deployment because any hope of building a credible second-strike capacity against a rival that is geographically

distant (e.g. China's capacity to deter the US or India's to deter China) may do without airborne or land-based missiles, but not without a strong submarine arm. India currently has no nuclear-reactor driven submarine and may be years away from developing a viable submarine-based missile arm.

Bombing Bombay

More Devastating than Hiroshima?

Nuclear weapons are unlike any other armaments in their physical impact and health effects. There is no military or civil defence possible against them. It is virtually impossible to intercept nuclear missiles with any degree of reliability, and civil defence methods such as underground air-raid shelters and hardened structures are basically useless in a nuclear attack. They cannot offer any protection against one of the main lethal releases from a nuclear bomb: radioactive fallout.

That is precisely why the slogan of the peace movement, for instance in the UK, was summed up in the title of a famous booklet, *Protest and Survive*—in contradistinction to the government's propaganda manual, promising false protection to the citizen, *Protect and Survive.*

There is reason to be extremely concerned at the likely effects of a nuclear weapons explosion over a population centrre anywhere in the Indian subcontinent. In any realistic scenario of mass destruction, which is even worse than the havoc caused in Hiroshima, where 140,000 people perished, Indian and Pakistani cities are prime candidates. Not only are they more densely populated; they also have poor civic infrastructures and medical facilities. In relation to Japanese or European cities bombed during World War II, the subcontinent's cities have a much higher number of poor-quality buildings and a higher concentration of motor vehicles.

A huge proportion of their population—half to two-thirds—lives in shanty-towns, in flimsy structures that cannot possibly withstand hurricane-speed winds, firestorms, or blast waves. Their inhabitants use large quantities of plastics and other inflammable materials which produce extremely toxic chemicals upon combustion.

Indian and Pakistani scientists and nuclear disarmament campaigners have tried to estimate the likely effects of a single explosion of a

Hiroshima-type first-generation bomb, with a yield of 15 kilotons, at an elevation of 600 meters over cities such as Bombay, Karachi, Delhi and Lahore, all vulnerable to aircraft or missile attacks. The most systematic study of this kind has been done for Bombay by M.V. Ramana, physicist, formerly at the Massachusetts Institute of Technology.[1]

Ramana's conclusions are extremely distressing: between 150,000 and 800,000 people would die depending on where the bomb is exploded. If a more powerful 150-kt weapon were exploded, the casualties could be an even more awesome 2 to 6 million.

The devastating damage caused by a nuclear explosion falls into three categories: prompt effects, delayed effects and long-term effects. The first includes the initial intense flash of heat and light, release of neutron and gamma radiation, and shock or blast waves.

Exposure to intense radiation is liable to lead to leukemia, thyroid cancer, breast cancer, and lung cancer, as well as non-fatal diseases such as birth defects, cataracts, mental retardation, and keloids. Winds accompanying the shock wave would reach velocities of more than 110 km/h to a distance of 3 km or more from the epicentre. The shock wave would destroy everything within a radius of 1.1 km. Up to 1.7 km from the point of explosion, all houses not built with concrete would be destroyed. Many buildings in Bombay, especially old ones, are either badly designed or constructed with raw materials that are of poor quality (such as adulterated cement). Every year several hundred buildings collapse by themselves, especially during the rainy season.

The delayed effects, beginning within minutes of the explosion, include firestorms and radioactive fallout. Firestorms would begin with the coalescing of individual fires started by the initial flash of light and heat. In a Hiroshima-sized explosion over a city like Bombay, the radius of the region under flames would be 1.7 to 2 kilometres. Due to its large area, the fire zone would act as a huge pump, sucking in air from the surrounding areas and driving heated air upwards. This pumping action would create winds with velocities as high as 50–80 kilometres/hour.

The temperature in the fire zone would reach several hundred degrees, making it almost certain that there would be no survivors. Furthermore, fire-fighting would be almost impossible due to the combination of hurricane-force winds, thick smoke, destruction of water mains by the shock wave, and the presence of debris blocking roads.

In industrial cities such as Bombay, Karachi or Calcutta, the damaging health effects would be greatly magnified with the additional release of potential toxins from factories and from nuclear installations. For instance, Bombay is home to India's highest concentration of chemical factories (over 2,000 of them) and storage units. The Bhabha Atomic Research Centre, with a number of nuclear reactors and chemical plants and other facilities, including reprocessing plants, is located in Bombay. (Karachi has Pakistan's sole nuclear power reactor).

The second delayed effect, radioactive fallout, must not be underestimated. When a nuclear bomb explodes, a large quantity of material is vaporized and forms a cloud of highly radioactive dust which can travel long distances depending on weather conditions, including wind direction and velocity. Even a wind velocity of 25 km per hour is liable to distribute the fallout over an area of 25 to 100 square kilometres. Areas which receive high levels of fallout are liable to have a large number of radiation-caused fatalities and sicknesses, but even people living in localities receiving moderate fallout will suffer from leukemia, and cancers of the thyroid, lung, breast and bone.

In Hiroshima and Nagasaki, the mortality rates for all diseases, and for leukemia, among people exposed to more than 200 rads, were respectively 1.2 and 17.6 times higher when compared to an unexposed control group. Increases in cancer rates from an atomic bombing of Bombay should be comparable to those among Hiroshima survivors.

Ramana estimates that the 'prompt casualties' in Bombay from just the blast and fire effects of one small 15 kt nuclear weapon would be 150,000 to 800,000, given an average population density of 23,000 people per hectare, assuming that the weapon is exploded in the atmosphere at a height of 600 metres and that fallout effects are negligible. In the case of a weapon exploding at ground level, the areas damaged by fire and blast would be somewhat smaller, but fallout would be a significant cause of deaths and sickness. The number of people dying of all causes could be as high as 350,000 to 400,000.

The number of deaths and serious complications from bomb injuries in a nuclear explosion would be far higher in Indian and Pakistani cities because of the weaknesses of the medical relief infrastructure and the inability of fire-fighters, emergency aid providers, doctors, nurses, and hospitals to reach out to the victims.

High levels of road congestion, prevalence of flimsy building structures, poor fire-fighting facilities, paucity of doctors and hospital beds (these, as a proportion of the population are respectively less than a fourth and a tenth of the level in developed societies) are likely to result in a sharp, but avoidable, increase in the number of casualties, and in greater suffering.[2]

The long-term effects of a nuclear bomb explosion need no emphasis. In Hiroshima and Nagasaki, the victims, or *hibakusha,* continue to die to this day from illnesses contracted during exposure to the fallout of the atomic bombing of 1945.

Notes

1. Summary published as M.V. Ramana, 'The South Asian Bomb: Effects of a Nuclear Blast Over Bombay', in *Medicine & Global Survival*, Boston, October 1998, Vol. 5, Issue 2, p. 74–77. The full report, made available to the authors, is to be published by International Physicians for the Prevention of Nuclear War. The discussion here is essentially a summary of Ramana's excellent analysis.
2. This does not contend that adequate or effective medical treatment or a cure is possible for the disorders and illnesses caused by a nuclear weapons attack. Usually, none is. In the Indian subcontinent, however, even elementary first-aid treatment of severe burns and other serious injuries would be virtually impossible given the appalling state of the healthcare infrastructure and official callousness.

CHAPTER NINE

From Abstinence, to Ambiguity, to the Nuclear Blasts

The greatest element of surprise in the May 1998 tests by India and Pakistan lay not so much in that they took place within a few weeks of a new government led by the Bharatiya Janata Party coming to power in New Delhi, but in the circumstance that there was no tangible 'provocation' for them. No single event or even a series of developments can be credibly cited as providing an immediate rationale for the crossing of the nuclear threshold by India and Pakistan. The world had long known that the two South Asian states were, at most, 'a screwdriver's turn' away from making nuclear bombs; they might even have had 'Bombs in the Basement' for some time. It was not, however, known that they were both more or less ready to conduct underground nuclear explosions, based on extensive preparations: drilling of shafts in the desert (in Rajasthan in India) or the mountain (Chagai hills in Baluchistan in Pakistan), lowering of explosive assemblies and electric cables, 'hardening' of ground-level bunkers, and perhaps putting in place 'containment' systems to shield the explosions' impact. Such preparations can take up to a year if not longer. Clearly, scientists and engineers in India's Department of Atomic Energy (DAE) and the Defence Research & Development Organization (DRDO) could carry out the detonation of nuclear explosions at short notice—less than two months after the Vajpayee government was sworn in—only because they had not just the Bombs, but a number of auxiliary technologies as well as the physical infrastructure for the tests more or less in place. Pakistan followed India by testing within a fortnight.

Pakistan: Teased into Testing

The delay is explained less by a lack of preparation than by the Nawaz Sharif government's *political* hesitation in crossing the nuclear threshold in immediate response to India. Prime Minister Sharif showed a distinct reluctance to test: refraining from nuclear testing would have helped Islamabad seize the moral high ground and overcome some of the stigma deriving from its support to Islamic extremist groups such as the Taliban in Afghanistan and Harkat-ul-Ansar in Kashmir. Besides diplomatic advantage, Pakistan also stood to gain heftily in military and economic terms if it refrained from testing. The US, which sent a delegation to Islamabad in May led by Deputy Secretary of State Strobe Talbott, offered a $5 billion package in economic and military aid to Sharif in return for showing restraint.

Sharif was clearly tempted enough by the offer, and by the calculus of costs and benefits of non-testing, for him to withstand heavy pressure from his political opponents as well as large chunks of the Pakistani establishment, including former high functionaries, diplomats, and generals, not to speak of radical Islamicists, in the Indian tests' immediate aftermath. By the end of the week of 11 May, it did seem that Pakistan would refrain from testing its nuclear weapons. Some extreme right-wingers in India took this to mean, quite simply, that Pakistan did not have the Bomb: why else would it not test one?[1]

That is when India's Home Minister, Lal Krishna Advani, known for his hardline views, opened a new front in the ongoing India–Pakistan hostilities: Kashmir. On 18 May, he warned Pakistan that with the Indian tests, the 'geo-strategic' situation had decisively changed. He said that India's 'decisive step to become a nuclear weapon state has brought about a qualitatively new stage in Indo-Pak relations, particularly in finding a lasting solution to the Kashmir problem'. He asked 'Islamabad to realize the change in the geo-strategic situation in the region and the world', and demanded that Pakistan must 'join India in the common pursuit of peace and prosperity in the Indian subcontinent', warning that: 'any other course will be futile and costly for Pakistan.'[2]

The response to this from Pakistan was one of ultra-nationalist outrage driven under strong Islamicist pressure. More inflammatory statements by Indian leaders, in particular Defence Minister George Fernandes, including some threatening 'hot pursuit' of Pakistani troops and Pakistan-backed guerrillas into its territory, followed. These could only be interpreted as India taunting, teasing, needling, cajoling Pakistan into testing.[3] Sharif could not withstand the pressure to test any longer, especially after the Pakistan army chief, following a visit to Azad Kashmir (the Pakistan-held part of Kashmir), reported that his troops' morale would be compromised if there was no nuclear test. Pakistan detonated what it claimed were five nuclear explosive devices on 28 May and yet another on 30 May, equalizing India's total of six, and 'getting even' with the enemy, as Sharif put it. Pakistan too announced it was now a nuclear weapons state. This was probably the first time in history that a nuclear state that had crossed the threshold actually encouraged its own adversary to follow suit.

The relative ease with which India and Pakistan crossed the nuclear Rubicon can only be explained in terms of a prolonged process, stretched over decades, involving technological preparations, creation of a physical infrastructure and acquisition of strategic materials, as well as a hardening of the two rivals' nuclear postures. India's transition from a state that campaigned for nuclear disarmament and practised nuclear abstinence, to one that suddenly embraced the doctrine of nuclear deterrence and self-avowedly tested these weapons of mass destruction, is naturally the more dramatic of the two stories. This transition was itself punctuated for a quarter-century by the policy of nuclear ambiguity. What enabled this transition to occur? At work here was the unfolding of both technological and political processes.

India was the first Third World country to launch a nuclear energy programme. Homi J. Bhabha, the programme's leader, played a major role in the founding of the Tata Institute of Fundamental Research in 1944 and in the creation of a high-profile scientific establishment committed to research in nuclear physics and related areas. This establishment was to form the core of the Atomic Energy Commission (AEC) set up in 1948. The AEC organized a survey of such natural resources relevant to nuclear energy as uranium, thorium, beryllium, and graphite, and established a special unit, the Rare Minerals Division. The Commission also emphasized the development of basic sciences and the training of high-quality research scientists as well as the indigenous production of special instruments and support facilities.

The first Indian nuclear reactor, *Apsara*, went critical in 1956, with help from the UK which supplied the enriched uranium fuel. Soon after, a second reactor, code-named CIRUS after Canadian–Indian–US cooperation, went critical in 1960, and a plutonium reprocessing plant was also established. The spent fuel from CIRUS and the ability to reprocess it, coupled with the expertise and experience Indian scientists had gained in the nuclear field, were to give India an independent nuclear weapons option. Since the mid–1960s, India has undertaken the construction of nuclear power stations and large research facilities and the establishment of independent 'unsafeguarded' sources of weapons-grade plutonium. The civilian programme encompasses the entire 'nuclear fuel cycle'.

Currently, India has an installed capacity to generate 1840 MW of nuclear power, and plans to raise nuclear electricity generation to 20,000 MW by the year 2020.[4] The mainstay of the nuclear power programme is the Canadian Deuterium-Natural Uranium (CANDU) reactor design, although the country's first nuclear power station, built as a turnkey project with US aid, at Tarapur near Mumbai, is based on an enriched uranium-light water design. India's CANDU reactor programme has not performed well; nor has India been able to innovate and stabilize an improved design. This lack of success and financial stringency recently impelled India to contract the import of two Russian-designed VVER-1000 reactors.

India has sought to develop its nuclear programme across a broad technological front that includes a space exploration programme and missiles, in addition to such components as material sciences and other auxiliary technologies. India's progress in the field of delivery systems needs to be especially noted. Its nuclear-capable aircraft include the Canberra, Ajeet, MiG–21, –23, –27, and –29, Jaguar, Mirage, and Sukhoi–30, which provide a combat radius from around 100 to over 900 miles (approximately 160–1450 kilometres). The Jaguar and Mirage, and possibly even the MiG–29, are equipped for in-flight refuelling.

India started working on space-launchers and rockets in the 1960s and by the early 1980s had 'established the basic technology required for missile systems in solid and liquid propulsion, control and guidance and precision fabrication'.[5] In 1983, it launched the Integrated Guided Missile Development Programme which aimed to produce five kinds of missiles. Nuclear-capable missiles being developed in India include the *Prithvi,* a surface-to-surface missile with a range of 250 to 350 km, now being serially produced, and the *Agni* (which has had three test flights and is still under development) with a range of 1500–2500 km. When fully developed, the *Agni* would be capable of bringing the area of the Persian Gulf and many Chinese cities into striking distance. The *Agni* was first successfully tested on 22 May 1989. After the third test, in 1994, all further development was put on hold until May 1998. A longer-range (2500–3000 km) version of the missile, *Agni-II,* is under development and was tested in April 1999. There is also a polar space launch vehicle under development which would be the equivalent of an intercontinental ballistic missile. The Orissa missile test firing range, located in the eastern part of India, is clearly for missile-related military purposes.

Pakistan was a late starter in the area of nuclear energy and missiles and launched its own nuclear programme only in the 1960s. The turning-point came in the mid-1960s after India had acquired a plutonium-producing 'research reactor' (1960) and built a reprocessing plant (1964). The first record of discussion of a nuclear weapons programme in the Pakistan cabinet is traceable to 1963. The issue of feasibility of such a programme was actively discussed during the 1965 war with India, especially in the light of the October 1964 statement of Homi Bhabha, following the first Chinese test, that India too could, if necessary, make a nuclear Bomb within 18 months. In 1966 and 1968, the Cabinet again discussed the issue. In 1968, at the instance of Bomb enthusiast and Foreign Minister Zulfikar Ali Bhutto, Pakistan commissioned a feasibility study—or rather two different studies, one by the Pakistan Atomic Energy Commission and the other by defence scientists. Their recommendations however contradicted each other and neither fructified.

Pakistan's nuclear programme was of course greatly influenced by developments in India, including the nuclear policy debate in that country. Following the Sino-Indian border war in 1962, and particularly after the Chinese Lop Nor test of October 1964, the nuclear weapons issue invaded parliamentary and public debate in India. The debate, especially the clamour for an 'Indian Bomb' by several MPs, appears to have provided an additional stimulus to Pakistani decision-makers to favour the pursuit of a nuclear weapons capability. It was however only after the fall of the Yahya Khan regime in the wake of the creation of Bangladesh in 1971, that the new premier, Zulfikar Ali Bhutto, could give a decisive fillip to the country's nuclear programme.

'We'll Eat Grass . . .'

In 1972, Bhutto made his famous 'we-will-eat-grass-but-we'll-have-our-Bomb' speech, emphasizing in his address to top scientists and engineers at Multan the critical importance of developing a Pakistani Bomb at any cost to 'safeguard the country's security' against India. After Pakistan's dismemberment at India's hands in the Bangladesh war, the rhetoric of militant nuclearism acquired a particularly sharp edge. There is reason to believe this was backed with a financial commitment. Pakistan by then had also approached Canada to build a small natural uranium CANDU reactor at Karachi (Karachi Nuclear Power Plant (KANUPP). KANUPP's function was related more to gaining familiarity and experience with the working of nuclear technology than power generation (of which it has a rather poor record).

In the initial stages, Pakistan explored the plutonium route to nuclear weapons manufacture. This is technologically simpler and far easier to manage, once a nuclear reactor is in place, and access to its spent fuel is secured. Pakistan in the 1960s and 1970s could not have designed or built such a reactor on its own; nor was it in a position to reprocess spent nuclear fuel so as to extract plutonium from it. Under Bhutto's leadership, Pakistan also began exploring the possibility of enriching uranium by the gas-centrifuge process. It first sought French assistance in building a plutonium reprocessing plant. France agreed. Although the plant was to be subject to international 'safeguards', it would nevertheless have enabled Pakistan to absorb the technology and possibly accumulate weapons-grade material on the sly.

By 1976, US concerns over Pakistan's nuclear intentions were translated into successful pressure on the French to stop their technology transfer. With the possibility of open external support for its nuclear programme effectively curtailed, Pakistan, both under Bhutto and his successor, General Mohammed Zia ul-Haq, embarked on a carefully coordinated clandestine effort to secure the components necessary for building a uranium enrichment plant at Kahuta, as well as New Labs, a small pilot plutonium extraction plant in Rawalpindi. It is the uranium enrichment programme that provided the decisive breakthrough for Pakistan in the area of weapons-grade material production.

From the outset, Pakistan's nuclear programme has essentially been a 'dedicated' one, that is to say having a clear military purpose as its principal *raison d'être*. In this respect, the programme mirrors Pakistan's much more 'reactive' foreign policy driven by an obsession with India. The Indian nuclear programme, on the other hand, has reflected a more complex constellation of pressures and motivations. Conceived originally as a purely civilian effort, India's programme nevertheless acquired a 'dual' character after the 1950s under a scientific leadership that was keen to preserve the weapons option despite the Nehru era policy of permanent nuclear abstinence.

The potential for military spin-offs and capabilities from the Indian civilian nuclear programme did not emerge either suddenly or after a certain technological threshold was crossed in the nuclear programme. It was the result of a conscious choice by the programme's leadership to build into it the possibility, of obtaining progressively greater militarily valuable technologies and products and to make the transition from civilian to military use of nuclear capabilities, if required, as quickly and as smoothly as possible. The built-in 'dual' character was reflected in the importance given to plutonium production—in addition to CIRUS, India built the 100 MW (thermal) *Dhruva* reactor—as well as to work on materials sciences and on auxiliary technologies.[6] Thus, the Pokharan test of 1974 could be organized within a relatively short period of time after the approval to produce a 'nuclear device' was granted—assessments vary from claims that this was in late 1969 to some time in 1972.[7]

India: Scientists' Pernicious Role

Most accounts of the relationship between the policy-making apparatus in India and the scientific leadership of the nuclear programme suggest that the latter has tended to enjoy at least in practice a certain degree of autonomy from the former. This was especially true of the early period of the development of the Indian nuclear programme under Bhabha. Although Bhabha was formally constrained by the Nehru policy of permanent nuclear abstinence—and was, ironically, a Nehru appointee close to the prime minister in science policy and planning—in actual practice, he appears to have pursued a different orientation. He organized the Indian nuclear effort in such a way as would enable him to keep the weapons option open indefinitely and, indeed, to sustain and develop it to the point of being able to stockpile unsafeguarded weapons-grade material.

Thus, Bhabha devoted a considerable amount of energy to the construction of CIRUS, the 'research reactor' built with Canadian and US assistance, but operated without the constraint of safeguards or sanctions. There is reason to believe that Bhabha strove hard to avoid signing a formal agreeement with Canada and the US that would in any way compromise, restrict, or limit India's complete control over the reactor and its output, including spent fuel. The agreements India signed in the 1950s committed it to limit the use of CIRUS and its products to 'peaceful purposes', but without safeguards or oversight by an external agency. The spent fuel from the CIRUS reactor was later reprocessed at a plutonium separation plant set up next to the reactor at Trombay (near Bombay) in 1964. Eventually, this became the source of the plutonium used in the Pokharan explosive device.

Bhabha was thus making neither an academic point nor an empty boast when he stated in a famous broadcast following China's first test in October 1964 that India could, given a political decision, manufacture the bomb in 18 months. By the late 1950s, Bhabha had apparently begun to shift towards the view that the policy of permanent nuclear abstinence was probably not in India's long-term interest. He argued that in a world without disarmament, the only effective means of countering 'atomic colonialism' (traceable to the nuclear weapons monopoly of the great powers) would be a Third World bomb. Whether or not Bhabha fully worked out the implications of this proposition in order to arrive at a comprehensive formulation that was radically opposed to India's official policy in the Nehru period is not clear. What is fairly clear is that he followed a direction that diverged significantly from the officially stated policy.

One reason why nuclear scientists have been able to pursue programmes that diverge in subtle ways from proclaimed policy is related to the structure of nuclear policy-making and implementation in India. The agency charged with this task is not, as in most policy matters, the Cabinet, but the AEC, which was constituted under a special Act of Parliament. Typically, the AEC is composed primarily of scientists and dominated by the top leaders of the Department of Atomic Energy. The AEC's chairman serves as the ex-officio secretary to the India government in the department of atomic energy and is rated on a par with the topmost bureaucrat. In practice, the minute details of the nuclear programme are probably not even discussed in the AEC, but are left to individual scientists to plan and execute in an environment that is relatively insulated from, and hostile to, public scrutiny. The Atomic Energy Act, 1962 institutionalizes secrecy and centralization of control within the AEC as few Indian laws do for any institution.

The specialized technical nature of the nuclear scientists' work and role in the nuclear energy establishment was yet another obstacle to 'outsiders', 'generalists' and political leaders acquiring effective control over the nuclear programme. This *de facto* autonomy of the scientists results from, and is further enhanced by, the overall prestige and high profile that modern science and its practitioners enjoy in most Third World countries, at least in the perception of and opinion among the élite. This is particularly the case with India and Pakistan where scientific achievements with even explicitly stated military implications or aims attract an exceptional degree of praise from within an élite that may be unfavourably disposed towards political leaders. Scientists are thus able to claim special status and unique importance for themselves and to demand effective autonomy from political leaders.

Until the early 1960s, India's official position, which was supported by the general consensus, was a policy of permanent nuclear abstinence. To explain how this policy came about, one must examine the particular inflexions of Indian non-alignment during the Nehru era. Non-alignment must be understood in two separate senses. First, non-alignment represented a particular world-view of the international system of states and conflicts between them. As such, the perspective manifested strong normative and moralist overtones, which were critical of alliance politics and the search for 'balances of power'. As the name of a broad movement of non-aligned nations suggests, it offered the prospect that the movement would play a positive role (under the leadership of certain countries) out of all proportion to its ability to impose sanctions of any meaningful kind. In the second and more fundamental sense, non-alignment was also the foreign policy framework of a particular country (in this case, India) which, by definition, sought maximum national autonomy to pursue its interests free from the constraints imposed by bloc membership.

The basic tension between these two senses of non-alignment was not really perceived until the 1962 Sino-Indian conflict. Through most of the Nehru era, India adopted a high-profile and diplomatically activist approach in international affairs and in such fora as the United Nations. This approach was reflected by India's active role in the disarmament negotiations of the 1950s and 1960s. This role reinforced the credibility and strength of the Indian government's decision not to go nuclear. The 1962 war with China marked a decisive watershed. After this, India's national interests became more sharply focused and defined, and were regarded as being essentially regional.

An involution of preoccupations took place: India became less concerned about having a high international profile in various fora, and more concerned about strengthening the components of its national power. Non-alignment became, more or less, a loose synonym for the traditional realpolitik approach of pursuing national interests through the projection and expansion of national power. To this extent, a re-evaluation of the role nuclear weapons could play in India's foreign policy could be expected. Earlier negative attitudes or outright rejection began to give way to more positive perceptions of the linkages between nuclear weapons, deterrence, and national security ambitions.

Despite early criticism from the West, inspired by the influential US Secretary of State, John Foster Dulles, India's non-alignment policy came to be accepted and endorsed by both major blocs; and India, unlike China, never had to face either, let alone both, nuclear-armed superpowers as a strategic adversary. China embarked on the nuclear weapons path earlier and with fewer signs of vacillation than India and was never inclined to remain 'only' a threshold nuclear state. Despite tensions linked to the US alliance with, and support for, Pakistan, Indo-US relations during the Cold War were of a complex and fluctuating character that never hardened into a posture of strategic opposition or open hostility. Even the perception of a Chinese 'threat' especially after the border war of 1962, was seen as qualified; of interest principally along the Himalayan crest. During the 1950s and 1960s, however, and even after the 1962 conflict, India did not display any immediate apprehension of a Chinese–Pakistan line-up, let alone the US–China–Pakistan 'axis'. The most important consequence of the 1962 war was its impact on India's self-perception and its stimulation of a new self-awareness concerning the aims and means of achieving national 'fulfilment'.

Pakistan: Reactive Consistency

Pakistan's nuclear preparations and thinking have been based on fairly clear and straightforward premises that, in some ways, lend to its nuclear policy a level of consistency and coherence that is absent in the Indian case. Pakistan does not have a general or universal (declared) policy that is independent of India. Islamabad's repeated declarations after 1971 that India is clearly the dominant power in the region have not prevented Pakistan from seeking military–political parity with India, whether this quest was motivated by prestige or defensive considerations or by ambitions over Kashmir.

Pakistan's nuclear preparations, of course, pre-dated the Pokharan nuclear test, but assumed added urgency in its wake. US pressure in this respect was of little avail until the late 1980s, when the stiff Pressler Amendment to the US Trade Act was enacted. Neither Zulfikar Ali Bhutto nor his successor succumbed to US pressure. Pakistan's recalcitrance during the Zia ul-Haq period (1977–88) came as a particular shock to Washington, which had reason to believe that the military regime's unpopularity and hence its greater reliance on US support would render it more pliable in regard to its nuclear programme. In reality, Zia ul-Haq's regime was completely successful in its clandestine efforts to secure classified designs of a centrifuge-based uranium enrichment plant and in obtaining a number of critical subsystems, components, and materials.

The key figure in all this was Dr Abdul Qadir Khan, a German-trained metallurgist who had worked at the centrifuge enrichment plant at Almelo, the Netherlands, where he almost certainly obtained access to key designs and to lists of suppliers of crucial components. Pakistan is believed to have begun to produce weapons-grade uranium some time in 1986, and stopped doing so under the threat of US trade sanctions between May 1989 and June 1990. It is believed to have resumed production for some time in 1991, but finally to have stopped production that year. This suggests that at the time of the tests, Pakistan had at least accumulated between 160 and 260 kg of highly enriched uranium—enough for eight to 20 Hiroshima-type first-generation bombs.

Pakistan has a range of nuclear-capable aircraft. It has developed two short-range missiles (*Hatf*-I and-II), with a range of 80 km and 300 km respectively, and is believed to have received some Chinese M–11 missiles (or at least their components) in clandestine transfer. The M–11, with a range of about 300–350 km, is a borderline case so far as restrictions under the Missile Technology Control Regime are concerned. In April 1998, Pakistan announced the 'successful' test flight of a 'medium-range' missile, the *Ghauri* (named after an Afghan invader of India during the Middle Ages). There is some confusion over its origin (whether it is Chinese or North Korean) and its capabilities, but if Pakistani official claims are correct, then many cities in peninsular India, not just the North, could come within the *Ghauri's* range.

Until the early 1990s, Pakistan pursued its own version of a two-track policy. On the one hand, it systematically sought to develop a clandestine nuclear weapons capability. On the other, it just as systematically put forward a variety of proposals for regional denuclearization which gave it the moral 'high ground' in the war of words against India. The proposals included mutual bilateral inspection of each other's facilities, third party verification, the conclusion of a bilateral treaty renouncing nuclear weapons, mutual and simultaneous signature of the NPT, and the establishment of a South Asian nuclear weapons free zone (NWFZ).

By the mid-1990s, the terms of Pakistan's engagement with India on matters nuclear had changed. The CTBT had emerged as a major issue. Here too, Pakistan's attitude was to follow India, rather than make an independent decision. When it became clear in 1996 that India would not sign the treaty, Pakistan too decided to keep out. Some Indian analysts have argued that Pakistan's nuclear weapons orientation and ambitions were not and are not fundamentally conditioned by Indian actions, but were and are to a large extent independently motivated. In addition to being implausible and unconvincing, these arguments are also somewhat self-serving in that they tend to obscure India's responsibility as the key referent or pole in the South Asian nuclear arms race.

That is not to say that there are no independent factors, such as Pakistan's search for prestige in the Islamic world, that affected its nuclear policies. The *decisive* factor, however, was India and its preparations. This provides the foundation of, and key motivation for, Pakistan's essentially narrow perspective. Pakistan's deliberations have never been encumbered by moral doubt. On the contrary, they have been based on a realpolitik approach to threat perceptions, in the narrowest possible sense of the term. Thus, there is no available evidence to suggest that Pakistan ever seriously considered not moving towards a threshold status once India had achieved it.

Until May 1998, Pakistan displayed a concern not to cross the nuclear threshold. This stemmed from the realization that once a nuclear arms race was launched on the subcontinent, the basic asymmetry in power and resources between the two countries would impose a disproportionately heavier burden on Pakistan, assuming that it could even successfully 'keep up', itself a contentious proposition. However, Pakistan's reluctance gave way within a fortnight after India's tests. It eventually followed India by testing itself, although this meant further jeopardizing its already fragile economy.

In contrast to Pakistan, Indian nuclear policy and preparations have been subject to more complex and divergent pressures. In some respects, the end of the Nehru era marked the closure of a period when an active nuclear policy was pursued. Since then until the mid-1990s, nuclear policy-making carried within a broad framework of deep reluctance to close the nuclear option bear the strong stamp of a series of tactical, ad hoc, responses rather than the hallmark of a carefully executed and coherent long-range policy. Every incumbent prime minister lent his or her own nuances to declared policy and undeclared activities.

During 1966–8, for instance, there was a short-lived flirtation with the idea of a US or Western nuclear weapon umbrella against China. It was also the period of government uncertainty over the NPT, in the drafting and preparation of which India had played a significant role. By 1968, however, every hope of quick progress towards disarmament had vanished as the nuclear arms race gained momentum. New Delhi's despair over the whole disarmament effort influenced its decision not to sign the NPT, although the primary consideration was that signing the NPT would have meant closing the nuclear option and also the fact that China would have nothing to do with the Treaty until much, much later. Again, much later under Rajiv Gandhi (1984–9), there were some hesitant, uncertain attempts at a pro-disarmament diplomacy, but these soon collapsed. Meanwhile, under Indira Gandhi's post–1971 government, nuclear policy underwent some hardening, symbolized above all by the 1974 Pokharan explosion.

Pokharan-I: From Abstinence to Ambiguity

What was the motivation behind India's first test at Pokharan? It is difficult to relate it to the existence of any real and present threat or danger. In 1974, less than three years after the dismemberment of Pakistan, India's pre-eminence in the South Asian region was as unchallenged as it was obvious. Although China first tended to side with Pakistan during the Bangladesh conflict, this did not turn China into India's strategic adversary. The USSR had proved a dependable friend of India and New Delhi had signed a Treaty of Friendship and Cooperation with Moscow in 1971. It was impossible to detect a deterioration in India's external security environment in that period.

The motivation behind the first Pokharan nuclear explosion was largely *internal*. Indira Gandhi, who had ridden a wave of popularity in 1971 on left-leaning slogans, suddenly found the sands shifting from under her feet a year later. By 1973, India had slipped into the century's highest-ever spiral of inflation, led by food prices. Government after state government led by Gandhi's Indian National Congress found itself confronting a rising tide of popular turmoil and protest at economic policy, corruption, and misgovernance.

The Congress party's base, already insecure especially in north India, began to erode rapidly. In two states, Bihar and Gujarat, students and youth, protesting against Congress-style corruption and patronage, had managed to cripple the functioning of the ruling party's governments, forcing one of them to resign. The popular mood against the Congress was most forcefully expressed in the railway workers' strike of May 1974, led, ironically, by none other than George Fernandes, defence minister in the BJP-led coalition government that conducted the 1998 nuclear blasts.

The precise timing of the first Pokharan test was determined by domestic political, as opposed to external, security-related, considerations—in addition to two other factors. One, the nuclear scientists' lobby exerted considerable pressure on Indira Gandhi to conduct the tests. Its anxiety that they be carried out was largely a function of shoring up and raising its falling profile in the science and technology (S&T) establishment, itself related to the hopelessly sub-standard performance of the nuclear power programme and its repeated failure to meet targets and stay within allocated (and often, very generous) budgets. Nuclear explosions, based on well-understood principles of physics all available in the public domain, offered the *easy option* of claiming that the DAE did have some technical competence and getting away with the claim among a cheerleading but largely ill-informed élite audience in search of tattered symbols of national greatness.

The second factor at work in the timing was simply that the Bomb had matured. As Gandhi told an American researcher: '[The PNE] was simply done when we were ready. We did it to show ourselves we could do it. We couldn't be sure until we had tried it .... But it was for peaceful purposes only .... We had to do it to demonstrate our independent capability'.[8]

To the extent there was an 'external' motive at all behind Pokharan-I, it was to announce and spread the message of new-found Indian power after the Bangladesh war. This was India's own kind of aggressive 'self-assertion', a diffused, unfocused 'protest' against exclusion from the Big League, and its rulers' determination—quite unrelated to domestic popular self-perception—that they would force the world to take cognizance of India's power despite her poverty, misery, deprivation, and illiteracy. That was India's own manifest destiny. Yet, India's leaders were not confident (or brazen) enough to want to claim that the state had crossed the nuclear threshold and become a nuclear weapons-state (NWS) on a par with the other five, by virtue of conducting the test. They slyly announced that the test was a 'peaceful nuclear explosion'.

This ambiguity, and the compulsion to tell a half-truth, was prompted in part by the constraints placed by the agreements India signed with Canada and the US in 1955 and 1956 in respect of assistance for the CIRUS 'research' reactor: namely, to use its products for 'peaceful purposes' only. However, in part, it reflected ambivalence in attitudes towards the Bomb among many in the Indian establishment. For one, the establishment was divided over whether to conduct the test and what its consequence might be. Going by Raja Ramanna's account, two of the small group of four key individuals who deliberated on the issue—both highly experienced senior civil servants and advisers to Indira Gandhi—were opposed to the test and its timing.[9]

For another, the test was not part of, or related to, a larger strategic game plan, nor subserved a greater diplomatic and political objective. There was no long-term policy calculation involved here. India did not follow up Pokharan-I with an immediate programme of repeated and systematic further testing. It did not even attempt to relate the claim of a 'peaceful nuclear explosion' to an actual application, such as creation of reservoirs or to stimulation of oil recovery, which could have conceivably been part of an Indian version of Project Ploughshares (for PNEs) in the US. The adverse international fallout of Pokharan-I was only one, minor, reason why India ceased nuclear testing for a quarter of a century after Pokharan-I. The absence of a larger game plan was the principal reason; indeed, the overwhelming one.

Pokharan-I marked a further degeneration of Indian nuclear policy: from permanent nuclear abstinence under Nehru to 'No Bombs Now' under Shastri and Indira Gandhi from 1967 to 1974, and then on to a deliberate policy of nuclear ambiguity.[10] Pokharan-I did not only represent a loss of nuclear innocence. It entailed legitimizing the acquisition of the capability to commit mass-scale murder; a capability not remotely related, even going by official pronouncements, to Indian security and real threats to it. So completely at odds with India's stated nuclear doctrine—rejecting nuclear deterrence and even possession, leave alone use or threat of use of, nuclear weapons—was this that it could only be projected in sober terms as the acquisition of the capability, or keeping the nuclear option open, but firmly drawing a line at exercising or implementing it. This took the form of a policy of nuclear ambiguity.

This policy had three fundamental components: (a) maintenance of the dual character of the nuclear programme, while simultaneously enhancing civilian and military capabilities and potential on a broad technological front; (b) keeping the weapon option open and sustaining it at progressively higher levels; and (c) deliberately sending out conflicting signals on whether and how India would go overtly nuclear. The first two components lent a degree of stability and continuity to the Indian nuclear weapons programme and policy, particularly after May 1974. There were however certain perceptible shifts. While Prime Minister Morarji Desai, who succeeded Indira Gandhi in 1977, was positively hostile to PNEs, he accepted the broad parameters of the Indian posture of refusing to foreclose the nuclear weapons option. The government of Charan Singh which followed emphasized the Pakistani threat as part of a more active defence of keeping the option open.

After her return to power in 1980, Indira Gandhi continued the policy of ambiguity. Under Rajiv Gandhi, the only variations were a change of tone with regard to the third factor and the greater frequency with which India delivered nuclear warnings. In other respects, the approach displayed remarkable stability throughout the years till the mid-1990s. Indian leaders, but more frequently, hawkish nuclear polemicists, tried to justify the retention of the nuclear weapons option by citing the Chinese 'threat' and the expansion of China's nuclear arsenal from the 1960s. Neverthless, the complete absence of any Chinese attempt at nuclear blackmail, the historical experience of 'living with the Chinese Bomb' and a sober appraisal of the supposed seriousness of the Sino-Indian border dispute, all helped to diminish the fear of and preoccupation with Chinese nuclear might.

In comparison to external threat perceptions, a much greater part was played in nuclear policy-making by India's self-perceptions about its potential political 'destiny' and future regional, Asian and global roles. The argument for accumulating an adequate nuclear arsenal as a counter-deterrent to China was never immediately pressing. From the early 1980s, Pakistan's progress towards a nuclear weapons capability and threshold status were far more important to Indian threat perceptions. The acquisition of nuclear weapons was not an 'urgent' response to a disturbing *existing* reality, but rather a longer-term perspective appropriate to the coming of age of an India 'on the march'.

Why did Pakistan aspire to a nuclear threshold status well before 1998? Pakistan's case was distinct from that of the other threshold powers: Pakistan acquired a threshold status because India had done so. The reverse, however, was not true. The Indian government thus found it difficult to justify the preservation of this status in terms of any immediate or urgent security danger. Instead, it cited dangers which were more remote and long-term in nature, such as the possibility of superpower blackmail. The impact of the one attempt to define a more concrete security risk—namely, the Pakistani nuclear threat—was blunted not only by the latter's willingness to explore the possibilities of regional denuclearization, but also by New Delhi's failure to effectively counter Pakistan's 'peace offensive'. While both India and Pakistan can be said to have practised a species of 'nuclear ambiguity', the Pakistani posture was less ambiguous because it had less difficulty in defining its insecurities and fears and therefore in discussing the ways in which nuclearization or denuclearization would be related to these insecurities.

'Recessed Deterrence' or Silent Arms Race?

One unanticipated consequence of India's ambiguous posture was that India was unable to prevent the emergence of a nuclear equation between itself and Pakistan. New Delhi repeatedly expressed its hostility to outsiders making such an equation, which implicitly suggests the notion of parity. Nevertheless, by constantly referring to Pakistani nuclear preparations in justifying its own status as a threshold power, India endorsed the validity of the equation that was often drawn.

Under Rajiv Gandhi, the diplomatic dilemma reflected itself more strikingly than in the case of any of his predecessors. Gandhi's government 'authorized' another sovereign nation—in this case, the US—to exert pressure on Pakistan to prevent it from pursuing its nuclear goals. This became the only active component of India's strategy to counter Pakistani and international pressures to take some action in preventing the outbreak of a regional nuclear arms race. Even within certain élite circles in India, this was viewed as demeaning because it tended to highlight Indian impotence. The only alternative to this could seem to be the advocacy by some in the Indian government of a pre-emptive aerial attack on Kahuta enrichment plant in Pakistan. In 1983–4, India considered launching such an attack, both on its own and in collaboration with Israel, to cripple Pakistan's nuclear weapons development at an early stage. There was even public advocacy of this, albeit by a nuclear hawk, and expression of strong opposition.[11] This was not, however, pursued.

The prolonged nuclear stand-off or silent nuclear competition between India and Pakistan since the late 1980s impelled many theorists, especially those belonging to the 'Realist' school, to posit the concept of 'non-weaponized', 'recessed' or 'existential' 'deterrence', hypothesized as a relatively stable situation which neither state wishes to disturb, because both feel relatively secure in it. Such 'non-weaponized deterrence' was, however, anything but stable; even less did it provide security in any sense of the term. For instance, the India–Pakistan nuclear balance changed significantly after Pakistan reportedly succeeded in 1986 in producing sizable quantities of highly enriched uranium; enough for A.Q. Khan to declare confidently, 'you can go tell them, we have it [the Bomb]'.[12] Given the policy of ambiguity, it was hard to tell where the line of demarcation lay between the acquisition of a weapons capability (central to 'non-weaponized deterrence' and any state marked by the absence of weapons deployment even in the rudimentary sense of the term), on the one hand, and actual weapons possession and induction, on the other. Given this fuzziness, there was bound to be much room for suspicion and strategic misperception, which could quickly erode stability and security.

Indeed, that is precisely what seems to have happened at least twice, in 1987 and 1990; years by which not just India, but even Pakistan, had almost certainly reached the nuclear threshold. In 1986–7, a major military crisis erupted during a routine large-scale exercise by the Indian army, 'Operation Brasstacks'. The exercise was seen as an offensive manoeuvre by the Pakistani army, which moved its troops to forward positions across the border. An eyeball-to-eyeball confrontation ensued, involving among other things, a Pakistani air exercise 'Hallmark', which could have led to an exchange of hostilities, with a potential for escalation to the nuclear level.

It is believed that Pakistan brandished its nuclear sword towards the end of the confrontation. The fact that 'Brasstacks' was planned and led by Gen Krishnaswamy Sundarji, known for a tough stance against Pakistan, and with a penchant for high technology devices and nuclear weapons—he was the first Indian army commander to plead openly in a semi-public forum, the College of Combat, Mhow for nuclear weapons—did not help matters at all. Eventually, the crisis led to the formal signature in 1988 of a confidence building measure, 'Agreement on the Non-Attack of Nuclear Facilities between Indian and Pakistan', which had been first verbally mooted in 1985.[13]

The second crisis, in Spring 1990, was by all accounts even more serious, and had an *explicit nuclear dimension*. It too was triggered off by misperceptions about each other's military manoeuvres, and escalation of tension along the 'hot' Kashmir border following Pakistan's large-scale 'Zarb-i-Momin' military exercise. The timing was crucial because it came on the heels of the eruption of the *azadi* ('freedom') rebellion in the Kashmir Valley. Pakistan reportedly felt threatened that India might be tempted to carry out a surgical strike against Kahuta. In response, according to one version, Pakistan made a deliberately demonstrative move, lining up a convoy of trucks at the gates of the Kahuta enrichment plant, thus signalling that it would be prepared to use its nuclear capability to pre-empt India. The stand-off impelled Robert Gates, then US deputy national security adviser, to embark on a special mission to visit New Delhi and Islamabad and defuse the crisis. He eventually succeeded, but barely in time.[14]

For the purposes of understanding the limitations of, and the high risks associated with, 'existential deterrence', it is less pertinent to ask if the course of the 1990 crisis has been fully documented, than to consider whether such episodes fall within the realm of possibility. The answer must be 'yes'. Scenarios of the kind painted for 1990 are wholly plausible. Political and strategic misperception, breakdown of communication at a crucial juncture, misreading of specific moves of the adversary, exchange of bellicose threats and warnings by political leaders, as well as military grandstanding, are all realities in the Indian subcontinent.

For instance, Gen Ayub Khan launched what he thought was a pre-emptive strike in Kashmiri in 1965 in the conviction that the Kashmiri population would rise in rebellion against India. He was disastrously mistaken. There is a 'hot line' between the Director Generals of Military Operations of the two states, but it is not regularly activated or used. To take another instance, there were no fewer than 350 cases of firing across the Kashmir border in 1998 alone. India and Pakistan both suffer enormous losses by prosecuting their strategically absurd war at Siachen Glacier at attitudes exceeding 6,000 metres. They have repeatedly failed to reach an agreement to defuse and resolve the conflict. There have been three wars between the same two combatants since 1947 which makes South Asia second only to the Middle East as the world's most war-prone region since the Second World War.

The characterization of the silent nuclear competition between India and Pakistan until 1998 as a situation of 'stable non-weaponized deterrence', then, was misleading and wrong. The stand-off had a powerful potential to degrade and degenerate, and degenerate it did. This, of course, did not happen spontaneously or automatically, nor even only because a major political change occurred in India with the nuclearly obsessed BJP coming to power in March 1998, important as that development was. It happened with the strengthening of the forces favouring nuclearism in both India and Pakistan in the course of the extremely important debate on the Comprehensive Test Ban Treaty while it was being negotiated in Geneva in 1994–6. It is vital to situate the further degradation of the Indian and Pakistani nuclear policies in the context of that debate and of the shifts in the general foreign policy perspectives of, particularly, India that emerged towards the end of the eighties.

The Turning Point of 1988

With the collapse of the Indo-Sri Lanka Accord in 1988, Indian ambitions to become the *acknowledged and permanent hegemon* of South Asia also collapsed. Though in November 1988, New Delhi flew in troops to put down a rebel coup in the Maldives, thereby sustaining its President Gayoom, this flexing of regional muscles could hardly compensate for its debacle in Sri Lanka. Nor could this be said to have retrieved some limited 'prestige' for India when in May of the same year India revealed itself impotent in the face of a coup in Fiji which brought in a government that began to seriously repress Fijians of Indian origin. New Delhi was reduced to making feeble protests but nothing else, barring a call on Australia and New Zealand to intervene. By the end of 1988, there was deep uncertainty within the Indian national security establishment about India's stature regionally and globally. Whatever foreign policy framework this establishment had become used to operating within was already tottering when in the next three years, 1989–91, the dramatic collapse of the former USSR and of the Soviet bloc turned the post-War world upside down!

In those tumultuous years India's foreign policy framework suffered a double blow from which it has never recovered. What value did the Non-aligned Movement (NAM) now possess when one bloc no longer existed? What value also was there in India now pursuing its traditional policy of an economic tilt towards the West and a strategic tilt towards the USSR when the latter was replaced by a smaller and far weaker Russia, itself abandoning all efforts at promoting non-alignment among third world countries, and more determined than ever to forge a 'strategic partnership' with the West, especially the US? What alternative did the Indian state now have but to abandon the 'third way' of non-alignment and go the whole hog of adopting the new form of neo-liberal economic globalization being assiduously peddled through what is called the 'Washington Consensus' or the collective ideology of the World Bank, the International Monetary Fund, and the US government. (The headquarters of the WB and IMF are in Washington and the single strongest influence on the WB/IMF is exercised by the US.)

Actually, there *were* alternatives, both economic and political. Economically, India could have turned its gaze eastwards to Japan and the 'Asian Tigers' for lessons in managing the globalization process. Politically, it could have continued to pursue a more independent path despite the new weakness of the NAM. However an élite, whose general mindset had become more right-wing and US-oriented than ever before, and which was more insecure and frustrated than ever, could hardly have been expected to pursue such alternatives. What emerged as a supposed foreign policy framework was a strange amalgam of shifting components.

There were four main ingredients to the brew. First, there was a 'soft Hindutva' (Hindu sectarian nationalism and communalism) affecting élite self-perceptions. This promoted a stronger desire than ever that India become a 'glorious' power retrieving its 'manhood' which in the eyes of a large section of the élite had been 'emasculated' by centuries of Muslim rule and invasion. Such views rested on a communal misrepresentation of India's actual history, but this was largely beside the point. The fact is that such views were widely spread and more strongly entrenched than ever before. This 'soft Hindutva' also fed and shaped another component—an aggressive and belligerent interpretation of what the so-called imperatives of realpolitik are.

The third component was a newer and stronger adherence to neo-liberal economic thinking on the supposed compulsions of globalization. For the Indian élite, the ideological recoil from the model of bad socialism represented by the USSR and its bloc was so strong that it promoted a virtual stampede into the adoption of a bad capitalism. It was the new Congress government of 1991 that adopted the Washington Consensus and its IMF-sponsored programme of 'Stabilization and Structural Adjustment' to cover a temporary though serious balance of payments crisis—what has aptly been called the application of a long-term 'solution' to a short-term problem. Throughout the 1980s, Indian economic policy had moved steadily to the right, but the 1991 reforms were nonetheless a *qualitative* acceleration in this direction. Naturally, such an economic reorientation strongly reinforced the desire, and the quest, for a much closer relationship than before with the West, particularly the US. The fourth and weakest component in this amalgam was the fast fading legacy of the non-alignment era; the lingering elements of third worldist solidarity.

Over the nineties, this last component has steadily shrunk in importance and the weights of the other three have shifted in relation to one another, depending both on changing external circumstances and changing internal developments such as which government has been in power. For all these confusions and drift (though clearly rightwards) in Indian foreign policy thinking since 1988–9, it was *not* inevitable that India would go openly nuclear. To explain why it eventually did so requires a systematic tracing of the historical process from which this emerged. Most of this has already been done in this and previous chapters. Here, it will suffice to bring the story up to date by briefly outlining the external developments of it in the nineties that shaped the overall Indian trajectory.

In one important sense it was the failure of certain expectations to materialize that helped pave the way for overt nuclearization. After the collapse of the former USSR and the dramatic rightward shift in India's economic policy from mid-1991, there was a widespread expectation among the Indian élite that the US would now re-evaluate its perspectives towards India and assign it a much more important place than ever before in its strategic thinking. More specifically, it was expected that the time was ripe for a 'new, strategic relationship' between India and the US. The former was in fact ready to forge a 'junior partnership' with the latter.

There were efforts on both sides to forge such a closer relationship. The neo-liberal economic reforms were warmly welcomed and endorsed in Western capitals. Indian shifts towards greater accommodation with GATT/ WTO, and for a freer global investment regime, were similarly applauded.

Military cooperation between the US and India reached levels inconceivable during all the previous decades of bloc rivalry and Non-alignment. Not only were exchanges of officers, regular meetings and discussions sought to be institutionalized, but joint military exercises were discussed and some limited forms of this even took place—a historic first in India–US relations. The 1992 'Kicklighter Proposals' (named after Lt. Gen. Claude Kicklighter, former Commander of the US Army in the Pacific) embodied this new turn. According to the Kicklighter agenda, there would be (a) annual visits in both countries of chiefs of staff; (b) the setting up of an Indian–US Army executive steering council; (c) reciprocal visits by other senior commanders; (d) combined training activities and information exchange; (e) regular talks between the two armies at staff level; (f) various other forms of joint participation at different levels of the military hierarchy.

The problem lay not in any clash in principle between the US and India about what the general future thrust and direction of mutual relations should be. It lay in the fact that what India expected or hoped to get out of the US from a 'junior partnership' or 'new, strategic relationship' was not something that the US would feel any serious need or reason to deliver. Before elaborating on this crucial point, it needs to be pointed out that the nuclear issue itself (at least before the CTBT negotiations which began in 1994 imposed their distinctive pressures) was not the principal bone of contention. To be sure, the US did not want India to be an overt nuclear power even in its role as a junior partner or strategic friend (not yet, or quite, an ally). In this respect, right up to the May 1998 tests, the US has behaved consistently. It has always wanted to ensure that South Asia did not get openly nuclearized. Indeed, it wanted at least to 'cap' the nuclear capabilities of India (and Pakistan), and at most to 'roll back and eventually eliminate' their existing capabilities.

The US–India–Pakistan Triangle

This India was never prepared to do (and Pakistan was, only if India was so prepared), though in the early nineties New Delhi showed a willingness to discuss these matters with the US that it had never shown before. Between 1992 and 1994, there were four rounds of bilateral talks which did not ultimately resolve mutual differences. Pakistan, of course, always had a running 'dialogue' with the US on nuclear-related matters. Thus, a curious scenario emerged in which both New Delhi and Islamabad were each prepared to talk to Washington on substantive nuclear issues but not to each other. Even today there is something of a continuity in US attitudes to India. After the tests and the early US surprise, anger, and irritation, things have settled down. The US is now prepared to accept the fait accompli of India's nuclear status (but not to formally or legally endorse it) and still wishes to keep both countries' nuclear capabilities at a level where they would not reach a scale where they might complicate nuclear politics played out on a larger, extra-regional or global arena. A proliferation of nuclearly armed states outside the US's orbit greatly disturbs and complicates its nuclear–strategic planning and options. Hence the *variable* nature of US pressure on different actual or threshold nuclear states and their preparations. The US has been consistently hostile to North Korea on this score, oblivious and condoning if not supportive, of Israel, negligent about India, and fluctuating in its attitude to Pakistan. The US is today still telling the Indians that it wants a 'partnership' with it.[15]

Thus, the India–US differences on the nuclear issue were an irritant but not a barrier in their mutual quest for a closer, more 'strategic' form of relationship. What was (and is) the principal problem is (and remains) the enormous disparity between the power and ambitions of the US and India, and therefore the much greater degree of flexibility and range of options available to the US. This meant that what each country expected out of a closer, 'strategic relationship', was different. India, in the post-Cold War era, and following its own economic and political shift towards the West, expected that the US, seeing India's greater strategic value and importance, would correspondingly shift from its alignment certainly with Pakistan, and perhaps to some extent from China. This the US was (and is) not prepared to do. Why should it? Why should it take India *that* seriously despite all the rhetoric about India being potentially a future great power? After all, India is not a great or major regional or world power yet, and may not even become one!

After the end of the Cold War, South Asia was downgraded in strategic importance by the United States. It was never as strategically important as say, the Middle East but even by the US's own previous standards, there has been a relative decline now that Russia is not the rival it was and cannot attempt to 'recruit' states in the South Asian region as part of its own global efforts to resist the US or isolate China. Thus, in a region now regarded by the US as of lower strategic importance in its list of high priority areas, less strategic value will also be attached to seeking friends or allies in the region. South Asia's nuclearization gives it much stronger 'negative' or disruptive salience, not strategic importance.

In the flux created by the end of the Cold War, the US has also to rethink its global strategic perspectives. It would be naïve to imagine that it has done so, and can do so for each and every part of the world. The five great constants of its general strategic thinking in the post-Cold War era, and which enjoy near-consensus from its domestic national security establishment, are the following: One, the US must secure and maintain strategic–political–military dominance over the oil-rich Middle East (Central Asian oil reserves are far lower by comparison and the region cannot ever have similar importance). Two, NATO enlargement must take place and NATO must remain the bedrock of European security. Three, there must be consolidation and calculated expansion of the North American Free Trade Agreement (NAFTA). Four, the US must maintain a military capacity to fight 'one-and-a-half' wars simultaneously, i.e. a war on the global level and another on the regional level. Five, the US-must maintain the kind of global 'open' economic system whereby the dollar remains the informal world currency (with all the benefits that accrue from this) and financial inflows from all sources (including US-owned multinationals) can come in to ensure that the structurally low-saving US economy can nonetheless be sure of high investment and steady growth.

South Asia is not an area that requires urgent strategic attention from the US. It suffices if the US has a clear idea of what it does not want in the region even if it does not have a clear idea of what it wants strategically from the region. What it does not want, however, is to accept some unequivocal regional hegemon when it does not have to, and particularly when India has still not shown the capacity to actually become such a hegemon. So why on earth should the US sacrifice or weaken its relationship with Pakistan just to please India? Even more ludicrous, why should the US give up its multiple options vis-à-vis China (and towards India) just to embrace the idea that a nuclear India would be an important ally in future US efforts to isolate the supposedly rising power of the twentyfirst century, China? Some right-wing Republicans or Democrats in the US may join in with some Indian strategists to engage in such speculation but that is all it is—speculation about possible benefits in the future. Such 'birds in the bush' possibilities cannot be allowed to override in importance (let alone overturn) the management of the 'birds in the hand' reality of the existing complex pattern of US–China relations.

Pakistan is important to the US both for its connection with Afghanistan and Central Asia, and for its long-standing relationship with Saudi Arabia. The latter link fits in very well with the paramount importance the US attaches to strategic control of the Middle East. Here, it is the informal US-dominated nexus pertaining to its influence and control over three states that is of vital significance—Saudi Arabia, Egypt and Israel. Moreover, Pakistan, unlike India, is a more pliable and reliable strategic ally for the future and it has proved to be so in the past. The US has no reason whatsoever to interpret the India–US relationship in the way that India's own strategic community understands or interprets it, or to draw the same corrollaries concerning the necessary 'rearrangements' or 'adjustments' attendant upon consolidating such a strategic link between the two countries. For this reason alone, tensions have continued to persist throughout the nineties in the post-Cold War era despite the new opportunities and inclinations that have arisen for forging a closer Indo-US relationship. It is hardly surprising, then, that a somewhat disappointed India should also currently see greater value than it did a few years ago in strengthening its traditional military–political relationship with a Russia also disappointed in its expectations and hopes regarding its new post-Cold War 'partnership' with the US.[16]

Throughout the 1990s, frustrations about unfulfilled aspirations and disappointed expectations have all played a role in augmenting the desire for nuclear status as a perceived short cut to India's achieving regional and global eminence. When the CTBT issue came along and put the sharpest possible spotlight on the distinctive incoherences of India's posture of nuclear ambiguity, it did so in a general political context where there was greater likelihood than ever before that the Indian stand on the nuclear question, held for over two decades, would be shaken and could be shattered. India's posture of ambiguity was not so much a policy as a non-policy.

The 'Chinese Threat': Myth or Reality?

India did not become a threshold nuclear state because it first formulated or systematized a policy of ambiguity and then followed it. Also, for most of the time it was a threshold state, it had no nuclear policy worth the name except for the bottom-line assurance that it would neither close the option nor exercise it. There were some feeble attempts to rationalize this posture pursued by some strategists both in India and abroad. Accordingly, concepts like 'recessed deterrence' and 'non-weaponized deterrence' were coined. However, for good reasons, they impressed few among the hawks and none among those opposed to all nuclear deterrence thinking. Despite the deep incoherence of the doctrinal justifications that some attempted to lend to the posture of ambiguity, one, nonetheless, had reason to be thankful that the more irresponsible and adventurist step of going openly nuclear was not taken till May 1998. Nonetheless, a non-policy it undoubtedly was.

One way of seeing this is simply to note that during all this time there existed *no nuclear equation relevant for serious diplomatic purposes, at least, between India and China.* Between 1974 and 1998, China did not perceive India as a nuclear security problem nor did Beijing see itself as posing such a threat to New Delhi. It was therefore impervious (though polite) to any attempt by India to put it in that role. Moreover, whatever pro-nuclear lobbyists outside the Indian government may have thought or said, India was (till the BJP-led coalition came to power in 1998) reluctant to officially postulate that China constituted a serious security threat because the logic of so postulating would be to highlight the importance of then engaging in systematic nuclear diplomacy between the two countries. This was however not possible. There cannot be proper nuclear diplomacy between two parties if either does not see the other as a nuclear threat to itself. India repeatedly refused all diplomatic efforts to improve regional security through progressive disarmament of itself and Pakistan citing its concerns vis-à-vis China. It was, however, unable to propose disarmament or nuclear arms restraint measures involving China because it did not want to openly acknowledge the great difference between them in nuclear status, and hence, the enormous asymmetry in their starting positions on the nuclear–diplomatic issue.

Nuclear diplomacy is only meaningful when both sides believe they have reason to fear each other and that mutual obligations to carry out arms control or disarmament are feasible and desirable. Nuclear bargaining means each side has a bank of bargaining chips whose 'value' is roughly related to the comparative strength of their respective arsenals. In regard to China, India did not in the past (and does not even now) come close to having the *minimum bank of such chips even to qualify for entrance* into the nuclear diplomatic game vis-à-vis China. An India whose own self-image demanded that it be recognized as a rough equal of China, entitled to equivalent treatment by the rest of the world community, found it impossible to officially acknowledge its great nuclear 'inferiority' and enter into negotiations with China on such a basis. The end result was that India had no positive or active framework of serious nuclear diplomacy to address its own professed security needs. Periodic citation of the 'China factor' was thus made into a negative obstacle against any nuclear diplomacy confined to South Asia, and that was all! Pakistan's nuclear diplomacy, as pointed earlier, was by contrast clarity itself. Islamabad proposed a series of measures for final elimination of nuclear-related tensions between itself and India through an effective de-nuclearization of the region only to be repeatedly rebuffed by a New Delhi incapable of offering any alternative diplomatic path to eliminating such tensions.

There were only two ways for India to resolve this diplomatic impasse. Either it could put the Chinese threat into proper perspective and recognize it for what it always has been—an abstract and remote threat, never exercised in any way—and consider it largely irrelevant in much the same way as the abstract nuclear threat of the other four NWSs is considered irrelevant. India could then move towards mutual nuclear disarmament vis-à-vis Pakistan. Alternatively, India should go openly nuclear, and over time seek to establish a nuclear balance of sorts with China thereby initiating some kind of 'relevant nuclear diplomacy' with China but with no guarantee that it would succeed in this venture.

After May 1998, it is this last course upon which India tragically and foolishly has decided to embark. The advent of the CTBT negotiations in early 1994 helped to severely weaken the official posture of ambiguity by revealing more clearly than ever the incoherences of this position, especially when, technologically speaking, the CTBT would, if India signed it, have limited the exercise of its option. Of course, as explained earlier, the pressures imposed by the imminence of the CTBT negotiations were a proximate cause, not a fundamental one, for India going nuclear. One should not, however, underestimate the way that debate increased domestic frustrations. The Entry Into Force clause that demanded Indian accession as a precondition for the Treaty coming into force was widely seen as a deliberate affront to the country. That the CTBT was nonetheless taken to the UN General Assembly and passed there despite the Indian veto preventing its passage in the Conference on Disarmament only poured more fuel on the burning embers of Indian resentment. Certainly, this resentment at how India was being treated during the CTBT negotiations was essentially a self-concocted one, but the resentment was real enough and unfortunately very widespread amongst the Indian élite. It was systematically fed by some of the most tendentious and dishonest reporting, editorializing, and commentary that has ever appeared on any issue in the India print and electronic media. When in 1996 the Indian efforts to secure one of the temporary berths in the Security Council of the UN was unsuccessful with an overwhelming majority of Non-aligned states supporting Japan's bid instead, the feeling of international isolation and 'revealed impotence' was almost palpable.

The fact that it was an élite nationalism frustrated by its own sense of impotence and not any presumed iniquity of the CTBT that constituted the deeper sources for India going openly nuclear, has been strikingly revealed by the Indian attitude to the CTBT after May 1998. Most of those 'strategic experts' who cried foul about the CTBT between 1994 and 1996 claiming that opposition to it was a matter of principle and genuine commitment to nuclear disarmament and not just of 'national security', now have no problems whatsoever with accepting it if India can get a good behind-the-scenes 'bargain' from the US as the reward. If the media overwhelmingly supported Indian opposition to the CTBT earlier, it now in its majority supports India joining the Treaty as a nuclear power with no qualms whatsoever about such a public display of cynicism. The Foreign Minister, Jaswant Singh, now uses the analogy of how one's view of the CTBT must change when you are a passenger inside the railway compartment, i.e. a nuclear power, from when you were outside, i.e. not a nuclear power. India's chief negotiator at the CTBT talks, Arundhati Ghose, declared at the UN General Assembly in 1996 that India refused to sign the CTBT not because it wanted to produce nuclear weapons but because it did not want to. However, after the tests, the same Ghose publicly declared that it should have been obvious when India refused to sign the CTBT that it was going to go ahead to test. She came out in support of the tests and India's decision to go nuclear but is now among a small minority of the hawks who still believe that India should not sign and ratify the CTBT.

Most hawks know signing the CTBT is the minimum price India has to now pay for ending its international isolation. The government can even hope to get a good deal from the US not because India has a strong bargaining position but because the US government may find it very difficult, perhaps impossible, to get Senate ratification unless it first ties up an Indian agreement to sign the CTBT. Thus, the same India whose spokespeople declared repeatedly that the country's 'security was not negotiable' and even that 'India does not have to explain' and its actions has sat down to negotiate with the US on precisely such issues. Whatever the outcome of these ongoing negotiations, whether or not by September 1999 India joins the CTBT regime, one thing should be crystal clear. India's break from its old posture of ambiguity is now final and irreversible. Though the mainstream Indian Left, namely the two large Communist parties, still cling to the illusion that India can, and should, go back to the posture of ambiguity, this is inconceivable. The true choices are moving forward towards nuclear sanity and disarmament, regional and global, while avoiding further weaponization, induction and deployment of nuclear weapons; or moving backwards towards such induction and deployment, emulating the other NWSs. Pakistan will follow the Indian path.[17]

Notes

1. This corresponds to the assessment of a sizable section of top scientists of the DAE, who for years believed and argued that Pakistan, with its 'considerably inferior' science and technology base, manpower and its generally backward infrastructure, could not possibly match India in mastering a 'difficult' and 'advanced' technology such as nuclear energy. Especially notable in this regard are Raja Ramanna, who headed the Bhabha Atomic Research Centre of the DAE at the time of the 1974 test, and P.K. Iyengar, who headed its physics

group at the time, both of whom went on to become chairmen of the Atomic Energy Commission. They are on record as saying that Pakistan could not have mastered a technology that was 'borrowed' or 'stolen', as opposed to one developed 'indigenously', as in the mis-stated case of India.

This assessment had less to do with a serious, considered, informed analysis of Pakistan's capabilities than with the combination of hubris, the 'we-are-superior-to-them' attitudes towards neighbours commonly encountered in South Asia, and to the DAE top brass's reluctance to concede that Pakistan could have mastered a technology—uranium enrichment by the centrifuge method—which India had failed to stabilize, leave alone industrialize. Some of these factors and the unsoundness of the assessment involved went beyond narrow S&T circles and into the media. Ramanna himself became a junior minister in a (non-BJP) government and has since been nominated a Member of Parliament.

2. L. K. Advani, quoted in 'Pak told to roll back proxy war', *The Hindu*, 19 May 1998.
3. Pervez Hoodbhoy, a Pakistan physicist and anti-nuclear campaigner, was among the first to point this out.
4. For the DAE, such targets have been largely meaningless, and they have always been missed. Thus, according to its 1970 long-term 'perspective' plan, it should have been producing 10,000 MW of nuclear electricity by 1980. Its actual performance was below 800 MW. It subsequently revised its target to forecast that it would reach 10,000 MW by 2000. The capacity at the turn of the century is likely to be only about a fifth of that figure. Ironically, India's own uranium resources are inadequate to sustain 10,000 MW of generating capacity in standard (thermal) nuclear reactors, as distinct from fast-breeders which have proved extremely problematic and dangerous everywhere, including France. France, once their most ardent advocate, closed down its much tom-tommed *Superphenix* fast breeder reactor in 1998.

   The DAE has long been notorious as the worst performing department of the Government of India. Its cost and time overruns are huge—typically, of the order of 200 per cent-plus—and its safety record is appalling. Two of the world's six most contaminated nuclear reactors are Indian. The DAE has exposed over 350 workers to radiation doses well above the maximum permissible limits that it itself stipulates.
5. Official brochure of the Missile Technology Centre quoted in *Nuclear Risk-Reduction Measures in Southern Asia*, The Henry L. Stimson Center, Washington, D.C, November 1998, p. 10.
6. Itty Abraham, *The Making of the Indian Atomic Bomb*, Zed Books, London, and Orient Longman, Delhi, 1998, p. 120
7. See Rodney Jones, 'India' note 47. p. 121 in *Non-Proliferation: the Why and Wherefore*, SIPRI, Taylor & Francis, London, 1985. Jones believes 'the decision to try to fabricate and test a nuclear explosive device almost certainly was made in late 1969, as a close perusal of two sources will make clear. The two sources in question are N. Seshagiri, *The Bomb: Fallout of India's Nuclear Explosion* (Vikas,

Delhi,1975) and J. Bandopadhya, *The Making of India's Foreign Policy,* Allied Publications, Bombay, 1970. P.N. Haksar, former principal secretary to Indira Gandhi, claimed the decision was taken in 1972. [Private conversation with the authors.]

8. R. Jones, op. cit., p. 114
9. R. Ramanna, *My Years of Pilgrimage,* Viking, Delhi, 1991, pp. 89–91.
10. It has been urged by some writers, including some who are strongly opposed to nuclear weapons, among them Itty Abraham, that there is an essential, immanent continuity in India's nuclear policy and doctrine right from 1947 to 1998. Abraham holds that the virtual certainty and inevitability of the May 1998 tests (mediated by specific conjunctures, of course) was written into the way the Indian nuclear programme was structured and operated (with its potential for dual use). More fundamentally, it derived from the science–state dialectic that developed in India in the early years of Independence, with all its links with military uses, its limitless faith in the ideology of developmentalism, in gigantic projects, in secrecy, and so on.

    There are several problems with this line of argument. First, it uncritically accepts the validity of, and works on the terrain of, the most right-wing, conservative and hawkish accounts of the evolution of India's nuclear policy, which too (disingenuously) posit such continuity, cutting across the Nehru period of abstinence, the post-1974 policy of ambiguity, and overt nuclearization in 1998. This elides sharp differences at the *doctrinal* level: namely, India's wholly unprincipled embrace of nuclear deterrence in 1998, a doctrine it had for 50 years described as 'abhorrent', 'repugnant', illegal and 'illegitimate'; or the contrast between the equally long-standing position that nuclear weapons are not essential to security, on the one hand, and on the other, the 1998 stand that 'national security' considerations, even 'compulsions', were the motive behind the tests. Second, it wrongly assumes or asserts strong homogeneity and uniformity in policy-making establishments where there is plurality and difference. For instance, although the Bhabha model of institution-building in science and technology was important for the DAE, it was *not* the sole model in India's S&T. Robert Anderson, *Building Scientific Institutions in India: Bhabha and Saha,* Centre for Developing Area studies, Montreal, 1975. Nor was there unanimity in the top policy apparatus on conducting the May 1974 test.

    Abraham is similarly wrong to contend that all India's major political parties welcomed the 1998 tests. They did not. The Left was the first to oppose them. By the end of year, democratic popular opinion had shifted against nuclearization.

    Third, Abraham's line of argument, following post-modernist discourse, overemphasizes the language of signs and symbols—e.g. fetishes in the form of gigantic nuclear reactors akin to the *lingam*—at the cost of substantive programmes and policies in identifying the key to legitimizing the state. It thus fails to understand the sources of the crisis of legitimacy and how it might be overcome. In reality, nuclear power and nuclear weapons have played a rather marginal role in resolving the systemic crisis of the state in India and Pakistan.

Fourth, it is factually wrong in inventing secrecy where it did not exist. In Abraham's book, the most glaring example of this is his description of the Indo-Canadian and Indo-US agreements of the 1950s in respect of the CIRUS reactor. The arguments did not have, as he claims, 'secret' appendices, nor was that the reason why the Canadians did not strongly accuse India of having breached the accords. Canada did not protest that there was a legal breach because India contended that May 1974 was a 'peaceful' explosion. What was involved, it emerged later, was blatant illegality and cheating: the 1974 explosion was a 'Bomb'.

11. Bharat Karnad, distinguished for extreme views, e.g, that India should build a nuclear force adequate to deter even the US, publicly urged that India should bomb Kahuta, if necessary with Israeli cooperation. See 'Thinking the Unthinkable: Knocking Out Kahuta' in *The Sunday Observer*, Delhi, 17 January 1988. This was strongly opposed by one of the authors (Praful Bidwai, 'Our Own Dr Strangelove', *The Sunday Observer*, Delhi, 24 January 1988.
12. Quoted in Kuldip Nayar, 'We Have the A-Bomb, say Pakistani's "Dr Strangelove".' *The Observer*, London, 1 March 1987. It has been alleged that Pakistan in 1987 managed to obtain from China vital nuclear weapons-related data (according to some, the design of a Bomb). This seems possible, but has been hard to prove. We will have to wait for some exceptional kind of disclosure before this can be conclusively established.

    Had New Delhi had proof, or even strong pointers to such technology transfer, it would have certainly used that information to demand that it be prohibited. At any rate, much of the data/design in question has long been widely available in the public domain. Pakistani engineers could have easily accessed it. It is difficult to argue that Sino-Pakistani collaboration in this regard, even assuming it has been strategic and of a long-term nature one and not occasional or sporadic, constituted a 'provocation' for India to radically alter its own nuclear stance.
13. The most detailed account of the 1986–7 crisis is to be found in Kanti Bajpai, PR Chari, et al. *Brasstacks and Beyond: Perception and Management of Crisis in South Asia*, (Manohar, Delhi, 1995). See also Lt Gen K M Arif *Working with Zia: Power Politics 1977–88*, Oxford University Press, Karachi, 1995.
14. There has been no official confirmation of the nature, degree of seriousness of, or sequence of events in, the 1990 crisis. The most detailed account is to be found in Devin Hagerty, 'Nuclear Deterrence in South Asia: the 1990 Indo-Pakistani Crisis,' *International Security*, 20. no. 3 (Winter 1995–6) and Michael Krepon and Mishi Faruqee, eds., *Conflict Prevention and Confidence Building Measures in South Asia: the 1990 Crisis*, Occasional Paper No. 17. The Henry L Stimson Center, Washington, D.C., April 1994. The latter is based on a special discussion which the Henry L Stimson Center organized among some of the key individuals involved in the episode, but the results were not conclusive.

    Since, then, Kanti Bajpai and Amitabh Mattoo have written an interesting article ('First Strike', *The Pioneer*, New Delhi, 23 April 1995) quoting an unnamed but 'highly placed' and 'authoritative' source as confirming that the Indian authorities did consider making a nuclear response to the Pakistani move, and that a major power had indeed intervened to defuse tensions between India and Pakistan.

15. Strobe Talbott, Deputy Secretary of State, in his address to Stanford University, California, on 'Dialogue, Democracy and Nuclear Weapons in South Asia', reported in all the major Indian dailies of 23 January 1999. For the full text of his speech, see, 'The Strands of a Spreading Cobweb' in *The Asian Age*, 26 January 1999. The US Assistant Secretary of State, Karl Inderfurth, has stated that both countries should not go much above the nuclear threshold, i.e. that they 'define those requirements in a way that are minimum but meet their needs'. See, 'No make-or-break affair: US' in *The Pioneer*, 28 January1999.
16. India and Russia have agreed to a 10 year 'strategic accord' which sounds more grandiose and important than it actually is. But it does mean that Russia continues to be India's most important supplier of military hardware.
17. For the importance of the CTBT and the character of the finalized treaty, see Appendix 1. This is based on the small book written by the authors entitled *Testing Times: the Global Stake in a Nuclear Test Ban*, Dag Hammarskjold Foundation, Uppsala, in May 1996 when the negotiations were reaching a final stage, and a more recent survey by the authors entitled 'Why India should Sign the CTBT: Returning to Our Own Agenda', *Economic and Political Weekly*, Mumbai, 19 September 1998.

    For a systematic refutation of the criticisms put forward by the anti-CTBT Indian lobby (some of which are shared by others including some anti-nuclear disarmament proponents), see Appendix 2. This is extracted from the authors' article, 'Why India Should Sign the CTBT', op. cit.

CHAPTER TEN

Challenges to the Global Nuclear Order

Whose Crisis? Whose Dilemma?

The crossing of the nuclear threshold by India and Pakistan confronts the world with a peculiar dilemma. On the one hand, the two have become nuclear weapons states (NWSs), or at least states that can go on to build and induct, and possibly deploy, such armaments (unless they voluntarily or through a negotiated arrangement agree not to do so). On the other, the existing, officially agreed, inter-state nuclear order cannot concede that status to them. Under the Nuclear Non-Proliferation Treaty, only the five countries that tested nuclear weapons prior to 1 January 1967 enjoy that status.

Thus, even those, including the United States, who formulated and voted for the Security Council Resolution (number 1172) which calls upon India and Pakistan effectively to roll back their nuclear programmes and undertake nuclear disarmament, concede that what was done in May 1998 cannot in practice be 'undone' or 'disinvented' (see Appendix 4). In that context, US Deputy Secretary of State Strobe Talbott says: 'We are confronted with a lamentable but for the foreseeable future, irreversible fact: India and Pakistan have formally and overtly demonstrated that they have nuclear weapons.'[1] Similarly, Assistant Secretary for South Asian affairs Karl, F. Inderfurth told the Foreign Policy Association, Washington, on 21 January 1999: 'in many respects, our major challenges in South Asia are not so much about prevention, but management of thresholds that have already been crossed'.[2]

At the same time, P–5 officials cannot possibly officially acknowledge India and Pakistan to be NWSs, for not only would that mean jeopardizing the stability of the existing global nuclear order but, in their view, it would be tantamount, as US Secretary of State Madeleine Albright put it, to 'rewarding' India and Pakistan despite their having breached the political norm against nuclear testing and overtly crossed the threshold. Besides, it would risk opening up a number of thorny issues, including, for example, the commitments made in the 1960s by Germany and Japan to renounce nuclear weapons and become signatories to the NPT as non-nuclear weapons states.

The nuclearization of India and Pakistan must be seen in some ways as signifying the second big question mark over the power arrangements among the globe's nation-states that were put together at the conclusion of the Second World War. The distribution of power broadly reflected the outcome of the war and was written into the structure and composition of the United Nations system, in particular, the Security Council. Of course, the first question mark appeared almost 10 years ago, with the coming down of the Berlin Wall and the end of the Cold War. However, in spite of the disintegration of the USSR and the collapse of state socialism in the East, the architecture of power built five decades earlier could more or less absorb the shocks sent out by the end of bloc rivalry, without coming down altogether. India's and Pakistan's nuclearization must be seen as carrying further the process of alteration of the post-War distribution of power. In conjunction with proposals to expand the Security Council and reform the working of the United Nations system, it acquires a new significance, even if no radical changes may be on the anvil.

The Skewed Global Nuclear Order

The greatest significance at the international level of the crossing of the nuclear threshold in South Asia lies in the challenges it poses to the advocates of nuclear disarmament, the vast majority of the world's peoples and states, the five recognized NWSs, and more generally, to the global nuclear order, itself skewed and unequal. For the world's non-proliferation regime, it is the first great breakout in 35 years. It is also the first time since 1964 that an Asian power went overtly nuclear, following China. The breakout does not, however, mean that the non-proliferation regime has failed or that the global nuclear order has been seriously weakened, leave alone undermined. In the next chapter, we shall deal with the challenge to the world as a whole, and especially to the nuclear disarmament and peace movement. We concentrate here on the global order, the responses of the P–5 states, and the dilemmas that India and Pakistan face.

The global nuclear order is non-proliferation-oriented, not disarmament-oriented. It is based on three foundations: the Nuclear Non-Proliferation Treaty (NPT) of 1968; the P–5 states' nuclear oligopoly and their continued reliance on nuclear weapons for security, and their reluctance to move quickly towards the abolition of nuclear weapons; and a number of specific arrangements that restrict the sale of nuclear materials or transfer of nuclear and related technologies, e.g. the London Suppliers' Group (LSG), the Zangger accords, or the Missile Technology Control Regime (MTCR).[3]

Agreements to establish nuclear weapons free zones, or measures of voluntary and unilateral nuclear arms reduction by any of the P–5, or de-mating and de-alerting nuclear warheads and delivery vehicles, and most important, the emerging Comprehensive Test Ban Treaty (CTBT) regime, are not foundational to or cornerstones of the present global nuclear order in the way the NPT is. Positive, transitional steps of this second category are fully compatible with, and part of progress towards complete nuclear disarmament. However partial a measure they may be, they do not freeze existing inequalities in the way the NPT does, not just by placing different obligations upon two different categories of states, but by rendering the obligations that pertain to real disarmament and elimination of nuclear weapons practically ineffectual. The NPT places no real, operational compulsions or injunctions upon the NWSs to demonstrate tangible progress towards the goal of nuclear abolition.

It might be argued that the LSG or Zangger accords, or some variant of these, may also be necessary in any disarmament-oriented global order that is making a transition towards a nuclear weapons-free world. There is indeed a strong case for restricting the supply of nuclear materials or missile and rocket technology, and not just to 'rogue' states or those suspected to be interested in or capable of transferring them directly or indirectly to military programmes. There is however every reason why such restrictions should be *multilaterally* negotiated as part of a *universal* and non-discriminatory agreement, rather than being imposed by already powerful, developed, if not hegemonic, states who have a strong temptation to define what is permissible for others, but who accept no restrictions on their own 'right' of access to these materials/technologies. In their present, unequal, asymmetrical form, these agreements do become an integral part of a skewed global nuclear order.

This non-proliferation-oriented global order is founded upon a flawed and unequal bargain, that lies at the heart of the NPT: not just objectively, but in the eyes of the vast majority of its signatories too, notwithstanding the partly self-serving Indian objection to the treaty. In the perception of that majority, there is a *political* relationship between the acceptance of nuclear abstinence on the part of the non-NWSs, and the process of nuclear disarmament, or progress towards it on the part of the NWSs. As Mueller, Fischer, and Koetter argue: 'If Article VI is removed from the NPT, the remaining obligations of the NWSs (essentially not to transfer nuclear weapons to NNWSs) cannot be said to establish an adequate reciprocal commitment for the renunciation of nuclear weapons by their non-nuclear weapon Treaty partners. For reasons of legal logic alone, Article VI has considerable weight in the overall framework of the Treaty.'[4]

This legal argument implies, of course, that the NNWSs are surrendering a valuable asset in renouncing nuclear weapons. This point is contestable. First, two-thirds of the parties to the NPT are still far removed from the technical ability to build nuclear weapons even if they wished to do so. However, more to the point, the vast majority of the NNWSs consider that their security interests are better served by not having nuclear weapons and that an effective worldwide legal barrier to horizontal proliferation is very much to their advantage. That is the chief reason why they acceded to the NPT, and it is this conviction which provides the basis of the 1967 Tlatelolco and 1985 Rarotonga treaties and of freely made renunciations such as that confirmed for all time by Germany in the 1990 Treaty on the Final Settlement with Respect to Germany (the 'Two-plus-Four' Treaty).

Yet, it is fair to conclude that

whatever may or may not be said about the 'bargain' between various articles of the NPT, there is no doubt that the history as well as the politics of the Treaty have made it abundantly clear that a majority of NNWS parties consider it the duty of the NWSs to abide by the letter of Article VI. Few expect them to dispose of nuclear weapons at once. Only a few more would insist on obliging them to a very strict timetable for nuclear disarmament. A vast majority, however, encompassing industrial as well as developing countries, call for tangible steps towards a distant goal of nuclear disarmament. The process may be very protracted, but it must go on.[5]

Regrettably, that process has not taken off. The reductions related to START-I and -II (of which the second faced prolonged delays in ratification), are separate from and do not express a P–5 commitment to the implementation of their Article VI obligations.[6] Because of this fundamental asymmetry, which persists three decades after the NPT came into force, the non-proliferation-oriented order still remains unequal and unfair, in effect freezing the P–5 states' nuclear oligopoly.

Nevertheless, it would be foolhardy to discount the importance of the non-proliferation regime. This derives not so much from the fact that the NPT 'has succeeded beyond the expectations of its founders', in reducing the number of potential proliferants from 20 or 30 to about half a dozen, as from the circumstance that without its basic discipline and constraints, including international safeguards—and despite its flaws—it would be considerably more difficult, if not impossible, to negotiate arms control, arms reduction and disarmament measures.[7] Freedom to proliferate would have led to multiple and potentially runaway, wild, nuclear arms races, undermining efforts at arms control and even peaceful resolution of disputes. The non-proliferation regime has a deeply contradictory and dualistic character. The NPT *is* discriminatory and yet, it cannot simply be thrown to the winds as some influential Indian leaders seem to be advocating. The contradiction can be resolved only if the discrimination is reduced through visible progress towards nuclear weapons abolition.

What, then, is the challenge that India's and Pakistan's nuclearization poses to the non-proliferation-oriented global order? Three kinds of danger are readily conceivable. First, the direct one: that other nations will be impelled, prompted, or tempted to go nuclear because they feel threatened or because India or Pakistan are likely to clandestinely transfer nuclear materials or technology to them. Second, the danger that other states, in search of prestige, may want to emulate India and Pakistan, especially because they know that the consequences of so doing, while unpleasant, may be far from unbearable. Third, South Asia's nuclearization will weaken the evolving political norm for nuclear restraint and disarmament, and reduce international support for the non-proliferation aspect of the present nuclear regime, without generating pressure on the P–5 to undertake nuclear arms reduction and disarmament.

The first two categories of risk are, thankfully, relatively limited. A nuclear India and a nuclear Pakistan do threaten each other, and India after May 1998 has got into a potentially adversarial relationship with China (about which more later). They do not, however, directly threaten their other neighbours, nor are they likely to spur them to seek to meet any realistic security threats by acquiring nuclear weapons themselves. There is no persuasive evidence that India and Pakistan ever transferred, or are prone to transfer, nuclear materials or technologies to non-nuclear states. On the contrary, there is evidence that when requested to do so, they (or rather, India) refused.[9]

India and Pakistan are poor examples to emulate. Nuclearization has not earned them prestige. Rather, it has lowered their global stature, decreased their moral authority, led to their political isolation, reduced their bargaining power, and narrowed their diplomatic–political options. The risk that states such as Iran or Libya will be more strongly impelled today than before May 1998 to acquire nuclear weapons is quite minimal. The considerations that determine their nuclear pursuits are largely independent of the effect of the crossing of the nuclear threshold by India and Pakistan. Besides, the international community has long known that India and Pakistan have been developing nuclear weapons at least since the 1970s. This does put them in a different category, especially after Pokharan in 1974, from Iran, Iraq, Libya, and North Korea with their far more limited or aborted nuclear programmes. This 'prior knowledge' effect in the South Asian case made, among other factors, for a relatively soft reaction to the tests from the international community. A totally new breakout would attract much greater opprobrium, stiffer sanctions, and more strategic hostility.

Dangers from Altered Security Equations

The most serious risk in India's and Pakistan's neighbourhood lies in the altered security equation between China and India. Immediately after May, India repeatedly named China as the source of the gravest threat to its security although China had made no belligerent gestures and despite the two major agreements it signed in 1993 and 1996 on 'peace and tranquillity' along the disputed border with India, and on a slew of troop reduction, risk limitation, and confidence-building measures. China was the last of the P–5 states with which India tried to open some kind of dialogue after the tests, largely unsuccessfully. China conveyed its dismay and resentment at being named a 'threat' in no uncertain terms, while 'strongly condemning' them.[10]

Even in early 1999, the Chinese response to India's offer to discuss the nuclear weapons issue was to demand compliance with Security Council Resolution 1172. This was a much tougher line than that of the US which had noted significant 'progress' in its bilateral talks with India and Pakistan and 'appreciated' the gestures towards nuclear restraint made by the two states in late 1998, primarily in the form of a No First Use (of nuclear weapons) commitment by India, and Pakistan's declaration that it would meet India half-way in defusing their mutual nuclear rivalry (although it does not offer No First Use).

If and when India fully develops and operationalises the *Agni* missile, and especially its extended-range version (*Agni*-II or *Agni*-plus), China is likely to feel impelled to factor India seriously into its nuclear–military calculations. If however, India slows down the pace of missile development and indicates that it has no plans to deploy intermediate-range missiles at least for an extended period of time, China may not respond by relaunching its intermediate-range *Dong Feng 25* missile development programme, by overtly targeting cities in the Indian heartland, stalling further progress on defusing tensions along the border, or obstructing negotiations for improved economic and diplomatic relations, or by making belligerent gestures.

In other words, the tests by themselves are not certain, even very likely, to alter the Sino-Indian security equation decisively. India would have to do *more*, e.g. proceed with rapid development of the *Agni* and explore the possibility of mating a warhead with it and deploying it before this happens. This danger is very real. Going by the poor outcome of the visit of India's Foreign Secretary K. Raghunath to Beijing (January 1999) and by the statements of Sha Zukang, head of China's department for arms control and disarmament, in early 1999, relations between the two states are not about to improve dramatically.[11]

Although India and China have not yet entered into a relationship of strategic hostility, they have moved towards an equation based on strategic rivalry; or more accurately, they now oscillate between strategic indifference or non-cognizance of each other as rivals in security terms, on the one hand, and strategic rivalry, on the other. This should underscore the importance of restraint on India's part in nuclear and missile development and deployment, as well as the salience of a strategic dialogue and further arms-reduction and confidence-building measures between China and India. In the absence of this, the danger could get significantly enhanced.

It is the third category of risk, that of a *weakening of the international moral–political norm* and will for nuclear restraint, that is truly grave and both of immediate and long-term consequence. This must be seen against the backdrop of the failure of the NPT review process and the utter cynicism with which the P–5 have treated it, resisting and dismissing all entreaties and appeals by the NNWSs to move towards nuclear disarmament. In 1998, just days before India's 11 May tests, the NPT preparatory conference in Geneva ended in bitter disagreement and mutual recrimination, with the P–5 stubbornly refusing even the suggestion that there is a legal obligation on them to undertake nuclear disarmament.

The Stockpile Stewardship programme in the US, Russia's deployment of the new *Topol-M* series of missiles, and the double standards employed by the Western nuclear powers, especially the US, in regard to Israel, on the one hand, and India and Pakistan, on the other, are so many indices of the persistence of wholly negative attitudes and deceits on the part of the Great Powers, which could lead to serious doubts about the possibility and feasibility of a world without nuclear weapons. The subcritical tests conducted by the US and Russia have further strengthened such doubts.[12] If these doubts grow, if there is no progress towards qualitative nuclear arms reduction and disarmament, and if only minor measures of restraint are successfully negotiated, such as an FMCT which only bans future production of fissile material and excludes existing stocks, the will of the world community to erect barriers to proliferation and to grapple with the means to bring about nuclear disarmament will weaken. That would be a serious, even historic, setback, with real and growing possibilities of breakouts from the non-proliferation regime. A world with more nuclear powers would be even more insecure and unsafe than today.

The overt nuclearization of India and Pakistan confronts the P–5 with a dilemma. It effectively, and in a *de facto* although not *de jure* manner, ends their oligopoly of possession of nuclear weapons, without, however, seriously undermining the non-proliferation regime. However, where and how do they accommodate India and Pakistan? Clearly, they cannot expect them to join the NPT as non-nuclear weapons state signatories when they already have the weapons. Nor can the P–5 officially admit them to the Nuclear Club as fully-fledged members.

The P–5 could at most succeed in pressuring India and Pakistan to stay fairly close to the nuclear threshold and to manage their mutual nuclear and conventional rivalry within 'acceptable' limits, in non-deployment mode. At least, they would have to create a new category: a third class of low-ranking nuclear states, or Nuclear Possessor states, as distinct from NWSs. To both these ends, the P–5 would have to engage the two states in a dialogue and seek some assurances of a stable strategic balance in South Asia and a commitment from both India and Pakistan not to enter into a fully-fledged nuclear arms race with each other, nor let the effects of their newly acquired nuclear status spread beyond the boundaries of the South Asian region. This is precisely what the P–5, with the US in the lead, are now engaged in.

The core P–5 agenda, as it is emerging, is threefold. First, it seeks to ensure that India and Pakistan do not disturb the global non-proliferation regime (however elevated their rhetoric against its iniquities and however loud their complaints against 'nuclear apartheid'). Secondly, their emergence as minor NWSs or Nuclear Possessor States must not radically upset regional and global strategic balances. This means containing the nuclear prowess and reach of India and Pakistan to the South Asian region as far as possible. This will require assurances that they will not rapidly stockpile huge quantities of fissile material or develop and test-fly nuclear-capable missiles, they will delay the mating of delivery vehicles and warheads, and desist from openly deploying missiles or positioning them close to each other's borders. Thirdly, and equally importantly, it involves a tacit agreement that the NNWSs are not allowed by the P–5 and India and Pakistan to seize effective control of the nuclear disarmament agenda. In other words, India and Pakistan must behave like 'responsible', status quoist, loyal junior partners of the P–5, *deserving* aspirants to, or candidate-or associate members of, the Nuclear Club, with the same stake as the P–5 in barring fresh entry and keeping all other aspirants as far away as possible from the Clubhouse.

This does not argue that all of the P–5 have identical agendas or that there are no differences in their approaches to the subcontinent, or individually to India and Pakistan. There are indeed significant divergences. For instance, Russia, France, and Britain all refused to impose economic sanctions upon

India. France was the first P–5 state that welcomed the visit of a senior level Indian emissary to meet President Jacques Chirac after the May tests. It later opened a 'strategic dialogue' with India, and India has since indicated, following a visit by defence minister Fernandes to Paris in January 1999, that it will make sizable arms purchases from France. (The two have had significant military and nuclear cooperative programmes in the past.)

Russia went even further. Soon after the tests, it supported India's candidature for permanent membership of the UN Security Council. It then signed wide-ranging security cooperation and arms purchase agreements with India during a visit by Prime Minister Yevgeny Primakov in December 1998. Similarly, China was considerably softer on Pakistan than on India; it only expressed 'deep regret' over Pakistan's tests, but had 'strongly condemned' India. It was also appreciative of Pakistan's 'compulsions' to test after India did so. The US tended, despite a growing relationship with India, to sympathize with Pakistan's economic plight in the wake of sanctions, and said so openly.[13]

A Multi-Class Nuclear Club

In the Nuclear Club, the first-class members by virtue of the size and range of their nuclear arsenals are the US and Russia. The second-class members are the UK, France and China. They have their points of tension vis-à-vis the former. China and France once declared that when US and Russia reduced their arsenals by 50 per cent, they would join the reduction/disarmament process. Once this became possible (after the Cold War) both resiled from their earlier commitments and declared, joined by the UK , that the US and Russia would have to reduce their arsenals by 95 per cent before they join in. China, in particular, resists the idea of even a 'no increase' pledge, wary as it is of future US theatre missile defence plans.

The third-class members, India and Pakistan, also have their points of tension and difference with the other NWSs, which could well surface in the FMCT negotiations. If these talks proceed too fast—and India, for example, is worried that it won't have accumulated 'enough' stocks by the time they are about to conclude—then New Delhi could well try to stall matters. Despite these other significant differences and tensions *within* the Nuclear Club, what unites its members *against* the NNWSs is much more important than what divides them. This must be borne in mind even as the NNWSs try to work on these differences to better pursue complete nuclear disarmament.

BOX 4

Where are They?

Worldwide Nuclear Deployments

A March 1998 report of the National Resources Defense Council (NRDC), the US-based NGO, provides, for the first time, authoritative estimates of the sizes and locations of the nuclear arsenals of the US, Russia, the UK, France, and China. The full report contains detailed descriptions, including maps and tables, of today's arsenals, and describes the events that have led to the consolidation of weapons storage sites. What follows is a summary (also prepared for the most part by the NRDC) of that report.

Though the end of the Cold War has transformed relations with Russia, and disarmament agreements have resulted in significant reductions in nuclear weapons worldwide, NRDC estimates that some 36,000 nuclear bombs still remain in the arsenals of the five nuclear powers: the United States, Russia, the UK, France, and China. Over the past decade, large-scale reductions in the size of the nuclear arsenals have resulted in significant shifts in weapons locations, shifts unequalled since the earliest days of nuclear deployments. Until now, however, no authoritative estimates of the sizes, locations and characteristics of worldwide nuclear arsenals have been available. In the mid-1980s, the five powers possessed nearly 70,000 nuclear weapons, widely dispersed in the Soviet Union, Eastern and Western Europe, and Asia, as well as on and beneath the high seas. Since then, an extensive consolidation has taken place, with a fivefold decrease in the number of storage sites to less than 150.

NRDC assesses the nuclear arsenals of the five countries as follows:

The United States: Nearly 12,000 nuclear weapons (deployed or stored) are located in 14 states. New Mexico, Georgia, Washington, Nevada, and North Dakota are the top five and account for about 70 per cent of the total. The other nine are Wyoming, Missouri, Montana, Louisiana, Texas, Nebraska, California, Virginia, and Colorado.

The number of US nuclear weapons land-based or airfield-based in Europe has shrunk dramatically, from over 6,000 of many types in the early 1980s to some 150 B61 bombs at ten air bases in seven countries (Belgium, Germany, Greece, Italy, the Netherlands, Turkey, and the UK) by the end of 1997. The US is the only country with nuclear weapons deployed outside its borders.

Russia: Some 22,500 weapons are deployed or stored at about 90 sites in Russia. In a little appreciated logistical feat, Soviet, and then Russian, members of the12th Main Directorate consolidated, over the past decade, a far-flung arsenal of tens of thousands of nuclear weapons at hundreds of locations in Eastern Europe and 14 republics to under a hundred sites in Russia today.

The United Kingdom: The UK stockpile is about to be composed of a single weapon type: the Trident-II missile on Vanguard-class submarines. According to the NRDC, the last WE-177 gravity bombs were scheduled for retirement by March 1998 when its Report was published. The Tornado bombers that once carried them will only conduct conventional missions.

France: The French stockpile totals some 450 warheads of three types at four locations, down from a dozen bases at the beginning of the 1990s.

China: The Chinese stockpile is estimated at about 400 located at some 20 sites.

SOURCE: Natural Resources Defense Council, Washington, DC, USA.

The existing five recognized NWSs do not want India and Pakistan to become examples for others to emulate; they must not be allowed to form independent tactical alliances and blocs of their choosing which can shake up the global nuclear status quo. Thus, whatever the claims of nuclear hawks and ultra-nationalists in the two countries, or at the other end of the spectrum, of some in the international peace and nuclear disarmament movement, India and Pakistan have not ended up defying the global nuclear order. All they seek is a place at its margins, in or close to the Nuclear Club. Their freedom of manoeuvre remains as limited or narrow as ever, and indeed they have lost some of their leverage. Their nuclearization does not represent the P–5's 'comeuppance', but is largely in conformity with the maintenance of the existing order.

So far as India is concerned, the US and China remain at two different poles. China has refused to engage India in substantive negotiations on the nuclear weapons issue. In fact, in early 1999, the head of China's department for arms control and disarmament, Sha Zukang, not only demanded that India and Pakistan 'stop and reverse' their nuclear development programmes, but also went so far as to implicitly accuse Washington of violating UN Security Council Resolution 1172 which condemned the tests: 'It is a direct violation [of the Resolution] to negotiate, or even discuss, with India on India's so-called minimum nuclear deterrence capability.'[14] According to another report from Beijing, China is opposed to any deal that would allow India to maintain a 'minimum nuclear deterrent' in return for 'joining the Comprehensive Test Ban Treaty . . . . China has conveyed its stand on the South Asian nuclear issue to the US in clearcut terms', according to Chinese officials who recalled the 27 June Sino-US joint statement issued after talks between the Chinese and US Presidents. [15]

Unlike China, the US has held substantive talks with India on the nuclear and missiles issues as well as on the more general question of security. By early February 1999, it had concluded eight rounds of talks each with India and Pakistan. At the same time, the US has followed a strategy of economic sanctions and trade embargoes on Indian military and nuclear-related research laboratories and public enterprises engaged in arms production. In November 1998, it released an 'Entities List', naming 200 institutions in India which were to be subject to such embargoes.

Washington's aims, as stated by Talbott himself at a Brookings Institution speech, and by other US officials, are to get India to agree to some measures of restraint, including signature of the CTBT, non-deployment of missiles and aircraft capable of carrying nuclear bombs/warheads in the immediate future, freeze production of fissile material, and institute strict controls on the export of nuclear materials or technologies. India has repeatedly indicated that it will sign the CTBT. In September 1998, four months after the test, Indian military scientists prepared the technical ground for this by declaring that no further tests were necessary to achieve reliable weaponization, and India could go ahead and sign the CTBT without compromising its security. They have since reiterated this position a number of times.

Indian officials have also indicated that India has no intention or immediate plans to deploy nuclear weapons openly in conflict mode with full command and control systems in place, but that it would like an acknowledgement of the legitimacy of its 'minimum credible nuclear deterrent' as the price for this. This 'minimum' deterrent proved a sticking point at least until the end of the eighth round of talks with the US. However, there were indications in early February 1999 that the US would move towards lifting some sanctions and stop voting against loans totalling $3.67 billion to India from the World Bank and other multilateral institutions if India signs the CTBT by mid-1999. To please the US, New Delhi also cancelled a test-flight of the *Agni* scheduled for 26 January, India's Republic Day but eventually carried it out in April 1999. Both sides noted 'forward movement' of their bilateral relations and agreed to create a 'positive atmosphere' to resolve differences.

If the negotiations succeed, there would come into being some compromise on accommodating India (and Pakistan) at the margins of the existing world nuclear order. This would mean conceding the legitimacy of their 'deterrent'. That would be a thoroughly undesirable state of affairs if, as is likely, it freezes and extends that order, rather than alters and radically reforms it so that it yields to a disarmament-oriented regime. An opportunity to make a major thrust forward towards both comprehensive and incremental approaches to nuclear disarmament would be lost. The P–5 would be united in bringing about and ensuring just such a loss. However, their own rationalizations for retaining their nuclear weapons state status and their arsenals, and their approaches to arms reduction and disarmament, all differ significantly from one another.

A Hardening US Posture

The US remains the most reluctant among the P–5 to make any meaningful commitment to nuclear disarmament, except as some kind of remote future goal, although President Clinton recently came close to acknowledging, however obliquely and without any reference to the US's own past policies, that nuclear weapons have little to do with achieving peace and security. Immediately after the first Pakistani tests of 28 May, he said: 'I cannot believe that we are about to start the 21st century by having the Indian subcontinent repeat the worst mistakes of the 20th century, when we know it is not necessary to peace, to security, to prosperity, to national greatness or personal fulfilment.'[16]

With the end of the Cold War, the fundamental rationale of US nuclear weapons, and of NATO strategic doctrine, simply collapsed. It became manifestly clear that the sheer magnitude and size of the US arsenal could in no way be justified in the absence of the Warsaw Pact. The US then invented other rationales for its nuclear weapons and their continued stewardship: first, through ideologists and pamphleteers positing, or rather, mostly exploiting, prejudices about, the 'Islamic threat', and peddling such notions of security as based on a 'clash of civilizations' and 'rogue' states or nuclear terrorists, and later, through official policies and programmes.

Of these last, the Nuclear Posture Review of September 1994, the Presidential Decision Directive-60, and the Science-Based Stockpile Stewardship and Management Programme (SSMP) are the most important. They address both the subjective and objective dimensions of 'security' based on nuclearism. Subjectively, the NPR and PDD-60 provide the rationale for *retaining* nuclear weapons while at the same time trying to make them do more things even though there will be fewer such weapons around than in the Cold War era. PDD-60 broadens the list of sites that can be struck in China, and allows use against 'rogue states' and against an attacker using non-nuclear weapons of mass destruction.

The introduction of a 'single integrated operational plan'(SIOP) in the flexible Strategic War Planning System (SWPS) of 1992, eliminated the distinction between strategic and tactical nuclear planning. Through what is called 'adaptive planning', the nuclear target list can be expanded even as the number of bombs continues to decline. In short, PDD-60 provides a series of nuclear attack *options*. Since not only a smaller number, but older warheads are being asked to do more, the SSMP must ensure their 'reliability'. Of course, the SSMP is meant not only to better *preserve* ageing nuclear weapons systems but also to better *prepare* for a future qualitative arms race if a breakout from post-Cold War constraints ever takes place!

The formulations that the NPR and PDD-60 offer are so dubious that it is difficult to believe they can sound plausible even to believers in America's 'manifest destiny' or to worshippers of its self-appointed leadership role in the world, especially to protect it from mass-destruction catastrophes engineered by fanatics, lunatics and assorted terrorists. It is not the intrinsic, logical value, or even strategic plausibility, of such reasoning, but the prevalence of terrible intellectual inertia, that prevents any rational thinking on issues of security. That alone explains why the NPR and PDD-60 went through with little criticism or discussion.

This inertia entails a refusal to countenance the possibility that the US could achieve adequate security without its thousands of nuclear warheads, missiles, submarines, and aircraft, or without dismantling powerful weapons laboratories, and without severely pruning its still gargantuan nuclear weapons budget which runs at $35 billion a year a decade after the end of the Cold War. Similarly, not only must the nuclear weapons labs be kept running; they must be given expensive facilities (some call them 'exercise machines') to play with in the shape of the SSMP and direct-fusion weapons experiments, etc. Indeed, in 1995–6, Clinton had to make a deal over the CTBT by giving in to pressure from the laboratories and from Pentagon lobbies, which meant accepting the SSMP as a quid pro quo.

Precisely because the security rationale for retaining huge stocks of nuclear weapons and continuing further nuclear weapons development, including possibly fourth-generation weapons, is so weak that South Asia's nuclearization has not provoked the least bit of rethinking or heart-searching in the US administration on its nuclear posture and policies. Subjecting these to scrutiny and discussion would open a Pandora's Box. All that the South Asian breakout has done is to prompt the US to co-opt India and Pakistan into the existing nuclear order, without questioning any of the assumptions or foundations of that order.

In Russia, the rationale for retaining the unwieldy nuclear arsenal, which that impoverished country can ill-afford, has had less to do with real security than with a subjective rationale, of shoring up that state's shrinking stature and declining image. Russia has moved in a retrograde direction since its 'independence' from the former Soviet Union: rescinding its No First Use pledge, embarking upon modernization of some of its nuclear warheads and missiles, and demonstrating a far greater reluctance than in the Brezhnev or Gorbachev period (when it was far more positive and flexible than the US) to move towards nuclear arms reduction and disarmament, and supporting initiatives to promote these in multilateral fora.

Russia, by no stretch of the imagination, has any need to conduct any more nuclear tests in order to develop new weapons or designs in the interests of greater security. Yet, in 1996, it (along with China) insisted on an entry-into-force clause being introduced into the CTBT text which was solely designed to get every other nuclear-capable state on board. The logic was: why should we alone suffer the 'disadvantage' of not being able to test? Let others suffer too. This, when even the US, normally ultra-conservative, was fairly relaxed about the issue, at least to begin with. Clearly, Russia is also trying to get its nuclear weapons (which are getting fewer in number) to do more and different things: from using them as bargaining chips to trying (futilely) to recover lost 'national honour' through them. It too has not been jolted by the new situation in South Asia into reconsidering its nuclear policies. On the contrary, the rather fanciful idea that Prime Minister Primakov threw up in December 1998 of a 'grand strategic triangle' or partnership between Russia, China, and India suggests that nostalgia for past glory, rather than hard-nosed strategic calculation, plays a significant role in policy thinking in Moscow.

As for the second-rank nuclear weapons states, France, China and the UK, the first two insist on waiting and watching the Big Two. It is the latter that have to set the pace of reduction and disarmament. France and China could take dramatic initiatives unilaterally to accelerate this momentum, but they won't. Britain does not pursue a fully independent nuclear policy of its own. China or France could take a somewhat autonomous stand and lend some support to the NNWSs' demand for implementing the recommendations of the International Court of Justice in favour of completing negotiations on the abolition of all nuclear weapons at an early date. However, controlled as they are by the nuclear mindset, they have not been jolted into action or new thinking even in the post-Cold War period. Clearly, unless pressure is brought to bear upon these second-rank nuclear states through friendly governments, through citizens' groups, and NGOs, and through mass campaigns and peace movements, it will very difficult to recruit them into a bold new initiative that favours nuclear arms reduction and disarmament. How this might be done is discussed in the next chapter.

The New Nukes' Dilemmas

Finally, what of the dilemmas of the New Nukes, India and Pakistan, themselves? Nuclearization has proved a Faustian bargain for them. Their entire foreign policy agendas have been largely narrowed down to controlling or limiting the damage caused by crossing the threshold. Their economies have suffered, as has their credibility. To hide its embarrassment, and in a desperate move to regain lost ground, India has embarked on a strategy of making largely tokenist gestures of nuclear restraint, and still reiterating some vague commitment to nuclear weapons abolition. For instance, in November 1998, it moved a resolution in the UN General Assembly calling for de-alerting nuclear weapons and separating warheads from delivery vehicles. After nuclear testing, and having made a number of incoherent statements of its nuclear policy, India in early 1999 fashioned some kind of doctrinal formulation that might sound reasonable and sober, if only to the naive: India does not want to amass and deploy large numbers of nuclear weapons. It only wants to build a 'credible minimum deterrent'. It unilaterally offers never to be the first to use nuclear weapons against an adversary, and never to use them against a non-nuclear state. And so on.

In reality, these are purely tokenist gestures. De-alerting nuclear weapons is a far cry from disarming them or dismantling them. India may even have been making a virtue out of necessity (its own limited capability for full deployment) by advocating that warheads and delivery vehicles be kept separated. This is at best a risk-reduction or arms control measure, not a disarmament measure. Moreover, one of the important aspects of de-alerting is that this is something that can be done bilaterally, and without international treaties. The US and Russia have been discussing and doing this to an extent. There have been genuine and reasonable worries that India's attempt to make a general resolution of this at this particular time would jeopardize such efforts by forcing a negative vote and a hardening of positions by some NWSs just because of the consideration that a cynical nuclear India wants to milk some diplomatic advantage out of a noble-sounding de-alerting resolution or posture. At some point, a general de-alerting posture makes eminent sense and must be pursued. The grounds for this have however to be carefully prepared. De-deploying nuclear weapons is a desirable *step* but hardly an *end* in itself, nor a *substitute* for genuine disarmament. The 'credible minimum deterrent' concept is too vague and shifting to mean very much. As discussed earlier, it is no assurance that India will not get sucked into a nuclear arms race of the classical Cold War type, albeit on a smaller scale.

India's No First Use commitment does not mark a radical break from nuclear deterrence-based thinking, it is fully compatible with it. True, a commitment to No First Use, even if unilateral and legally unenforceable, even meaningless, is better than the absence of such a commitment, or a doctrine that advocates or allows pre-emptive use of nuclear weapons even when one is not threatened with nuclear weapons.[17] However, a No First Use commitment by India can always be overruled in a situation of conflict or of rapid escalation of hostile exchanges, by invoking 'military necessity' and citing the 'supreme national interest' or a 'national emergency'. Within the dread logic of nuclear deterrence-based thinking, it can be persuasively argued that the threat of use of nuclear weapons, backed by a stark demonstration of preparations and the will to use them, if not the *actual use* of them, would ultimately be less 'costly' than the consequences of staying stuck to No First Use. This is true *a fortiori* when the adversary (in India's case, Pakistan) has made no such commitment and would perhaps have—or so many in the Indian élite at least believe—no compunctions in using its nuclear bombs first. In a situation of 'use them or lose them', military considerations of a fairly crude nature are likely to prevail, rather than cautious, sober, principled thinking based upon a recollection of noble offers made in the past in 'different' circumstances.

The force-of-circumstances argument apart, Indian and Pakistani strategic moves on the ground are bound to be substantially affected by military personnel who are trained to think of battles and wars in terms such as 'element of surprise', 'overwhelming the enemy', and establishing not just decisive 'superiority', but real 'supremacy' over the adversary at an early stage in a conflict. Such generals, admirals, and air marshals can be expected to be loath to surrender the vital option to use, or at least threaten to use, nuclear weapons first. In the Indian subcontinental context, the prevalent uncertainties about each other's intentions, preparations, even doctrines, can only add to the strategic uncertainties and tensions involved in a situation of conflict. War is after all about establishing or re-establishing certainties, about creating decisive, violent shifts in power balances and strategic equations. Few generals are likely to pass up all these options which are effectively denied them by strict, unflinching, unconditional, and categorical adherence to a No First Use commitment. In short, a No First Use declaration by India in *current circumstances* is diversionary and hollow, but a No First Use declaration by the existing NWSs is of real importance, and will be discussed in the next chapter.

There is, besides, a credibility problem which the Indian government faces here. It has so brazenly, so violently, so comprehensively, and so irredeemably, breached and betrayed its own stated and well-established positions and policies on the question of nuclear weapons, especially at the *doctrinal* level, that its word can no longer be taken to mean what it says. There is a double *credibility gap* in the Indian case. New Delhi has often spoken in the 1990s from the moral high ground, only to do the opposite of what it says, especially on the nuclear issue. It would be extraordinarily naive to think that just because it crossed the nuclear threshold, it has shed its hypocrisy and double standards once and for all. Just the contrary. The world and all those Indians who stand for integrity and honesty in the conduct of public affairs must treat New Delhi as being just as capable of double standards and hypocrisy as any other state, including the most hegemonistic ones.

Pakistan is less hypocritical, and does not profess the same adherence to universal and noble values as does India. However, as discussed earlier, that does not make it less immoral or politically more respectable either in its pursuit of nuclear weapons or in its courtship of the United States as a potential ally and friend which, it urges, should favour it over India. Pakistan, with its economy crumbling, and its state structures in an advanced stage of decay and disintegration, faces a dilemma: manufacturing and deploying nuclear weapons and missiles is liable to impose an unbearable burden on the government and the people in the name of whose security the weapons were to be made. On the other hand, not 'matching' India, almost Bomb for Bomb, could lead to Pakistan's civilian rulers being discredited in the eyes of the extremely powerful military and also make its elected governments more vulnerable to the depredations of fanatical Islamicist forces.

Pakistan, for the moment, is trying to convert its weakness (fear of its collapse as economy or state) into a strength in its bargaining with the US. It has a stake in limiting its nuclear rivalry with India, but the horizons of its ruling élite are limited to the South Asian region. It cannot be expected to take a bold initiative in favour of nuclear disarmament at the global level.

South Asia's nuclearization, then, presents different dilemmas, challenges, and problems to the different actors concerned and involved. The most important of these are the challenges it presents to the advocates of nuclear disarmament and to the peace movements in different parts of the world. It is to these challenges that we now turn.

Notes

1. Talbott's remarks in this address to the Conference on Diplomacy and Preventive Defense, 16 January 1999, Stanford University, *Official Text*, US Information Service, New Delhi, 25 January 1999).

2. Quoted in *Official Text,* US Information Services, New Delhi, 25 January 1999.
3. The London Suppliers' Group was established in 1975, following India's first nuclear explosion, by seven industrially developed countries working behind closed doors. It was the result of a US initiative to set up a broad-based group to ensure that sensitive nuclear plants and technologies are not supplied to future tactical proliferators. When the 'Guidelines for Nuclear Transfers of 1977' (London Guidelines) were published in 1978, 15 countries adhered to them. The LSG now has over 30 members, including European Union states, many members of the former Warsaw Pact, and most members of the Organization for Economic Cooperation and Development (OECD).

   The Zangger Committee, named after its first chairman, Professor Claude Zangger of Switzerland, was established to define what was meant in the NPT's Article III not only by 'source or special fissionable material' but also by 'equipment or material especially designed or prepared for the processing, use or production of special fissionable material,' since the parties were required not to export such items to any NNWS 'unless the source or special fissionable material' is 'subject to safeguards'. The committee completed its first 'trigger list' in July 1974.

   The MTCR is a closed-door group set up in 1987 by different states to restrict transfers or sales of missiles or components of missiles above the range of 300 km. It is essentially a non-proliferation measure.
4. *Nuclear Non-Proliferation and Global Order,* Oxford, SIPRI/OUP, 1994, p. 7.
5. ibid. p. 7–8.
6. Article VI reads: 'Each of the Parties to the Treaty undertakes to pursue negotiations in good faith on effective measures relating to cessation of the nuclear arms race at an early date and to nuclear disarmament, and on a treaty on general and complete disarmament under strict and effective international control.'
7. George Perkovich, 'Nuclear Proliferation', *Foreign Policy,* New York, Fall 1998, p.12. Perkovich recalls: 'Back in 1963, President John Kennedy had feared that 20 to 30 states would build nuclear weapons by the 1970s.' ibid.
8. For instance, India's foreign minister Jaswant Singh, when asked, 'If countries like Iraq, Iran were to conduct tests, would you deny them their right to test?', said: 'No, this is the principle. Do you deny that nations on this earth have not right to equal and legitimate security?' Interview with *Indian Express,* 28 January 1999.
9. For instance, India after the 1974 nuclear test was reportedly approached by countries such as Libya, Iran and Iraq with requests for assistance in the nuclear field. It turned down these requests. However, as a minister in the Janata Party government of 1977–8, George Fernandes is believed to have strongly lobbied for transferring nuclear technology to Libya. He was overruled by Prime Minister Morarji Desai.
10. China's initial reaction to the India's tests was the angriest of all the responses of the P–5 states. It accused India of 'undermining the international effort in banning N-tests so as to obtain begemony in South Asia in defiance of world opinion . . . . ' It said that the tests reveals 'nothing but an outrageous contempt for the common will of the international community for the CTBT . . . and [would]

entail serious consequences to peace and stability'.'India turns to an old comrade as China talks tough', *Indian Express,* New Delhi, 15 May 1998.

Later, in an exclusive interview, on the eve of Clinton's visit to China in June, President Jiang Zemin said: 'In November 1996, I paid a successful visit to India . . . I was accorded a very friendly reception by the government and people of India. That visit has left me with very good memories. I was very surprised that they conducted the nuclear tests. I was even more surprised that they cited China as a reason for their nuclear testing. I really don't know what kind of threat China poses'. Cited in *The Hindu,* 22 June 1998.

However, the assessment of Chinese experts, quoted in *Jane's Defence Weekly,* is that India will take at least 10 more years to establish an 'operational nuclear strike capability', and cannot yet pose a grave or 'immediate threat' to Chinese security. This follows a review by China's security planners over whether they should upgrade their rating of the threat from India. Cited in *The Hindustan Times,* New Delhi, 30 December 1998.

11. For Sha's statements, see. 'China jolts India with nuclear blast', *The Telegraph* Calcutta, 14 January 1999. Also, note 14.
12. By February 1999, the US had conducted six subcritical tests at the Nevada test site, and in late December, the Russians officially admitted to having carried out five such tests at an Arctic testing range between 14 September and 13 December 1998, according to the Interfax agency. Cited in *The Hindu,* Delhi, 25 December 1998.
13. US Assistant Secretary for South Asian Affairs Karl F. Inderfurth said on 21 January 1999, on the eve of the eighth round of talks with India and Pakistan, that 'the US supports the International Monetary Fund's approved economic plan for Pakistan because it would assist Pakistan to get through this rough economic time . . . . We did not want to see economic collapse in Pakistan.' Cited in *Backgrounder,* US Information Service, New Delhi, 27 January 1999.
14. op. cit. See Endnote 11 above.
15. 'China opposes minimum n-deterrence for India', *The Hindu,* Delhi, 28 January 1999.
16. Quoted widely, among others by Zia Mian and M.V. Ramana, 'Stepping Away from the Nuclear Abyss', *INESAP Bulletin* Darmstadt, November 1998, p. 13).
17. The NATO doctrine of pre-emptive first use of nuclear weapons to eliminate the possibility of an adversary attack with non-nuclear weapons of mass destruction such as chemical or biological weapons, is utterly reprehensible and violative of the principle of proportionality in ethics, and in the laws of warfare.

CHAPTER ELEVEN

The Struggle for Nuclear Weapons Abolition

Them and Us

They are the upholders of the existing nuclear order. *We* are the opponents of that order. *We* comprise all those individuals, groups movements, and governments that are most seriously, honestly, and unequivocally committed to rapid global disarmament. This distinction between *them* and *us* is vital and must be borne in mind if we are even to understand what are the tasks that lie ahead of humanity as well as who it is that must be relied upon to pursue their fulfilment most strongly and energetically. The Pakistani and Indian tests are not a wake-up call for *them*. They are a wakeup call and challenge to *us*! The problems created for the existing nuclear regime are of a much lower and qualitatively different order than the problems created for us.

For *them*, the problems are of the in-house variety. To transpose and somewhat mutilate a famous remark from another, spy-thriller, context, the existing nuclear order has been stirred but not seriously shaken, let alone weakened or altered, by the recent Indian and Pakistani actions. For *them*, the central concern remains what it was earlier: keeping the focus and thrust of anti-nuclear activities and negotiations on non-proliferation, not on rapid and steady disarmament. Contrary to the belief that such a situation cannot continue to last, it most certainly can. The existing nuclear order cannot 'absorb' ten or twenty new entrants, but it can accommodate to the new reality of India and Pakistan (and a few more) becoming *de facto* nuclear states. If a state with apparently strong anti-US sentiments like Iran or Iraq were to acquire such a weapons capability or cross the threshold, it will certainly complicate matters. The anti-US 'red bombs' of the USSR and China did.

Newer entrants such as these will create a qualitatively higher danger of Bombs being used or nuclear hostilities breaking out, e.g. through a pre-emptive US nuclear strike, or a terrible new Middle East face-off. These are, however, *fundamental* challenges to *us*, not to *them*. The existing NWSs have been prepared to live with the dangers of a nuclear bombing or exchange for decades and will keep on doing so. They will continue to stress the importance of maintaining some kind of non-proliferation regime as their primary goal even if the nuclear club was to be further extended to informally include a total of ten countries or thereabouts.

What has been called the non-proliferation regime is not about to unravel under the weight of its supposed contradictions. That kind of thinking is an illusion that anti-nuclear disarmament activists would do well to avoid. This is often expressed in the misplaced emphasis given to, or more accurately, the misplaced conclusion drawn from, the existence of nuclear hypocrisy. The offensiveness of this hypocrisy is self-evident. It is also written into the very nature of today's unequal nuclear order. Hypocrisy, however, never drives other countries also to go nuclear. The existing NWSs are not 'penalized' for their hypocrisies by such additions. Hypocrisy provides no comeuppance for NWSs through the route of unwanted but limited proliferation. That is why the NWSs continue in their deceits, with their basic orientations persisting, but now joined by newer and junior hypocrites.

If the hypocrisies of the NWSs are to provide a source of possible comeuppance for them, that can only happen through another route. It is only when the existence of such hypocrisies can be harnessed by the real agents of disarmament to tap the wider public anger against the NWSs that pressure can be imposed on nuclear élites to weaken their ranks and erode their power and influence. The central question for us, then, remains effectively what it has been for the last decade. How do we use the window of opportunity created by the end of the Cold War to shift the fulcrum of existing anti-nuclear negotiations from non-proliferation to disarmament? What are the lessons we must learn from the past, especially from our past of anti-nuclear activity and mobilization? Who are the principal agents of that struggle today? How do we go about defining and pursuing our goals, transitional and final? These are the very difficult and complicated issues that this chapter will address, howsoever inadequately or incompletely.

Lessons from Our Past

Certain evils can disappear for good from human societies, never to reappear. This has happened with colonialism and apartheid. It can happen with nuclearism and nuclear weapons. In each of these cases, successful achievement rests on two cruces. The mindset that would legitimize such evil practices in the name of national or élite power and influence is thoroughly delegitimized, morally and politically. There emerges a contextual or situational alternative that persuades more and more of those earlier defending such practices to abandon this because it no longer makes sense to do so. This is usually partly because resistance to, and disapprobation of, those practices has become stronger than ever and therefore the 'costs' are ever higher, and it is partly because the 'value' of giving up colonialism, apartheid, and nuclearism becomes obvious and tangible. That is to say, the struggle against an evil like nuclearism and nuclear weapons, if it is to be sustained through its inevitable downturns, lapses, and fatigues, cannot simply be connected to something so intrinsically 'negative' as the mere striving for survival or peace, even when it is the survival of the planet and of the human species that is at stake.

The goal of lasting nuclear peace, i.e. permanent freedom from the threat of nuclear war, must have some kind of material and social content and shape if it is to *inspire* millions and arouse them from their myriad problems of everyday life to practically engage, in howsoever a modest way, in the struggle to bring about global disarmament. The problem has never been achieving popularity for, or acceptance of, the ideal of a nuclear-free world but of convincing enough people to join in the race against time to bring it about before it is too late for some, or all of us, on this planet. The issue has been how to generate the sense of urgency and the collective action that together can forge a tool of protest sufficiently powerful to make a political difference, and then to keep on pressing for positive changes thus creating a cumulative dynamic of actual disarmament.

That sense of *urgency* and that kind of collective *action* cannot be generated by simply ringing the alarms. No amount of warning about the dangers or possibility of a nuclear war will suffice. We have the means to bring about a global holocaust and a possible end to the human species, but the sheer unspeakable horror and incomprehensibility of such a denouement makes the danger appear remote and abstract. Or else, how do we live and get on with our lives? The value of nuclear peace must be made tangible in some way, and to do that it has to be connected to the prospects of achieving concrete and visible forms of *progress,* i.e. to the realization of more livable alternatives, all the better and clearly so for being freed from the evil in question. If colonialism and apartheid can disappear forever because there is both the promise and the evidence that a post-colonial and post-apartheid society is better, then we have to generate that same persuasive promise and evidence for a post-nuclear world.

The force of this logic, if accepted, necessarily takes us in a particular direction. The lowest and widest common denominator of anti-nuclearism has to be the collective moral sentiment against such life-threatening evil. However, the vision of a collective and shared humanity that this arouses must also be linked, at least in some informal and indirect sense, to a broader agenda of struggle for collective human progress in the twenty-first century. It is in this vital sense that it remains as true now as in the past, that to fight successfully for peace we must fight for more than peace. To fight successfully against nuclearism, we must fight against more than nuclearism. To fight successfully for a nuclear-free world, we have to be internationalists. To continue to deepen and strengthen our internationalism on this front, we will have to be internationalists on many other fronts.

What all this means is that the efforts at, and prospects of, moving progressively nearer to a nuclear-free world is unavoidably connected, *but never in any simple or straightforward way,* to the efforts at, and prospects of, moving towards a better world in general. The rhythms and tempos of struggle are different on different fronts. The extent of retreats and advances will also similarly vary, and the networks of mutual influence are complex. It is certainly possible to make very significant advances on, say, the anti-nuclear front but not in many other areas. However, insofar as defeating nuclearism for good means defeating a particular mindset and replacing it with a new, internationalist and humane one, such a new mindset will shape, and be shaped, by the values, beliefs, and emotions that emerge from other struggles against other injustices and inhumanities.

The nuclear mindset must, however, also be attacked and delegitimized on its own terrain and terms. The lessons of history on this score are clear. First, there has to be the clearest moral perception that nuclear weapons are the closest thing to an absolute evil. Second, there has to be complete consistency in opposing their possession. The idea that nuclear deterrence in some circumstances is justified should be rejected. This consistency is important not because the principle of consistency is a virtue in itself but because both logic and the historical record endorse such consistency. Third, no virtue or positive attribute or property of any kind should be accorded to the possession of nuclear weapons, nor even to the capability to develop, possess, induct, and deploy them. Fourth, there is no place whatsoever for *any* form of nuclear nationalism.

Many otherwise committed and progressive anti-nuclear disarmament activists and supporters have not fully absorbed all of these four fundamental precepts and in failing to do so, directly or indirectly, provide props for the nuclear mindset. This is true of sections of the international Left (among others) and is most obviously so of the organized Indian Left, their parties, leaders, and many of their members. This constitutes a particularly serious dilemma because the two principal Indian Communist parties, the CPI and CPM, are among the strongest such parties anywhere in the world, and no mass anti-nuclear disarmament movement worth the name in South Asia can do without their commitment, support, and participation. (See Box 5)

BOX 5

Marxists and Nuclear Weapons

Amibiguity and the 'Red Bomb'

Of all the various activist currents—socialists, Marxists, liberals, pacifists, ecologists, feminists, etc.—that have gone into the making of the mass anti-nuclear movements and activities over the second half of the twentieth century, many Marxists have been among the most ambivalent in their moral attitudes. This ambivalence comes not just from the 'charity' with which they have viewed the 'red bomb' of the USSR or China but has its source in a weakness within Marxism itself. Marxist discourse has always been replete with moral passion, rhetoric and appeal. A practical Marxist commitment has always entailed and required moral anger against injustice. Some of its central theoretical concepts such as 'exploitation' have an inescapable moral dimension. However, Marxism has always had an underdeveloped ethical theory which has often promoted a certain moral insensitivity especially to the question of the relationship between means and ends.

In the absence of such sensitivity, a class relativism towards ethical issues has often superseded the commitment to universalist principles of justice regardless of class position.[1] Thus many Marxists have displayed disturbing equanimity, even an unruffled complacency, in the face of Soviet and Chinese possession of the bomb. The 'red bomb' is as morally unacceptable as the capitalist bomb but has not always been seen as such. It is really only in the course of the mass anti-nuclear movements—the CND of the fifties and sixties in the UK, and then the peace movements of the seventies and eighties in Europe and the US—that some Western Marxists confronted head-on the distinctive dilemmas posed for Marxist theory and politics by the nuclear question in general, and the 'red bomb' in particular.[2]

Western Marxists brought into the anti-nuclear peace movement a vital emphasis–seeking to give a positive content to the otherwise 'empty' notion of peace. In doing so, they helped raise consciousness of the linkages between nuclear behaviour and imperialist attitudes, and of the relationship between peace and socialism. Many Western Marxists also learnt from the broader peace movement. They learnt to recognize the importance of a moral universalism, the fact that the politics of nuclear disarmament in certain ways transcended class politics, and that it could not simply be reduced to a component of, or 'fitted into', the anti-imperialist struggle. These are lessons that have never really touched Indian Marxists or the Left parties of India. The Russian bomb was welcomed with no moral or political qualms. Much of the organized Left also welcomed the Chinese tests of 1964 and where they didn't, it had to do with nationalist sentiments not internationalist ones. This Left has remained insouciant in its defence of the unmistakably immoral but long time Indian stance of nuclear ambiguity.[3]

Notes

1. It is no coincidence that the landmark advance in ethical political theory came not from the domain of Marxism but from liberal political philosophy: the work of John Rawls. However, many Marxists have engaged constructively with Rawls and post-Rawlsian philosophy and political theory to deepen and further develop Marxist ethical thinking. Among notewrothy works in this regard, see M. Cohen, T. Nagel, and T. Scanlon, (eds.), *Marx, Justice and History,* Princeton, 1980; K. Nielsen and S.C. Patten (eds.), *Marx and Morality,* vol. III of the *Canadian Journal of Philosophy,* 1981; A. Buchanan, *Marx and Justice,* London, 1982; R. W. Miller, *Analysing Marx,* Princeton, 1985; N. Geras, *Discourses of Extremity,* Verso, London 1990; A. Gilbert, *Democratic Individuality,* Cambridge, 1990; S. Lukes, *Marxism, Morality and Social Justice,* Princeton, 1990; D. McLeilan and S. Sayers (eds.), *Socialism and Morality,* London, 1990.
2. The 'red bomb' has been defended in the name of proletarian internationalism not just of a general or non-class internationalism. That is to say, the Soviet and Chinese bomb was said to have constituted a powerful defence of the international working class including those sections of it in the US and other capitalist NWSs. To argue or believe however that the 'red bomb' best defends the US working class by first having to threaten its complete extinction, does require the ability to perform mental calisthenics of the highest order.
3. For a representative sample of such thinking, see the booklet, *Against Nuclear Jingoism,* National Book Centre, New Delhi, July 1998, published by India's largest Communist party, the Communist Party of India-Marxist or CPM. It contains the party's official statements and contributions by senior leaders and publicly prominent sympathizers.

In opposing the mindset of deterrence, the Indian Left, like much of the international Left, has been seriously deficient. It has subscribed to the view that there are circumstances in which the possession of nuclear weapons has played a progressive role. Thus the socialist bomb has been seen as a progressive weapon against the capitalist or imperialist bomb. The adjective has been made more important than the noun in a perverse understanding of the history and politics of nuclearism. This Left's claim that deterrence has *sometimes* worked is simply a self-serving delusion. It is not supported by the historical record.[1] On the contrary, the Soviet Bomb (as well as that of the US) spurred China to develop its own and then to justify its possession against the US's 'capitalist–imperialist' bomb and against the Soviet 'social–imperialist' bomb. Once nuclear weapons emerge and are justified for whatever reason—as an expression of anti-imperialism or whatever—they prove extraordinarily difficult to eliminate even when the conditions that initially 'justified' them disappear. The nuclear genie should never be let out of any 'national' bottle.

This second precept is also, obviously, connected to the fourth precept that rejects nuclear nationalism. There are, (especially) in these days of neo-liberal globalization hype, *progressive* forms of political, economic, and cultural nationalism. This means nationalism remains a crucial terrain of struggle: that imperialism exists and therefore the anti-imperialist effort must continue. This should not, however, be allowed to obscure the fact that there is no progressive form of nuclear nationalism. It is precisely because this is the case that an intransigent internationalism always informs the struggle for disarmament. One of the most obvious expressions of this intrinsic internationalism in a world of nation-states is that the adoption of a *unilateralist* disarmament perspective is *always* and *everywhere* (in any and every NWS) a morally impeccable and politically appropriate principle of struggle.

However, being politically appropriate is not the same as being politically most appropriate. There are circumstances in which, from the point of political tactics or strategy, some non-unilateralist perspectives could be wiser. This is most obviously the case in South Asia where the perspective of securing a South Asian NWFZ or mutual bilateral renunciation would be a more effective mobilizing principle. This is not to dispute either the moral grandeur of Indian and Pakistani unilateralism or the political courage and usefulness of such a stand in either country; only to make a judgement of relative political efficacy in the struggle for regional disarmament.

The point that is more germane to the present context of discussion is, however, that neither the possession of nuclear bombs nor of nuclear capability can serve a progressive nationalist purpose or function. The organized Indian Left supported ambiguity (it welcomed Pokharan-I) precisely because it considered India's nuclear capability to be the expression of a progressive nationalist form of anti-imperialist resistance (it considered India's opposition to the CTBT to be the same). This Left, at least in the view of some of its spokespeople, was persuaded to assign deterrent capacities to ambiguity, and even to assign other positive virtues to threshold status, thereby violating the third precept. Thus the Left insisted that retaining nuclear capability was vital because it constituted a powerful symbol of national independence and sovereignty in a world where 'nuclear hegemony' and 'nuclear imperialism' was said to hold sway.

However, any claim that a nuclear capability alone can deter NWSs indirectly endorses the general principle of seeking security through nuclear deterrence. Only, instead of arguing that actual nuclear weapons possess this security-enhancing deterrence capacity, it gives nuclear capability this attribute. Of course, even by the limited 'logic' of deterrence thinking, nuclear ambiguity has a distinctive problem: it is a half-hearted and particularly confused form of deterrence thinking that impresses neither the opponents nor the proponents of nuclear weapons. Similarly, to believe that nuclear capability is a valued symbol of national sovereignty is an argument that is different only in degree, *not in kind*, from the argument that Indian possession of actual nuclear weapons is a valued symbol of sovereignty and independence. As long as the organized Indian Left continues to hold such views, and desires a return to ambiguity, it can hardly be expected to be an intransigent and fully committed protagonist in the struggle to completely and permanently defeat and delegitimize the nuclear mindset.

The Fallacy of 'Nuclear Imperialism'

One of the most significant mistakes made by this Left and, indeed, by many other disarmament activists, is to confuse intentions with reality. That certain NWSs seek to impose nuclear hegemony or pursue a nuclear imperialism or try to integrate nuclear weapons into imperialist strategizing is undeniable. To believe, however, that they have succeeded in doing so is another thing altogether. To argue or claim as much is to believe that nuclear weapons do have real political efficacy; so much so that at the two ends of the nuclear relationship between an NWS and another country there is a structured distribution of 'gains' and 'losses' that is integrally connected, i.e. they are two sides of the same coin. It is to claim that an NWS in some way *oppresses* or *exploits* an NNWS *through* its nuclear weapons. Such a view necessarily implies belief in either the efficacy of nuclear deterrence or in the status of nuclear weapons as a 'currency of power' providing significant and tangible benefits at the expense and *deprivation* of the non-possessor of nuclear weapons. Such beliefs precisely replicate the mindset of nuclearism, except that the advocate of nuclear weapons in the name of anti-imperialism awards a minus rather than a plus sign to such claimed properties!

However, the great and distressing irony for the NWSs is that deterrence doesn't work, that nuclear weapons are not a currency of power which delivers significant tangible benefits over non-nuclear countries. Nuclear hegemony or imperialism does not exist. Mere possession of nuclear weapons, or even flaunting them, does not a nuclear hegemony or imperialism make! It is the astrategic nature of nuclear weapons that is their most striking political characteristic. It is also, and precisely, because diehard and arch-US imperialists like the McNamaras and Butlers recognize this reality that they advocate total abolition with confidence that this would not politically weaken the US.

For nuclear disarmament activists and supporters, the real problem is not the existence or persistence of nuclear hegemony/imperialism. It is the danger represented by the presence of nuclear weapons and their 'control' by morally sclerotic and politically misguided nuclear élites. The refusal or failure to recognize this reality, and instead to make a bogey of nuclear imperialism, has led many sections of the Left, particularly in India, into dangerous dead-ends. It has made them see devils where there are none, thereby opposing what they should not have opposed, e.g. the CTBT.[2] It has made them defend the indefensible, e.g., the 'red bomb' or nuclear ambiguity. These are the lessons that the South Asian Left needs to learn if its efforts are to be harnessed in an uncompromising fashion to the struggle for regional and global disarmament.

For example, what if, as is very possible, India and Pakistan do soon enough deploy their nuclear weapons systems? That would mean that the current position of all those opposed to the May tests (which includes the organized Indian Left) of demanding no further weaponization and deployment would have become redundant. At this point there will be three fundamental disarmament perspectives to choose from. One will be unilateralist. A second will be a regional (South Asian NWFZ) or bilateral perspective demanding mutual Indian and Pakistani renunciation. There will be a third perspective strictly counterposed to the first two: Indian renunciation only as part of a global disarmament process. It will not entirely be a surprise if the Left parties in India were to choose the third in order not to 'strengthen Western/US nuclear imperialism'. This, of course, is exactly the position that the pro-bomb lobby in India would adopt. The only difference is that the Left would want to return to ambiguity and claim it as the most viable 'fourth position' when it is the most untenable position of all. It would be incapable of generating strong and growing support from nuclear disarmers since as a posture it has no moral stature whatsoever and as a practical perspective impresses no one with its feasibility or desirability.

For all practical purposes concerning the continuation of anti-nuclear and disarmament activities, it is the first three perspectives that would dominate discourse and practice. If the Indian Left aligned itself with the pro-nuclearists in making steps towards regional disarmament *conditional* on equivalent steps elsewhere, then an unbridgeable strategic chasm would open up between itself and other Indian disarmament activists, and also the overwhelming majority of anti-nuclear activists worldwide. One hopes that this will not happen, but it could well come to pass.

These are not the only lessons to be learnt. There are others, too, that have to be absorbed from our past, particularly those provided by the remarkable legacy of the mass nuclear disarmament movements of Europe, US, and Japan from the fifties to the eighties. One important lesson (already discussed) is the connection between the struggle for peace and those for achieving other progressive goals. There are two more. For an anti-nuclear movement of truly mass proportions to emerge, there are certain necessary (but not sufficient) conditions. The danger embodied in the existence of nuclear weapons, or in an arms race, or in nuclear rivalry must be a *felt* danger, not an abstract one. The people of the country in question must feel that they are under siege, as it were. The possibility of a nuclear assault or exchange must be widely believed to be real. Without the existence of a felt danger there is no emotional–political foundation for a mass movement. Thus, the end of the Cold War with its welcome ebbing of popular fear has also rendered the regeneration of anti-nuclear mass movements in Europe and the US much more unlikely in the near future.

No mass movement is possible without an *agitational focus* against one's own government and state apparatus. A mass movement cannot be sustained on the basis of general or vague appeals to global disarmament. It must have certain specific demands directed against its own government or against a number of governments (including one's own) that are wedded to some common project that the movement opposes. Thus the movements have focused (besides other demands) on the central demand for unilateral disarmament in the UK, for non-nuclearization in Japan (which because of the unique Japanese experience of Hiroshima and Nagasaki was not an abstract demand), for a nuclear freeze in the United States, for dismantling Euromissiles, etc. Since we live in a world of nation-states, and it is this unit that constitutes the arena where citizenship rights and electoral choice prevail, it is on this terrain that some sense of popular empowerment and peoples' sovereignty is felt and exercised. It is, therefore, here that the organized struggle for change in nuclear policies must most strongly be situated. This is the true dialectic of the national–international on the nuclear issue, not the idea of a nuclear nationalism versus nuclear imperialism! A 'non-proliferation regime' is not equivalent to a 'nuclear imperialist' or 'nuclear hegemonic' order, although loose and imprecise thinking, even by disarmament activists, often treats them in just this way.

Public Policy and Popular Consciousness

No independent mass movement for peace is possible under strongly authoritarian political systems. A minimal requirement is that some reasonable space and freedom be allowed in civil society for mass protests, at least for those kinds that for the most part threaten specific policies but not necessarily regime rule as a whole. By such a reckoning, anti-nuclear mass movements were not possible in the USSR or in China past and present. It would, however, be possible in Pakistan today, and of course in democracies from the US to India. Finally, in the generation and sustenance of a mass peace movement, the widest and strongest unifying factor is always the moral dimension. Political sophistication in arguing the anti-nuclear case and countering nuclear theologies is necessary for the leadership of such movements. It is, however, moral outrage that keeps a mass movement together despite inevitable differences over strategies and tactics of building or keeping its momentum going. A moral universalism, then, always lies at the heart of any anti-nuclear movement and is its single most potent attribute.

How do we measure the success or failure of the great anti-nuclear mass movements of the past decades? On the one hand, in terms of sheer numbers, the mobilizations associated with this cause have dwarfed those of any other cause, certainly in the First World. Literally millions were persuaded to march in the streets and protest. On a global scale, only the Iranian Revolution of 1977–9 that overthrew the Shah, compares with, or exceeds in scale and frequency, the popular mobilizations of the First World anti-nuclear movements. On the other hand, in terms of actual demands fulfilled, the paucity of their achievement is most striking. Does this mean the great peace movements must be deemed a comprehensive failure? Only if the narrowest of criteria for evaluating success are used. The dialectic between changes in popular consciousness and changes in public policy is complex and subtle. Mediations between the two are never straightforward. The filtration process is osmotic and capillary rather than direct and sharply funnelled. Unanticipated side consequences and delayed or lag effects on official policy are often much more important, thereby rendering misleading any judgement of success or failure based on direct comparison of the explicitly stated demands of the peace movement with their degree, or lack, of fulfilment.

The great peace movements helped change the whole discourse surrounding nuclear weapons, breaking the monopoly on public common sense that pro-nuclearists sought to establish. The movements educated a whole generation of activists, some of whom are today carrying on work that is central to the cause. Many are to be found working within what is now an international network of anti-nuclear NGOs. As such, they are among the principal actors today in the disarmament effort. The movements forced senior officials in state apparatuses to be publicly accountable and question more deeply than ever before their own rationalizations for retaining such weapons. Thus, when the Cold War ended and earlier nuclear rationales disappeared, there was strong support among decision-makers themselves for a winding down of the nuclear arms race. Among many, there was a stronger commitment to total disarmament. As the struggle for global disarmament moves into the twenty-first century, there has to be unstinting praise and admiration for the pioneering efforts of those great anti-nuclear mass movements. It is on their shoulders that we stand today surveying a socio-political terrain very different from their own.

Unless there is some quite dramatic and unexpected shift in current trends in Europe, or in the US–Russia–China triangle, we are not going to witness the emergence of mass peace movements in the First World for some time to come. However, the necessary (if not sufficient) conditions for the possible emergence of mass-scale opposition to nuclear weapons could surface in South Asia, if India and Pakistan over the next few years go ahead to erect, improve, and openly deploy weapons systems against each other. It is then, when the likelihood of nuclear conflict breaking out becomes a widely felt danger, that it may become possible for activist groups in the two countries, operating till then at the level of small-scale propaganda, to make the transition to large-scale agitation.

In the wake of the Indian and Pakistani tests, what has so far emerged is a collection of small, urban-based groups that have engaged themselves in anti-nuclear activity from symbolic forms of public protest to organizing demonstrations, to seeking to institutionalize the production and dissemination of anti-nuclear perspectives through written materials, audio-visual aids, meetings, etc. The peace and nuclear disarmament movement in India and Pakistan is not yet strong enough to influence or alter nuclear policy directions. If the molecular forms of resistance to nuclearism in Indian and Pakistani civil society grow into wider, stronger, and connected pockets of opposition, then they can coalesce to form a national network of resistance and struggle. They could then become the foundations on which mass agitation in the future can be built. (See Box 6.) The regional, South Asian perspective for disarmament, if both India and Pakistan deploy nuclear weapons, is an issue that will be discussed later.

BOX 6

No Peace in the 'Land of the Buddha'?
Disarmament Movements in South Asia

The stereotypical impression of the 'popular'or 'mass' reaction to the nuclear blasts in India and Pakistan which is embedded in the minds of large numbers of people around the world is the initial 'CNN image': groups of male youth dancing with joy in Delhi's streets, or waving saffron flags to congratulate the Hindu-nationalist Bharatiya Janata Party. Pakistan was presented as the exact, symmetrical, obverse. There too, the dominant impression is that of jubilation over 'standing up to' and 'getting even with' India.

In reality, such currents of strongly pro-Bomb opinion, while telegenic, only represented a small, urban, vocal minority in India. Opinion even within the urban majority was sharply divided. Many tentatively supported the tests, without enthusiastically welcoming them, because they saw them as acts of defiance against the nuclear hegemony of the P–5, not because they believed that nuclear weapons are necessary for India's security or have enhanced her prestige.

The enthusiastic support of the minority for the tests soon ran out: the Pakistani tests that followed, India's diplomatic isolation, sanctions, and the growing realization that nuclearization has done little for India's security while diverting scarce resources away from real priorities, all wrought a major shift in public opinion. Within two months of the tests, a clear majority of people polled spoke against the Bomb. As many as 72.8 per cent said India must not make, deploy, or use nuclear weapons.[1]

In Pakistan, there was a stronger link in the popular mind between a possible threat from an 'inimical' and now-nuclearized India, and Pakistan's own tests. There too, however, opinion was divided. The Bomb did not shore up Nawaz Sharif's sinking credibility or create a consensus.

However, it must be admitted that popular opposition to the tests was relatively weak to start with. The anti-nuclear current was a minority. It has since expanded manifold. One of the most significant effects of the tests was to *ignite* a peace and nuclear disarmament movement in India and Pakistan on a significant scale.

Prior to May 1998, the peace and nuclear disarmament movement in India and Pakistan was relatively weak and scattered. It did not have a major political impact in shaping policies or party agendas although it had strong and organic roots in the environmental, human rights, civil liberties, and women's movements and in a range of non-governmental organizations (NGOs).

One reason for this was the pursuit of nuclear ambiguity in both countries for a decade or more. This bred complacency about the viability of 'non-weaponized' or 'recessed' deterrence. Since nuclear weapons did not actually exist, and their existence was not admitted, they did not represent a *felt danger*.

Two deeper reasons explain the relative weakness of the peace movement in the subcontinent. The first is the strength of Third World anti-colonial or post-colonial nationalism in both India and Pakistan. At least in the public discourse of the two states, which gained independence in 1947, such nationalism made it difficult for political leaders, intellectuals, and ordinary citizens to be advocating the narrowing or closing of the nuclear weapons option, which was wrongly seen as an instrument of national sovereignty and a repository of pride.

Such is the strength of this nationalism, particularly in the more belligerent and aggressive form it has taken in the past decade or so, that even the parties of the Left have succumbed to it, often by pleading that for 'tactical' reasons it would be dangerous to allow the Right to monopolize the nationalist space. In a situation where globalization and pursuit of neo-liberal policies are seen to be eroding the space for indigenous paths to development, the defence of national sovereignty acquires some legitimacy.

The second factor at work in the pre-May 1998 period was public disillusionment with the prospect for rapid movement towards global nuclear disarmament. Although it would be ludicrous, and utterly dishonest, to make this an excuse for crossing the nuclear threshold as New Delhi did, large numbers of people in India and Pakistan saw few signs of willingness on the part of the nuclear weapons states—themselves seen as pushy powers—to do anything to reduce the nuclear danger, and delegitimize and marginalize their dependence on nuclear weapons, leave alone abolish them. Had the NWSs 'led by example', the case for India and Pakistan too moving in the direction of closing the nuclear option would have become persuasive, if not pressing.

In India, there has been an additional factor at work. That is the steady erosion and collapse of one significant current of pacifism in the region—the Gandhian movement that espoused non-violence, universal brotherhood and peace. The bulk of Mahatma Gandhi's spiritual disciples who did not join the Congress party regrouped themselves into the 'Sarvodaya' movement. 'Sarvodaya' (literally, rise, upliftment and progress of all) too preached non-violence, but did not concern itself specifically with nuclear issues, or with other contemporary questions of war, peace, and social strife. It was content to advocate non-violence and peace in the abstract, as spiritual values, *not political goals* seen as worthy by citizens who relate them to their own priorities.[2]

The task of building public opinion in favour of peace and nuclear disarmament has now been taken up by relatively young people, drawn from varied backgrounds, who see the struggle for nuclear disarmament as being related to the defence of decency, humanity, and democracy, and espousal of the cause of peaceful resolution of conflicts. The current of opinion represented by such people sees nuclearism as a perversion bound up with aggressive militarism and religion-based nationalism in South Asia. It is in the process of constructing a campaign for nuclear disarmament, and peace and conciliation with India's neighbours. Especially noteworthy here is the support which nuclear disarmament groups have received in both countries from a number of initiatives in favour of friendly and improved relations between India and Pakistan, with a special emphasis on people-to-people contacts and exchanges. Many such initiatives were set up and have grown since the mid-1990s in both countries.

Three aspects of the growing nuclear disarmament and peace movements in India and Pakistan, especially India, are noteworthy. First, they have strong links with NGOs and 'people's movements' structures active in a number of areas. Thus, their 'natural' or 'organic' constituencies include activists fighting for the right to livelihood, for rehabilitation (of project-displaced people), for equal access to environmental resources, and defence of the natural environment. Equally important are those fighting for empowerment of the underprivileged, for secularism, against religious fanaticism and intolerance, and campaigners against child labour.

Second, there is strong and spontaneous participation of women in the peace movement. This link has been established in India and Pakistan—and indeed in the rest of South Asia—at an early stage of evolution of the struggle for nuclear disarmament. Feminists in India and Pakistan have a strong awareness of the connections between nuclearism and patriarchy, and between militarism and suppression of women's rights, (see Box 2). Feminists were among the first group of movement-rooted activists to condemn the nuclear tests. They held an impressive march in Pune in western India in late May 1998 to coincide with the Indian Women's Studies Conference, which had participants from the South Asian region as a whole.

Third, the subcontinent's peace and disarmament movement has a remarkably holistic and comprehensive perspective. Its activists relate their objectives and methods to the larger struggle for a humane, egalitarian, gender-just, ecologically sound, non-hierarchical, free, and open society. They are broad-minded and internationalist in outlook, and acutely aware that the arena of activism must at once be national, Asian and international. The nuclear disarmament agenda by its very nature, has to be addressed at the national level, regionally, and above all, globally.

Several groups, networks and organizations dedicated to nuclear disarmament have sprung up in Indian and Pakistani cities, although their activity at the village level is feeble. They made their presence felt through the impressive number of marches, meetings, and cultural events that they organized on 6 August, Hiroshima Day, in 1998. This was a large and energetic mobilization of people on a non-party basis, comparable in strength, for instance, to the pro-secular and anti-sectarian initiatives witnessed on the Ayodhya mosque demolition issue or on the harassment of Christians.

A sign of the growing strength and moral force of the Indian and Pakistani nuclear disarmament movements is the support they have won from several highly regarded former generals, admirals, and air marshals, from senior diplomats and civil servants, as well as from eminent intellectuals and artists. Despite its late start, and its weaknesses, the peace movement has become an inalienable component of grass-roots civil society organizations in India and Pakistan. Its fate is inextricable from the future of the broader agenda of democratization and popular empowerment.

Notes

1. Press Trust of India, the country's principal news agency, reported, quoting an opinion poll, '72.8% opposes use of N-weapons, says survey', *Economic Times*, New Delhi, 24 June 1998.

   Most opinion polls, especially the early ones, were limited to the urban areas, and thus tended to exaggerate the popular support for the tests. The more systematic broad-sample polls done later suggest that large numbers of rural Indians were not even aware of the tests. According to an *India Today*–MARG poll, published in that magazine on 25 December 1998, 47 per cent of people had not even heard of the May tests.
2. Soon after the initial burst of enthusiasm, and the setting up of a number of spartan ashrams in rural areas in the early 1950s, the 'Sarvodaya' movement turned conservative. It became increasingly oblivious of social reality, which is dominated by intense inequalities in wealth, income, access to land, and entitlements to public goods in rural India, where it primarily worked. Instead of taking the side of the landless, the poor, and women in their struggle for justice, it advocated that the landed rich generously donate a part of their land to the landless: 'Bhoodan'. 'Bhoodan' will go down as one of the greatest hypocrisies and frauds in twentieth-century India. It did not, predictably, result in land reform or redistribution. Minuscule quantities of arid and degraded land were all that was donated by the rich.

   Failure to engage with social reality was to marginalize 'Sarvodaya'. Its worst degeneration however came in the 1970s, when its most prominent leader, Vinoba Bhave, became an apologist for Indira Gandhi's Emergency regime, rationalizing it as the Era of Discipline. Since then, most old Sarvodayis have individually strayed into various irrelevant or trivial pursuits, some even joining forces with the BJP and its cohorts in attacking Christians in Gujarat.

   There are exceptions, such as Narayan Desai, Thakurdas Bang, and Nirmala Deshpande, but as a group, the Gandhians have totally failed to build public opinion in favour of peace and nuclear disarmament.

What is to be Done?

Who is to control the agenda of disarmament and shift it from its current focus on non-proliferation? How is this to be done? Where are the main sites of this struggle? While there is always a welcome place for the symbolic politics of public protest and opposition, some of the principal sites of sustained disarmament activities have shifted in the post-Cold War period from outdoors to indoors; from the streets to institutionalized diplomatic settings of inter-governmental negotiations and discussions. The principal forms of disarmament activities have shifted from pressurizing through mass actions to pressurizing through informed lobbying; from fervent public denunciations to calculated exposures of the fallacies and weaknesses in the briefs of the NWSs, and through the provision of practical and carefully worked out projects for accelerating disarmament.

There are three key actors in today's world of disarmament activities. There are the mass movement structures. Then there are the anti-nuclear NGOs possessing various kinds of expertise. This can be in an understanding of the intricacies of disarmament negotiations, in the technical skills they bring to the discussion of possible restraint and reduction measures, in the deftness with which they can communicate with a wider public both through and besides the public media networks. Finally, there are certain governments that have become thoroughly fed up with the procrastinations and deceits of the NWSs and their non-nuclear allies, and have taken it upon themselves to play a more aggressive activist role in global nuclear diplomacy.

The first are to be found in certain countries, most notably the UK, US, Germany and Japan. They have some kind of functioning national network or structure of propaganda, membership lists in the thousands, capacities to periodically or occasionally play a major role in organizing mass actions. In some cases, they have living links with major national political parties or mass organizations such as trade unions. Perhaps the more important examples of this are the Campaign for Nuclear Disarmament (CND) and its links with the Labour Party in UK, and the current Greens-SPD coalition government in Germany. Under the umbrella of the Greens, there exist strong anti-nuclear and environmental groups.

The second set of actors are scattered throughout the First World, but again mainly in the US, Western Europe, and Japan. Not all are single-mindedly focused on the nuclear issue. And many pursue multiple agendas. Some possess expertise of such high quality that they are valued sources of informational and analytical inputs for governmental delegations of many NNWSs in the various fora for ongoing disarmament-related negotiations in Geneva and New York.

The third set of agents are a select group of governments strongly committed to disarmament. For the first time, an informal concert of countries has emerged that has broken with the fixed mould set by the Cold War of First, Second and Third World blocs. It was the formation of the eight-member New Agenda Coalition that really signalled this important development. Seven of those countries (Slovenia dropped out of the eight), plus Canada and Australia, and a few others like Costa Rica and Norway are the governments now most determined to take the lead in promoting disarmament. Those seven are South Africa, New Zealand, Egypt, Brazil, Mexico, Sweden, and Ireland.

Lobbying for disarmament is not just a question of those countries working in greater cooperation with one another, it is also a matter of closer and better coordination between mass movement structures, activist NGOs, individual disarmament 'experts', and these governments. This is the organizational challenge that has to be addressed and overcome. Even as a possibility yet to be concretized, this kind of loose association or informal partnership is something new in the history of disarmament efforts, but if it comes to fruition, the arrangement possesses a real potential for achieving what is needed—accelerating the global momentum towards disarmament.

Any serious effort at disarmament must *simultaneously* follow two tracks. It must pursue comprehensive or 'absolute' measures of total disarmament as well as transitional and incrementalist measures of restraint and reduction. Going along the second track but ignoring the first is to fall into the trap happily laid by the NWSs. It risks making each incremental measure a goal in itself and failing to see it as part of a larger process whose direction must be controlled and momentum accelerated. It is to risk following the tempo and pace laid down by the NWSs which will not only enormously lengthen the time-scale over which total disarmament can be achieved but risks forever postponing that goal to an ever more distant and difficult-to-see horizon. The longer we postpone total disarmament, the more we risk nuclear disaster. It is also to risk entrapment in a non-proliferation order rather than to fight to break that order and shift matters towards disarmament.

However, following the first track without pursuing the second is hopelessly impractical. The momentum towards global disarmament cannot be sustained without partial successes. Convincing the governments and peoples of the NWSs to accept *total* disarmament is itself a process that will require partial successes. It is these advances that help generate the realization that a world completely free of nuclear weapons is not just desirable but feasible: this is not just a workable global order but a *reachable* one.

In this quest for total global disarmament, the first step must be the institutionalization of some body that is multilateral in character and is collectively acknowledged and authorized to carry out negotiations leading to total disarmament. Bilaterally negotiated arms reductions between Russia and the US or restraint and reduction measures agreed upon between the NWSs are fine. They are, however, no substitute for the institutionalization of such a multilateral body. Disarmament is too important an issue to be left to the NWSs alone. It is every country's right and need to participate in the process and to make their voices heard on an issue that affects all countries and peoples. Moreover, the NWSs cannot be trusted to carry out total disarmament by themselves. It is silly even to imagine that.

Three Routes

At present there would seem to be three possible routes to bring into existence or functioning a multilateral body suitably empowered to carry out such negotiations. None of these approaches excludes the others. They can all be pursued concurrently and separately. However, different disarmament activists and groups have different priorities and hopes in this regard. We will spell out the reasons for our own choice of priorities but this is not meant to be read as some kind of injunction to other activists to forgo their own efforts and priorities. The front of disarmament activities is a very broad one. Different people perceive different points of potential and promise and work where they will to bring about a breakthrough. If there was one very obvious point of weakness where a breakthrough is most self-evidently likely, then a call for collective concentration could be justified. There is however no such obvious point where the limited resources of activist groups and individuals or governments *must* be concentrated. Disarmament activists are still in the process of creating that most obvious weak point and thus there is no escape at present from having a general and ecumenical approach. Nonetheless, we do hope that others may be persuaded to give our choice of priorities more serious consideration. It is the first two approaches that we consider most likely to deliver positive results.

The first approach is to seek to establish a Nuclear Weapons (Abolition) Convention (NWC) that deals with the process and time scale of disarmament. Already an international consortium of lawyers, scientists, and disarmament experts led by the Lawyer's Committee on Nuclear Policy (LCNP) has drafted a Model Nuclear Weapons convention (MNWC) which was circulated by the UN in its six official languages in November 1997.[3] This is not meant to be a final draft, but it stimulated discussions and sought further refinement and clarifications. These can be embodied in future drafts. This model draft represents an invaluable service. It is not necessary to wait for a body to be institutionalized before discussions with a substantive thrust, i.e. on the actual content of a global disarmament treaty, take place.

Already there has been intense discussion on the political, technical, and legal requirements for verifiable and coordinated large-scale nuclear disarmament. The ICJ Advisory Opinion has prompted a UN Resolution (52/38) calling for commencement of such negotiations. Many Western states (including some allies of the US), China, and the UK have responded with cautious and qualified welcome to this call for multilateral negotiations—something that France, the US, and Russia continue to oppose. Perhaps the most important point to emerge from the discussions so far is that the comprehensive approach embodied in the MNWC should be integrated with the incremental approach possibly through a treaty that takes the form of a 'framework agreement' incorporating 'general principles' that all can agree upon, a phased pattern of progress and not excluding unilateral and bilateral initiatives by the NWSs, but providing for multilateral processes of review and accountability.

The main stumbling block, however, remains. When will an NWC come about and start getting implemented? Does one wait till all the NWSs agree to participate in it, which does not seem at all possible in the foreseeable future? Does one wait till some or at least one of the NWSs join in, which may still mean waiting for an unacceptably long period, apart from perhaps retaining the illusion that the nuclear club will break ranks on so vital an issue? Do the NNWSs go ahead on their own to set up such an NWC as a way of putting public pressure on the NWSs to join in? The last is probably the most promising route. It does not require all or most NNWSs to agree to set up and participate in a NWC. Before such a Convention can however be organized and expected to sustain itself, it will require acceptance from, and involvement by, a *critical mass* of NNWSs, including the most pro-active of them on the disarmament issue.

Negotiations between governments that do not include the NWSs have their obvious limitations. However, discussions aimed at refining working drafts, and reaching agreements among a growing circle of NNWSs in a formalized set-up like the NWC, would amount to institutionalizing the existence of such a multilateral body and legitimizing its role as the desirable locus of future negotiations involving the NWSs. All this would also exercise very powerful public pressure on recalcitrant NWSs whose international isolation would be more sharply highlighted than ever before. The principal task of the three set of agents currently pursuing global disarmament would be to bring about this critical mass of NNWSs willing and able to set up a functioning NWC.

The second approach that needs to be concurrently explored is the possibility of setting up an Ad Hoc Committee on global disarmament in the CD. To begin with it would almost certainly have to settle for a discussion or 'deliberative' mandate with no power to actually negotiate. Even this is difficult, but far from impossible to bring about. The US remains opposed so far to the formation of such a body and the Russians will follow the US lead in this matter. Washington has however acknowledged that such a Committee with a discussion mandate cannot be accused of usurping the functions it believes should only reside with the NWSs. It is also possible to work on the differences between the NWSs in this regard. China is open to the idea of such an Ad Hoc Committee. The new Labour government in the UK has been more positive about this initiative than its Tory predecessor. France has also shown sympathy for the idea.

Much will depend on the fate of the currently stalled negotiations on fissile materials cut-off treaty (FMCT) in the CD proceed. The most proactive NNWSs are determined that the FMCT be connected to the issue of stockpiles so that it is a genuine restraint measure on the five NWSs which have already stopped fissile materials production because they have accumulated enough stockpiles to meet conceivable future needs. These NNWSs are also determined that the FMCT be integrated into the disarmament process. One way of doing this is to barter their support for it in return for just such an Ad Hoc Committee being set up. It is the actual process of negotiations that will determine the final outcome, but the current indications are that the NWSs will have real difficulty in not conceding some kind of linkage between the FMCT and wider disarmament concerns. The NNWSs must hold together a very large section of their own ranks as well as win over the allies of the NWSs and even some NWSs. If South Africa and Egypt are leading the charge for the formation of such a committee, five NATO members—Belgium, Germany, Italy, Netherlands, and Norway—have now called for the formation of an 'Ad Hoc Working Group' to 'study ways and means of establishing an exchange of information and views within the Conference on endeavours towards nuclear disarmament.'[4]

What approach India and Pakistan will take is as yet uncertain. Traditionally, Pakistan has wanted both the issue of stockpiles to feature in the FMCT negotiations (unlike India and the five recognized NWSs) and for it to be linked to the formation of an Ad Hoc Committee. However, Pakistan, along with India, now wants to establish its 'reliability' and 'bona fides' as an NWS by showing its 'sensitivity to the concerns of the other NWSs, especially the US. At the same time, if either government believes it is in its interest to stall the pace of negotiations so as to build up its stockpiles to some requisite level before a final production cut-off, then either or both might see virtue in joining more strongly with the demand of some NNWSs for such a Committee or Working Group. In any case, by doing so they would be posing as NWSs with a relatively greater concern and respect for disarmament and concerned with winning diplomatic points amongst the NNWSs.

The third approach attempts to use the provisions of the NPT to generate pressure to initiate a disarmament process. The principal idea here is to take advantage of the fact that only one-third of the membership of the NPT have to agree for an amendment conference to be called. There, substantive amendments to put much stronger teeth into, say, Article VI, can be put forward. Of course, they will not be passed because each of the member NWSs has veto power on all substantive amendments. However, the very procedure of convening an amendment conference, putting forward such proposals, and having them rejected by the NWSs, would have a valuable effect in putting political pressure on the latter. Moreover, such amendment conferences can be repeatedly called to continue the pattern of public embarrassment and exposure of the NWSs.

This approach is obviously an effort to salvage something of the original spirit and purpose of the NPT and to make it move away from being simply the pillar of the non-proliferation regime that it has long since become. Though the attraction of the proposal is that it should be relatively easy to get a one-third consensus to call such amendment conferences, this has not happened so far. This provides a message of its own. Moreover, the idea that in spite of failures to fulfil the substantive purpose of calling such conferences, member NNWSs would still remain enthused to regularly and repeatedly call such conferences merely to constantly repeat the exposure process, is unconvincing. In part, the reason for putting forward such a proposal is also to counter another attitude to the NPT which is not only wholly dismissive of the NPT but seeks to fully undermine it.

Some disarmament activists and groups, in utter frustration with the NPT regime, have called for a threat of a mass walk-out by the NNWSs from the NPT if the NWSs do not agree to begin a process of genuine disarmament negotiations.[5] This is one step further than the authors would go, although we share its protagonists' anger and disillusionment with the NPT. However, threatening the total dismantlement of the NPT, and then in all probability having to carry out this threat, makes very little sense. The threat is a huge gamble. It is a dramatic one-off gesture that will almost certainly fail. More important, disbanding the NPT altogether eliminates a forum where some kind of diplomatic–political pressure, no matter how feeble, can repeatedly be exercised against the NWSs because of their commitment (their only such legal commitment anywhere) to obey Article VI. While sharing the frustration of those who rail against the NPT and see it as the central pillar of non-proliferation, not disarmament, we would not go so far as calling for its total dismantlement, nor for expending efforts to work through it, but for working around and besides it. This is a strategy of ignoring the NPT rather than seeking either to break it, or energize it, in our search for avenues of movement towards global disarmament.

Before turning to an exploration of those transitional and incremental measures that must also be pursued, it would be pertinent to survey what prospects there are that any of the existing NWSs may give up their nuclear weapons even though the rest of the club does not. One of the tragedies of the nuclear age is that once a country goes nuclear, getting it to fully renounce its weapons is very difficult. The experiences of Belarus, Kazakhstan, and the Ukraine, though welcome, were unusual and are to be largely explained by the exceptional circumstances in which they simultaneously came into existence as modern, independent nation-states and as NWSs. For the UK and France, there is today even by the benighted standards of conventional nuclear security thinking, no security rationale for their remaining NWSs in preference to giving up their nuclear arsenals. France however continues to pursue its delusions of national grandeur and European eminence even though it is non-nuclear Germany that is the hub of new Europe. The idea of an independent (from NATO) European nuclear deterrent, for which the French *force de frappe* might have been the foundation, has fewer takers than ever before. If either France or the UK were to unilaterally disarm, this would give a tremendous fillip to the cause of global disarmament. In one stroke, either or both of these countries would raise their global stature immensely, indeed become the undisputed moral and political leaders in the crusade for global disarmament. The prospects for this coming about are however virtually nonexistent.

The real disappointment has been the UK because expectations from it have been higher. Unlike France, the UK experienced mass anti-nuclear movements of enormous scale and considerable duration. The UK also had a strong connection between these movements and one of its two principal political parties. Indeed, the Labour party in opposition did once officially adopt as party policy the posture of unilateral disarmament. The great failure to cash in on this history can be ascribed not so much to the peace movement or to any of its components as to weaknesses and limitations of the Labour party's organizational structure and its ideology of Labourism. Internally, it has always suffered from an undemocratic set-up in which the conservative sections of the parliamentary wing have had a disproportionately larger influence than either ordinary members or grassroots activists or the trade unions.

The result has been that, time and again, genuinely popular aspirations and pressures from below that emerged because of the historical character of the Labour party as also something of a 'broad church movement', have repeatedly been throttled from above. The British experience is a classic example of how extra-nuclear factors can have decisive consequences on the anti-nuclear struggle itself. The 'New Labour' of current leader and Prime Minister, Tony Blair, is a decisive departure even from Old Labour. Blairism is the most conservative form of social democracy found anywhere in Western Europe and is the closest cross-Atlantic cousin to President Clinton's 'New Age Republocrats'. This makes even more unlikely the prospect of Britain being the country most likely to break the disarmament logjam through adoption of a unilateralist posture. Blair's party is different from the Tories on the nuclear question, but all this amounts to is that a Labour government is willing to be more transparent in declaring what it has by way of nuclear preparations, and more flexible than the Tories and the US in responding to the concerns of the NNWSs. There are however no signs that it will break fundamentally from US tutelage on nuclear and foreign policy.

Denuclearization of South Asia

What about the prospects for denuclearization of India and Pakistan? As the weakest and newest entrants to the nuclear club, what chances are there that they might be prepared to give up their nuclear status and preparations? Dim as the prospects must seem for the near future, there are possibilities here which do not exist in the other five NWSs, even if in the next few years both countries induct and deploy rudimentary weapons systems against each other. The reason for this is because of all the NWSs, Pakistan was the most reluctant to acquire this status, the most worried about the sacrifices involved in maintaining it, and the NWS still most willing to give it up if just one other NWS—India—were to do the same. A unilateralist renunciation by Pakistan is very difficult to envisage. However, though the struggle for a South Asian NWFZ has become more difficult than it was before May 1998, this perspective continues to retain a relevance and feasibility that makes its prospects of achievement considerably greater than the full and rapid denuclearization of any other NWS or set of NWSs.

This is the case for three reasons. First, though that section in the pro-nuclear lobby of Pakistan, which sees possession of nuclear weapons as a hedge for its inferiority in conventional military strength vis-à-vis India, has become stronger, the prospect of non-nuclear parity between the two countries, if it again appears feasible, will always be strongly attractive to the larger part of the Pakistani élite. Indeed, it may well prove to be the case that a popular anti-nuclear movement in Pakistan will be the initiating factor in generating a similar popular response in India. The greater the number of ordinary Pakistanis who call for an end to the regional nuclear madness, the more likely are ordinary Indians to respond in kind.

Second, for all India's determination to build a credible second-strike capacity against China, not only can this take much longer than currently anticipated, but it may not even properly materialize. For all its ambitions, India's nuclear capabilities may remain effectively confined to the South Asian region. If such a situation were to coincide with growing public unease, then the call for regional disarmament in the shape of a South Asian NWFZ will achieve a stronger and growing resonance. Such an unease can develop both because of the dangers of the regional face-off with Pakistan and because of the sacrifices entailed in preserving the nuclear arsenal given the demands on resources that other problems and priorities—fighting poverty and illiteracy, or maintaining internal stability, etc.—will make.

The third is not so much a reason as a condition of possibility. Post-1998 is not the same as post-1945. There is more international anger and greater public delegitimization of such weapons and of the countries that have them. If there are further incremental advances in the process of nuclear restraint and reductions, then both India and Pakistan will come under severer pressure for being the only two NWSs which, as newer entrants, are seeking to increase the size and sophistication of their arsenals when on the whole the others are slowing down and moving in the opposite direction. Thus, the prospects for denuclearization of South Asia, say, in the form of a South Asian NWFZ, are clearly tied to the prospects for the successful achievement of other valued restraint and reduction measures. It is to these that we now turn.

NWFZs have both symbolic–political importance and practical value. As a symbolic measure, they announce in a dramatic fashion the renunciation of nuclear weapons in a certain region. When municipalities and towns announce themselves to be nuclear-free zones, often in NWSs or in allied countries, they symbolize resistance by the people and authorities in that locality to official national policy. NWFZs of this kind become mechanisms for raising consciousness and can sometimes require direct action to prevent the passage or movement of materials related to weapons systems. When an NWFZ covers a group of countries or a continent it symbolizes renunciation by the governments in question.[6] When at least some of the countries are nuclear capable or could become so, the renunciation is even more significant.

As a disarmament measure, membership of an NWFZ is a more comprehensive and less contradictory a commitment than membership of the NPT. The latter allows NNWSs to have stationed on their territory the weapons of allied countries, e.g. US-controlled NATO missiles on German soil. The NPT allows this 'crypto-nuclear status' while NWFZs do not allow or sanction it. Furthermore, there is no carrot-stick contradiction of the kind prevalent under the NPT regime in the creation and sustenance of NWFZs. The NPT 'rewards' NNWS members for their renunciation by facilitating their acquisition of the wherewithal to develop nuclear weapons capability clandestinely, if they so wish.

The Importance of NWFZs

That is not to say that NWFZs have not had their problems. An NWFZ invokes three principles: non-possession of nuclear weapons by member states, non-stationing, and non-use or threat of use by outside NWSs. The thorny issue in regard to the principle of non-stationing is the matter of naval or airborne transit, especially the former. Coastal states enjoy full jurisdiction only over internal waters, i.e. up to 12 nautical miles, but have no such jurisdiction over exclusive economic zones or in the high seas. Any flag state enjoys right of 'innocent' transit in zonal waters. The real problem, however, is 'hostile' transit or passage that is perceived not to be innocent despite protestations to the contrary. This problem has not been satisfactorily resolved by any NWFZ and it has been left to individual member and coastal states to decide as they wish on the matter of naval or airborne transit by NWSs of their nuclear carrying platforms. The third principle enjoins upon the NWSs not to target, use, or threaten to use their weapons against member countries of the zone in question. This matter has usually been handled through the addition of separate protocols to the NWFZ Treaty in question.

There have been four NWFZs, three other treaties of equivalent nature, and one near-NWFZ. In 1959, the Antarctica Treaty was signed and subsequently came into force. Apart from prohibiting placement of nuclear weapons, it bans nuclear explosions and disposal of radioactive waste on the Antarctic subject to future agreements. Its signatories include all the five NWSs. China and India acceded in 1983. In 1967, the Outer Space Treaty was signed and later came into force. It has been signed by all the five acknowledged NWSs, India, and 58 others. It prohibits the placement of nuclear weapons or other weapons of mass destruction in space or earth orbit.

In 1967, the Treaty of Tlatelolco became the first treaty to denuclearize an inhabited region of the globe: virtually the entire continent of Latin America. Two former threshold powers, Brazil and Argentina, eventually gave up threshold status and signed and ratified the Treaty. Cuba joined in 1995, and now the Treaty covers every country in Latin America. The Treaty prohibits possession, testing and stationing of nuclear weapons and all the five NWSs have signed the protocols demanding non-use and non-threat of use against member countries. The Treaty does permit 'peaceful nuclear explosions'. This first NWFZ treaty was a landmark that set the standards for subsequent NWFZ treaties which learnt from and in some ways improved upon it.

In 1971, the Seabed Treaty was signed and ratified by the US, the UK, and the USSR and entered into force the following year. China acceded in 1991 but France so far has not. Sixty-six states have so far ratified it. The Treaty forbids the placement of nuclear weapons and WMDs on seabed and ocean floors beyond the 12 nautical mile limit.

In 1985, the Treaty of Rarotonga covering the South Pacific was signed and entered into force the following year. Protocols I, II, and III have been signed by the US, the UK, and France. Russia and China have so far acceded to Protocols I, II and III. The Treaty prohibits all possession, manufacture, stationing of nuclear weapons, all tests including PNEs, and disallows dumping of nuclear waste.

The Bangkok Treaty making Southeast Asia nuclear free was signed in 1995 and came into force in 1997. Apart from the usual prohibitions, the Treaty denies transit in seas adjacent to territorial waters, i.e. all zonal waters. The five NWSs have not yet given their support because they (particularly the US and China) contest its claim of not violating the right of transit in exclusive economic zones or on high seas. The Bangkok Treaty prohibits everything that the Treaty of Rarotonga does.

The 1996 Treaty of Pelindaba makes Africa nuclear weapons free. It has 49 regional signatories. France has approved all three protocols, the other four NWSs, the first two protocols. The Treaty has not yet been fully ratified nor come into force. Apart from the usual prohibitions, it outlaws research into nuclear weapons production and testing. The near-NWFZ is the 1992 declaration by both Koreas to make their peninsula nuclear weapons free. However, the monitoring mechanisms have not been implemented and the US maintains its suspicions about secret North Korean bomb preparations.

The Southern hemisphere is, apart from transit outside territorial waters (and with permission, within such waters), nuclear free. However, not a single one of these NWFZs has required any major sacrifice from the NWSs. France which tested in Africa and the South Pacific, supported the relevant treaties after it eventually decided to renounce explosive testing. The Treaty of Pelindaba avoids the question of Diego Garcia (jurisdiction over which is disputed between the UK and Mauritius) and so the island remains on lease to the US which uses it as a nuclear storage base. Nonetheless, the emergence of these NWFZs is an important gain because of the precedents they have set, for the impetus given to the creation of further NWFZs, and for the concrete advances they express in the effort to make the world totally nuclear free.

The challenge is also to have NWFZs that will entail the practical dismantling of nuclear weapons actually placed or of nuclear weapons capability or of some degree of jurisdictional control by any of the NWSs. So while NWFZs covering the Nordic region or one in Central Asia (very much on the anvil), or in the Balkans (there are suspicions about missiles in Turkey) are certainly desirable and to be welcomed, a real breakthrough would be provided if an NWFZ could be created in any of the following areas: in South Asia (already discussed), Central Europe, North-East Asia, the Middle East.

A Central European NWFZ would substantially counter the negative effects of NATO enlargement. Russia would strongly welcome this for it would mean the effective denuclearization of Germany. The first step before such a zone becomes feasible is however progress in the effort to get NATO to drop its hitherto hallowed First Use of nuclear weapons doctrine. Some NATO members, most importantly Germany, have called for just such a reconsideration. This has badly shaken the US, France, and the UK. Although Germany has said it would abide by a majority NATO decision on this score, the call for re-evaluation has led to the release of intra-NATO pressures that cannot now be easily submerged.

In Northeast Asia, such a proposed zone would cover Japan, the two Koreas and parts of Russia and China. Even if it excluded those Russian and Chinese areas where its missile bases are located, the very idea poses an unwelcome challenge to the two NWSs regarding the issue of their nuclear territorial sovereignty. When a Central Asian NWFZ emerges, as it most likely will, this will give a boost to the efforts to put a Northeast Asian NWFZ on the agenda. If however Japan, as a key player in this regard, really wants such an NWFZ, then its government must realize that any hopes of moving ahead on this front will be completely dashed if it goes ahead and participates in the Theatre Missile Defence or TMD project that Tokyo and Washington are currently contemplating. Contrary to Chinese hopes that the Russians would hold the line and prevent any watering down in the interpretation of the 1972 ABM Treaty, this has happened. An economically desperate Russia has not mustered sufficient political will to prevent a partial victory of the right-wing in the US. The US will now plan a deployable

National (Ballistic) Missile Defence (NMD) System in three years, but will defer the actual decision about whether or not to deploy an NMD system for another three years to 2003. It may still be that an NMD of the kind that would upset China may not come about, but the chances of this happening have become stronger than at any time in the post-Reagan era. START-II ratification by the Russian Duma and the regularization of START-III reductions, along with other positive restraint measures, can still hope to reverse the negative developments that have taken place on the ABM Treaty front.

In the Middle East, a zone free of all weapons of mass destruction—nuclear, biological, chemical—is an idea whose time has surely come. Israel insists on linking this to its desire for an overall peace settlement, i.e. a resolution of the Palestine problem and of the possible challenge that Iran and Iraq might pose. It is not however inconceivable that either way—whether or not the political situation improves—more Israelis may be persuaded that such a zone (stretched to include Iran and Iraq) is greatly in their interest. Once again, positive advances in this direction are probably contingent on the degree of progress that is made elsewhere in the general restraint and disarmament process.

The CTBT and Beyond

That the CTBT must come into force as soon as possible is obvious common sense. India, Pakistan and North Korea are the current hold-outs. India is the principal problem, but the chances are good that it will eventually accede making Senate ratification in the US easier. If that happens, Russian and Chinese ratification will follow. (By summer 1999, however, it is far from certain that the US senate will take up CTBT ratification in a positive fashion.) The coming into force of the CTBT will not shift the current order from its non-proliferation mode to a disarmament one, but it will represent a significant step forward (See Appendix 1). The next step after the CTBT's entry into force is to push for the permanent closure of all test sites. France has done this with its Moruroa site in the South Pacific and China with the Lop Nor site. The UK relies on the US Nevada test site. Russia now has only the Novaya Zemla site. Indian and Pakistani test sites must also be included in such a general closure. This would go a long way in foreclosing subcritical tests although some of these can be done in the laboratory. Getting the demand for international monitoring of weapons laboratories accepted is much more difficult, but it is a demand that can be raised more strongly after a successful closure of all test sites.

The FMCT is another matter. Three issues of great salience arise here. One, the question of linking it to a wider disarmament process through the call for an Ad Hoc Committee. This has already been discussed. The second issue is stockpiles. The old and new NWSs (apart from Pakistan) will not agree to its incorporation in current negotiations. It may well be that a production cut-off will have to be agreed upon first. One way to attempt to get around divergences in approach among different countries is to go for a 'framework agreement' and therefore to get general acceptance of a continuing but phased approach. Rather than a treaty solely focused on production cut-offs, which is finalized after agreement, the negotiation process would have to be broader, more complex, and prolonged but in the course of which whatever is collectively agreed upon would still be registered as an advance.

Besides the issue of destroying stockpiles, there is also the matter of commercial production and reprocessing of weapons-usable radioactive materials. In the face of the adamant refusal of the NWSs to take up the problems of military stockpiles and commercial production/accumulation, a possible interim proposal that would nevertheless advance matters positively, is to set up an international and open register of plutonium and enriched uranium. At the very least, such public transparency would pave the way for eventual and collectively agreed reductions from stockpiles of all NWSs. However, the initial demands would be for the NWSs and all nuclear capable states to submit full information about stocks, military and commercial; allow for a process of clarification and confirmation regarding these stocks; and for international inspection and monitoring to ensure that withdrawals can only be for non-military purposes.[7]

A No First Use Pledge

There can be no gainsaying the importance of obtaining such a pledge from the five NWSs. There is an important distinction to be noted between First Use and first strike. First strike refers to an initial strike aimed at destroying all or most of the enemy's nuclear weapons system. It is what is called in the jargon, a counterforce strategy, i.e. one aimed at military-industrial-nuclear targets and capacities, not at cities or population centres that are called countervalue targets. First Use covers all situations of first use including the first strike scenario. However, the Chinese pledge of No First Use is qualified by not excluding the option to use its nuclear weapons first on its own territory in response, say, to an external intervention. This has some pertinence because Chinese nuclear behaviour vis-à-vis Taiwan is thereby left unclear.

On the whole though, a No First Use pledge is more encompassing and, therefore, more valuable than a No First Strike pledge. However, as it stands, such a pledge is unverifiable and capable of being reversed either informally or formally. There is nothing to stop a country that has given such a pledge from violating it in practice. Russia, which had held this position as its declared policy for over a decade, officially dropped it in 1993. If in spite of these limitations such a pledge must be deemed to have great value, then it is because of the shift in political–strategic thinking that such a change would represent. Once all NWSs publicly declare a No First Use commitment then they are at least officially stating that nuclear weapons possession is meant *only* to deter a nuclear attack from another country.

Of course, countries that do give such a pledge do not simply think that the only value of nuclear weapons is deterrence against a nuclear assault. Nuclear élites invariably invest all sorts of wondrous properties in such weapons to justify their possession. However, the very fact that they are making such a pledge provides a powerful point of entry for opponents of nuclearism. Two public pronouncements that all such NWSs make can then be conjoined to demand that they live up to the logic of their public commitments. The other pronouncement that all NWSs make is that they do believe *ultimately* in global disarmament. Now if all the NWSs agree to this, and also agree that the only purpose of having such weapons is to deter a nuclear attack (the meaning of a No First Use pledge), then no country has reason to retain them and all should be much more amenable to the idea of progressive disarmament down to zero.[8]

NATO's resistance to the adoption of this pledge makes less sense today than it ever did. Its First Use doctrine was articulated with the idea of deterring a massive conventional military attack from the USSR or from Soviet-led Warsaw Pact forces. After the end of the Cold War, the Warsaw Pact no longer exists, there is no longer Soviet control over Eastern Europe, and the conventional balance of military power, always misconstrued as favouring the Soviet side, is now so obviously 'reversed' that it cannot even be plausibly misconstrued as being the opposite. Indeed, a major reason why Russia has dropped its earlier No First Use pledge is because it is adopting the earlier NATO tripwire principle to compensate for its perceived inferiority vis-à-vis NATO's conventional military might. The absurdity of retaining NATO's First Use doctrine is so obvious that many NATO members, most importantly Germany, Canada and Belgium, are calling for a review of this policy stasis. This is only the beginning of rumblings on this count within NATO. There will be more to be heard. A NATO declaration of No First Use will also go a very long way in getting Russia to make a similar pledge part of its official policy once again.

De-Alerting Nuclear Weapons[9]

Measures of de-alerting have multiple possible effects or functions. They can improve the general political atmosphere by easing nuclear tensions. They can be important practical steps to lessen the likelihood of a nuclear outbreak whether by accident or miscalculation. In their strongest forms, they shade into becoming concrete disarmament measures. They can also make a pledge of No First Use and the promise of no first strike contained within it not merely of political–symbolic value, but a commitment that also becomes in practical terms verifiable. These positive consequences of de-alerting arise out of its two principal technical attributes. De-alerting is about removing warheads from delivery vehicles as well as disabling but not destroying or fully dismantling the warheads themselves, and also about extending missile firing time.

The best way to prevent accidental war and also to ease some of the tensions associated with institutional nuclear rivalries/hostilities is through sequestration, i.e. separating warheads from delivery vehicles and storing them at a distant depository. Even better is to tag and disable such warheads and to store them in conditions where these warheads can be internationally monitored (e.g. in national depositories) under genuine multilateral authority. Such sequestration is easiest to carry out for airborne bombs, not particularly difficult for land-based missiles, but much more difficult for submarine-launched nuclear-tipped missiles.

The most likely form that First Use would take is first strike. Strong and effective sequestration, which is also put under multilateral monitoring, is tantamount to establishing a verifiable no first strike or use capacity. Even minor cheating (secretly hiding a few warheads) would not enable an effective first strike. Only massively successful cheating would, but a properly monitored sequestration programme effectively eliminates this possibility. Certain kinds of SLBMs, that are extremely accurate, such as the W-88 SLBMs of the US, can double up as first strike weapons. Once a programme of major de-alerting so as to eliminate the first strike option is adopted, then logically such accurate SLBMs should be verifiably replaced by much less accurate and lower yield SLBMs.

A further step in de-alerting is to disable the warheads in a way that is not irreversible but whose reversal would take considerable time. One way of doing this is to remove tritium bottles from all boosted fission and thermonuclear bombs. If the tritium is mixed with helium and stored under multilateral/international monitoring conditions, then even more time is bought. Removing the tritium in this way eliminates the booster. This does not prevent the primary explosion but it does prevent the secondary (thermonuclear) explosion, thereby greatly reducing the yield and making the warhead concerned far less effective as a first-strike weapon.

Quite apart from its weakening of first-strike possibilities, a generalization of such a policy of tritium removal would reduce the explosive power of the world's stock of nuclear weapons from thousands of megatons to around a hundred megatons or less. The consequences of a nuclear attack or exchange would still be horrific but qualitatively less than it would have otherwise been. Removing tritium also nullifies those parts of the US stockpile Stewardship programme that deal with thermonuclear reactions. Most of the rationale (though not all) of inertial confinement fusion programmes would be eliminated. Nuclear warheads after tritium removal can be further disabled by a technical procedure called 'pit stuffing'.[10] Finally, de-alerting, if it takes place before the end of 1999, would reduce the risks of the Year 2000 or Y2K problem affecting computer hardware and software. The Y2K problem perhaps cannot really cause an accidental launch, but it can affect computer warning signals and screening so as to suggest an enemy attack or launch, provoking a mistaken response. De-alerting, along the lines suggested, buys much more time for all the NWSs concerned.

Missile firing can too be handicapped and thus delayed by a variety of methods. Again, it is easier to do this for land-based or airborne missiles than for SLBMs. The motor ignition switches of missiles can be pinned and these pins would have to be manually removed first. The opening of the silos or of the places where missiles are housed can be made more difficult and awkward in a number of ways, from affixing barriers of various kinds on the roofs to covering silos with large mounds of earth. Crews preparing SLBMs can be ordered to forgo removal of flood plates from launch tubes or to carry out routine inspections. This would delay launches by many hours.

The great advantages of de-alerting measures and procedures, given the strong technical aspects involved, is that some of the measures can be carried out unilaterally while others can be agreed upon bilaterally with or without formalized treaty obligations. Thus, should Pakistan and India, for example, move towards open deployment some such measures will become of paramount importance. Best of all, of course, are those measures, wider and deeper, that can also be connected to procedures for international/multilateral monitoring by bodies representing both the NWSs and many NNWSs. This would be a major breakthrough, but prospects of achieving these are still some way down a long road ahead.

Even as anti-nuclear activists press for such deeper and wider multilaterally supervised de-alerting commitments, they must be sensitive to the possibilities for implementing unilateral and bilateral de-alerting measures that currently exist. These must not be jeopardized but strengthened even as disarmament activists press for more and better ones. Today, only the US and Russia have combat-ready alertness of a large part of their arsenals vis-à-vis each other. Some progress in de-alerting procedures has, however, been made. Those deeper and wider de-alerting measures become semi- or near-disarmament measures in themselves. No struggle to shift the agenda from non-proliferation to disarmament can afford to do anything else but treat the issue of de-alerting with the utmost care and seriousness.

Conclusion

What prevents the outline of transitional measures given above from being little more than a wish-list? Only the will and determination of the various agents in the struggle for disarmament and their reservoirs and catchment areas of public support! In the more than fifty years since the nuclear age began, the critical lesson of history is that it is open-ended. Nothing is certain—failure or success. In that respect, Karl Marx was wrong when he declared that humanity only sets those problems for itself that it can resolve. It can fail to resolve the problem of nuclearism in time although we hope it will not. However, Marx also said that even in historical circumstances not of one's choosing, one can still hope to shape the general course and direction of human society and future history more progressively and humanely .

As we approach the third millennium, humanity is confronted with certain problems ever more universal and international in character which also cry out for universal commitments and universal struggles and solutions. Nuclearism is one such problem, but there are others and each and all of them have to be tackled. How strong or weak the successes or failures on each front will be we cannot know, any more than we can know how these successes and failures will reinforce or counteract each other. That these efforts will however be connected in some way we can be certain. There are growing economic and social inequalities between and within countries. The obscenity of extreme wealth and extreme poverty not only persists, but the distance between the two is widening. By 2050 the world's population will reach the incredible figure of 10 billion or thereabouts. The pressures this will impose are not today fully imaginable. While there is some consolation to be had from the fact that liberal democratic forms of political governance have spread to cover more countries and peoples than ever before, the bad news is that democracy, like butter, has also thinned as it has spread.

With the rise and spread of right-wing ideologies and right-wing parties and organizations, even in the First World of advanced industrial democracies, it can scarcely be disputed that these societies are less humane, less economically and socially caring, less democratic than they were in their Golden Age of the late forties to the early seventies. An unbridled and rampant form of capitalism is exacting the kind of ravages of our eco-system which, if it is not checked, promises irreversible damage of certain kinds, even possible disaster, some time in the twenty-first century.

Indeed, there is something of a race between what might come first: a global ecological crisis of the first magnitude or a nuclear disaster of the same order of magnitude. One aspect of the ecological dilemma was thought to have been overcome when over half a century ago, the power of the atom was sought to be harnessed to provide a near-inexhaustible source of safe, plentiful, and constant energy. That is one illusion that a larger part of the comity of nations seems to have recognized and acknowledged. Today, nuclear energy production is in the process of being widely discredited. The anti-nuclear movements had a major role in helping to do this. It is no longer possible for most First World countries to undertake further construction of nuclear power reactors to replace older ones, let alone to extend their role in power and electricity generation.

Like most things, however, the lessons are unevenly absorbed. Even as there is no longer any major First World market for nuclear reactors (even Russia after Chernobyl cannot dare take the route of building more reactors), the five big potential markets for nuclear reactors and components are all in Asia: China, South Korea, Taiwan, Indonesia, India. Clearly, discrediting the claims of the nuclear energy lobby is something that should have fed more strongly into discrediting nuclear weapons and their support lobbies worldwide. Surely a world without nuclear reactors for commercial generation, by running down the 'plutonium economy', would make a world free of nuclear weapons easier to attain. So, along with all those incremental measures aimed at disarmament, should we not also be proposing measures to run down and eventually end commercial nuclear energy production worldwide? Can a nuclear disarmament movement afford to downplay the need to have alternative sources of energy?

This is a view that deserves much sympathy. Accordingly, there is hardly any problem in endorsing the idea of establishing an international energy agency promoting the development of sustainable and eco-friendly energy sources as part of the nuclear disarmament agenda itself. However, if a world free of nuclear energy production will greatly help in *sustaining* a world already free of nuclear weapons, the fact remains that in *bringing that world about,* the winding down of civilian nuclear energy production plays a lesser role. That is partly the reason why this book has not focused on that issue. The other part of the reason is that doing otherwise would have resulted in a work even more unwieldy and scattered in its diverse preoccupations than this one may already have become.

Some time in the next fifty years, and certainly before the twenty-first century ends, the world has to eradicate the evil of nuclearism and achieve total disarmament. If it cannot be done over this time span, then it is virtually inconceivable that it can be done over a longer one assuming all the while that someone, somewhere, still does not pull that nuclear trigger. The danger of a nuclear apocalypse tends to provoke a dismally pessimistic note in ruminations about possible futures. It need not and should not. What has happened over the past fifty years and more provides at least as many sources of hope and optimism as it does of despair and pessimism. Indeed, the cause of nuclear disarmament, in comparison with so many other worthy causes, starts with an inestimable advantage. Apart from a small handful of nuclear diehards, the vast, overwhelming majority of humanity genuinely believes that a nuclear free world is desirable, necessary, and feasible. The crucial collective project is to make that pervasive sentiment the political force it can and should become. This is the crucial struggle of our times. If it succeeds, there is everything, indeed literally a whole world, to be gained.

Notes

1. For example, throughout the fifties, the USSR had no nuclear deterrent capacity to speak of vis-à-vis the US. Cuba did not show that the Soviet deterrent worked but that the belief of both sides in the efficacy of deterrence was nearly suicidal. See also Chapter 2.
2. See *Against Nuclear Jingoism*, op. cit., and the article by the CPM's senior leader, Prakash Karat, 'Once Again on CTBT' in the party's English language weekly, *People's Democracy*, 10 January 1999. The article is partly directed against the authors' stand on the CTBT and follows their rebuttal of all Indian criticisms of the CTBT including those advanced by the CPM and other sections of the Indian Left. That rebuttal was carried in their article in the *Economic and Political Weekly* of 19 September 1998 entitled 'Why India Should Sign the CTBT'.

   Civil in tone and fraternal in spirit, Karat's article is nonetheless deeply disappointing. Karat avoids engagement with even a single substantive argument or rebuttal made by the authors, preferring simply to assert older claims and to justify this by claiming that the authors 'seem to forget or ignore that we are talking of nuclear weapons in the era of imperialism'. The expected then follows: the CTBT is an instrument of imperialism, etc. What is most depressing in all this is not so much what is revealed about the CPM's understanding about the

CTBT or Karat's failure to engage in a genuine dialogue or debate with the authors, but the party leadership's total lack of awareness that, in the light of all that has happened, it might need to carry out serious soul-searching and self-criticism of its entire approach to the nuclear issue, including of its presumed relationship to imperialism.

There is not even a hint of remorse that after 11 May the party's official statements, even as they criticized the tests, implicitly applauded the performance of Indian science and scientists for their work which made the tests possible. There is not the slightest recognition that the nature and general thrust of the 1994–6 CTBT debate (which the CPM defended in the name of a 'national consensus') helped pave the way for the 1998 tests. There is not the least acknowledgement that ambiguity is an immoral position, nor any attempt at explaining why the party failed to understand that Indian ambiguity, in comparison to that of all other threshold countries, was the most unstable. Nor, of course, is there any hint of self-doubt that the CPM's whole understanding of nuclear imperialism might be deeply flawed or that its historical defence of the Red Bomb was, and is, untenable—a judgement that many other anti-Stalinist Marxists and Marxist organizations in the West and Japan arrived at long ago.

3. The MNWC is available in English on the following websites: www.ngo.org/coraweiss/UNDOC.html and www.ddh.nl/org/ialana_www.ddh.nl/org/ialana. See also J. Rotblat, J. Steinberger, B. Udgaonkar, and F. Blackaby (eds.), *A Nuclear-Weapon-Free World: Desirable? Feasible?*, Westview Press, (Pugwash), San Francisco, Oxford, 1993; and Box 7 on pp.55–8 of P. Bidwai and A. Vanaik, *Testing Times: the Global Stake in a Nuclear Test Ban*, Dag Hammarskjold Foundation, Uppsala, 1996, where the five basic attributes of any such draft treaty or convention are highlighted: an international authority with powers to override national sovereignty, societal verification, universality of membership, effective technical monitoring, and power of enforcement.
4. There are three distinct proposals and one variation. (1) South Africa has proposed an Ad Hoc Committee with a discussion mandate (19 January 1999). (2) Egypt has called for an Ad Hoc Committee with a negotiating mandate (26 January 1999). (3) Belgium has called for an Ad Hoc Working Group (2 February 1999). The variation is an attempted precursor to the South African proposal in the shape of a call on the CD's President (rotating every four weeks) to appoint a 'special coordinator' to consult on the issue.
5. This is the proposal of the former Director of SIPRI (Stockholm International Peace Research Institute), Frank Blackaby, in 'Time For a Peasant's Revolt' in the November/December 1997 issue of *The Bulletin of Atomic Scientists*, Chicago.
6. The UN General Assembly in 1975 defined an NWFZ as follows:
   1. A nuclear weapon-free zone shall, as a general rule, be deemed to be any zone, recognized as such by the General Assembly of United Nations, which any group of States, in the free exercise of their sovereignty, has established by virtue of a treaty or convention whereby:
   (a) The statute of total absence of nuclear weapons to which the zone shall be

subject, including the procedure for the delimitation of the zone, is defined;

(b) An international system of verification and control is established to guarantee compliance with the obligations deriving from that statute.

Regarding the obligations of the NWSs:

1. In every case of a nuclear weapon free zone that has been recognized as such by the General Assembly, all nuclear weapon States shall undertake or reaffirm, in a solemn international instrument having full legally binding force, such as a treaty, a convention or, a protocol, the following obligations:
   (a) To respect in all its parts the statute of total absence of nuclear weapons defined in the treaty or convention which serves as the constitutive instrument of the zone:
   (b) To refrain from contributing in any way to the performance in the territories forming part of the zone of acts which involve a violation of the aforesaid treaty or convention:
   (c) To refrain from using or threatening to use nuclear weapons against the States included in the zone.

UNIDIR/96/24, p.36.

7. See Martin Kalinowski, 'Fissile Cutoff: Overcoming the Disarmament Deadlock', in *INESAP Bulletin,* Issue no. 13, July 1997, pp.7–10.
8. C. Raja Mohan, Strategic Affairs Editor of the Chennai-based Indian English language daily, *The Hindu,* has supported the No First Use pledge given by India and has also said that India may need to retain nuclear weapons even if all other NWSs including the US were to give them up so as to counter US dominance in a nuclear-free world. The last was stated in a public meeting (among other places) at Jawaharlal Nehru University in Autumn 1998 to which one of the authors (A. Vanaik) was also invited. The breathtaking cynicism displayed here should occasion no surprise, but Raja Mohan is considered to be a 'moderate' among Indian pro-nuclearists and is a member of the advisory committee of the National Security Council.
9. This section draws on a useful article by Arjun Makhijani, 'De-Alerting: A First Step', in *Science for Democratic Action,* October 1998 issue pub. by Institute of Energy and Environmental Research (IEER), Tacoma Park, Maryland, USA.
10. Here the warhead is disabled by stuffing a wire into the tube where tritium is otherwise introduced. The wire fills up the hollow of the warhead pit and gets tangled up. After this the warhead cannot be reactivated without re-manufacturing the pit.

APPENDIX 1

The Comprehensive Test Ban Treaty

The Importance of a Test Ban

1. The health and environmental benefits to humanity and the world of a permanent end to all nuclear test explosions are self-evident and significant. The political–psychological impact of not ever again having any such test explosions, or having to worry about them, are truly dramatic and valuable. The existing but fragile momentum of global arms restraint and disarmament will be strengthened.
2. The CTBT, when it comes into force, will weaken the technological push that has fuelled the arms race. It will weaken the malign influence of the weapons laboratories as an autonomous lobby.
3. The CTBT will break the 'talk–test–build' format. At least until START-I and START-II were negotiated, the arms control process followed a typical pattern: negotiating measures to control the competition, while simultaneously intensifying it through active testing and construction of new weapons systems.
4. The CTBT will have a major effort on what has been called the 'fear factor'. If all NWSs agree to restrict the push for technological advance in nuclear weapons, one major source of fear can disappear. Knowing that nothing new or exotic will suddenly emerge makes it easier to deal sensibly with existing problems.
5. A CTBT would help create a new climate for further arms limitation and reduction by opening up the door to other logical or natural steps such as a convention to freeze fissile materials production and reduce stockpiles to zero, end flight-testing of new missile systems, a No First Use treaty for all NWSs, a treaty to end deployment of new weapons systems, and de-alerting, etc.
6. The CTBT sets vital precedents for the future of negotiations on other arms restraint, reduction, and disarmament measures.
   (i) The CTBT negotiating process, for all its weaknesses, and despite

the unavoidable reality that different countries had differing bargaining and leveraging capacities, was nonetheless the most genuinely multilateral and the most democratic process among all nuclear arms-related treaty processes in history.

(ii) It was the first Treaty the negotiation of which was concluded in accordance with the set deadline and in which there had to be full consensus in the Conference on Disarmament (CD) on all provisions. These were excellent precedents providing, through the principles of formal equality of veto power and unanimity, at least some kind of check for weaker countries against more powerful ones, and for the NNWSs against the NWSs.

(iii) The CTBT, when it comes into force, will have set up, for the first time ever, a truly international monitoring system, which in certain respects overrides all national authorities. In doing this, it sets a crucial and practical operating precedent for the kind of supranational structures of authority and supervision that will be necessary to ensure that the world of nation-states not only becomes nuclear-free, but remains that way.

The Final Treaty: Strengths and Weaknesses

The final Treaty was not passed as it should have been by the Conference on Disarmament (CD) because of an Indian veto, ostensibly cast because of India's desire to alter Article XIV of the Treaty on Entry into Force, but actually to weaken the CD since India was fully aware that its veto would not alter the Article in question. It was passed by an overwhelming majority in the UN General Assembly.

The Treaty comprises a Preamble, seventeen Articles, two Annexes, and a Protocol. As would be expected from a multilaterally negotiated treaty, the final agreed text represented a compromise in which no country got everything it wanted and all major players had to make concessions of one sort or the other to arrive at a final consensus document. The real character of the final Treaty, then, is at variance from the view adopted by Indian critics that it was essentially an artefact of the NWSs (led by the US) to perpetuate their 'nuclear hegemony'.

Precisely because this was not the case, the Preamble of the finalized Treaty has had to be misinterpreted and misrepresented by the US executive so as to make it more amenable to manipulation in line with its possible future and contemporary interests. In this Preamble, the key statements are the following: (1) the 'objective' of the Treaty is 'to contribute effectively to the prevention of the proliferation of nuclear weapons in all its aspects, to the process of nuclear disarmament, and therefore to the enhancement of international peace and security,'; (2) 'that the cessation of all nuclear weapon test explosions and all other nuclear explosions, by constraining the development and qualitative improvement of nuclear weapons and ending the development of advanced new types of nuclear weapons, constitutes an effective measure of nuclear disarmament and non-proliferation in all its aspects.'

The US President in his message to the Senate of 23 September 1997, presented an interpretation that sought to obliterate the distinction in the Preamble between 'development and qualitative improvement of nuclear weapons' and 'development of advanced new types' in order to obscure the fact that the CTBT recognizes that the treaty will *'end* (emphasis added) the development of advanced new types of nuclear weapons'and thus reduce it to what the current US executive would like the Treaty to be but is not (namely, that the CTBT merely constrains such activities). In short, for US hawks to get their way, they have to try and undermine the CTBT's provisions in letter and/or spirit; they cannot scrupulously obey a treaty supposedly fashioned to promote their interests. Incidentally, even these hawks acknowledge that the CTBT 'constrains' the US's qualitative weapons advancement.

Regarding the seventeen Articles, the most important that need to be briefly outlined and explicated are Articles I, II, IV, VII, VIII, IX, and XIV.

Article I refers to the scope or basic obligations of all signatory members. Each such signatory must abjure 'any nuclear weapon test explosion or any other nuclear explosion' no matter how small in yield on its territory and prevent any such occurrence under its jurisdiction. Besides no state party can cause, encourage or participate in any way in such test or other nuclear explosion. This is what is meant by the famous'zero yield' formulation that was, after much wrangling, advanced during the negotiations in August 1995 and became the basis of the, till then elusive, agreement on scope by the five major nuclear weapons powers, each at a different level of nuclear weapons, technological and scientific capability and potential.

Article II gives the character, functions, and distribution of powers and responsibilities of the different tiers of the organization of the CTBT or CTBTO. The three levels of the organization are the Conference of States Parties, the Executive Council (EC) and the Technical Secretariat which includes the International Data Centre. While the CTBTO will cooperate with other international organizations such as the International Atomic Energy Agency (IAEA) it is an independent body. The supreme decision-making body is the Conference of States Parties in which each member has one vote only. This Conference will meet (once the Treaty comes into force) regularly (annually if accepted) besides any special sittings that may be requested by the Executive Council, the Conference, or any State Party if supported by a majority of members. On 'matters of substance' decisions 'shall be taken as far as possible by consensus'. If this is not possible than it has to be by two-thirds majority of members present (a majority constituting a quorum). The single most important official position is that of the Director-General of the International Secretariat. S/he will be appointed by the Conference with each term lasting four years and renewable for one more term only.

Between the Conferences of States Parties, the decision-making within the parameters set by the Treaty will be by the Executive Council consisting of 51 members, on which each member has the right to serve in due course and by rotation taking into account geographically distributed quotas. There are no permanent members of the Executive Council and all members are treated as equal and eligible regardless of their weapons status. The EC membership will be selected by the Conference with reference to stipulated geographical and technical criteria laid down in the Treaty and the EC is accountable to the Conference. The EC is charged with seeing to the 'effective implementation of, and compliance with, this Treaty' and with supervising the activities of the Technical Secretariat as well as with organizing the regular and other meetings of the Conference.

The Technical Secretariat is responsible for carrying out the practical verification of compliance, i.e. to ensure that there is no cheating by any member signatory regarding a nuclear explosion—test explosion or otherwise. The Technical Secretariat supervises and coordinates the International Monitoring System (IMS) comprising variant forms of monitoring stations and activities as well as operating the International Data Centre and to process, analyze, evaluate all relevant data.

Article IV deals with the character of the proposed verification regime which has (a) an International Monitoring System; (b) provisions for consultation with and clarification from requested and requesting States Parties; (c) on-site inspections (OSI); (d) confidence-building measures.

All monitoring facilities of the IMS shall be owned and operated by the states hosting them or otherwise responsible for them in accordance with the protocol of the Treaty. They will, however, be placed under the authority of the Technical Secretariat and their functioning cannot be impeded by national governments. All data, raw and processed, is available to all States Parties.

No State Party is 'precluded from using information obtained by national technical means of verification' (e.g. satellites) to judge whether a demand, for example, for on-site inspection of a particular country should be made.

This information must, however, be obtained 'in a manner consistent with generally recognized principles of international law, including that of respect for the sovereignty of States'. This is generally interpreted to mean that information from illegal spying activities will not be permitted.

The crucial issue, of course, is the impartiality and rigour of the procedures for sanctioning and then carrying out on-site inspections. Any State Party has the right to request (from the Director-General and the EC) an on-site inspection of another member country's facilities only for determining whether Article I has been violated. Even so, the requesting country must obey established procedural norms regarding the provision of adequate information about the environment of the event triggering the request and the estimated time of the triggering event. And it must provide all data on which the request is based. Before the question of whether or not to sanction such a request arises, there is a stipulated procedure concerning the communication of the request to the said country as well as to all other States Parties, the awaiting of the said country's clarifications and communication of that to the requesting country. If the requesting country is still not satisfied and insists on an on-site inspection, then this will be undertaken only if 30 or more out of the 51 members of the EC agree. It can take up to eight days for this procedure of initial request–clarification–sanction of the OSI to be completed.

If an OSI is sanctioned, this must be carried out in accordance with strictly laid down procedures in the Treaty. There can be no simultaneous OSIs on a given territory. The inspected State Party has the 'right to take measures it deems necessary to protect national security interests and to prevent disclosure of confidential information not related to the purpose of inspection'. Representatives of the inspected State Party will be present throughout the inspection and the inspection team will wherever possible 'begin with the least intrusive procedures and then proceed to more intrusive procedures only as it deems necessary to collect sufficient information to clarify the concern about possible non-compliance with this Treaty'.

The final report of the inspection team will be transmitted to the requesting State Party, the inspected State Party, the EC, and to all other State Parties. The EC will decide whether there has been non-compliance and whether, even if there is deemed to be compliance, the request for OSI was an abusive request or not. In the event of an abusive request, the EC can require the State Party concerned to defray the costs of preparations of the Technical Secretariat. It can go further and suspend the requesting State Party's right to request future OSIs for a period of time determined by the EC. It can further suspend the right of the requesting State Party to serve on the EC for a period of time.

Regarding the issue of non-compliance with Article I deemed to have been shown by an OSI, it is the Conference that will decide what to do taking into consideration the EC recommendations. The rights and privileges of a State Party can be restricted or suspended by the decision of the Conference. The Conference can recommend collective measures to the States Parties against the non-complying country, but these have to be 'in conformity with international law'.

Article VII concerns amendments to the Treaty. This can only be done by an Amendment Conference. Such a Conference can be called if a majority of States Parties want it, but no substantive amendment to the Treaty can be carried out unless there is a positive majority vote with 'no State Party casting a negative vote'. That is to say, each State Party has veto power. Everybody doesn't have to say yes, a majority will do, but nobody should say no, not even a single country!

According to Article VIII, there will be (unless a majority decide otherwise) a review conference ten years after the Treaty comes into force. This review will take into account any new scientific and technological developments relevant to the Treaty. Every ten years thereafter, or even at lesser intervals, there can be a review conference if so decided by the Conference of States Parties.

Article IX concerns duration of, and withdrawal from, the Treaty. The Treaty is of unlimited duration. As is standard in treaties whose signatories are sovereign national states, each State Party has the right to invoke jeopardization of its 'supreme interests' in order to withdraw from the Treaty.

Article XIV deals with entry into force. Here the key point is that the Treaty can only enter into force if it is signed and ratified by 44 countries listed in Annexe 2 of the Treaty, which countries are deemed by the IAEA as having nuclear power or research reactors. Specifically, this means the CTBT cannot enter into force unless two countries, India and Pakistan, which have so far refused to accede to it, sign, and ratify it. This is clearly unfair to the two countries concerned and seeks to coerce India and Pakistan into going along with a Treaty they have rejected, as is their sovereign right to do.

However, far worse than this unfairness to India and Pakistan—an earlier hold-out, Israel, has now signed the CTBT—is the unfairness of this provision to the Treaty itself. Its coming into force should not have been made contingent on the accession to it of countries that did not wish to accede to it. It should have been allowed to come into force excluding India and Pakistan, leaving it to them to decide whether or not they wish to reconsider their decision at some later date. The sooner a CTBT comes into force covering most of the world, the better.

Regarding the powers of the review conference that is supposed to take place in September 1999, three years after the CTBT was passed in the UN, these are strictly defined. Only ratified member-signatories have voting power with non-ratifying but signing members only enjoying observer status. This Conference cannot impose sanctions on countries that are not so far signatories to the CTBT like India and Pakistan. It can only consider what measures 'may be undertaken to accelerate the ratification process in order to facilitate the early entry into force of this Treaty'. However, such 'measures' have to be decided by 'consensus' and in a manner 'consistent with international law'. International law, and the Vienna Convention on the Law of Treaties, does not allow for any Treaty to endorse collective punishment of any sort on a country or countries which refuse to be a party or parties to the Treaty in question!

APPENDIX 2

Self-Serving Sanctimoniousness

Indian Criticism of the CTBT

There have been five main lines of criticism of the CTBT in the Indian debate. (i)The CTBT was not linked to a time-bound schedule for global nuclear disarmament as it should if it is to be acceptable. (ii) The CTBT is discriminatory in character. (iii) The CTBT is decisively flawed and rendered effectively worthless at least for the US and perhaps France and possibly for Britain, China, and Russia. This is because, in its present form, it allows subcritical testing, does not prevent advances in computer simulation techniques that will set up a 'virtual testing regime' or 'informational test ground', and allows research and development of direct fusion weapons to continue through such institutions as the planned National Ignition Facility in the US and the Laser Megajoule facility in France. (iv) The CTBT is another building block, after the NPT, in the perpetuation and strengthening of 'nuclear hegemony' practised by the nuclear haves against the nuclear have-nots, led above all by the US. (v) Specific criticisms of some provisions of the CTBT, most notably Article XIV on Entry Into Force; the supposed pressure likely to be imposed on India by the 1999 review conference and the 'intrusive' dangers of the verification procedures embodied in the Treaty. Each of these criticisms will be taken up in turn and refuted.

1. Take the first line of criticism. Time and again, countries opposed to positive nuclear restraint or reduction measures have used a standard argumentative technique. Commitment to a grand goal, e.g. global nuclear disarmament, with which every sane person can agree, is cited precisely in order to block the *process* of incremental steps by which we can move towards that goal. India was doing exactly this with its demand for a time-bound schedule. India has a past record as a country more committed than most to the cause of nuclear disarmament. This, and the fact that for so long it did not go openly nuclear despite having proven its nuclear weapons capability, had given it a certain moral capital that inclined a large number of non-nuclear

weapons states (NNWSs) to give India the benefit of the doubt as to its motives in proposing this linkage. The important point, however, is that the other NNWSs did not join India in making or endorsing this explicit linkage between a time-bound schedule for global disarmament and the CTBT. They did not do so because they valued the CTBT in itself sufficiently so as not to try to make the best the enemy of the good and thus jeopardize the very possibility of a CTBT coming into existence.

In a sense, there were three basic positions during the CTBT negotiations which can be elaborated in the form of an analogy. If the relationship between a measure like the CTBT and global nuclear disarmament is visualized as a descending staircase at the bottom of which is the common goal of complete disarmament, with the CTBT representing the first step down towards this goal, then the position of the NWSs, especially of the US, could be characterized as follows: they are prepared, in their words, to go this first step down, but are not prepared to be pressured any further. They will decide whether, when, or how they will take further steps down this staircase. The second position was that of the overwhelming majority of NNWSs barring India. The value of the CTBT in their eyes lies not simply in its specific merit but also as a measure promoting the momentum towards further disarmament. In short, they wanted the NWSs to give a more serious commitment to moving further down this staircase and not just stopping after the CTBT.

The third position was India's. Not only did India not regard the CTBT as a step downwards (at least for the US and possibly France), but it would not itself take this one step unless the NWSs gave a categorical commitment not only to move all the steps down towards total global disarmament but provide a definite time schedule for doing this! India cannot, of course, give a time-bound schedule for solving the Kashmir problem or its own problems of poverty, communalism, or illiteracy, but it demanded on so difficult an issue as getting global nuclear disarmament that the NWSs provide just such a timetable right away!

The absurdity of this position was reinforced by the fact that the Indian government was effectively putting the cart before the horse. Before one can sensibly talk of securing a time-bound schedule for global disarmament, one has *first* to secure and institutionalize a genuine multilateral body that has a mandate *accepted* by the NWSs as well as the NNWSs to negotiate such universal disarmament. Getting such a body into existence or effectively preparing the ground for this is going to take many years of arduous diplomacy and struggle on the part of NNWSs, given the current reluctance of the NWSs to countenance such a body. One does not jeopardize the efforts to secure such a crucial breakthrough by insisting that the *very birth* of such a body be made contingent on the NWSs now agreeing to accept a time-bound schedule for total disarmament. Indeed, the two most important efforts to secure such a body are the pursuit of the formation of an Ad Hoc Committee on Global Nuclear Disarmament in the CD, and the setting up of a Nuclear Weapons (Abolition) Convention or NWC.

Both efforts need to be pursued simultaneously and continuously. The first was exactly what the large majority of the NNWSs in the CTBT negotiations were pursuing, hoping that they could get a commitment from the NWSs on agreeing to such a body at least with a discussion mandate, if not a negotiating one, to begin with. Such a commitment could have been embodied in the Preamble of the CTBT. Had India been serious about helping to institutionalize such a body, then it could have employed powerful leverage to get this as the price of its acceptance of the CTBT. This emerged as a real opportunity in the crucial weeks before India's June 1996 rejection of the CTBT. However, opposing the CTBT because it would affect its (wrongly) perceived national security interests, India was never interested in seriously negotiating to bring about a stronger or better CTBT even more in line with the aspirations and hopes of the majority of the NNWSs and other anti-nuclearists worldwide.

Regarding the NWC, India pays lip service to it. Insisting, however, that the NWC's very inception be made dependent on the NWSs accepting a time-bound schedule within it for disarmament is nothing but obviously ill-motivated, shallow, and hypocritical moral posturing out of synchronization even with those NNWSs most committed to rapid global disarmament, which make no such demand. This is an outrageous and ridiculous 'big bang' conception of how global nuclear disarmament must take place. The Indian government has now dropped this demand, but not from any sophisticated or deep-seated new-found commitment to disarmament. Rather, it now wants to pose as a 'responsible and moderate' nuclear weapons power.

2. The second criticism pertains to the supposedly discriminatory character of the CTBT. It is one thing to consider a treaty flawed. On this there can then be a debate on how significant are the flaws and whether the treaty is thereby rendered worthless for one or more of its signatories. It is another thing altogether to make the more *morally charged* accusation that a treaty is discriminatory. Who after all wants to be on the side of discrimination? Such a criticism has a much more general appeal to a public otherwise unfamiliar with the technical dimensions of nuclear arms development, which is necessary to assess how technically flawed the CTBT is. To call something discriminatory is therefore a politically damaging accusation, which is why the sheer irresponsibility of the charge is so great.

The claim that the CTBT is discriminatory betokens precisely that imprecision of language and thought that can often bedevil a proper assessment of an issue. The CTBT imposes the *same* obligations on *all* member signatories. In this respect, it is fundamentally and decisively different from the NPT which has discrimination legally enshrined within it by having *differential* obligations for different classes of members to the treaty. In the NPT, the two different classes of members are the NWSs and the NNWSs, and the treaty refers to them as such, as well as spelling out a range of different obligations and privileges for each. In the CTBT, the very language shows the absence of any such enshrined discrimination. The only terms used for all members are 'States Parties' or 'States Members'. There are no separate obligations nor separate classes of members.

It can, of course, be argued or claimed by critics of the CTBT that behind the formal or legal 'impartiality' and 'non-discrimination' of the treaty in question, there exists a *prior* context or situation on the ground of discrimination between the nuclear haves and have-nots which the CTBT does not adequately address. This is, however, *fundamentally* and *conceptually* different from the claim that the CTBT itself is *inherently*, or by its nature, discriminatory. It is, in fact, an implicit claim that the real problem with the CTBT is not that it is discriminatory but the very opposite! It does not do what its critics think it should do: to discriminate *positively*, or in favour of the nuclear have-nots, so as to help rectify the real situation of discrimination that exists regardless of, and prior to, the CTBT!

Perhaps the appropriate analogy here is the celebrated comment of Anatole France that the law in its impartial majesty equally penalizes the rich and the poor for sleeping under a public bridge! The point here is that the rich don't have to so sleep and therefore the effects of this law are so uneven as to cause no problems for the rich but many for the poor. Is the CTBT, then, something like this, having strong and genuine restraining effects on the NNWSs, on nuclear threshold countries like Israel and India and Pakistan (before their tests), on possibly some of the NWSs, but not on others most notably the US? This in fact, is also a misleading analogy. The CTBT powerfully restrains *all* the NWSs including France and the US.

3. This brings us to the third line of criticism about the supposedly fatal technical loopholes that exist in the Treaty because it allows subcriticals, computer simulation, and R&D on direct fusion or fourth-generation nuclear weapons. This is related to, but distinct from, the previous line of criticism. Does the pursuit of such activities violate the letter of the CTBT? It does not, but it certainly violates the general spirit informing the Treaty which intends to move away from efforts to qualitatively enhance nuclear weapons development.

Of course, no treaty can effectively monitor and thereby curb computer simulation. Does the existence of these possibilities for carrying out subcriticals, computer simulation, and direct fusion R&D weaken the CTBT to the point of making its restraining effect on all NWSs, including the US, effectively nugatory or inconsequential or of little consequence? Here, the answer is a categorical and emphatic no! The CTBT remains a powerful and worthwhile restraint measure.

The refutation of the claim that these activities constitute fatal loopholes in the CTBT relies on arguments and evidence of a technical nature as well as on evidence of a non-technical and political nature which can plausibly convince non-specialists about the efficacy of the Treaty. We will take the more technical arguments first. Subcriticals, computer simulation, and direct fusion weapons R&D must each be dealt with separately because of their quite different purposes and aims.

Subcritical experiments (SCEs) are those that do not lead to a nuclear chain reaction but remain below that critical point. Their nuclear yield is therefore zero. These experiments are designed to study the dynamic properties of ageing nuclear materials. They can incorporate what is called hydrodynamic testing which helps in the study of the other non-nuclear components in a weapons assembly. Neither hydrodynamic tests nor other kinds of SCEs are however of much use in weapons designing beyond first-generation weapons, knowledge regarding which is already widely available in the public literature.

The real danger represented by SCEs is that they can 'creep up' to the level of hydronuclear testing (HNEs), which is of significant help in the designing of very small yield weapons. HNEs, because they achieve slight supercriticality, are banned by the CTBT. Preferably, there should be no SCEs. If they are carried out, however, the central problem with them is that their conduct should be sufficiently *transparent* so that there is public assurance that they have not been allowed to 'creep up' to the level of HNEs. SCEs *in themselves* are not however a serious problem, let alone a fatal loophole in the CTBT in regard to qualitative nuclear weapons advancement.[1]

What about computer simulation and the possibility of establishing an 'informational test site' or 'virtual testing' that would effectively do away with the need for explosive testing? Here, the crucial issue is whether or not computer simulation alone can lead to the emergence of a new generation of *sufficiently accurate* weapons codes that are crucial to developing a new generation of nuclear weapons or making significant qualitative advances in weapons designing even within the existing generation of weapons.

What are weapons codes? It is best to think of weapons codes as something like a shelf or even shelves of a very large number of books which provide or attempt to provide a deep and integrated knowledge of an extremely complex and vast array of issues. Nuclear weapons codes establish linkages between the empirical evidence gained from previous explosive tests and laboratory work, the existing (though incomplete) state of knowledge about the basic physical processes involved in a nuclear explosion, and the specific design parameters of the device under consideration. They are, in fact, the *principal tool* of nuclear weapons designers.

The US, unsurprisingly, is the country that has invested the most in the effort so far to develop an 'informational test site' through its Accelerated Strategic Computing Initiative (ASCI) which is being carried out in collaboration with five major US universities. What has now been realized from ongoing efforts is that though computer simulation most certainly helps in the development of such weapons codes it nonetheless suffers from insuperable problems. The issue is not whether a new weapon will work or not but whether it will work in the way its designers want it to work, i.e. whether it will properly fulfil the function for which it has been designed.

Such is the limitation of existing knowledge about what takes place in advanced nuclear weapons explosions (especially regarding what are called the 'secondaries') and the complexity of the way various processes are connected, that codes generated by computer simulation alone are simply inadequate. These connections are so complex and their basis still so poorly understood that if weapons codes are made or adjusted to be more accurate in one direction, then for reasons unknown, they become more inaccurate in other directions. The significance of these 'fudge factors', as they are called, has been repeatedly affirmed by the comparison of results achieved by computer simulation alone when compared to *known* parameters of devices already established through previous explosive testing.

The effort to establish 'virtual testing' is thus deeply ironic. It has led to the *greater* recognition of the importance of *ultimately* resorting to actual proof-testing or explosive testing in order to finally design advanced or new generation weapons.[2] Far from *substituting* for explosive testing, such simulation efforts create pressure for eventually resiling from the CTBT if the US is ever to make serious qualitative advances in nuclear weapons development and weaponization. Thus, what the existence of facilities for carrying out SCEs, direct fusion weapons R&D, and ASCI do is to keep the necessary software (the small pool of highly specialized scientists) and much of the hardware in operation, so that if in the future the US decides to *break out* of the CTBT it can move towards the development and deployment of a new range of weapons in the shortest possible time. What all this indicates is not the irrelevance of the CTBT but, in fact, the vital importance of securing it and keeping it *permanently* in place.

Finally, there is the issue of fourth-generation or direct fusion weapons such as laser beam weapons, etc. The CTBT and the banning of explosive testing does not theoretically present an obstacle to the development of such weapons, so the treaty does not render their development impossible. To claim however that the CTBT is rendered worthless on this count is absurd. The leap from third-generation to fourth-generation weapons is far greater than from first-generation to third-generation weapons. Indeed, nobody can say with any confidence that such a leap will ever be made. The physics is simply unknown.

The US National Ignition Facility seeking to develop the key technology of Inertial Confinement Fusion (and France's Laser Megajoule) are *deeply speculative* ventures to produce 'pie-in-the-sky wonder weapons' whose chances of success are regarded as small. The overwhelming majority of knowledgeable nuclear physicists give these facilities less than a 10 per cent chance of success. The very small minority who are most committed to these projects are themselves not prepared to give it more than a fifty-fifty chance of success.[3]

With a CTBT in place, today's US can do, and not do, the following: it *cannot* go ahead to develop any third-generation nuclear weapons such as particle beam weapons, enhanced or reduced radiation weapons or battlefield micro-nukes, electromagnetic pulse bombs, etc. It cannot *certify* any nuclear weapon. Within the range of second generation weapons, which is where the US is currently situated (but ahead of any other country in this range), it can, even with the CTBT in place, develop weapons that represent *new applications* of existing or known designs such as 'deep penetration earth bombs', etc. In respect of newer weapons (but not new generation weapons), the closer their designs are to known ones, the easier they are to make even if the CTBT prevents certification of all weapons. However, the further away the new designs are from existing designs, the more difficult they become to make, and indeed after a shortly arrived point of distance from existing knowledge, they are effectively not possible to design with the necessary confidence that they will work as they are supposed to.

It is, however, not necessary to be a nuclear physics expert in order to realize that the CTBT is a genuine and powerful restraint measure on all the NWSs. The non-technical evidence is there for all to see except those most determined not to see it. In all the NWSs, there exist powerful lobbies primarily centred around sections of the weapons laboratories, defence forces and ardent arms-racers (usually positioned on the hard right of the political spectrum) that have resolutely opposed the CTBT *precisely* because they have understood fully well its powerful restraining effect. In the US, they have gathered around a section of the Republican right with the result that Senate ratification of the CTBT remains deeply uncertain. How is it that the more right-wing, gung-ho section of the US establishment is so reluctant to support the CTBT if it is a measure that is meant to serve US imperialist interests and is not a serious restraint on that country's qualitative weapons advancement?

The effective answer of Indian critics of the CTBT, notably the Left is, and has to be, the absurd argument that the Democrats and supporters of the CTBT in the US are the more intelligent and sophisticated imperialists, but these right-wing Republicans and others are the more stupid imperialists who don't properly understand how US imperialist interests should be best pursued. Such critics of the CTBT have hardly been swayed, dismayed, or even shaken out of their complacency by the fact that virtually the whole of the international anti-nuclear movement and the overwhelming bulk of the international Left have, with varying degrees of enthusiasm, supported the CTBT! The overwhelming majority of international anti-nuclear groups and activists, most of whom have a more consistent record than the Indian left in their opposition to all nuclear weapons-related activity (whether by capitalist or Communist countries) and which include top world-class nuclear physicists, including former nuclear weapons designers have also supported the CTBT with varying degrees of enthusiasm.

However, the division between pro- and anti-CTBTers in the US does not correspond to the absurd and artificial division between smart and naive imperialists. Rather, it reflects the obvious fact that after the end of the Cold War, there is a division between arms-racers in the US, on one hand, and arms reducers/arms moderators, on the other. There is no significant or powerful section of arms-eliminators amongst the US nuclear élite, although the number of voices demanding complete arms elimination is growing.[4] After the end of the Cold War, however, the category of those who no longer see the purpose of continuing with the quantitative and qualitative advancement of nuclear weapons by the US or any other country has grown stronger. Most of them want an end to this race and favour considerable reductions in nuclear weapons even though they do not countenance their complete elimination on the part of the US, and are far from becoming opponents of US political imperialism.

There is further non-technical evidence. The idea that other NWSs like Russia and China would ever have agreed to a CTBT which was fatally flawed is absurd. Indeed, the CTBT only became a possibility when the 'zero yield' formulation was agreed upon by the US on 11 August 1995. Before that, the US had been pressing for a very small loophole allowing explosive testing up to 2 kg yield. The position of the other NWSs, particularly Russia and China, was that if a loophole of any sort was to be allowed, then it had to be large enough so that they themselves, at a lower level of weapons technology than the US, would nonetheless be able to benefit.

Thus the Russians demanded a loophole of ten tons while the Chinese wanted an allowance of up to several hundred tons. It should be self-evident to Indian critics of the CTBT that the nuclear and scientific establishments of Russia and China (which can safely be assumed to be far more advanced than that of India) went on board after the zero-yield proposal because they recognized that anything else would have constituted a debilitating flaw in the CTBT from which the US alone would significantly benefited. But a treaty allowing SCEs, computer simulation, and direct fusion R&D was not similarly flawed.

Unfortunately, as in the case of the Republican right opposing the CTBT in the US, the fact of Russian and Chinese acceptance of this Treaty despite these presumed flaws has only led to tortuous Indian efforts at rationalization. Among the more ridiculous of such attempts are claims that the US so badly wanted a CTBT that they were prepared to share knowledge and equipment, i.e. give away their technological edge in these areas, with Russia and China. Thus, whereas once it was argued the US so badly wanted this 'flawed' treaty because it alone could monopolize the benefits of its failings, later it was argued (often by the same critics) that the US was so keen on the Treaty that it was willing to give up its monopoly of benefit from its supposed flaws! Other equally desperate and far-fetched explanations claimed that the Chinese were primarily bent on sustaining the imbalance in their nuclear relationship with India. So long as this was on the anvil the Chinese were not too bothered about allowing the qualitative nuclear technological imbalance between themselves and the US to grow, calculating that they had enough of a minimum deterrent against America.[5]

Some such critics also claim that the Russian and Chinese insistence that the CTBT only enter into force if India, Pakistan and Israel join it, constituted a second line of defence against the Treaty ever coming into existence. This would thus prevent the US from monopolizing the benefit of its 'biased' operation. This is, of course, an extraordinary argument, for its logic, strictly speaking, must lead to the conclusion that should Indian and Pakistani accession to the CTBT become likely in the future (and thus its entry into force) then the Russians and/or the Chinese will resile from the Treaty! In fact, Russian, Chinese, and British insistence on Indian, Pakistani, and Israeli accession to the Treaty before it could come into force simply and obviously reflected their concern that the 'sacrifice' imposed by the CTBT upon them would not be shared by the nuclear capable threshold states if they stay out of the Treaty, and that given the strength of the anti-CTBT lobbies within their own countries, this was a way of stalling the Treaty's operation, though certainly not of guaranteeing that it would never come into operation. For such a period then, the CTBT would constitute a moral–legal norm of restraint and behaviour on its signatories, but not a punitive one.

The behaviour of the other NWSs, notably Russia and China, indicates by all reasonable and balanced inference, that the CTBT was perceived by them as a genuine restraining measure on all countries including the US. The whole controversy over the Entry Into Force clause (Article XIV) thoroughly undermines the argument that the CTBT was primarily (or even secondarily) a US-led 'trap' aimed at containing the threshold nuclear powers and especially India which unlike Pakistan and Israel is not deemed a formal or strategic ally by any section of the US foreign policy establishment.

Indian critics who have claimed as much have never bothered (understandably, since it so seriously weakens their case) to either state or emphasize the following facts. India formally announced its refusal to sign the CTBT in June 1996. A month earlier, in May, when it became increasingly clear that India was going to reject the Treaty, the US was the *first* and *only* NWS to publicly appeal to India that it would accept India's rejection but that it should not block the passage of the Treaty in the CD.[6]

Moreover, the US did not attempt to coerce India by insisting on its signature as a precondition for the Treaty to enter into force. The US initially opposed the stands of Russia, China and the UK in this regard and even sought to get these countries to withdraw this demand in the interests of enabling the Treaty to go through. Curious behaviour indeed for a country supposedly aiming to 'trap' India through the CTBT! While the US could have handled the UK, the Russians and Chinese were adamant, the Russians as much as, if not more so, than the Chinese. The US then accepted the Russian and Chinese condition because it was important to get these two countries on board the Treaty and because even if this condition was withdrawn, India would still have nothing to do with the CTBT. Incidentally, Russia, China, and the UK insisted on this clause only *after* India made its rejection of the Treaty clear in late June 1996.

4. The fourth line of criticism is that the NPT is the central pillar of the non-proliferation regime sought to be sustained by the NWSs (led by the US) and that the CTBT is another building block in the effort to perpetuate and strengthen this regime. The first part of this claim is fundamentally correct but the second part is not, being based on a gross misrepresentation. Before investigating the true nature of the relationship between the CTBT and the NPT, it is necessary to say something about the NPT, in particular about the utterly unbalanced and inaccurate way in which it has been criticized in India.

In the mid-sixties, India played a major role in pushing for the NPT and in seeking to draft it. The final draft represented the consensus view of the US, UK and USSR (China and France only joined the NPT in the early nineties) brought about by their own separate discussions, and as such had formulations that were not satisfactory to a number of NNWSs of the time including India. However, the standard criticism that the NPT is inherently discriminatory was not—to begin with, nor at the time of signing—the real problem for the NNWSs, including India. It subsequently became convenient for Indian critics to make this discriminatory character the centrepiece of its case against the NPT, but this represents a misleading simplification.

At the time the proposed NPT was being drawn up, there were only two choices. One was that the treaty should be completely non-discriminatory with equal obligations for all member signatories—in which case the NWSs would never accept it and would have to be excluded from the treaty. Alternatively, in order to get the NWSs in, the proposed treaty would have to have two classes of member-signatories with the principle of differential obligations enshrined within it. This was because, at least for some period, the NWSs would not renounce their possession of nuclear weapons while this would be the condition demanded of all other signatories. Sensibly enough at the time, most NNWSs felt there would be no purpose in having a treaty that excluded the NWSs. A basic bargain was thus established when the treaty was finalized in 1968 and came into force in 1970. In return for the NNWSs accepting the enshrinement of the principle of discriminatory obligations in the treaty, the NWSs would commit themselves to move eventually towards complete nuclear disarmament. It is this bargain that is embodied in Article VI of the NPT.

The failure of the NPT since its inception—and the principal reason why it has become over the years the central pillar of a limited non-proliferation regime (and thus deserves criticism and condemnation)—is not so much its inherently discriminatory character but the fact that the NWSs failed to live up to their end of the bargain by their perfidious disregard for the letter and spirit of Article VI in the NPT. Whatever disarmament has since taken place (after the end of the Cold War) is certainly not because of the NPT but despite it.

The subtle but important difference between highlighting the central weakness of the NPT as lying in the perfidious behaviour of the NWSs and not in its discriminatory provisions becomes acutely relevant when it comes to assessing why India did not sign the NPT. This was *not* primarily because it was discriminatory and India was initiating some sort of moral-political crusade against the 'pernicious' NPT. While the principle of discrimination between nuclear haves and have-nots was accepted within the Treaty, this did not mean that there had to be as much of an imbalance as there was in regard to other differential obligations between the NWSs and NNWSs in regard to technology transfers, IAEA safeguards, etc. This too, however, was not a sufficient explanation for the Indian refusal.

Like a number of potential nuclear powers close to the threshold of achieving weapons capabilities, e.g. Brazil and Argentina, India, too, did not want to foreclose this option at the time. Already, after the death of Nehru, there had been a subtle shift in official thinking from a posture of 'no bombs ever' to one of 'no bombs now' as well as the emergence of a new kind of official discourse in which it was now being simplistically claimed by New Delhi that continuing vertical proliferation would be the direct cause of further horizontal proliferation instead of acknowledging that the latter also had an independent dynamic.

Article II of the NPT prohibits NNWSs from manufacturing or acquiring all 'nuclear explosive devices', also including 'peaceful' ones, as in Pokharan-I. All this weighed heavily in shaping the Indian decision. The decisive factor in leading to the Indian rejection of the NPT was however almost certainly the Chinese refusal at the time to sign the NPT even as an NWS. Nonetheless, any balanced assessment of the NPT (rarely present in the Indian debate and certainly never during the hysteria of the 1994–6 anti-CTBT period) would have to point out that it was also initially directed against Japan, Germany, and Italy, the losers in the Second World War, each with the capability to produce nuclear weapons. This was something to be supported, not opposed. Later it became a way for the NWSs to maintain non-proliferation amongst the NNWSs and to rationalize in the longer term (after its unwarranted and condemnable permanent extension in April 1995) their own possession of nuclear weapons.

However, it is also necessary to note that the NPT still contains *the only international legal commitment that has ever been made by the five major NWSs to carry out complete nuclear disarmament.* Not surprisingly, many anti-nuclear activists feel that this does provide an important point of legal-moral international leverage, which, in the absence of anything else, can still be of some use in the struggle for global disarmament. They are thus not prepared to go so far as to call for the treaty's dismantlement or to declare its complete irrelevance, or to condemn it totally. This is not a view of the NPT shared by the authors of this article who reject it on much more comprehensive grounds than most Left critics in India.[7] This position, when coming from anti-nuclearists, should not be seen as simply dishonourable or 'supporting nuclear imperialism' or other such over-simplifications advanced by Indian critics with a much less balanced or sophisticated understanding of the NPT and the historico-political context surrounding it.

Let us come now to the question of the real nature of the relationship between the NPT and the CTBT. So strongly committed are the NNWSs to the idea of the CTBT that even during the effort to draft the NPT, countries like Mexico, Burma, and Ethiopia wanted a CTBT to be reached in conjunction with the NPT. Indeed, for the NNWSs which were considering signing the NPT, a CTBT was seen as the single most important expression of the NWSs' commitment to pursue disarmament as embodied in the terms (Article VI) of the treaty. The three NWSs preparing to be a party to the NPT—the USSR, US and UK—adamantly opposed this.

Subsequently, at every five-year review conference of the NPT, in 1975, 1980, 1985, 1990, the issue of the CTBT was repeatedly raised by NNWSs and consistently opposed by the NWSs. Indeed, in the view of many countries, the NPT would itself only survive in the long run if there were effective international safeguards, and a CTBT. Thus there has always been a historical connection between the CTBT and the NPT, but of a kind very different from that which has been made out by Indian opponents of the CTBT. When in 1995 the issue of the NPT's extension came up, it was inevitable that the issue of the CTBT would also surface. The NWSs only succeeded in getting what they wanted—the permanent and indefinite extension of the NPT—by resorting to very considerable behind-the-scenes arm-twisting of many NNWSs. This permanent extension was extremely unfortunate because it eliminated that degree of leverage the NNWSs would have continued to possess had they agreed only to the NPT's short-term and conditional extension before reviewing it again in the future.

Although the NWSs got what they wanted, they *had to pay a price.* That price was an explicit and time-bound commitment for the first time ever to completing a CTBT. In the 1995 review conference, new 'Principles and Objectives' were established whereby a CTBT had to be completed before the end of 1996. Far from the CTBT being another building block after the NPT in the NWSs' supposedly calculated attempt to promote their 'nuclear hegemony', it was a *concession* forced upon them by the NNWSs which the NWSs had to make because otherwise the NPT's permanent extension and its authority would have been gravely undermined.[8] As it is, a number of NNWSs had become deeply critical and frustrated by the NWSs' behaviour inside and outside the NPT, with some like Mexico even threatening to withdraw from the NPT.

The Indian government had no reason to explain to its public what actually went on in the 1995 review conference attended by numerous anti-nuclear groups, NGOs and individuals so that the pattern and manner of negotiations were public knowledge. However, the refusal of the Indian Left to even look seriously at what actually happened in those negotiations, let alone at the general history of the relationship between the NPT and the CTBT, is deeply disturbing.

5. The fifth line of criticism centres around certain claims regarding the iniquity of Article XIV on Entry Into Force in the CTBT; on the supposedly pressing danger to India of the 1999 review conference, thereby justifying the timing of the Indian nuclear tests; and on the putative dangers of excessive 'intrusiveness' embodied in the CTBT's verification regime. The first has already been covered in this text. Regarding the second, there is no way that the review conference, which is confined to seeing how it can accelerate the ratification process so as to bring the Treaty into force as early as possible, can penalize India or Pakistan if either refuses to accede to the Treaty by then. Not only do substantive decisions have to be taken by consensus but the decisions must be in accordance with international law. Such law cannot allow for punitive measures against any country not party to the Treaty in question. Regarding the third point, the basic parameters have also been laid out in the discussion on Articles II and IV in the CTBT. The Chemical Weapons Convention (CWC) served as an important precedent for the CTBT in regard to how the principle of balancing between concerns of 'national sovereignty' and 'effectiveness' of international monitoring could be handled. India endorsed the CWC procedure without serious reservations.

It only needs to be added here that Israel and China are the two most secretive nuclear regimes. There were hard negotiations before the specific provisions concerning verification procedures and authorization of OSIs were arrived at. The result was a compromise consensus, but one that was acceptable to Israel and China so that both have signed the CTBT precisely because the final outcome was deemed reasonable by them. On this terrain too, the Indian objections have been couched in vague terms carefully avoiding specifying which provisions are unacceptable and why, let alone why Indian concerns about the dangers of intrusive spying are sharper than Israel's and China's or why these countries are prepared to be 'taken in' by a supposedly flawed verification regime. Incidentally, inspections are confined to the site of explosions only. Is it not obvious that once again India was resorting to self-serving deception in order to justify its opposition to the CTBT?

Notes

1. An Indian staple is that subcriticals and computer simulation constitute fatal flaws. Although it has taken a principled stand against the May 1998 tests, the

left-wing Indian fortnightly magazine, *Frontline*, has long been carrying on a campaign against the CTBT based on precisely the kind of arguments that have been criticized here. However, in its 17 July 1998 issue it carried a rare technical article entitled 'Matters of Authority' by a 'Special Correspondent', of genuine authority and worth about these tests which also accurately portrayed the essential character of SCEs, reinforcing the argument presented here. Prior to this article, *Frontline* had not carried anything of comparable technical authority on CTBT-related matters by any Indian writer.

Periodically, Indian critics have cited, very selectively, the technical criticisms of subcriticals and computer simulation by Western experts known for their general anti-nuclear stance, such as C. E. Paine, Ted Taylor, and Frank N. von Hippel (a particular favourite) but without ever pointing out that these experts have, with various reservations, supported the CTBT; they indeed, have been advocates of it as well as of rapid nuclear disarmament. Such activities in the US also come under the umbrella of the government-sponsored 'science-based stockpile stewardship and management programme' (SBSS&MP) which, too, has been severely and correctly criticized as intending more than it formally says, i.e. to help in weapons designing and not just to check the 'safety and reliability' of the existing ageing stockpile.

The authoritative and regular reports of the Natural Resources Defense Council (NRDC)—a Washington-based NGO—have been of particular importance in this regard. What has not been pointed out is that the SBSS&MP has been attacked by the NRDC not just for promoting efforts at weapons designing despite the CTBT, but also for being financially wasteful and promising more than it can deliver. For an authoritative account of the post-CTBT subcriticals carried out by the US in 1997, emphasizing the importance of ensuring transparency, see Suzanne L. Jones and Frank N. von Hippel, 'Transparency Measures for Subcritical Experiments under the CTBT', *Science & Global Security*, Amesterdam, vol. 6, 1997, pp. 291–310.

2. See, in particular, the 'Nuclear Weapons Databook' series published by the NRDC, especially *Explosive Alliances: Nuclear Weapons Simulation Research at American Universities* by M.G. McKinzie, T.B. Cochran, C.E. Paine, Washington, January 1998; and *End Run: The U.S. Government's Plan for Designing Nuclear Weapons and Simulating Nuclear Explosions under the CTBT* by C.E. Paine and M.G. McKinzie, Washington, April 1998.
3. The SBSS&MP justifies the development of facilities such as the Dual Axis Radiographic Hydrodynamic Test Facility (DARHT) at Los Alamos and the National Ignition Facility (NIF) at Lawrence Livermore. The key area of dispute is over the possible relationship of NIF and Inertial Confinement Fusion (ICF) techniques to the development of fourth-generation fusion weapons. The theory behind ICF is that giant lasers (yet to be built at NIF) will produce concentrated pulses of ultraviolet light to explode a tiny capsule called a hohlraum, itself comprising a pellet of deuterium and tritium. Just before the hohlraum explodes, it is supposed to emit a powerful beam of X-rays that will compress and heat the

pellet to more than a 100 million degrees Celsius, causing the deuterium and tritium to fuse as in a nuclear bomb but on a very much smaller scale.

The chances of this ever working are, as pointed out, very dim. However, the NIF is obviously one of those 'big science toys' that keeps weapons labs and their scientists and administrators active and happy. Promising these facilities was one way of overriding, and buying off, much of the opposition from these quarters to the CTBT and getting them to reluctantly accept the latter. See J. Bairstow, 'Switch Off the National Ignition Facility', in *Laser Focus World,* Sept. 1997.

4. The *Nuclear Posture Review* pubished by the US government in September 1994, and the *Presidential Decision Directive-60* (which was the outcome of a seven-year review process and officially declared in November 1997) are key documents in this regard. Their purposes are to officially rationalize the retention of nuclear weapons for the future but in recognition of the changed post-Cold War context in which a new nuclear strategic doctrine would have to be established. New enemies have to be found, hence 'rogue states'; and a much smaller number of nuclear weapons are being asked to fulfil newer, yet to be fully worked out, strategic tasks. PDD-60 is the first such directive relating to nuclear weapons after Reagan's last directive in 1981 and reverses that earlier commitment to fighting 'winnable' nuclear wars. The US has now accepted that such weapons are for deterrence only.

   The point is not that the US will not continue to elaborate nuclear strategic perspectives (the 'pursuit of nuclear imperialism') but that these changes of perspective have been very substantially pushed upon it by the post-Cold War reality of a new momentum towards disarmament and restraint that the US finds difficult or undesirable to buck completely but can seek to dilute or outflank as best it can. The relationship of these particular planning perspectives to restraint measures like the CTBT must be clearly understood. They are not efforts at reorganizing strategic nuclear perspectives *through* the CTBT but *despite or apart from* the CTBT.

5. This extraordinary claim, along with a series of tendentious, politically mistaken, and technically ill-informed attacks on the CTBT, is to be found in S. Varadarajan, 'Testing the World Order' in *Seminar,* New Delhi, no. 468, August 1998. The Chinese have always been concerned about their imbalance with the US. Their strike force—of an estimated mere 13 to 20 long range land-based ballistic missiles capable of hitting the US mainland—has always been theoretically vulnerable to a US first strike, located as it is in only two north-eastern bases. So much for their possessing at the moment an 'adequate' or 'credible' second-strike capacity against the US.

   The Chinese are currently particularly disturbed by possible developments in regard to the US's Theatre High Altitude Area Defence (THAAD) preparations which in conjunction with right-wing efforts to undermine the 1972 ABM Treaty might eventually lead to that 'pale' or 'soft' version of a 'Star Wars' system of defensive missile interceptors, etc. that in its stronger version was once so seriously pressed for by President Reagan. Should this happen, and such a ballistic missile defence system be established, then even if the currently feeble Chinese capacity to hit the US in a second strike was somewhat strengthened, it could well be rendered worthless.

6. India did not have to block the passage of the CTBT in the CD after rejecting it. It claimed it had to do so after the emergence of the new Entry Into Force clause so as to put pressure on changing it. New Delhi was however fully aware that blocking the Treaty's passage in the CD would have no effect in this regard. It did so for two reasons; as a symbolic gesture of defiance; but more importantly, to deliberately weaken the stature of the CD in keeping with an evolving diplomacy. To be sure, if the Entry Into Force clause had not been changed in the way it was, the CTBT text would probably not have been blocked by India in the CD.

   However, this still does not excuse what India did. India even went to the extent of vetoing the passage of an otherwise consensus *factual* report of the CD on its activities over the previous two and a half years. This report would merely have concluded that there was a consensus that there was no consensus! The report's acceptance and formal passage would however have salvaged some credibility for the CD by recognizing and acknowledging its efforts and workings despite its failure to reach the desired final consensus.

7. The NPT has a built-in contradiction. To soften the stick of renunciation of nuclear weapons by NNWSs, it offers the carrot of technical support on the civilian side of nuclear energy production: thus helping to provide the wherewithal for building nuclear bombs. This contradiction has been taken advantage of by, at least, Iraq and North Korea. Moreover, the very fact that the NPT promotes the civilian nuclear energy programme can be condemned by those who believe that as an energy and power source this too is unacceptable for the innumerable problems, dilemmas, inefficiencies, and dangers it poses.

   The Indian Left does not oppose the production of nuclear energy for civilian purposes. It should take a second, critical look at the issue. The NPT is also a weaker disarmament measure than NWFZs because unlike the latter, it allows NWSs to station nuclear weapons on the territory of NNWSs.

8. Throughout the 1995–6 debate on the CTBT, it was rare indeed to find an Indian critic of the Treaty who was even prepared to acknowledge that it was a concession forced upon the NWSs to secure the NPT's permanent extension, let alone that without this concession the NPT regime could have unravelled. More recently, this has been more widely acknowledged but in such a manner as to try and rob the point of its legitimate impact. Some such critics (belonging to the Left) insisted wrongly for so long that the CTBT was effectively a building block after the NPT in the general architecture of the non-proliferation regime through which 'nuclear hegemony' was to be strengthened.

   In order to somehow preserve the basic thrust of this charge, they now have to carry out a desperate intellectual–political contortion by simultaneously acknowledging that the CTBT was indeed a *concession* (purely token, according to them, but still a concession) to ensure the consolidation, even the continued survival, of the NPT, and yet insisting that the CTBT is an integral part of the architecture of 'nuclear imperialism' centred on the NPT. It was as though the difference between a Treaty that is sought after by the NWSs (most notably the US) because it will *enhance* the NPT regime and one that is finally conceded in order to *preserve* this regime, is not a fundamental one, providing two *distinctive* judgements on the character of that Treaty itself. See S. Muralidharan, 'Unequal Bargain' in *Frontline,* Chennai, 3 July 1998; and S.M. Menon, 'The Nuclear Imperium and its Vassal Kings', in *Economic and Political Weekly*, Mumbai, 1–7 August 1998.

Nuclear Weapon Treaties

TREATY AND YEAR	SIGNATORIES	COMMENTS	STATUS
'Nuclear Umbrella'			
North Atlantic Treaty Organization (NATO), 1949	Original: Belgium, Canada, Denmark, France, UK, Iceland, Italy, Luxembourg, the Netherlands, Norway, Portugal, and the US. Added later: Greece, Turkey, Germany, Spain, Poland, Czech Republic, and Hungary.	US provides 'security' assurances including possible first use of nuclear weapons.	Expanding
Warsaw Pact, 1955	Albania, Bulgaria, Czechoslovakia, East Germany, Hungary, Poland, Romania, and USSR.	Soviet response to NATO.	Dissolved in July 1991.
Bilateral Security Agreements			
US–Japan Security Treaty, 1952	US, Japan	Similar 'security' assurances as NATO.	In force

(Contd...)

(Appendix 3 contd...)

Intermediate Nuclear Forces Treaty (INF) 1987	US, USSR	Bans intermediate range and shorter-range missiles	Entered into force June, 1988.
Strategic Arms Reduction Treaty (START-I), 1991, 1992	US, USSR	Limits number of heavy bombers, ICBMs and SLBMs; also limits ICBM and SLBM launchers and warheads.	In force. Most reductions in Russia due to removal of warheads in Belarus, Kazakhstan and Ukraine.
START-II, 1993	US, Russia	Limits US and Russian strategic arsenals to 3500 warheads tactical and spares not included)	US ratified 1996; Russia not yet ratified citing, in part, NATO expansion and US ballistic missile defense programmes. Implementation period extended to 2007.
Comprehensive Test Ban Treaty (CTBT), 1996	Signed by 150 countries, including five major nuclear powers and Israel. Ratified by 20 countries (as of 9/98), but not yet by US, Russia, or China.	Bans all nuclear explosions, including 'peaceful nuclear explosions.' Objections raised over allowances for computer-based and subcritical testing	India, Pakistan and North Korea are not yet . signatories. Their signatures and ratification are required for entry into force.
START-III (framework agreement only), 1997	US, Russia	If implemented, it would reduce strategic weapons to 2000–2500	In early stages of discussion. Stalled by US as Russia has not yet ratified START-II.

(Contd...)

Restrictive Treaties and Nuclear Weapon Free Zones (NWFZ)

TREATY AND YEAR	SIGNATORIES	COMMENTS	STATUS
Antarctic Treaty, 1959	12 signatories, including France, US, UK, USSR. China and India acceded in 1983.	Prohibits nuclear explosions and disposal of radioactive waste on Antarctica, subject to future agreement.	In force
Outer Space Treaty, 1967	Signed, ratified by US, UK, USSR France, India, 58 other countries. China acceded in 1983.	Prohibits nuclear or other weapons of mass destruction from being placed in space (including Earth orbit). Peaceful uses OK.	In force
Treaty of Tlatelolco (Treaty for the Prohibition of Nuclear Weapons in Latin America), 1967	Begun by Mexico, Brazil, Chile, Bolivia and Ecuador. 29 regional signatories, US party to Protocols I and II.	Prohibits testing, production, possession or acquisition of nuclear weapons in Latin Am. Protocol I: states with territorial interests keep Latin Am. nuclear weapon-free zone. Protocol II: NWS parties to treaty cannot 'use or threaten to use' nuclear weapons against parties to protocol.	First to exclude n. weapons from inhabited region of globe.
Seabed Treaty, 1971	Ratified by US, UK, USSR. China acceded in 1991. France did not sign. 66 states ratified.	Prohibits placement of n. weapons or weapons of mass destruction on seabed and ocean floor beyond a 12-mile coastal zone.	Entered into force in 1972. Multiple review conferences have upheld the treaty.

(Contd...)

Restraint on Use or Development

TREATY AND YEAR	SIGNATORIES	COMMENTS	STATUS
Limited Test Ban Treaty (LTBT), 1963	US, USSR, UK, France, China are not signatories.	Banned all but underground nuclear explosions.	Attempts to make this a comprehensive ban failed.
Nuclear Non-Proliferation Treaty (NPT), 1968	US, USSR (Russia), UK, France China are signatories. India, Pakistan, and Israel are not. Total signatories: 185 (as of January 1997).	Limits ownership of nuclear weapons to five states, requires progress on nuclear disarmament, promotes commercial nuclear technologies.	Extended indefinitely in 1995.
Strategic Arms Limitation Treaty-I (SALT-1), 1972	US, USSR	Limits nuclear weapons, but allowed for some arsenal expansion.	Ratified and implemented.
Anti-Ballistic Missile Treaty (ABM), 1972 Protocol, 1974	US, USSR	Bans development of more than one anti-ballistic missile system. Bans development of space-based systems.	US wants to loosen to allow certain space-based anti-missile systems.
Threshold Test Ban Treaty (TTBT), 1974	US, USSR	Limits nuclear explosions to 150 kilotons	
Underground Peaceful Nuclear Explosions Treaty (PNE), 1976	US, USSR	Governs nuclear explosions outside declared test sites. Limits yield to 100 kt. No use of data for weapons purposes.	Entered into force December 1990.
SALT-2, 1979	US, USSR	Increasing limits on ICBMs, SLBMs and heavy bombers. Other limits on MIRVs, bombers with long-range missiles, and MIRVed ICBMs.	Was to remain in effect through 1985. Not ratified.

(Contd...)

South Pacific Nuclear Free Zone (Treaty of Rarotonga), 1985	Protocols I, II, and III signed by US, UK, France in 1996.	Prohibits manufacture, possession or testing of nuclear devices, prohibits dumping of nuclear waste.	Entered into force in 1986. Russia (1986) and China (1987) acceded to protocols II and III.
Southeast Asia Nuclear Weapons Free Zone (Treaty of Bangkok), 1995	Brunei Darussalam, Cambodia, Indonesia, Laos, Malaysia, Myanmar, Philippines, Singapore Thailand and Vietnam.	Prohibits development, testing, stationing, transport, manufacture, possession of nuclear weapons. Also prohibits dumping n. waste. Allows nuclear energy ('peaceful use').	Entered into force in 1997. But US, UK, Russia, France China do not yet support it.
African Nuclear Weapons Free Zone (Treaty of Pelindaba), 1996	49 regional signatories. US, France, UK, Russia, China signatories to Protocols I and II. France to Protocol III.	Prohibits all nuclear weapons in NWFZ, and requires destruction of any existing nuclear devices. Calls for NWS to provide negative security assurances. Bans research into nuclear weapons	Not yet ratified.
Mutual Defence Treaties			
Australia, New Zealand, US (ANZUS), 1951	Australia, New Zealand, US.	Nuclear security guarantee to NZ, Australia.	Effective, 1952. NZ nuclear weapons free law enacted in 1984. US suspended security obligations to NZ in 1986.

NOTES : ICBM = Intercontinental Ballistic Missile; SLBM = Submarine Launced Ballistic Missile; MIRV = Multiple Independently-Targetable Re-entry Vehicle; NWS = Nuclear Weapon State

SOURCE : *Science for Democratic, Action,* Tacoma Park, Md, US, vol. 6, no. 4 & 7 no. 1 October 1998.

APPENDIX 4

International Resolutions

India, Pakistan at the Receiving End

A stunned world was quick to react to the Indian, and then the Pakistani, tests in strong terms. The element of surprise—and outrage—in the reaction was greater in the Indian case because there was no visible rationale for New Delhi's decision to cross the threshold. Pakistan was widely seen to be reacting to New Delhi, and goaded into testing by Indian ministers.

The reactions from the neighbourhood and the major powers all noted the adverse impact of India's and Pakistan's nuclearization on regional and global security, on their own international stature, and on their external relations. Perhaps the most important reaction was Resolution 1172 of the United Nations Security Council, reproduced below—the strongest such reprimand received by any South Asian state.

The individual reactions of the five NWSs varied in emphasis. China's was the most strongly worded. The P–5 positions were harmonized in their joint statement issued from Geneva on June 4, 1998, in response to 'the grave situation': 'The [P–5] ministers condemned these tests, expressed their deep concern about the danger to peace and stability in the region, and pledged to cooperate closely in urgent efforts to prevent a nuclear and missile race in the subcontinent, to bolster the non-proliferation regime, and to encourage reconciliation and peaceful resolution of differences between India and Pakistan.'

The statement called upon India and Pakistan to adhere to the CTBT 'immediately and unconditionally, thereby facilitating its early entry into force,' and to participate in FMCT negotiations. It reiterated the P–5 goal to be 'adherence by all countries, including India and Pakistan, to the Nuclear Non-Proliferation Treaty (NPT) as it stands, without any modification.'

For the short run, the P–5 foreign ministers affirmed 'their readiness to assist India and Pakistan, in a manner acceptable to both sides, in promoting reconciliation and cooperation. The Ministers pledged that they will actively encourage India and Pakistan to find mutually acceptable solutions, through direct dialogue, that address the root causes of the tension, including Kashmir . . . In that connection, the Ministers urged both parties to avoid threatening military movements, cross-border violations, or other provocative acts.'

The P–5 resolution fell short of calling for economic sanctions against India and Pakistan, but confirmed their members' 'policies to prevent the export of equipment, materials or technology that could in any way assist programmes in India or Pakistan for nuclear weapons or for ballistic missiles . . .'

The Neighbourhood Reacts

In the neighbourhood, Bangladesh had the strongest early reaction. The Sri Lankan foreign minister originally lent verbal support to the Indian tests, but a subsequent statement by the foreign ministry expressed 'concern' at the South Asian tests.

All other regional states expressed 'regret' or 'concern' in varying degrees. At the summit meeting of the South Asian Association for Regional Cooperation (SAARC) in Sri Lanka, in July 1998, the tests overshadowed all other issues. But given that its charter prohibits SAARC from raising contentious bilateral issues, the summit adopted 'recent developments' as the 'code name' for the nuclear tests, without specifically mentioning the explosions or naming the two states.

Beyond this, the tenor of the statements varied. Shaikh Hasina, Bangladesh Prime Minister, was the most explicit: 'the recent nuclear tests in our region is a development that we all wish could have been avoided.' Sri Lankan President Chandrika Kumaratunga said that the atmosphere of confidence in South Asia . . . 'could be affected by recent developments.' Similarly, Nepal Prime Minister G.P. Koirala said: 'recent events have given rise to the fear of an arms race in the region. Statesmanship and vision is required to counter this fear of a setback to the painstakingly created atmosphere of confidence in our region . . .'

The G–8 Position

The June 12, 1998 statement of the foreign ministers of the G–8 (comprising the seven most industrialized Western states, and Russia) was far more explicit.

It was issued by a 'special meeting' in London to consider the 'serious global challenge' posed by the nuclear tests. It condemned 'the nuclear tests carried out by India on 11 and 13 May 1998 and by Pakistan on 28 May and 30 May. 'These tests have affected both countries' relationships with each of us, worsened rather than improved their security environment, damaged their prospects of achieving their goals of sustainable economic development, and run contrary to global efforts towards nuclear non-proliferation and nuclear disarmament.'

The G–8 built on the P–5 statement and Resolution 1172, reminding India and Pakistan that 'the negative impact of these tests on the international standing and ambitions of both countries will be serious and lasting. They will also have a serious negative impact on investor confidence.'

Noting Indian and Pakistani statements that they 'wish to avoid' a nuclear and missile arms race, the statement said India and Pakistan 'should stop all further nuclear tests and adhere to the CTBT', they should 'refrain from weaponization or deployment of nuclear weapons and from the testing or deployment of missiles capable of delivering nuclear weapons', 'refrain from any further production of fissile material for nuclear weapons', and 'confirm their policies not to export equipment, materials and technology that could contribute to weapons of mass destruction or missiles capable of delivering them'.

The G–8 asked India and Pakistan to 'undertake to avoid threatening military movements, cross-border violations, including infiltrations or hot pursuit, or other provocative acts and statements; discourage terrorist activity and any support for it; implement fully the confidence- and security-building measures they have already agreed and develop further such measures'. They should 'resume without delay a direct dialogue that addresses the root causes of the tension, including Kashmir . . .'

The G–8 statement sternly said: 'We believe it is important that India and Pakistan are aware of the strength of the international community's views on their recent tests and on these other subjects. Several among us have, on a unilateral basis, taken specific actions to underscore our strong concerns. All countries should act as they see fit to demonstrate their displeasure and address their concerns to India and Pakistan. We do not wish to punish the peoples of India or Pakistan as a result of actions by their governments, and we will therefore not oppose loans by international financial institutions to the two countries to meet basic human needs. We agree, however, to work for a postponement in consideration of other loans in the World Bank and other international financial institutions to India and Pakistan, and to any other country that will conduct nuclear tests.'

ASEAN Regional Forum

Besides the G–8, the Indian and Pakistani tests came in for another multilateral reprimand, from the ASEAN Regional Forum, a grouping including the U.S., China, Japan, etc., of which India too is a partner. At its meeting at Manila on July 27, 1998, the ARF through its Chairman's statement said: 'The ministers recalled that as early as 1995 the ARF put emphasis on the importance of non-proliferation of nuclear weapons in promoting regional peace and security. They also noted that the ARF subsequently welcomed the overwhelming adoption of the CTBT ... In this connection, the ministers recalled the United Nations Security Council Resolution 1172.

'The ministers, therefore, expressed grave concern over and strongly deplored the recent nuclear tests in South Asia, which exacerbated tension in the region and raised the spectre of a nuclear arms race. They called for the total cessation of such testing and urged the countries concerned to sign the Treaty on the Non-Proliferation of Nuclear Weapons and the Comprehensive Nuclear Test Ban Treaty without delay, conditions, or reservations. They asked the countries concerned to refrain from undertaking weaponisation or deploying missiles to deliver nuclear weapons, and to prevent any transfer of nuclear weapon-related materials, technology and equipment to third countries. In the interest of peace and security in the region, the ministers called on the countries concerned to resolve their their dispute and security concerns through peaceful dialogue.'

India had put in considerable high-powered lobbying effort prior to the ARF meeting to change the original wording from 'condemn' to 'strongly deplore' and to replace an explicit reference to 'the tests by India and Pakistan' to 'nuclear tests in South Asia'.

The NAM Resolution

A little later, in early September 1998, India and Pakistan received yet another rebuke, from the Non-Aligned Movement, of which India was a founder, and of which it considered itself a 'natural' leader. At the opening ceremony of the NAM summit at Durban, President Nelson Mandela commented on the South Asian nuclear tests, linking them with Kashmir. He said all NAM states 'remained concerned over the problem in Jammu and Kashmir' and should be 'willing to lend all our strength for the peaceful solution of this problem.' India protested loudly, its anger all the greater because of New Delhi's earlier close relationship with Mandela. It claimed that Mandela's deputy offered an apology to India the next day. This claim was denied by South Africa.

In the summit resolution itself, India succeeded in altering the original paragraph (number 109) on disarmament. The original read: 'The recent nuclear tests conducted in the subcontinent of South Asia have inevitably added to the complexities of issues relating to non-proliferation and nuclear disarmament. [The NAM countries] further expressed their deep concern at the re-emergence of the nuclear arms race and called for all states which have the capability to produce nuclear weapons to refrain from weaponising their capability and to desist from placing them on delivery systems.'

In the final version,

'[The NAM countries] noted the complexities arising from nuclear tests in South Asia, which underlined the need to work even harder to achieve their disarmament objectives, including elimination of nuclear weapons. They considered positively the commitment by parties concerned in the region to exercise restraint, which contributes to regional security, to discontinue nuclear tests and not to transfer nuclear weapons-related material, equipment and technology.' However, the resolution also further 'stressed the significance of universal adherence to the CTBT, including by all nuclear weapon states, and the commencement of negotiations in the Conference on Disarmament on fissile materials . . .'

Security Council Resolution 1172

Following is the verbatim text of Security Council Resolution 1172, at its 3890th meeting on June 6, 1998, deploring the nuclear tests.

The Security Council,

Reaffirming the statements of its President of 14 May 1998 (S/PRST/1998/12) and of 29 May 1998 (S/PRST/1998/17),

Reiterating the statement of its president of 31 January 1992 (S/23500), which stated, inter alia, that the proliferation of all weapons of mass destruction constitutes a threat to international peace and security,

Gravely concerned at the challenge that the nuclear tests conducted by India and then by Pakistan constitute to international efforts aimed at strengthening the global regime of non-proliferation of nuclear weapons, and also gravely concerned at the danger to peace and stability in the region,

Deeply concerned at the risk of a nuclear arms race in South Asia, and determined to prevent such a race,

Reaffirming the crucial importance of the Treaty on the Non-Proliferation of Nuclear Weapons and the Comprehensive Nuclear Test Ban Treaty for global efforts towards nuclear non-proliferation and nuclear disarmament,

Recalling the Principles and Objectives for Nuclear Non-Proliferation and Disarmament adopted by the 1995 Review and Extension Conference of the Parties to the Treaty on the Non-Proliferation of Nuclear Weapons, and the successful outcome of that Conference,

Affirming the need to continue to move with determination towards the full realization and effective implementation of all the provisions of the Treaty on the Non-Proliferation of Nuclear Weapons, and welcoming the determination of the five nuclear-weapon states to fulfil their commitments relating to nuclear disarmament under Article VI of that Treaty,

Mindful of its primary responsibility under the Charter of the United Nations for the maintenance of international peace and security,

1. *Condemns* the nuclear tests conducted by India on 11 and 13 May 1998 and by Pakistan on 28 May 1998;
2. *Endorses* the Joint Communique issued by the Foreign Ministers of China, France, the Russian Federation, the United Kingdom of Great Britain and Northern Ireland and the United States of America at their meeting in Geneva on 4 June 1998 (S/1998/473);
3. *Demands* that India and Pakistan refrain from further nuclear tests and in this context calls upon all states not to carry out any nuclear weapon test explosion or any other nuclear explosion in accordance with the provisions of the Comprehensive Nuclear Test Ban Treaty.
4. *Urges* India and Pakistan to exercise maximum restraint and to avoid threatening military movements, cross-border violations, or other provocations in order to prevent an aggravation of the situation;
5. *Urges* India and Pakistan to resume the dialogue between them on all outstanding issues, particularly on all matters pertaining to peace and security, in order to remove the tensions between them, and encourages them to find mutually acceptable solutions that address the root causes of those tensions, including Kashmir;
6. *Welcomes* the efforts of the Secretary-General to encourage India and Pakistan to enter into dialogue;
7. *Calls* upon India and Pakistan immediately to stop their nuclear weapon development programmes, to refrain from weaponization or from the deployment of nuclear weapons, to cease development of ballistic missiles capable of delivering nuclear weapons, to confirm their policies not to export equipment, materials or technology that could contribute to weapons of mass destruction or missiles capable of delivering them and to undertake appropriate commitments in that regard;
8. *Encourages* all states to prevent the export of equipment, materials or technology that could in any way assist programmes in India or Pakistan

for nuclear weapons or for ballistic missiles capable of delivering such weapons, and welcomes national policies adopted and declared in this respect;

9. *Expresses* its grave concern at the negative effect of the nuclear tests conducted by India and Pakistan on peace and stability in South Asia and beyond;
10. *Reaffirms* its full commitment to and the crucial importance of the Treaty on the Non-Proliferation of Nuclear Weapons and the Comprehensive Nuclear Test Ban Treaty as the cornerstones of the international regime on the non-proliferation of nuclear weapons and as essential foundations for the pursuit of nuclear disarmament;
11. *Expresses* its firm conviction that the international regime on the non-proliferation of nuclear weapons should be maintained and consolidated and recalls that in accordance with the Treaty on the Non-Proliferation of Nuclear Weapons India or Pakistan cannot have the status of a nuclear-weapon state;
12. *Recognizes* that the tests conducted by India and Pakistan constitute a serious threat to global efforts towards nuclear non-proliferation and disarmament;
13. *Urges* India and Pakistan, and all other states that have not yet done so, to become Parties to the Treaty on the Non-Proliferation of Nuclear Weapons and to the agreed mandate, in negotiations at the Conference on Disarmament in Geneva on a treaty banning the production of fissile material for nuclear weapons or other nuclear explosive devices, with a view to reaching early agreement;
14. *Urges* India and Pakistan to participate, in a positive spirit and on the basis of the agreed mandate, in negotiations at the Conference on Disarmament in Geneva on a treaty banning the production of fissile material for nuclear weapons or other nuclear explosive devices, with a view to reaching early agreement;
15. *Requests* the Secretary-General to report urgently to the Council on the steps taken by India and Pakistan to implement the present resolution;
16. *Expresses* its readiness to consider further how best to ensure the implementation of the present resolution;
17. *Decides* to remain actively seized of the matter.

Select Bibliography

1. Books, Reports, Monographs, etc.

Abraham, Itty, *The Making of the Indian Atomic Bomb,* Zed Books, London, and Orient Longman, Delhi, 1998.

Acronym Institute, The, *Various Acronym Reports,* London.

Anand, Y.P., *What Mahatma Gandhi Said about the Atom Bomb,* National Gandhi Museum, New Delhi, 1998.

Anderson, Robert, *Building Scientific Institutions in India: Bhabha and Saha,* Center for Developing Area Studies, Montreal, 1975.

Andrew, Lichterman and Cabasso, Jacqueline, *A Faustian Bargain: Why Stockpile Stewardship is Fundamentally Incompatible with the Process of Nuclear Disarmament,* Western States Legal Foundation, California, 1998.

Arif, K.M., (Lt Gen.), *Working with Zia: Power Politics 1977–88,* Oxford University Press, Karachi, 1995.

Arkin, W.M., Norris, R.S., Handler, J., *Taking Stock: Worldwide Nuclear Deployments, 1998,* Natural Resources Defense Council, Washington, March 1998.

Babbage, R. and Gordon, G. (eds), *India's Strategic Future: Regional, State or Global Power,* Macmillan, London, 1991.

Bajpai, Kanti and Chari, P.R. et al., *Brasstacks and Beyond: Perception and Management of Crisis in South Asia,* Manohar, Delhi, 1995.

Ball, Desmond, *Can Nuclear War be Controlled?* Adelphi Paper 169, IISS, London, 1981.

Bandopadhya, J., *The Making of India's Foreign Policy,* Allied Publications, Bombay, 1970.

Barnet, R.J. and Falk, R.A. (eds), *Security in Disarmament,* Princeton University Press, Princeton, N.J., 1965.

Bennett, John, *Nuclear Weapons and the Conflict of Conscience,* Charles Scribner's Son, New York, 1962.

Bernal, J.D., *Social Functions of Science,* London, 1939.

Betts, Richard K., *Nuclear Blackmail and Nuclear Balance,* Brookings, Washington, D.C., 1987.

Bhabha, Homi J., 'The Role of Atomic Power in India and Its Immediate Possibilities', Paper presented at the First International Conference on the Peaceful Uses of Atomic Energy, Geneva, August 1955; Reprinted in Jain, J.P., *Nuclear India*, vol. 2.

Bird, Kai, and Lifschultz, Lawrence, *Hiroshima's Shadow,* The Pamphletteer's Press, Connecticut, 1998.

Blair, Bruce G., *The Logic of Accidental Nuclear War,* Brookings, Washington, D.C., 1993.

Blight, James G. and Welch, David A., *On the Brink: Americans and Soviets Reexamine the Cuban Missile Crisis,* Hill and Wang, New York, 1989.

Bose, D.M. and et al. (eds), *A Concise History of Science in India,* New Delhi, Indian National Science Academy, 1971.

Bottome, Edger, *The Balance of Terror,* Beacon Press, Boston, 1971.

Bracken, Paul, *The Command and Control of Nuclear Forces,* Yale University Press, New Haven, CT & London, 1983.

Brodie, Bernard, *Strategy in the Missile Age,* Princeton University Press, Princeton, N.J., 1965.

———(ed.), *The Absolute Weapon: Atomic Power and World Order,* Harcourt Brace, New York, 1946.

Buchan, A. (ed.), *A World of Nuclear Powers,* Prentice Hall, New York, 1966.

Buchanan, A., *Marx and Justice,* London, 1982.

Bull, H., *The Control of the Arms Race: Disarmament and Arms Control in the Missile Age,* Praeger, New York, 1961.

——— *The Anarchical Society: A Study on the Order of World Politics,* Macmillan, London, 1977.

Bundy, McGeorge, *Danger and Survival: Choices about the Bomb in the First Fifty Years,* Random House, New York, 1988.

———(ed.), 'The Unimpressive Record of Atomic Diplomacy', *The Nuclear Crisis Reader,* Vantage, pp. 42–54 in Gwyn Prins, New York, 1984.

Buzan, B., *People, States and Fear: The National Security Problem in International Relations,* Wheatsheaf Books, Brighton, UK, 1983.

Calder, Nigel, *Nuclear Nightmanes*, Penguin, Harmondsworth, 1981.

Carnegie Task Force on Non-Proliferation and South Asian Security, *Nuclear Weapons and South Asian Security,* Carnegie Endowment for International Peace, Washington, D.C., 1988.

Carr, E.H., *The Twenty Year's Crisis,* Harper Torchbook edition, New York, 1964.

Cohen, M., Nagel, T. and Scanlon, T. (eds), *Marx, Justice and History,* Princeton, 1980.

'Common Security', *Report of the Palme Commission,* 1982.

Cortright, David, and Mattoo, Amitabh (eds), *India and the Bomb: Public Opinion and Nuclear Options,* Notre Dame Press, Notre Dame, Indiana, 1996.

Cousins, Norman, *In Place of Folly,* Washington Square Press, New York, 1962.

Department of Atomic Energy, Government of India, *Annual Reports,* various years.

———, *Performance Budget*, various years, DAE, Government of India.

Disarmament: India's Initiatives, Ministry of External Affairs, Government of India, New Delhi, 1988.

Elliot, David, et al., *The Politics of Nuclear Power,* PPU Press, London, 1978.

Ellsberg, Daniel, *The Crude Analysis of Deterrence Choices,* The Rand Corporation, Santa Monica, CA, 1960.

Enloe, C., *Bananas Bases and Beaches: Making Feminist Sense of International Relations,* Pandora, London, 1989.

Exterminism and the Cold War, New Left Review, (ed.), Verso, London, 1982.

Feaver, Douglas Peter, *Guarding the Guardians: Civilian Control of Nuclear Weapons in the United States,* Cornell University Press, Ithaca, 1992.

Fetter, S., *Toward a Comprehensive Test Ban,* Ballinger, Cambridge Mass., 1988.

Fischer, D.A.V., *Stopping the Spread of Nuclear Weapons,* Routledge, London and New York, 1992.

Fursenko, A. and Naftali, T., *One Hell of a Gamble: Krushchev, Castro, and Kennedy 1958–64,* W.W. Norton, 1997.

Geras, N., *Discourses of Extremity,* London, 1990.

Giddens, A., *The Nation-State and Violence,* Polity Press, Cambridge, 1985.

Gilbert, A., *Democratic Individuality,* Cambridge, 1990.

Goldblat, J. and Cox, D., SIPRI, *Nuclear Weapon Tests: Prohibition or Limitation?* Oxford University Press, Oxford, 1988.

Goldschmidt, Bertrand, *The Atomic Complex,* American Nuclear Society, La Grange Park, Illinois, 1982.

———, *Atomic Rivals,* Rutgers University Press, New Brunswick, 1990.

Gopal, S., *Jawaharlal Nehru: A Biography, Volume Two: 1947–1956,* Oxford University Press, Delhi, 1979.

Gowing, Margaret, *Independence and Deterrence: Britain and Atomic Energy, 1945–1952, Vol. 1, 'Policy Making',* St. Martin's Press, New York, [1964] 1974.

Gregory, Shaun, *The Hidden Cost of Deterrence: Nuclear Weapons Accidents,* Brassey's, London, 1990.

Halliday, Fred, *The Making of the Second Cold War,* Verso, London, 1983.

———, *Rethinking International Relations,* Macmillan, London, 1994.

Halperin, Morton H., *Nuclear Fallacy: Dispelling the Myth of Nuclear Strategy,* Ballinger, Cambridge, MA, 1987.

Hart, David, *Nuclear Power in India: A Comparative Analysis,* George Allen and Unwin, London, 1983.

Healey, Denis, *The Race against the H-Bomb,* Fabian Tract, London, 1960.

Hersey, John, *Hiroshima,* Vintage [1946], New York, 1985.

Holloway, David, *Stalin and the Bomb: The Soviet Union and Atomic Energy, 1939–1956,* Yale University Press, New Haven, 1994.

Honderich, Ted, *Violence for Equality,* Penguin Books, Harmondsworth, 1980.

Jain, J.P. (ed.), *Nuclear India,* vols. 1–2, Radiant Publishers, New Delhi, 1974.

Jaipal, Rikhi, *Nuclear Arms and the Human Race,* Allied Publishers, New Delhi, 1986.

Jervis, Robert, *The Illogic of American Nuclear Strategy,* Cornell University Press, Ithaca, N.Y., 1984.

———, *The Meaning of the Nuclear Revolution: Statecraft and the Prospect of Armageddon,* Cornell University Press, Ithaca, N.Y., 1989.

Jungk, Robert, *Brighter than a Thousand Suns,* Harcourt, Brace, Jovanovitch, New York, 1956.

Kaku, M., and Axelrod, D., *To Win a Nuclear War,* Zed Books, London, 1987.

Kaplan, Fred, *The Wizards of Armageddon,* Simon & Schuster, New York, 1983.

Kennan, George, *The Nuclear Delusion,* Pantheon, New York, 1982.

Keohane, R.O. (ed.), *International Institutions and State Power: Essays in International Relations Theory,* Westview Press, Boulder, Colo., 1989, pp. 132–214.

Klein, Bradley, *Strategic Studies and World Order: The Global Politics of Deterrence,* Cambridge University Press, Cambridge, 1994.

Krass, Allan, 'The Evolution of Military Technology and Deterrence Strategy', in *World Armaments & Disarmament: SIPRI Yearbook 1981,* Taylor & Francis, London, 1981.

Krepon, Michael and Faruqee, Mishi (eds), *Conflict Prevention and Confidence Building Measures in South Asia: The 1990 Crisis,* The Henry L. Stimson Center, Washington, D.C., Occasional Paper No. 17, April 1994.

Leonard, S., *The New Nuclear Nations,* Vintage Books, New York, 1985.

Lewis, John, and Xue Litai, *China and the Bomb,* Stanford University Press, Stanford, CA, 1988.

Lifton, Robert Jay, and Falk, Richard, *Indefensible Weapons,* Basic Books Inc., New York, 1982.

Living with Nuclear Weapons, Harvard Nuclear Study Group, Harvard University Press, Cambridge, Massachusetts, 1983.

Lukes, S., *Marxism and Morality,* Oxford, 1985.

Mandelbaum, Michael, *The Nuclear Revolution,* Cambridge University Press, Cambridge, 1981.

Mann, M., *The Sources of Social Power,* Vol. II, Cambridge University Press, Cambridge, 1983.

Maxwell, Neville, *India's China War,* Penguin Books, Harmondsworth, Middlesex, 1972.

May, E.R. and Zelikow, P.D., *The Kennedy Tapes,* Belknap Press of Harvard University, Cambridge, Massachusetts, 1997.

McKinzie, M.G., Cochran, T.B. and Paine, C.E., *Explosive Alliances: Nuclear Weapons Simulation Research at American Universities,* Washington, January 1998.

McLellan, D. and Sayers, S. (eds), *Socialism and Morality,* London, 1990.

Medvedev, Zhores Aleksandrovich, *Nuclear Disaster in the Urals,* (Translated by George Saunders), Vintage Books, New York, 1980.

Menon, M.G.K., *Homi Jehangir Bhabha, 1909–1966,* Royal Institution of Great Britain, London, 1967.

Meyer, Stephen M., *The Dynamics of Nuclear Proliferation,* University of Chicago Press, Chicago, 1984.

Miller, R.W., *Analysing Marx,* Princeton, 1984.

Montgomery, B., *The Ethics of War,* Collins, London, 1968.

Nader, Ralph and Abbots, John, *The Menace of Atomic Energy,* Norton, New York, 1977.

Nadis, Steven J., *Nuclear Power: Time for Reassessment,* Union of Concerned Scientists, Cambridge, Mass., 1979.

Naim, S. Rashid and Aadhi Raat Ke Baad, 'After Midnight', in Stephen Philip Cohen (ed.), *Nuclear Proliferation in South Asia Prospects for Arms Control,* Westview Press, Boulder, CO, 1991.

Nair, Vijai K. (Brigadier), *Nuclear India,* Lancer International, New Delhi, 1992.

Non-Proliferation: The Why and Wherefore, SIPRI, London, Taylor & Francis, 1985.

Nuclear Futures: The Role of Nuclear Weapons in Security Policy, British American Security Information Council, London, Washington, D.C., 1996.

Nuclear Non-Proliferation and Global Order, Oxford, SIPRI/Oxford University Press, 1994.

Nuclear Weapons Databook, Natural Resources Defense Council, Washington, D.C., various volumes publishers.

Out of Nuclear Darkness: The Indian Case for Disarmament, MIND (Movement in India for Nuclear Disarmament), New Delhi, 1998.

Paine, Christopher E. and McKinzie, Matthew G., *Ebd Run: The U.S. Government's Plan for Designing Nuclear Weapons and Simulating Nuclear Explosions under the Comprehensive Test Ban Treaty,* Natural Resources Defense Council, Inc., New York, 1997.

Peffer, R.G., *Marxism, Morality and Social Justice,* Princeton, 1990.

Penny, [Lord] 'Homi Jehangir Bhabha, 1909–1966', *Biographical Memoirs of Fellows of the Royal Society,* vol. 13, The Royal Society, London, 1967.

Perrow, Charles, *Normal Accidents: Living With High-Risk Technologies,* Basic Books, New York, 1984.

Potter, W.C. (ed.), *International Nuclear Trade and Nonproliferation: The Challenge of the Emerging Suppliers,* Lexington Books, Lexington, Mass., 1990.

Radioactive Heaven and Earth, International Physicians for Prevention of Nuclear War, Zed Books, London, 1991.

Rajan, M.S., *Non-Alignment: India and the Future,* University of Mysore Press, Mysore, 1970.

Ramana, M.V., *Bombing Bombay: Effects of Nuclear Weapons and a Case Study of a Hypothetical Explosion,* IPPNW Global Health Watch, Cambridge, Massachusetts, Report No. 3, 1999.

Ramanna, Raja, *Years of Pilgrimage,* Viking, Delhi, 1991.

Rhodes, R., *The Making of the Atomic Bomb,* Simon & Schuster, London, 1986.

Rosenberg, J., *The Empire of Civil Society: A Critique of the Realist Theory of International Relations,* Verso, London, 1994.

Rotblat, J. and Goldanskii, V.I. (eds), *Global Problems and Common Security: Annals of Pugwash 1988,* Springer-Verlag, 1989.

Rotblat, J., Steinberger, J., Udgaonkar, B. and Blackaby, F. (eds), *A Nuclear-Weapon-Free World: Desirable? Feasible?,* Westview Press, (Pugwash), San Francisco, Oxford, 1993.

Russell, Bertrand, *Has Man a Future?* Unwin Bros., London, 1961.

Sagan, Scott D., and Waltz, Kenneth N., *The Spread of Nuclear Weapons: A Debate,* W.W. Norton & Co., New York, 1995.

Scheer, Robert, *With Enough Shovels,* Random House, New York, 1982.

Schell, Jonathan, *The Fate of Earth,* Knopf, New York, 1982.

———, *The Gift of Time,* Metropolitan Books, Henry Holt and Company Inc, New York, 1998.

Schwartz, Stephen, I. (ed.), *Atomic Audit: The Costs and Consequences of US Nuclear Weapons since 1940,* Brookings Institution, New York, 1998.

Scott, R.T., (ed.), *The Race for Security: Arms and Arms Control in the Reagan Years,* Lexington Books, Lexington, Mass., 1987.

Seaborg, G.T., *Kennedy, Khrushchev, and the Test Ban,* University of California Press, Berkeley, 1981.

Selected Works of Jawaharlal Nehru, Second Series, Vols. 1–2, 4–5, Jawaharlal Nehru Memorial Fund, Delhi.

Sen Gupta, Bhabani, *Nuclear Weapons: Policy Options for India,* Center for Policy Research and Sage Publications, New Delhi, 1983.

Seshagiri, N., *The Bomb: Fallout of India's Nuclear Explosion,* Vikas, Delhi, 1975.

Sethna, H.N., *Atomic Energy,* (25 Years of Independence: India Series), Publications Division, New Delhi, 1972.

Sharma, Dhirendra, *The Indian Atom: Power and Proliferation,* Philosophy and Social Action, New Delhi, 1986.

Sidhu, W.P.S., Cloughley, Brian, et al,. *Nuclear Risk—Reduction Measures in Southern Asia,* The Henry L. Stimson Center, Washington, Report No. 26, November 1998.

Sinha, P.B. and Subramanian R.R., *Nuclear Pakistan,* Vision Books, New Delhi, 1980, pp. 35, 121.

SIPRI Yearbook, Stockholm International Peace Research Institute, various years, Oxford University Press, New York.

Sivard, Ruth Leger, *World Military and Social Expenditures 1996,* World Priorities, Washington, D.C., 1996.

Spector, L.S., *The Undeclared Bomb,* Ballinger Publishing Co., Cambridge, Mass, 1988.

Sreekantan, B.V., Singh, Virendra, and Udgaonkar, B.M. (eds), *Homi Bhaba: Collected Scientific Papers,* Tata Institute of Fundamental Research, Bombay, 1986.

'Status of Nuclear Weapons in International Law: Request for Advisory Opinion of the International Court of Justice', Mimeo., Ministry of External Affairs, Government of India, New Delhi, 1995.

Strange, S., *The Retreat of the State: The Diffusion of Power in the World Economy,* Cambridge University Press, Cambridge, 1996.

Stutzle, W., Jasani, B. and Cowen, R., *The ABM Treaty: To Defend or Not To Defend,* SIPRI Publications, Oxford University Press, Oxford, 1987.

Thomas, Raju, *Indian Security Policy,* Princeton University Press, Princeton, 1988.

Thompson, E.P., *Protest and Survive,* Monthly Review Press, New York, 1981.

———, *Beyond the Cold War,* Merlin Press, London, 1982.

Thompson, G., 'Verifying a Halt to the Nuclear Arms Race', in Barnaby, F. (ed.) *A Handbook of Verification Procedures,* Macmillan, Basingstoke and London, 1990, pp. 264–309.

United Nations, *Comprehensive Study on Nuclear Weapons,* UN General Assembly document A/33/392, UN, New York, 1980.

Vanaik, Achin, *The Painful Transition: Bourgeois Democracy in India,* Verso, London, 1990.

———, *India in a Changing World,* Orient Longman, New Delhi, 1995.

Venkateshwaran, A.L., *Defence Organisation in India,* Publications Division, Government of India, New Delhi, 1967.

Walker, R.B.J., *Inside/Outside: International Relations as Political Theory,* Cambridge University Press, Cambridge, 1993.

Walker, William and Loennorth, Mans, *Nuclear Power Struggles,* George Allen & Unwin, London, 1983.

Wallerstein, I., *Geopolitics and Geoculture: Essays in a Changing World System,* Cambridge University Press, Cambridge, 1991.

Waltz, Kenneth N., *Man, State and War,* New York, 1959.

———, *Theory of International Politics,* Addison Wesley, Reading, Mass., 1979.

Walzer, Michael, *Just and Unjust Wars,* Basic Books, New York, 1977.

Weart, Spencer R., *Nuclear Fear: A History of Images,* Harvard University Press, Cambridge Mass., 1988.

Weinbaum, M.G., and Kumar, Chetan (eds), *South Asia Approaches the Millenium: Reexamining National Security,* Westview, Boulder, CO, 1995.

Weissman, S.R. and Krosney, H., *The Islamic Bomb,* Times Books, New York, 1981.

Wight, G., and Porter, B. (eds), *International Theory: The Three Traditions,* Leicester University Press, Leicester, 1991.

Wittner, L., *One World or None: The Struggle Against the Bomb,* Vols I & II. Stanford University Press, Stanford, USA, 1993 and 1997.

World Council of Churches, *Before It's Too Late,* WCC Publication, Geneva, 1983.

World Health Organisation, *Effects of Nuclear War on Health,* W.H.O. Publication, Geneva, 1984.

York, Herbet K., *Race to Oblivion,* Simon & Schuster, New York, 1970.

Zukerman, Solly, *Scientist and War,* Harper and Row, New York, 1967.

2. Journal Articles

Ahmad, Aqueil and Sen, Falguni, 'Scientists and Science Policy Formulation', Indian Scientists view of Indian Nuclear Explosion, *Journal of Scientific and Industrial Research,* vol. 35, August 1976, pp. 497–501.

Anderson, Robert, 'Growing Science in India—2: Homi J. Bhabha', *Science Today,* Bombay, November 1976.

Bidwai, Praful, 'Lid Off Atomic Energy', *Business India,* Bombay, 4-17 September 1978.

Gupta, Vipin, and Pabian, Frank, 'Investigating the Allegations of Indian Nuclear Test Preparations in the Rajasthan Desert', *Science & Global Security,* Amsterdam, vol. 6, 1996.

Jayaraman, K.S., 'The Leak that Leaked to the Press', *Science Today,* May 1980, p. 17.

Jones, Suzanne L. and N. von Hippel, Frank, 'Transparency Measures for Subcritical Experiments under the CTBT', *Science & Global Security,* Amsterdam, vol. 6, 1997.

Kaushik, B.M., 'India's Nuclear Dilemma', *Strategic Analysis,* 1 (8), November 1977, pp. 1–4.

Marwah, Onkar, 'India's Nuclear and Space Programme: Intent and Policy', *International Security,* vol. II, no. 2, Fall 1977, pp. 96–121.

Mueller, John, 'The Bomb's Pretense as Peacemaker', *Wall Street Journal,* 4 June 1985.

Official Text, US Information Service, New Delhi, 25 January 1999 Nielsen, K. and Patten, S.C. (eds), 'Marx and Morality', vol. III of the *Canadian Journal of Philosophy,* 1981.

Rosenberg, David A., 'The Origins of Overkill: Nuclear Weapons and American Strategy, 1945–1960', *International Security,* vol. 7, no. 4 (Spring 1983), pp. 3–71.

Sagan, Scott, 'Why do States Build Nuclear Weapons: Three Models in Search of a Bomb', *International Security,* vol. 21, no. 6 (Winter 1996/97).

Sankaran, M.P., 'Brain Drain—Do We Need More Scientists or more Science?' (Ref. to training programme at BARC) *Science Today,* April 1980, p. 9.

Sharma, Dhirendra, 'India's Nuclear Options', *Indian Express,* 14 September 1979.

———, 'India's Energy: Policy Omissions & Commissions', *Philosophy & Social Action,* VII (1), January–March 1981.

———, 'Time to Move Away from Nuclear Power', *The Times of India,* 21–22 August 1980.

Strange, Susan, 'The Future of the American "Empire"', *Journal of International Affairs,* vol. 42, no. 1, pp. 1–77, 1990.

Sundarji, K. (General), 'Nuclear Deterrence: Doctrine for India, part 1', *Trishul,* vol. 5, no. 2 (December), Defence Services Staff College, Wellington, India, 1992c.

———, 'Nuclear Deterrence: Doctrine for India, part 2', *Trishul,* vol. 6, No. 3 (July), Defence Services Staff College, Wellington, India, 1993.

———, 'Nuclear Weapons in Third World Context', *Combat Papers,* No. 2 (August), College of Combat, Mhow, India, 1981.

'The Architects of Nuclear India', Special Issue of *Nuclear India,* vol. 26, October 1989.

Tomer, Ravindra, 'The Indian Nuclear Programme: Myth and Mirages,' *Asian Survey,* vol. xx, no. 5 (May 1980), pp. 517–31.

Trust and Verify, Verification Research, Training and Information Centre, London, Issue 84, April 1999.

Waltz, Kenneth N., 'Nuclear Myths and Political Realities', *American Political Science Review,* vol. 84, no. 3 (September 1990), pp. 731–45.

3. Special Documents, Unpublished Papers and Miscellaneous Sources

Atomic Energy and Space Research: A Profile for the Decade, 1970–1980, Atomic Energy Commission, Bombay, 1970.

Bose, D.K. and Mohan, S., 'The Cost of Nuclear Power in India', Technical Report No. ERU/3/80, Social Science Divison, Indian Statistical Institute, Calcutta, 1980.

Morehouse, Ward, 'Science in India', Administrative Staff College on India (ASCI) Occasional Papers, Hyderabad, 1971.

Nuclear Explosions and their Effects, A Government of India Publication, 1956.

Ramanna, Raja, 'Development of Atomic Energy in India: 1947–73', A Talk Delivered at the Nehru Memorial Museum, New Delhi on 29 July 1974, (mimeo.).

———, 'Inevitability of Atomic Energy in India's Power Programme', 39th J.C. Bose Memorial Lecture Delivered on 30 November 1977 at Calcutta.

———, 'On Some New Possibilities of the Peaceful Use of Atomic Energy', 11th Founder Memorial Lecture, 1975, Shri Ram Institute for Industrial Research, New Delhi, 1975.

Sarabhai, Vikram A., and et al., 'An Agro-industrial Complex in the Gangetic plain', Proceedings of the Seminar on Nuclear Power, 17–18 January 1970, edited by B.P. Rastogi, pp. 1–29, Department of Atomic Energy, Bombay.

Sethna, H.N. and Srinivasan, M.R., 'India's Nuclear Power Programme and Constraints Encountered in Its Implementation', *Nuclear Power and Its Fuel Cycle,* vol. 6, IAEA-CN-36/385, Vienna, IAEA, 1977.

Waltz, Kenneth N., 'The Spread of Nuclear Weapons: More May Be Better', Adelphi Paper 171, 1981, pp. 1–32.

4. Periodicals Referred To:

Arms Control Today (Washington, D.C.)

Chazov, Evgueni I., Ilyin, Leonid A., and Guskova, Angelina K., *The Danger of Nuclear War—Soviet Physicians' Viewpoint,* Novosti Press Agency, Moscow, 1982.

Disarmament Diplomacy (London)

Down To Earth (New Delhi)

Drell, Sidney D. and von Hippel, Frank, 'Limited Nuclear War', *Scientific American,* 235, November 1976.

Economic and Political Weekly (Mumbai)

Feld, Bernard T., 'Consequences of Nuclear War', *Bulletin of the Atomic Scientists,* 32, June 1976.

Frank, Jerome D., *Sanity or Survival in the Nuclear Age,* Random House, 2nd ed., New York, 1982.

Frontline (Chennai)

Dolan, Philip J. and Glasstone, Samuel, (eds), *The Effects of Nuclear Weapons,* Department of Defense and U.S. Department of Energy, 3rd ed., Washington, D.C., 1977.

Himal (Kathmandu)

India Today (New Delhi)

INESAP Information Bulletin (Darmstadt)

Jane's Weapons Systems, Jane's Publishing Co., Ltd., London.

Lifton, Robert Jay, *Death in Life: Survivors of Hiroshima,* Random House, New York, 1967.

Mack, John E., 'Psychosocial Effects of the Nuclear Arms Race', *Bulletin of the Atomic Scientists,* 37, April 1981.

Mainstream (New Delhi)

Medicine & Global Security (Cambridge, Mass.).

Military Balance, International Institute of Strategic Studies, London.

Nuclear India, Department of Atomic Energy, Bombay.

Outlook (New Delhi)

Peoples Democracy (Calcutta)

Piel, Gerard, Aronow, Saul and et al. (eds), 'The Illusion of Civil Defense', *The Fallen Sky,* Hill and Wang, New York, 1963.

Security Dialogue (Oslo)

Seminar (New Delhi)

The Asian Age (New Delhi)

The Bulletin of the Atomic Scientists (Chicago)
The Economic Times (New Delhi)
The Hindu (New Delhi)
The Hindustan Times (New Delhi)
The Indian Express (New Delhi)
The Nation (New York)
The Organiser (New Delhi)
The Pioneer (New Delhi)
The Statesman (New Delhi)
The Telegraph (Calcutta)
The Times of India (New Delhi)

Index